# A Taste for
# BROWN SUG

# A Taste for
# BROWN SUGAR

Black Women in Pornography   *Mireille Miller-Young*

Duke University Press   Durham and London   2014

© 2014 Duke University Press
All rights reserved
Printed and bound at Grafos SA, Barcelona, Spain
Typeset in Minion Pro by Tseng Information Systems, Inc.

Library of Congress Cataloging-in-Publication Data
Miller-Young, Mireille, 1976–
A taste for brown sugar :
black women in pornography / Mireille Miller-Young.
pages cm
Includes bibliographical references and index.
ISBN 978-0-8223-5814-5 (cloth : alk. paper)
ISBN 978-0-8223-5828-2 (pbk. : alk. paper)
1. Pornographic films—United States—History and criticism.
2. African American women in motion pictures.
3. African American motion picture actors and actresses. I. Title.
PN1995.9.S45M55 2014
791.43′6538082—dc23
2014013060

Cover art: Jeannie Pepper during her tour of Europe, Cannes,
France, 1986. Courtesy of JohnDragon.com.

# Contents

This is the first book about black women's images, performances, and labors in the porn industry. Most criticism of pornography excludes the position of the black female pornographic producer or consumer. Still less discussed are the ways in which black women producers and consumers have sought pleasure, subjectivity, and agency in pornographic representations. This book takes on the important challenge of talking about one of the most controversial businesses (pornography) through the lens of its most marginal workers (black women). To illustrate the sexual economy I am presenting, and to provide readers with a shared vocabulary of visual culture, I have chosen to include images of the films, events, and people I discuss throughout the book.

In over ten years of researching black women in pornography, I have grappled profoundly with issues of representation, racism, and violence in pornographic images. I have been called a pervert and a pornographer not only for writing about the history of black women's images, performances, and sex work in pornography, but for showing images from this history in various presentation formats. In this way, I have joined a history of what Sander Gilman has termed "academic pornographers." When Gilman first published his groundbreaking work on the iconography of the Hottentot Venus and early nineteenth century racial-scientific inquiry into black female sexuality, he was also accused of being a pornographer. Gilman's amply illustrated study, published in the famed special issue of *Critical Inquiry* from autumn 1985, and his own monograph *Difference and Pathology* (1985), displayed images of Saartjie (Sara) Baartman's genitals as they were studied and eventually dissected and exhibited by French scientists.

Although Gilman was accused of "bringing black women into disrepute"[1] by showing these images, his work revolutionized the study of black female sexuality, inspiring scores of black feminists to theorize (and argue about) Sara Baartman's iconicity as urtext for emergent thinking on racialized sexuality and discourses of black female sexual deviance.[2] Gilman reflected on being labeled an academic pornographer in his foreword to artist Kara Walker's book *My Compliment, My Enemy, My Oppressor, My Love* (2007). Responses to Walker's controversial art had ignited similar accusations about her role as exhibitor-purveyor of "negative images" that pandered to the racism of white audiences.[3]

Because this book reproduces and circulates images of black women in pornography, perhaps to the greatest degree ever accomplished in an academic work, I find myself considering Sander Gilman's embrace of the pejorative title of pornographer, and his argument that we must look at and engage in discussion about sexualized images of black women, even if this is at times traumatic. I represent and analyze the complex iconography of race found in pornography, both on behalf of those in the image, and in order to understand the enduring power of these images in our lives.

This is not to deny how sexualized images of black women are saddled with notions of dirtiness, or how they might produce a visceral response in the reader because they reveal a history and an imaginary of the black body as pornographic object. However, as a critic I am interested in challenging my readers to question their probable gut reaction to the images. By offering my own analysis of this iconography, I aim to expose the conflict and inspire conversation. I want to spotlight the ways in which the overwhelming focus on stereotypes and damaging images ignores the people involved in their creation.

The visual representation of black sexuality is a powerful concern for black feminists. Indeed, black visual artists including Kara Walker, Renee Cox, Carrie Mae Weems, Lyle Ashton Harris, Zanele Muholi, and Carla Williams use sexuality, and sometimes their own bodies, in their art in ways that forcefully illuminate how the process of making visible black sexuality necessarily invokes a collective racial trauma.[4] It is in this collective racial trauma that black feminists find ourselves groping for a language to talk about our own pleasure and for a set of practices for living within and against all the contemporary forms of exploitation, alienation, and objectification that make up life under advanced capitalism and sexualized racism.

To accuse scholars who reproduce sexualized images of black women of being pornographers is to follow a line of discourse dating to the 1970s about the role of images and representation in black women's lives. Many members of the academy are concerned that our culture is overwhelmed by, and indeed teeming with, injurious images of black womanhood. Because these images are so titillating and profitable, they tend to replicate themselves, crowding out the wide, complex reality of black women's lives. This anxiety about the damaging role of images in popular and political culture is so profound for black feminists that it may lead us to censor ourselves for fear of opening up our wounds, allowing taboos to further annihilate our humanity.

A politics of African American women's respectability first emerged in the late nineteenth century in post-emancipation Christian women's activist circles. This "respectability politics" seeks to counter the racist stereotype of the lascivious and deviant black woman by upholding and embodying an image of gender and sexual normativity evocative of a patriarchal ideal of feminine virtue.[5] Black women have adhered to respectability politics as part of an effort to resist and dismantle representations and social structures that cast them as sexually promiscuous, and hence—according to the racist and patriarchal logic of American social life—deserving of rape, abuse, and stigma. In addition to the politics of respectability, black women have learned a "culture of dissemblance," which Darlene Clark Hine describes as tactics of masking, secrecy, and disavowal of sexuality that allow black women to shield themselves from sexual exploitation.[6] The culture of dissemblance produces a cloak of silence around black women's sexual life. These twin cultural traditions—the politics of respectability and the culture of dissemblance—framed sexuality itself as hazardous and contributed to the sexual policing of black women.

In black communities, those who deviate from respectability and dissemblance politics by participating in nonnormative or nonconforming sexualities, including queer, contractual, or public sexuality, are promptly censured. They are accused of undermining African American claims to citizenship and belonging based on sexual respectability, and of giving cause to harmful discourses of black pathology. In this framework of respectability-dissemblance, black women in pornography—as well as those who write about it—are thought to invite further criticism and control of black women's sexualities.

Perhaps for this reason, black feminist critics since the late 1970s have largely dismissed pornography as inherently violent and dangerous. Tracy Gardner posits that pornography is "brutal and deadly" for women, and Aminatta Forna writes: "Images of black women are exploited by pornography and black women are exploited by pornographers."[7] Patricia Hill Collins asserts that black women in pornography "embody the existence of victim and pet" and engender a "totally alienated being who is separated from and who seemingly does not control her body."[8] Alice Walker posits the centrality of the pornographic as an idiom for the sexual consumption of black women during slavery: "For centuries the black woman has served as the primary pornographic 'outlet' for White men in Europe and America."[9] These black feminist analyses contend that pornographic representation continues a history of sexual violence against black women's bodies.[10] In addition, for Audre Lorde, pornography is the polar opposite of eroticism, and as the epitome of superficiality and individuality, rather than subjectivity and intimate relations, completely lacks the potential for truly progressive political work by black feminists and others.[11]

This book is not a rejection of the important feminist works outlined above. We cannot elide the historical role of slavery and colonialism in producing a scopophilic and coercive relationship to black women's bodies, one that is foundational to their depiction in pornographic images. Yet there is another tradition of black feminism that I wish to prioritize. This tradition provides a new lens to read the work of pornography on black women's bodies. Barbara Smith, Cheryl Clarke, and Jewelle Gomez write: "Even pornography which is problematic for women can be experienced as affirming women's desires and women's equality. . . . The range of feminist imagination and expression in the realm of sexuality has barely begun to find voice."[12] My work takes seriously this charge to find the voices of black women in pornography. I have used ethnographic methods to help these voices be heard — including interviews, participant observation, set visits, and my own years-long relationships with performers, some of whom I call friends. By reproducing these images of black women in pornography, I hope to honor their performances and document their interventions into the complicated history of black women's sexuality.

I assert that black women in pornography do other kinds of cultural work beyond representing injury, trauma, and abuse. I draw on black feminist critics whose work challenges the silences and erasures of the respectability-dissemblance framework and who show a particular interest in theorizing what Cathy Cohen calls the politics of deviance.[13] For Cohen, marginalized people's so-called deviant practices and behaviors are productive because they offer the potential for resistance. When "deviant groups" fight for "basic human goals of pleasure, desire, recognition, and respect," they open up and mobilize a queer politics of dissent with prevailing norms that deny the value of their lives.[14] Like Cohen, Ariane Cruz argues for the queer political potential in deviant acts, theorizing a "politics of perversion" that sees sexual pleasure as a subversive force.[15] "The stripper, prostitute, video vixen, gold digger, and sexual exhibitionist," L. H. Stallings contends, "cannot continue to be the deviant polarity to the working woman, wife, mother, lady, and virgin."[16] For Stallings, black feminists ought not to invest in the moral policing of outlaw women, for this only sustains binaries and deadens the rich and deeply political nature of black sexual expression. What if we explore pornographic deviance as a space for important political work? This means creating new scholarship that looks at pornographic sexuality as not simply a force of abuse, but as a terrain of strategic labor, self-making, and even pleasure in women's lives.

"By concentrating on our multiple oppressions," argues Deborah King, "scholarly descriptions have confounded our ability to discover and appreciate the way in which black women are not victims . . . [but] powerful and independent subjects."[17] Evelynn Hammonds agrees: "The restrictive, repressive and dangerous aspects of Black female sexuality have been emphasized by Black feminist writers while pleasure, exploration, and agency have gone underanalyzed."[18] This book accounts for the exploitative, repressive, and even violent aspects of black women's representation in pornography as delineated by black feminist critics and the black women informants themselves. Surely, black women's erotic autonomy is powerfully constrained and assaulted by industries like pornography, and a priori by broader frames of American social life such as racial capitalism, state repression, torture and incarceration, heterosexist and homophobic cultural nationalism, and political disenfranchisement. What remains under-theorized, however, is how black women catalyze sexual freedom in their everyday lives and in their imaginations.

Characterizing porn only as bad representation dismisses an arena in which black women and men are actually working hard to create their own images, express their own desires, and shape their own labor choices and conditions. There do exist black feminists who are also pornographers, who challenge the representational, physical, and psychic violence done to black women's bodies in pornography from within. This book is about them. Black feminist labors in the porn industry do not simply challenge individual instances of representation; they radically redefine the field of pornography and expand what it can be. Pornography is always wrapped up with questions of commodification and exploitation, and it is these very issues that this book takes up, as it asserts the absolute necessity of conceptualizing porn as a powerful and important site for black women's own imagination, and, yes, feminist intervention. Although I am not working in the adult industry, I do not entirely reject the label of academic pornographer, as I write this book in solidarity with the black feminist pornographers who have inspired and supported my research.

When I began this project, I believed that issues of representation and issues of labor were separate. However, I have come to see that these issues are profoundly interrelated. As I viewed thousands of sexualized images of black women's bodies, I began to ask how the women in the images experienced these images' production, and how they thought about their own work as image-makers. This book is my attempt to begin a conversation about the vital ways that pornography shapes black women's lives, and how black women also shape the life of pornography.

## Acknowledgments

I still remember the exhilaration I felt when I saw my first pornographic image. It was Vanessa Williams's famous layout in the issue of *Penthouse* magazine published in November 1984 when I was eight years old. My friend and I had taken the magazine from her stepfather's secret hiding place in the back corner of a closet when her mother was at work one day. Seeing Williams in an array of erotic poses with another woman was both shocking and titillating. She was the first African American woman to be crowned Miss America, so when the news broke it was a big deal. My friend and I had overheard our parents talking about the scandal and wanted to see what all the fuss was about. The images were absolutely thrilling to me. Williams was so beautiful and, though I did not yet understand fully what the term meant, sexy. I instantly became captivated with everything about sex, and I wanted to see more nude pictures, even though I knew that it was not allowed!

This book emerges from my longtime fascination with porn and the women in the images. In my over ten years of research into the history of black women in pornography, I have been humbled by the generosity and sisterly affection that my informants have shown me and greatly moved by their powerful courage, wisdom, and grace. This book would not have been possible without these incredible women, many of whom I proudly call friends. I am so grateful for the generosity of Jeannie Pepper, Angel Kelly, Sinnamon Love, Vanessa Blue, Diana DeVoe, Lola Lane, Marie Luv, Sasha Brabuster, Sierra, Carmen Hayes, India, Midori, Mya Lovely, Lollipop, Candice Nicole, Lacey Duvalle, Spantaneeus Xtasty, Damali X Dares, Lexi, Kitten, Obsession, Ayana Angel, Angel Eyes, Aryana Starr, Capri, Loni, Adora, Precious Tia, Phyllis Carr, Tony Sweet, Stacey Cash, Black Cat, Crystal, Sandi Beach, Honney Bunny, Lady Cash, Monica Foster, Serria Tawan, Dee, Dior Milian, Jade

Stone, Skyy Black, Ms. Panther, Misti Love, Pinky, Betty Blac, and Vanessa Del Rio. I try not to speak for these performers but instead to collaborate with them in theorizing the complexities of black women's sexualities in pornography. I appreciate their extraordinary thoughtfulness and candor. I learned so much.

A major element of my work has been to unearth the lost archive of black pornography dating back to early erotic photography and film. I wish to thank the archivists and collectors who have helped me to discover a trove of photographs, postcards, film reels, videos, and magazines. I am especially grateful to Catherine Ann Johnson-Roehr, Curator of Art, Artifacts, and Photographs, and Shawn Wilson, Library and Archives Public Services Manager at the Kinsey Institute for Research in Sex, Gender, and Reproduction. This book would not have been possible without their guidance and generosity.

I would like to acknowledge Alexandre Dupony of Editions Astarte and Archives d'Eros in Paris, France, who gave me access to his enormous collection of pornographic images of women of African descent, some of which are reprinted in this book. Albert Steg kindly welcomed me into his home for a private screening of his wonderful collection of stag film reels, many of which he painstakingly restores to their original condition. I thank him for his lovely hospitality and for providing stills of the films. David Copeland of Global Media International Films also generously shared his Historic Erotica archive with me, and I look forward to bugging him more about viewing his nine-thousand-reel collection. Finally, many private collectors and fans online were instrumental in this research. I would especially like to thank "VideoSan" and "Gregg" for providing rare copies of videos to me, and the online communities at Vintage Erotica Forums, Adult DVD Talk, and the Rec. Arts.Movies.Erotica forum for sharing their expertise, contacts, and collections with me.

I would also like to express my appreciation for the many other performers, producers, directors, journalists, photographers, agents, historians, activists, and adult-industry experts who offered the materials, information, and access that have been essential to my research: Tyler Knight, Mr. Marcus, Byron Long, Lexington Steele, Sean Michaels, Justin Long, Julian St. Jox, Ron Hightower, Shorty Mac, Orpheus Black, Nevin Washington, Laurence Christian, Lil Jon, Shock G, Money B, Fly Eli, Johnnie Keyes, Nina Hartley, Porsche Lynn, Sharon Mitchell, John Leslie, Jim South, Mark Kearnes, Jane Hamilton, Dian Hanson, Gino Colbert, Sarah Harter, Cindy Cheer, Scott Ross, Mike Ramone, Paul Fishbein, John Stagliano, Ron Jeremy, Randy West, Diane Duke, Mark Davis, Michael Fattorosi, and Ashley West. A very special thank you goes to filmmakers Shine Louise Houston, Nenna Feelmore Joiner, Abiola Abrams, Cheryl Dunye, Candida Royalle, Roy Karch, Kiki Rockstar, and Tristan Taormino. In addition to being big supporters of this project, John Dragon, Bill Margold, Suze Randall, and Christian Mann very generously provided images.

Ken Wissoker, my editor at Duke University Press, has been an advocate for my work since I was just beginning to conceptualize the manuscript. He understood immediately the value of the story I wanted to tell and championed it. I thank him for his invaluable guidance and patience during this process, and for allowing me to express my vision. Elizabeth Ault, my associate editor, has been a dream to work with. I am grateful for her care for the book and for me.

I have received numerous fellowships and grants that made my research possible, particularly from the University of California system and my own campus of UC Santa Barbara, including the University of California President's Postdoctoral Fellowship; the UC Regents' Junior Faculty Fellowship; the UC Regents' Humanities Faculty Fellowship; the UCSB Academic Senate Faculty Research Award; the Social Science Research Grant from the Institute for Social, Behavioral, and Economic Research; the UC Faculty Career Development Award; and the Faculty Release Time Award from the Interdisciplinary Humanities Center. In addition, support for the publication of this book was provided by the UCSB Office of Equal Opportunity and Sexual Harassment/Title IX Compliance as well as the Associate Vice Chancellor for Diversity, Equity, and Academic Policy.

In 2007–8 I held a visiting appointment in the Department of Women's Studies at the Ohio State University. I valued the chance to share my work with such an energetic community of scholars who so generously supported it. In 2003–4 I became a Dissertation Fellow in the Department of Black Studies at UC Santa Barbara. It was a great honor to be invited to UCSB by the esteemed Dr. Cedric Robinson, and I decided not to leave. The next year, when I won the UC President's Postdoctoral Fellowship, I was mentored by Dr. Anna Everett in the Center for Black Studies Research at UCSB. In 2005 I was hired into the Department of Feminist Studies, which has been an ideal space to do the work that I do. I also had the privilege to attend the Summer Institute on Sexuality, Culture, and Society at the University of Amsterdam in 2001, organized by Carol Vance and Han Ten Brummelhuis. The feedback that I received at the Summer Institute has been crucial for my thinking in this project as it evolved from dissertation to book.

I am grateful that I had the opportunities I have had to develop parts of this book in publications and conference presentations. I thank the Institute of Network Cultures and Geert Lovink for putting on a fun conference called Netporn, and for sponsoring the *C'Lick Me* volume that brought together work by a remarkable collection of scholars, artists, and porn activists and was edited by Katrien Jacobs, Matteo Pasquinelli, and Marjie Janssen. I was pleased to be included in Susanna Paasonen, Kaarina Nikunen, and Laura Saarenmaa's book *Pornification*, and parts of that essay were revised for this book. I appreciated being a part of Michelle Wright's collection, *Blackness and Sexuality*, in which I first published my ideas about video porn of the 1980s.

I first developed my thinking about the interface between hip-hop and porn in an article for a special issue of *Meridians* edited by Janell Hobson and Diane Bartlow. In this cutting-edge collection of scholarship, I had the chance to present theories that I now expand on here. My article in the special issue of *Sexualities* on Intimate Labors, edited by Eileen Boris, Rhacel Parreñas, and Stephanie Gilmore, served as the foundation for my chapter on performers' motivations for pursuing porn work. I also am indebted to the Feminist Press at CUNY for publishing my coedited volume *The Feminist Porn Book*, in which I experimented with arguments about black women's self-authorship that I explore in this book.

I have had the opportunity to present my work at numerous universities where I greatly benefited from helpful feedback: the Center for the Study of Women and Society at the University of Oregon; the Department of Women and Gender Studies at University of Illinois, Chicago; the Department of Women's Studies at UC Riverside; the Center for the Study of Women at UC Los Angeles; the Department of Community Studies at UC Santa Cruz; the Department of Communication at UC San Diego; the Africana Research Center at Pennsylvania State University; the Department of Women and Gender Studies and the Beatrice Bain Research Group at UC Berkeley; and the Humanities Institute at SUNY Buffalo to which Tim Dean invited me to be a keynote for the conference "At the Limit: Pornography and the Humanities."

That I earned a doctorate in history at New York University with a controversial project like this one is all thanks to my stellar doctoral committee members, who saw the importance of the work even before I did. Robin D. G. Kelley brought me to NYU to work with him, and to study in the most dynamic and innovative community of scholars possible. I thank him for nurturing my intellect and imagination. Lisa Duggan was the first person to tell me that I could write a dissertation on porn, challenging me to bravely become the academic that I wanted to be. Her caring advice and rigorous reading of drafts along the way helped me grow as a scholar. Walter Johnson and

Barbara Krauthamer are scholars of slavery whose work I admire, and I thank them for being attentive and generous committee members. Finally, I owe my discovery of this topic to Simone Weil Davis who taught a brilliant course on pornography that changed my life. From the paper I did for her seminar on black women in porn, and through the dissertation and the book, Simone has inspired and sustained my intellectual development.

New York University was an amazing place to be a graduate student in the late 1990s and early 2000s. I appreciated learning from the professors there, especially Sinclair Thomson, Jeffrey Sammons, Thomas Bender, Michael Gomez, Martha Hodes, Kamau Braithwaite, Tricia Rose, Richard Hull, and Ed Guerrero. A huge hug and thank-you to my closest comrades Suzanna Reiss, Jamie Wilson, and Eric McDuffie. Thanks to my fantastic classmates from whom I learned so much: Christina Hanhardt, Richard Kim, Carlos Decena, Adria Imada, Julie Sze, Dayo Gore, Betsy Esch, Kim Gilmore, Aisha Finch, Sherie Randolph, Tanya Huelett, Orlando Plaza, Peter Hudson, Njorage Njorage, Sujani Reddy, Daniel Widener, Alyosha Goldstein, Rachel Scharfman, Seth Markle, Hillina Seife, Maxine Roach, and Greg Johnson. I miss all of the dissertation study groups, beers on Bleecker Street, beef-patty breaks, and parties on someone's rooftop in Brooklyn.

I would not have had all these wonderful opportunities without mentors at each and every step of my life. In middle school, thanks to the mentoring of Vivien Alemani and Reginald Jones, I earned a place in the Albert G. Oliver Program. The program helps talented inner city kids like me apply to private schools in New York City and the Northeast. The head of the Olivers, John Hoffman, was a magnificent man who urged me to attend his alma mater, the George School in Newtown, Pennsylvania. George School was a magical place that allowed me to thrive. Headmaster David Bourns was my Gandalf, and John Davison, my history teacher, made me fall in love with the subject. At Emory University I studied history under the guidance of mentors Judith Miller, Leslie Harris, Leroy Davis, and Ron Brown. Their encouragement inspired me to apply to graduate school.

I have always enjoyed building community. I had the chance to do so with some dear friends whose scholarship I deeply admire in the emerging field of black sexualities studies. I am indebted to Adrienne D. Davis, the William Van Cleve Professor of Law at Washington University, for not only becoming a trusted mentor, but for pulling together resources to create the Black Sexual Economies Project. With generous funding from Vice Provost Marion Crain and the Center for the Interdisciplinary Study of Work and Social Capital at WU Law School, and staff support from Gail Boker and Shelly Henderson, Adrienne and I chose some of the best up-and-coming scholars in the field: Marlon M. Bailey, LaMonda Horton Stallings, Xavier Livermon, Matt Richardson, Jeffrey McCune, and Felice Blake. Our three-year collaboration culminated in an exciting conference, "Black Sexual Economies: Transforming Black Sexualities Research," in fall 2013. I am grateful to my BSE Project Research Scholars and our conference attendees for being my community and sustaining me.

I thank all my colleagues in the Department of Feminist Studies for their support over the years, but I especially wish to acknowledge Eileen Boris and Leila Rupp. They have championed me, pushed me, and cared for me. It was a great pleasure to celebrate tenure with them and I look forward to the book party. I also thank our department staff, Lou Anne Lockwood, Christina Toy, Rosa Pinter, Blanca Nuila, and April Bible. Many campus administrators helped me with this project, but special credit goes to Barbara Walker, Emily Zinn, and Sherri Barnes. Melvin Oliver, the Sage Miller McCune Chair of Social Sciences, has been exceptionally generous and supportive. Finally, Chancellor Henry Yang allows me to call him Henry and hugs me when he sees me. He even bailed me out of jail once. Enough said. Thank you, Henry!

The University of California, Santa Barbara, is a special place to work because we have the best community of scholars anywhere. I am especially thankful for my colleagues Constance Penley, Paul Amar, Celine Parreñas Shimizu, Lisa Hajjar, Lisa Parks, Jennifer Holt, Bishnupriya Ghosh, Bhaskar Sarkar, Stephan Miescher, Julie Carlson, France Winddance Twine, Cristina Venegas, Paul Spickard, Amit Ahuja, Claudine Michel, Cedric Robinson, Stephanie Batiste, Gaye Theresa Johnson, Ingrid Banks, Chris McAuley, Jeffrey Stewart, Anna Evertt, Cynthia Hudley, Nikki Jones, Roberto Strongman, Mary Bucholtz, Dolores Ines Casillas, Tania Israel, Elizabeth Weber, Kum Kum Bhavani, Chris Newfield, Avery Gordon, Howard Winant, Verta Taylor, Nelson Lichtenstein, Alice O'Connor, Horacio Roque Ramirez, Victor Rios, Carl Gutierrez Jones, Diane Fujino, Catherine Nesci, Christina McMahon, Beth Schneider, Dick Hebdige, Nadege Clintandre, and the late Clyde Woods.

I am fortunate to work in the University of California system, where I have an outstanding network of colleagues and friends across the ten campuses. I wish to recognize my colleagues and thank them for their warm support all these years: Deborah Vargas, Erica Edwards, Leigh Raiford, Darieck Scott, Juana Maria Rodriquez, Jane Ward, Maylei Blackwell, Grace Hong, Sarah Haley, Tammy Ho, Tracey Fisher, Setsu Shigematsu, Sara Clark Kaplan, Kristie Dorr, Rhoshanak Kheshti, Kalindi Vora, Jillian Hernandez, Gina Dent,

Felicity Amaya Schaeffer, Herman Gray, Tiffany Willoughby-Herard, Mark Sawyer, James Lee, Sora Han, David Theo Goldberg, Lisa Cartwright, and the late Lindon Barrett. I had the chance to meet many of these stellar scholars through the UC President's Postdoctoral annual retreats, and I thank Sheila O'Rourke and Kimberly Adkinson for their stunning success in keeping this important program going and maintaining it as a space for former fellows to stay connected with their peers.

I have received further support from colleagues across the nation who have invited me to speak at their institutions or collaborate on projects, offered useful advice on professional challenges, asked about my health and well-being, and told me to hurry up and get the book out. Particular thanks must go to Rinaldo Walcott, E. Patrick Johnson, Cathy Cohen, Jennifer DeVere Brody, Dwight A. McBride, Jennifer Morgan, Carol Stabile, Piya Chatterjee, Erica Rand, Jennifer Brier, John D'Emilio, Nan Alamilla Boyd, Nayan Shah, Fred Moten, Rebecca Wanzo, Erica Williams, Janell Hobson, Elizabeth Currans, Jane Haladay, Lynn Fujiwara, Tamara Lea Spira, Wendy Smooth, Francille Wilson, Shana Redmond, Zakiyya Jackson, Imani Kai Johnson, Kai Green, Philomena Essed, Nicole Fleetwood, Zakiya Adair, Jafari Sinclaire Allen, Christopher Parker, Johari Jabir, Fanon Wilkins, Derrick White, Kirby Gookin, Karl Bryant, Vicki Callahan, Brandi Summers, Kimberly Springer, Michelle McKinley, Tanisha Ford, Deborah Willis, Carla Williams, and the late Jose Esteban Muñoz.

When I began this project on the story of black women in porn I felt like I was out there alone. Therefore I was so pleased to discover a community of scholars doing work on pornography and sex work. Many of them have become my friends, collaborators, and advisers. I wish to acknowledge Ariane Cruz, Jennifer Nash, Lynn Comella, Kevin Heffernan, Chuck Kleinhans, Mindy Chateauvert, Svati Shah, Stephanie Gilmore, Becki Ross, Susan Dewey, Kerwin Kaye, Ronald Weitzer, Carolyn Bronstein, Nguyen Tan Hoang, Clarissa Smith, Feona Attwood, Tim Dean, Zeb Tortorici, Katrien Jacobs, David Squires, Andy Owens, Jennifer Moorman, Jill Bakehorn, Julie Levin Russo, Naima Lowe, Chauntelle Tibbals, Shira Tarrant, and Siobhan Brooks.

One of the most rewarding things about becoming an expert on pornography is learning about all of the artists and activists who have been doing the radical work of creating sexual culture. This community has welcomed me with open arms and I am extremely indebted to them for their care, insight, and creative inspiration. Thanks to Carol Leigh (aka Scarlot Harlot), Audacia Ray, Melissa Hope Ditmore, Rachel West, Robin Byrd, Yosenio Lewis,

Juba Kalamaka, Dee Dennis, Annie Sprinkle, N'Jaila Rhee, Charlie Glickman, William Winters, Jaclyn Friedman, Carol Queen, Reid Mihalko, Jiz Lee, Dylan Ryan, Kelly Shibari, Madison Young, Courtney Trouble, Danny Wylde, Rae Threat, Buck Angel, April Flores, and the late Carlos Batts. I loved my collaboration on *The Feminist Porn Book* because of the way it brought together many of these feminist artists and activists with feminist scholars, allowing us to have an important and unprecedented conversation. It has been such a pleasure to publicly present the work with the contributors to the volume and my coeditors Constance Penley, Celine Parreñas Shimizu, and Tristan Taormino, at the first annual Feminist Porn Conference at the University of Toronto and elsewhere.

I have revised this book many times. I had an enormous amount of material and so much to say. For these reasons I am more grateful than I can express for my colleagues who read various drafts and provided comments, corrections, and fresh ideas. I want to express my eternal gratitude to Constance Penley, the Editing Dominatrix, for her strict reading of the manuscript. But it was the nice Connie who brought me delicious food in care packages when I was on lockdown with the manuscript. The Black Sexual Cultures Working Group—Matt Richardson, Xavier Livermon, and Marlon M. Bailey—met at the "Columbus Estates" every month for several years to workshop chapters amid much hilarity and good food. Thanks as well to Nicole Starosielski, LaMonda Horton Stallings, Felice Blake, Rebecca Wanzo, Heather Tirado-Gilligan, and Heather Berg for their attentive readings of various parts of the book.

Invaluable copyediting assistance was provided by Diana Pozo, who solved some lingering issues like the brilliant editing wiz she is. I also wish to thank Anitra Grisales for her professional editing assistance. In addition, my research assistants were indispensable to the process. My gratitude goes to Diana Pozo, Amanda Phillips, Jade Petermon, Regina Longo, Nicole Starosielski, Sarah Whedon, Brandon Pineda, Vanessa Ramos, Toby Blakeney, Janai Harris, Samantha Kramer, and Amara Allenstein.

At UCSB I get to teach classes on pornography and sex work, which is fun but also a fantastic education for me. I want to thank my graduate students for their sharp thinking and enlivening discussions, which have helped advance my thinking about the scholarship: Heather Berg, Carly Thomsen, Rolondo Longoria, Lauren Clark, Kristie Soares, Pawan Rehill, Rosie Kar, Brett Esaki, Stacie Furia, Hareem Khan, Lillian Jungleib, Michelle Baca, Andrew Seeber, Kenley Brown, Randy Drake, Emily Crutcher, and Laurica Brown. I learned from several stellar undergraduate students as well, including Jessica

Hammond, Amieris Lavender, Elizabeth Canico, Sophia Armen, Tuquan Harrison, Scarlet Chan, Jessica Moore, Mor Weizman, Doug Wagoner, and Nathaniel Burke.

For over ten years I have been living between Santa Barbara and Columbus, Ohio, where my partner lives. It has not always been easy but it means that I have double the friends and support network. My Ohio family gets a big shout out: Perry Mickley, Darla Hollingsworth, Jo Anne Mickely, Tom Weiland, Damon Whitfield, and Brian and Christa Neill. My Santa Barbara family gets tons of love too: Anita David, Fred Backman, Tiye Baldwin, Morris Anderson, Mahsheed Ayoub, Lane Clark, Mike Long, Luca and Rori Trovato, Jenny Scholl, Donald and Peggy Canley, Ana Lozoya, Alyce Harris, Sharon Hoshida, Master Mel at MAFF, John Cervantes, and Terrie Furukawa.

My friends have supported me through the long process of getting this book out and now I am so thrilled to share its publication with them. My fierce love and thanks go to them and their families: Margaret Warren and my beautiful goddaughters Maya and Savanna, Nadia Wynter, Leon and Barella Kirkland and baby Grant, Erin Zimring and Dan Pipski and their sweet Felix and Juniper, Terri Paine-Cameron, Mirjam and Ethu Ukpabi, and Sophia Mann and Andrea Fiasco and their Iole and Niccolo.

My life is made rich by my family: Melody, Judy, Laurie, Rebekah, Jackie, Gitta, Jürgen, and many others. Thanks to my family angels watching over me and blessing me, especially Lannie, Wiley, Coley, and Bea. My love and appreciation to Rob "The Nose" Smith, who brought me to school every day and year, and took such good care of us. I am happy that I got to finally connect with my father, David Young, during the process of writing this book, and that he has been so open-minded and loving. But the lion's share of my appreciation goes to my mother, Beatrice Miller. She gave me the tools to dream and then go make my dreams a reality. She raised me to have a passion for learning and excellence, and to adore black culture and history. She is beautiful, brilliant, and the fiercest woman I have ever met. I hope this work makes her proud and that she enjoys reading it. Finally, I might not have continued on this path and now be realizing the wonderful feeling of accomplishment I have in this project were it not for the love of my life, my Samwise, Dorian. You are everything Dori. I celebrate this with you.

# Introduction Brown Sugar

## Theorizing Black Women's Sexual Labor in Pornography

You are not supposed to talk about liking sex because you are already assumed to be a whore. —JEANNIE PEPPER

In a private gathering following the East Coast Video Show in Atlantic City in 2002, legendary performer Jeannie Pepper received a special achievement award for twenty years in the porn industry, the longest career for any black adult actress. "It's been a long, hard road," she said to the audience of adult entertainment performers, insiders, and fans as she accepted the award from popular adult film actor Ron Jeremy. "There weren't many black women in the business when I started."[1] In 1982, when Jeannie Pepper began her career as an actress in X-rated films, there were few black women in the adult film industry. Performing in more than two hundred films over three decades, Jeannie broke barriers to achieve porn star status and opened doors for other women of color to follow.[2] She played iconic roles as the naughty maid, the erotically possessed "voodoo girl," and the incestuous sister in films like *Guess Who Came at Dinner?*, *Let Me Tell Ya 'Bout Black Chicks*, and *Black Taboo*. She traveled abroad as a celebrity, working and living in Germany for seven years.

In a career that spanned the rise of video, DVD, and the Internet, Jeannie watched the pornography business transform from a quasi-licit cottage industry into a sophisticated, transnational, and corporate-dominated industry. In 1997 Jeannie was the first African American porn actress to be inducted into the honored Adult Video News (AVN) Hall of Fame. By all accounts, Jeannie had an exceptionally long and successful career for an adult actress: she was well liked by her colleagues, and was a mentor to young women new to the porn business. Yet, as her acceptance speech reveals, her experience of being a black woman in the porn industry was shaped by formidable challenges. As in other occupations in the United States, black women in the adult

FIGURE I.1. Jeannie Pepper during her tour of Europe, Cannes, France, 1986. Courtesy of JohnDragon.com.

FIGURE I.2. Jeannie Pepper poses in the nude before onlookers outside of the Carlton Hotel, Cannes, France, 1986. Courtesy of JohnDragon.com.

film industry are devalued workers who confront systemic marginalization and discrimination.

Jeannie became a nude model and adult film actress in her twenties because she enjoyed watching pornography and having sex, and she was keen to become a path-maker in an industry with few black female stars: "I just wanted to show the world. Look, I'm black and I'm beautiful. How come there are not more black women doing this?"³ She felt especially beautiful when in 1986 she did a photo shoot with her photographer husband, a German expatriate known as John Dragon, on the streets of Paris. Dressed only in a white fur coat and heels, Jeannie walked around, posing in front of the Eiffel Tower, Arc de Triomphe, cafés, luxury cars, and shops. Coyly allowing her coat to drape open (or off altogether) at opportune moments, she drew the attention of tourists and residents alike. She imagined herself as Josephine Baker, admired in a strange new city for her beauty, class, and grace. Finding esteem and fearlessness in showing the world her blackness and beauty, even in the cityscapes of Paris, Hamburg, or Rome, Jeannie felt she embodied an emancipated black female sexuality.

Still, she remained conscious of the dual pressures of needing to fight for recognition and opportunity in the adult business, especially in the United States, and having to defend her choice to pursue sex work as a black woman.⁴

As Jeannie asserts in the epigraph, she perceived that part of the difficulty of being a professional "whore"—in photographs and films—was the expectation that she was not supposed to talk about or inhabit her sexuality in ways that would seem to exacerbate harmful stereotypes about black women, namely their alleged hypersexuality. Black women sexual performers and workers have had to confront a prevailing stigma: if all black women are considered to be sexually deviant, then those who use sex to make a living are the greatest threat to any form of respectable black womanhood.

"Brown sugar," this popular imaginary of African American women, saturates popular culture. In songs, films, music videos, and everyday life, the discourse of brown sugar references the supposed essence of black female sexuality. It exposes historical mythologies about the desirable yet deviant sexual nature of black women. Publicly scorned and privately enjoyed, the alluring, transformative, and supposedly perverse sexuality of black women is thoroughly cemented in the popular imaginary. Seen as particularly sexual, black women continue to be fetishized as the very embodiment of excessive or non-normative sexuality. What is most problematic about this sticky fetishism—in addition to the fact that it spreads hurtful and potentially dangerous stereotypes with very real material effects—is that the desire for black women's sexuality, while so prevalent, is unacknowledged and seen as illegitimate in most popular discourse.

As a metaphor, brown sugar exposes how black women's sexuality, or more precisely their sexual labor, has been historically embedded in culture and the global economy. Now a key component of the profitable industries of entertainment and sex in the United States, brown sugar played a central role in the emergence of Western nation-states and the capitalist economies. Across the American South and the Caribbean, black slaves cultivated and manufactured sugar that sweetened food, changed tastes, and energized factory workers in the Industrial Revolution.[5] In addition to physical labor, their sexual labor was used to "give birth to white wealth,"[6] and was thus the key mechanism for reproducing the entire plantation complex. "Sugar was a murderous commodity," explains Vincent Brown, "a catastrophe for workers that grew it."[7] The grinding violence and danger that attended sugar's cultivation in colonial plantations literally consumed black women's labor and bodies.[8]

Brown sugar, as a trope, illuminates circuits of domination over black women's bodies and exposes black women's often ignored contributions to the economy, politics, and social life. Like sugar that has dissolved without a trace, but has nonetheless sweetened a cup of tea, black women's labor and the mechanisms that manage and produce it are invisible but nonetheless *there*.

To take the metaphor a bit further, the process of refining cane sugar from its natural brown state into the more popular white, everyday sweetener reflects how black women, like brown sugar, represent a raw body in need of refinement and prone to manipulation. The lewdness and raw quality associated with brown sugar in popular discourse today thus shows how ideas about black women as naturally savage, super-sexual beings have flavored popular tastes even as they have driven a global appetite for (their) sweetness. While processed white sugar is held up as the ideal, there remains a powerful desire, indeed a taste, for the *real thing*.

The metaphor of brown sugar exposes how representations shape the world in which black women come to know themselves. But stereotypes usually have dual valences: they may also be taken up by the oppressed and refashioned to mean something quite different. Although brown sugar has been used as a phrase to talk about black women as lecherous, prurient sex objects, unlike other tropes such as the Mammy, Jezebel, or Sapphire, it conveys sweetness, affection, and respect. In African American vernacular speech and song, brown sugar often expresses adoration, loveliness, and intimacy even as it articulates lust, sensuality, and sex (along with other illicit, pleasure-giving materials like heroin or marijuana).[9] As in the saying, "the blacker the berry, the sweeter the juice," brown sugar is sometimes used by black people to speak to the complex pleasures they derive from their own eroticism. In this book brown sugar references a trope that black women must always broker. Sometimes they refashion this trope to fit their needs. As Jeannie Pepper shows, some black women choose to *perform* brown sugar—the perverse, pleasurable imago projected onto black women's bodies—in an effort to express themselves as desired and desiring subjects. Given the brutal history of sexual expropriation and objectification of black bodies, these attempts by black women to reappropriate a sexualized image can be seen as a bid to reshape the terms assigned to black womanhood. In this case, brown sugar might be a realm for intervention in their sexualization.

Some black women might view Jeannie Pepper, the porn star, as a menace to the hard-fought image of respectable womanhood they have sought to create for more than one hundred years.[10] Nevertheless, even though black sex workers know that their labor is seen to constitute a betrayal of respectable black womanhood, some pursue it. Their reasons may be purely economic: it's a job, and they must survive and take care of their families, after all. Or, in Jeannie Pepper's case, their motivations could be to take pleasure in "show-[ing] the world" a beautiful and sexually self-possessed black woman. While such a move to represent oneself may be viewed, especially by many in the

African American community, as perpetuating historical and ongoing stereotypes born out of horrible abuse, it is a powerful statement about how some black women redefine what respectable womanhood means for them. For Jeannie, more important than respectability, is respect.[11] Respect means being acknowledged and valued for her performative sexual labor and treated as a star. Jeannie Pepper's story illustrates how the perception of black women as hypersexual, which has persisted since the slave trade, has made it extremely difficult to acknowledge that some black women have an interest in leveraging hypersexuality. But it is possible to leverage this treacherous discourse and the black women who speak to us in *A Taste for Brown Sugar* explain how. They use the seductive power of brown sugar to intervene in representation, to assert their varied sexual subjectivities, and to make a living. In the process of making tough choices about how and when to commodify their sexualities, these women offer more complex readings of black gender and sexual identity than now prevail in the academy and popular culture. Porn is an important terrain in which this alternative sexual politics can emerge.

## Pornography as Culture and Industry

Pornography is a highly controversial category, not just for its content but because it sparks heated debates about its role in society. Most often pornography is defined as a genre of mass-produced written or visual materials designed to arouse or titillate the reader or viewer. A facet of entertainment culture and a domain of the commercial sex industry since its modern circulation in literature, photography, and film in the nineteenth century, pornography has been powerfully regulated as the explicit, obscene edge of acceptable forms of sexuality. It is also more than a kind of object or media; pornography is an idiom that communicates potent, blunt, and transgressive sexuality operating at the boundaries of licit and illicit, sacred and profane, private and public, and underground and mainstream culture. Hence, as Walter Kendrick argues, "'pornography' names an argument, not a thing."[12] Pornography becomes a map of a culture's borders, a "detailed blueprint of the culture's anxieties, investments, contradictions,"[13] and a site of cultural contest about social access and social prohibition.[14] Focusing on pornography since the rise of the modern adult film industry in the 1970s, *A Taste for Brown Sugar* analyzes the operation of black women's sexuality—its conditions of production, modes of representation, and strategic performances— in both the industry and idiom of pornography. This book traces the work of the black female body in pornography as a material object, but it also delves into pornography's function as a cultural discourse about racialized sexuality.

Does pornography really make much of an impact on how we view sex, race, and gender? One argument about porn's relevance is that it is big business with big cultural effects. Many critics have cited the broad impact of pornography on American life since its legalization during the sexual revolution of the 1960s and '70s.[15] With revenues of nearly $8–$10 billion a year, the adult entertainment industry is one of the largest entertainment industries in the United States.[16] Pornographic films, videos, and websites are one part of this larger industry that includes exotic dance clubs, phone sex, magazines, peep booths, and sex toys. While Hollywood makes nearly four hundred films each year, the adult industry makes more than ten thousand.[17]

This book focuses on photographic film and digital media from the turn of the twentieth century to the early twenty-first, a period during which pornography became a "phenomenon of media culture and a question of mass production."[18] Indeed, mechanisms of mass production and consumption have become central to the growing convergence of sexual aesthetics and media industries, and their prominent role in defining private fantasies and public spaces. In recent years we have seen this convergence happening within popular culture, from "porno chic" fashion, to reality TV shows such as *The Girls Next Door*, to mainstream films like *Zack and Miri Make a Porno* and *Boogie Nights*, to adult actress and entrepreneur Jenna Jameson being interviewed on *Oprah*. Porn as an entrance into everyday consumer life can be seen as producing what many critics have termed the "pornification" or "pornetration" of culture.[19] Previously illicit subcultures, communities, and sexual practices have been brought into the public eye through pornography, and in the process they have made their way into other modes of culture, including fashion, art, mainstream film, music, and television. Celebrity sex tapes, political sex scandals, and popular sex panics around issues like youth "sexting" have popularized the idea of public sex as a symptom of a pornographic mainstream media; they ignite worry that what is being projected and amplified is the worst of American sexual experience in terms of taste, values, and politics. Indeed, based on documentaries such as Chyng Sun's *The Price of Pleasure*, one would imagine that the biggest threat to society is not war, torture, poverty, or environmental degradation, but the proliferation of pornography and its representation of "bad sex."[20] Rather than an act of romance, intimacy, or love, bad sex is seen as the product of the narcissistic, self-interested character of our culture. This unfeeling, vulgar kind of sex rubs up against expectations of personal morality and rational social values rooted in traditional, bourgeois views of sex for the reproduction of proper families and citizens. Thus, fears of bad sex expose powerful anxieties about how changing meanings and practices around sex might lead to a downward spiral, a debasing of social life and the nation.[21] More than a debate about how sex is represented in our culture, porn is a site of moral panic about sex itself.

As an act of speech that speaks the unspeakable, pornography has been defined by what the state has tried to suppress.[22] In the process of pushing against censorship and obscenity regulation, porn presses and redefines the limits of the culture of sex. Media technologies have played a leading role in making porn increasingly accessible and part of the public domain. With so many genres and subgenres of erotic fascination making up pornography's "kaleidoscopic variorum" we might even think of it in a plural sense: as *pornographies*.[23] Yet despite its vast proliferation, increased pluralism, and rich potential for the reimagining of allowable forms of desire, pornography's commodification of sex has produced what Richard Fung notes as a "limited vision of what constitutes the erotic."[24] That porn reproduces predictable, indeed stereotypical, representations of sexuality for an increasingly niche-oriented marketplace is not surprising given its profit motive. This limited erotic vision may also be the result of sexually conservative regulatory systems, such as obscenity laws, which have defined what may or may not be broadcast via media technologies like television or the Internet or sold in stores, whether locally or across state lines.[25] In addition to affecting media policy, the regulation of sexual culture has reinforced severely narrow representations of gender, desire, and sexuality that make it difficult to construct alternative imaginaries, even in supposedly transgressive spaces like pornography.[26] Nevertheless, pornography reliably takes up the challenge of subverting norms, even as it catalyzes and perpetuates them. The fantasies it produces offer fertile spaces to read how eroticism, proliferation, commodification, and regulation get played out at the very heart of our public consciousness.

In many ways porn is a political theater where — in addition to gender, sex, and class — racial distinctions and barriers are reiterated even as they may also be manipulated or transformed.[27] Race, or more properly racialization, the process by which meanings are made and power is structured around racial differences, informs the production side of commercial pornography in at least two important ways: in the titillating images themselves and in the behind-the-scenes dynamics where sex workers are hired to perform in the production of those images.[28] Black women, and other people of color, have historically been included in pornography to the extent that its producers seek to commoditize, circulate, and enable the consumption of their images. Their bodies represent stereotypes of racial, gender, and sexual difference and the fantasies or deeper meanings behind them.[29] Until recently, when black women and men started to produce and circulate their own pornographies, those fantasies were seldom authored by black people.

Black women's images in hardcore porn show that the titillation of pornography is inseparable from the racial stories it tells. A central narrative is that black women are both desirable and undesirable objects: desirable for their supposed difference, exoticism, and sexual potency, and undesirable because these very same factors threaten or compromise governing notions of feminine sexuality, heterosexual relations, and racial hierarchy. Pornography did not create these racial stories, these fraught imaginings of black being and taboo interactions across racial difference, but it uses them. What interests me is the *work* of racial fantasy, particularly fantasy involving black women. Given our racial past and present, what is the labor of the black female body in pornography? As my informants show, the players of pornography's racial imaginarium are the ones who can best discern the crucial implications of these fantasies for black women's sexual identities and experiences. They reveal how some black porn actresses tactically employ the performative labor of hypersexuality to intervene in their representation, "contest it from within,"[30] and provide a deeper, more complex reading of their erotic lives.

### Working On, Within, and Against

Historically, enslaved black women were marked as undesirable objects for white men due to their primitive sexuality. These women, as the myth went, were so supersexual that they virtually forced white men into sex they ostensibly did not want to have.[31] Enslaved black women needed their sexual powers because otherwise these unwitting white men would never desire them. This myth concealed, denied, and suppressed the plain sexual exploitation of enslaved and emancipated African American women by casting the demand for their sexuality, both in images and as labor, as impossible. Chief to the racial fetishism of black women in pornography, then, is a *double focus*: a voyeurism that looks but also does not look, that obsessively enjoys, lingers over, and takes pleasure in the black female body even while it declares that body as strange, Other, and abject.[32]

Black women are of course aware of this regime of racial fetishism in representation (and the social and legal apparatus that sustains it), which licenses the voyeuristic consumption of their bodies as forbidden sex objects.

As Jeannie Pepper noted, black women are always "already assumed to be" whores. She, then, uses this insistent myth in her own work. That is, Jeannie Pepper employs her own illicit desirability in a kind of sexual repertoire. By precisely staging her sexuality so as to acknowledge and evoke the taboo desire for it, she shows that racial fetishism can actually be taken up by its objects and used differently. Standing nude on the beach in the South of France as throngs of tourists look on, Jeannie takes pleasure in presenting herself as irresistibly captivating and attractive in the face of the denial of those very capacities. In this way, Jeannie Pepper exposes the disgust for black female sexuality as a facade for what is really forbidden desire. It is a myth that can be reworked and redeployed for one's own purposes.

Jeannie Pepper shows us how black women—particularly sex workers—mobilize what I term "illicit eroticism" to advance themselves in adult entertainment's sexual economy.[33] Actively confronting the taboo nature and fraught history of black female sexuality, black sex workers choose to pursue a prohibited terrain of labor and performance. Illicit eroticism provides a framework to understand the ways in which black women put hypersexuality to use. They do so in an industry that is highly stratified with numerous structures of desire and "tiers of desirability."[34] Black women's illicit erotic work manipulates and re-presents racialized sexuality—including hypersexuality—in order to assert the value of their erotic capital.[35]

In an industry where they are marginal to the most lucrative productions, and where the quality of productions are largely based on demand, black women, along with Latinas and Asian women, face a lack of opportunities, pay disparities, and racially biased treatment in comparison to white women.[36] Black women are devalued in terms of their erotic worth, and they are critical of how they are made lesser players in pornography's theater of fantasy. These women seek to mobilize their bodies to position themselves to the greatest advantage. This mobilization requires a complex knowledge of what it means to "play the game" and to "play up" race by moving and performing strategically. However, because not everyone is able to increase their status in the established hierarchies of desire, black women employing illicit erotic labor face a complicated dilemma: lacking erotic capital, how can they produce more, and in the process enhance their erotic power, social significance, and economic position?

One strategy for black women in pornography is to work extremely hard to carve out space and fabricate themselves as marketable and desirable actors. Their appearance is important to them; they invest a great deal of time and money on self-fashioning and taking care of their bodies in order to achieve

FIGURE I.3. Jeannie Pepper standing before the Eiffel Tower in Paris, France, during her European tour in 1986. Courtesy of JohnDragon.com.

competitiveness. Performance is critical; most performers attempt to portray seductive eroticism and sexual skill, which may give them an edge with consumers and added appreciation by other actors and producers. In addition to appearing in adult videos, they actively cultivate themselves as "porn stars," which includes creating a captivating persona and becoming a savvy financial manager and entrepreneur. Selling themselves as brands or commodities means spending a great deal of time on promotion, including at photo shoots, appearances at trade conventions and entertainment-industry events, and on their websites, social networks, and chat rooms, to foster a fan base. All these spaces are spaces of work and contestation where black women must fight for their worth. Even more important, these primarily young, working-class black women do all this while also acting as mothers, aunts, daughters, sisters, and partners called upon to play important caretaking roles in their families. They are women who use their bodies as resources and their determined intellect as tools to make a living, and sometimes make a name too.

Marginalized and exploited in the labor market, many young, working-class black women today identify the sex industries as preferred spaces to make a living for themselves and their families.[37] This is not new. As the history of black sexual labor attests, this choice has been recorded as part of their negotiations of the labor market since slavery and through the Great Depression.[38] Black sex workers make a living when they take sex, which is associated with leisure and play, and turn it into what Robin D. G. Kelley calls "play-labor."[39] In commodifying sexuality, play-labor does not necessarily resist or overturn hegemonic institutions of power like patriarchy and racial capitalism. That is not its purpose. Play-labor is one strategy by which black women (and others) try to negotiate the existing political economy by using their corporeal resources, which are some of the only resources many black working-class women may in fact possess. Given that the other options open to working-class black women appear in service, care work, or other contingent labor industries, the "choice" to pursue sex work is of course constrained within a modern capitalist system where all work is exploited work, and black women's work is super exploited.[40]

Part of a continuum of sex work—including streetwalking, private escorting, erotic dancing, modeling, phone sex, and s/m role play—and part of a history of black women working in underground or gray economies as "mojo women . . . bootleggers, numbers backers and bawdy house operators," black women's work in pornography maneuvers within illicit and licit sexual economies to pursue what Sharon Harley describes as "personal and community survival."[41] Their maneuvers are generally prompted by market concerns, like porn's relatively flexible and high-income work, but also by nonmarket motives, such as sexual pleasure and the enjoyment of erotic performance. Garnering fame in the adult entertainment industry is often regarded by performers as a viable aspiration and a stepping-stone to more opportunities in entertainment. For young black women, attaining fame could also reflect a desire to harness the erotic capital possessed by recognized black entertainers and actresses such as Beyoncé, Nicki Minaj, Halle Berry, Pam Grier, and Josephine Baker.

Jeannie Pepper's identification with Josephine Baker indicates that some black women working in porn understand the historical depictions of their bodies as containing dynamic possibilities for reinterpretation and re-creation through performance. These women *work on* representations of black sexuality by using their own bodies and imaginations. These representations—painful, punishing, or pleasurable—are part of what Asian American studies scholar and filmmaker Celine Parreñas Shimizu terms the "bind of representation."[42] As for Asian American women and other women of color in the United States, racialized sexual representation forms black women's "very self-recognition every day and every minute."[43] Because black women are tethered to ontological concepts of sexual deviance, it is vital to acknowledge hypersexuality as a disciplinary instrument that effects pain, trauma, and abuse in their lives, and which, like other problematic representations of race, gender, and sexuality, is extremely hard to escape.[44]

Black women are not just victims of representation, however. Referencing three black Oscar-winning Hollywood actresses—Hattie McDaniel, Whoopi Goldberg, and Halle Berry—feminist literary and media scholar Rebecca Wanzo shows how many black women entertainers recognize the potentially recuperative nature of their performances. "Familiar with stereotypes about black female identity," writes Wanzo, "they have attempted to reconfigure themselves as central agents of a particular project and then see themselves as making themselves objects in relationship to this racist history on their own terms."[45] Like actresses in the racist and sexist Hollywood film industry, some black actresses in the adult industry also recognize their performances as spaces to negotiate the overdetermined and reductive depictions, and try to engage them on their own terms. White American women are not judged in the same way, nor are they accused of representing the "hypersexuality of white womanhood."[46] Yet black women, as individuals, often come to stand for their entire racial group. Not only are black women performers burdened with representing every other black woman, they are seen to depict only simplistic and denigrating types.[47] Black porn actresses understand that they are seen as archetypical whores and bad women by both the black community and the broader, categorically white, culture.

Crucially, these women often assert themselves within these archetypes. Performers who not only fit the stereotype, but also boldly put it to work in their performances can be read as having more sophisticated understandings and counterresponses in relationship to representation than previously acknowledged. In discussing her role as the "voodoo girl" in *Let Me Tell Ya 'Bout Black Chicks*, Jeannie explained that she chose a role that, though still a stereotypical representation of exotic, supernatural, and hypersexual black womanhood, she saw as an alternative to the then-standard role of the maid: "So I played the part of the voodoo girl. I wanted that part. I was glad to have [it]. I loved the way they dressed me up, with the costume. They made me look very exotic with all the makeup and feathers, and I was running around [acting possessed]. But I didn't want to play the maids. Those other girls were playing maids. . . . But I like my part." By playing the exotically fetishized black woman instead of the recognizable fetish of the servile black maid, Jeannie negotiated what she saw as a demeaning representation.[48] The voodoo girl was not necessarily a positive representation against the maid's negative one, but it allowed space for Jeannie to take pleasure in what she identified as a more complex performance. Dressed as the primitive, magical savage in a tinsel skirt that looks more fitting for a luau than a voodoo ceremony, colorful neon bangles, and 1980s eye-shadow-heavy makeup, Jeannie's voodoo girl uses a magic spell to conjure two white men to satisfy her sexual appetite. Jeannie brings erotic charisma and skill to her enthusiastic performance, stretching it beyond its impish and narrow construction. And, as she attests, her choice to perform a playful, mysterious, and (literally) self-possessed female character was a strategic move. Even though this move did not fully dismantle racist regimes of representation for black women in pornography, Jeannie's tactics for self-representation are important to recognize.

Angel Kelly, a contemporary of Jeannie Pepper in the 1980s, was the first black woman to win an exclusive contract from an adult film production company, Perry Ross's Fantasy Home Video. An A-list actress like Jeannie, Angel desperately wanted to make choices in her career that would show her in what she saw as a positive light: as glamorous, sexy, and beautiful. However, sometimes the nature of the industry meant that she became mired in the stereotypical construction of black women's sexuality. Like Jeannie, Angel was pressured to portray a "voodoo woman":

There is one video called *Welcome to the Jungle*, where I look like an African, I look like voodoo woman [on the video box cover]. I hate that picture. I hated it. I hated it! And that's why I wouldn't do the movie for it. So there was no movie, but there was a [video box] cover called *Welcome to the Jungle* and what [the producer, Perry Ross] did was he just made it a compilation tape. See, they can screw you that way anyway because when they are shooting pictures they got footage on you, and they can take all your scenes out of one movie and put it with another cover in another movie.

As Angel describes, she importantly chose to stand up to the demands of her producer by refusing to star in the production. Yet she did feel pressure to dress like an "African voodoo woman" for the *Welcome to the Jungle* (1988) photo shoot, because as she told me during our phone interview in 2013, "Sometimes if you wanted to work you had to swallow it. I tried to hold on the best I could." Angel felt bitterly about the experience, noting her lack of power in relationship to the greater power of studios to use and manipulate her images. For Angel, who had on occasion played the shuffling maid to a white family (see *The Call Girl*), negotiating porn work included evaluating the terms of each production and deciding how she might infuse the role with her own desires. Angel expressed to me the pleasures she gained in her work: "I had a chance to play all types of great characters a man could fantasize about. I was surprised that I had as many female fans as I did male fans. I had the opportunity to be a star."

Black women's counterstrategies of representation involve at times attempting to play the stereotype in order to reverse or go beyond it. At other times they offer alternative, more complex images of black sexuality, or they may refuse the roles altogether.[49] In my analyses of black women's participation in pornography, I identify where they tell stereotypical stories in their performances, but also where performers appear to tell stories about themselves that aspire to go beyond stereotypes, the "immediately available" stories told about black women.[50] Illicit eroticism, like José Esteban Muñoz's concept of "disidentification," describes how cultural workers enact a repertoire of skills and theories—including appropriating or manipulating certain stereotypes—to "negotiate a phobic majoritarian public sphere that continuously elides or punishes the existence of subjects who do not conform to the phantasm of normative citizenship."[51] Unlike disidentification, illicit eroticism describes a repertoire of appropriations distinct to the realm of sexual and sexualized labor, available to those whose sexuality has been marked specifically as illicit, including people of color, and queer folk, including queer people of color. Illicit eroticism conceptualizes how these actors use sexuality in ways that necessarily confront and manipulate discourses about their sexual deviance while remaining tied to a system that produces them as marginalized sexual laborers. For Jeannie Pepper and others, leveraging one stereotype can mean avoiding another. Yet these performers' layered work as black women remains connected to their very survival within a punishing field of representation and labor.

Both Jeannie and Angel tell of their aspirations to be seen as more complicated subjects than the pornographic script allowed. Playing up, against, and within caricature, Jeannie, who delved into a stereotyped role, imagined herself as an actor depicting a woman with power, one who magically and mischievously produces men to service her sexual desires, while generating a kind of glamour and joviality. Imagining a black female pornographic sexuality as joyful, subversive, and attractive, Jeannie's performance asserts *erotic sovereignty*. Her performance attempts to reterritorialize the always already exploitable black female body as a potential site of self-governing desire, subjectivity, dependence and relation with others, and erotic pleasure.[52] Erotic sovereignty is a process, rather than a completely achieved state of being, wherein sexual subjects aspire and move toward self-rule and collective affiliation and intimacy, and against the territorializing power of the disciplining state and social corpus. It is part of an ongoing ontological process that uses racialized sexuality to assert complex subjecthood, inside of the overwhelming constraints of social stigma, stereotype, structural inequality, policing, divestment, segregation, and exploitation under the neoliberal state. Jeannie's interventions are never separate from the conditions that propelled and shaped her work in the porn industry during the 1980s, including the impact of Ronald Reagan's devastating economic policies on African Americans, and the porn business's interest in capturing white consumers for black-cast products during the video era.

By foregrounding the testimonies of black porn actresses like Jeannie Pepper and Angel Kelly, I hope to explain how black porn actresses might simultaneously challenge and conform to the racial fantasies that overwhelmingly define their representations and labor conditions. Their negotiations offer a view into black women's needs, desires, and understandings, and into the deeply felt conflict between what stories about black women exist and what stories they long to imagine for themselves. Agency, a central concept in feminist thought, is generally understood as a person's ability to achieve freedom or "progressive change" in the context of everyday and manifold forms of oppression. I draw on postcolonial scholar Saba Mahmood's productive conceptualization of agency as a "capacity for action that historically specific relations of subordination enable and create."[53] Not eliding the role of subordination, Mahmood reveals agency as existing along a continuum. At times agency enables progressive change or resistive action, and at other times and contexts it is the "capacity to endure, suffer, and persist."[54]

Rethinking the meaning of agency in relationship to black women's sexuality, I propose to open up the concept of agency by moving away from readings of its equivalence with resistive (sexual) freedom. We might instead read agency as a facet of complex personhood within larger embedded relations of subordination. Depending on the historical moment, agency emerges differently and operates along divergent nodes of power. Agency then might be seen as a dialectical capacity for pleasure and pain, exploration and denial, or for progressive change as well as everyday survival. Through my close readings of interviews with black performers in the pornography industry, we can observe their differing forms of agency given changing contexts of representation and circuits of sexual economy.

The tension described above between aspiration and inescapable constraint forms the critical spine of this book. Although it is impossible to decipher what early black pornography actors imagined and desired as they performed during the rise of pornographic photography and film in the late nineteenth and early twentieth century, it is important to think through the foundational nature of early pornography as it set the terms for the later performances, labor conditions, and forms of negotiation deployed by black adult actresses. Chapter 1 examines the fetishization of black women's bodies in early pornography and considers how those bodies served as objects of spectacle, fascination, and disdain within the visual regimes of slavery, colonialism, and Jim Crow. A compulsive desire to sexualize race and to consume sexual images of black women and men intersected with the rise of commercial pornography, creating a distinct genre that I call "race porn." Photographs and films concerning black and black-white sex illuminate how discourses of racial and sexual difference became calcified during this period. Even in the most intimate interactions in early pornography racial-sexual borders are erected, permeated, and then built up again. Deploying what I call a black feminist pornographic lens, I read the archive of early race porn to contemplate the ways in which early black models and actresses may have reached past the confines of porn texts to provide performances that give us a surprising view of black female sensuality, playfulness, and erotic subjectivity.

Chapter 2 explores the performances of black porn actresses, like Desiree

West, during the "Golden Age" of pornography in the 1970s. Not only did large-scale social transformations alter racial-sexual borders in the United States during this period, they also transformed meanings and interactions around pornography itself, such that newly popularized sexual media became an important site for black women. A combination of white fascination with black sexuality and African Americans' desire to express a new, assertive sexual politics resulted in what I call "soul porn," a genre that powerfully shaped black women's performances and labor. Yet as black actresses became agents in the production of an emergent porn industry, they faced the anxieties and subjugations of racial fetishism and were sidelined by the extreme focus on black male sexuality as the archetype for racial-sexual border crossing.

Throughout its history, technological and social forces have continuously altered the landscape of the adult industry. In the process technology has transformed the kinds of texts and modes of production black porn actresses encountered. Chapter 3 investigates how the adult industry's adoption of VHS allowed for the growth of specific markets for black and interracial video. In this new interracial subgenre black actresses like Jeannie Pepper and Angel Kelly negotiated ways to assert their performances and professional personas into a restrictive formula and sometimes hostile terrain. In the early 1990s, digital media began to shift the production, marketing, and consumption of pornography, just as the rise of hip hop music began to shift the representations, discourses, and aesthetics associated with black female sexuality.

Chapter 4 interrogates how the convergence of hip hop and pornography helped establish the trope of the black working-class woman as "ho." Deploying this figure, the porn industry maintained a segregated, niche-oriented market for black sexuality based on commercial hip hop aesthetics. In the process, the ho became an inescapable text that black women in porn must decipher, and an archetype that speaks to black women's battles to prevail in the sexual economy. Using what I call "ho theory," I analyze the representation of working-class black women's corporeal labors to insert themselves in the marketplace of desires, and to both take pleasure in and benefit from the fetishization of black women's bodies. In addition, I explore the roles of black men in hip hop pornography as they are called upon to perform the roles of pimp or stud in their sex work.

Chapter 5 focuses on the labors of black women performers by asking what socioeconomic or other forces catalyze them to pursue pornography as a field of work and site of imagination. How does illicit eroticism, the process by which subjects convert sexuality into a usable resource in the face of a number of compelling forces and constraints, factor into their motivations to become porn stars? What do black women in porn identify as the most desirable, pleasurable, and powerful aspects of the industry? Because money, sex, and fame are the hydraulic factors in my informants' articulations of the need and desire for this work, it is important to unpack how the realities of the business meet with these expectations.

If chapter 5 is concerned with how aspirations collide with real-life experiences, chapter 6 analyzes these real-life experiences and the particular kinds of entanglements and pressures black porn actresses report as constitutive elements of their illicit erotic work. Former and current black porn actresses speak about the undeniable hurdles pornographic labor poses, and about how they grapple with issues of marginalization, discrimination, and abuse as they seek to promote their erotic capital under tremendous constraint in a business that profits from their objectification and exploitation. Ultimately, these sexual laborers expose how black women are made vulnerable by—yet critically intervene in—the larger sexualized economy of advanced capitalism in the United States. Black porn workers offer an alternative moral economy that sheds light on how marginalized people within industries like porn can cocreate social meanings, challenge conditions, and imagine other worlds.

This book identifies pornography as an important location to think about sexual culture and racial ideologies, particularly in the context of the sexualization of both popular culture and economic opportunities for women. As such, it is necessarily in conversation with feminist critics and provides a launching pad to advance the conversation about the role of pornography in women's lives. Pornography is a hugely controversial topic for feminists. For more than thirty years, feminists have been engaged in a fierce debate, widely known as the Sex Wars, about pornography's role in society. The feminist antipornography movement emerged out of radical feminist activism during the 1970s, against what was viewed as the proliferation of explicit, misogynistic images in the media. Antipornography feminists like Andrea Dworkin and Catharine MacKinnon defined pornography as equivalent to gendered violence, believing that pornography was the "subordination of women perfectly achieved."[55] For them, pornography commodifies rape and endorses and encourages men's abusive sexual desires and violent behaviors toward women.[56]

Alternately, a diverse coalition of queer, anticensorship, liberal, and sex-positive feminists rejected the claims of radical antipornography feminists, citing porn as a convenient scapegoat for social-conservative attacks on sexual dissent. These critics and activists identified pornography not as a "unified (patriarchal) discourse with a singular (misogynist) impact," but rather, as Feminist Anti-Censorship Taskforce member Lisa Duggan contends, as sexual discourse that is "full of multiple, contradictory, layered, and highly contextual meanings."[57] In other words, viewing practices for pornography are varied and dynamic; viewers are not solely abused by porn or trained for violent, misogynistic behaviors. While the adult industry is shaped by the problematics of heteronormative, homophobic, transphobic, and racist corporatist practices, pornography is not a monolithic or static entity. Porn is dynamic, diverse, and open for revision, including by those on the margins such as women, sexual minorities, and people of color.

Black feminists have often followed the antiporn feminist critique described above, arguing that pornography as an industry perpetuates harmful stereotypes about black women's sexuality.[58] While these black feminist writers are not wrong, the story is more complex, and black women's performances deserve a more nuanced analysis. Not only do black women's representations in porn include portrayals that sometimes undermine stereotypes, black actresses often try to capture something quite different from the meanings normatively attached to their bodies. Moreover, black women in porn often try to revalue their images and work by fighting for better representations, asserting themselves in their roles, attempting to take control over their products, and helping other black women in the industry. Black women in porn also see themselves as a mirror for black women porn viewers. They imagine their relationship with black female porn fans—the group from which many of these performers came—as empowering and challenging to black women's sexual politics. By including the performers' voices in the discussion we can address questions that are vital to black feminisms, such as the critical significance of pornography for black women's sexual labor and its significance for their own fantasy lives.

Before she started working in porn, Jeannie Pepper was a porn fan. She had watched sex films in X-rated theaters and imagined seeing more black women like her represented. Yet she also knew that such a move into the industry would mark her with a deviance that was overdetermined by the historical construction of black gender and sexuality. While Jeannie has remained critical of the limits placed on black women in the adult industry and by black respectability politics, she found affiliation with the iconic celebrity of Josephine Baker. Baker, for Jeannie, represented a story of financial success, glamour, mobility, autonomy, and sexual rebellion. Baker, like Jeannie, was an erotic performer who became an icon. It is crucial to understand the attractions that draw black women to the pornography business. I suggest that porn work is part of a long struggle by black women to *occupy* their bodies.[59]

The primary methodological interventions of this project are twofold: first, I converse with porn actresses directly, listening to their voices and taking seriously their descriptions of their experiences; second, I read the complexity of their performances in pornographic imagery. Even as more attention is given to the workings of race in pornography, few have endeavored to learn about porn's meanings by looking at the self-presentations and self-understandings of black women working inside the industry.[60] Over more than ten years of fieldwork, I conducted ethnographic research with nearly sixty black women, and more than forty others involved in the porn business. My research included directors, producers, distributors, agents, crew, and actors. I talked to black women porn performers while they made dinner at home, signed autographs at industry conventions, networked and partied at social events, and prepared for sex scenes on porn sets. As a black woman, I discovered an affinity with my informants that unsettled the traditional methodological division between researcher and object of study. My informants trusted me, called on me, and embraced me in their lives. I also became an advocate for them: I brought my informants to speak to my classes, published their essays, and strategized with them about how to overcome career and family hardships. What I found during this decade of fieldwork and personal interactions challenged the views I had at the start.

For instance I, like many people, thought that women in porn were primarily survivors of sexual abuse who got off a bus in Hollywood and were whisked away to Porn Valley by some shady pimp. Reading nostalgic accounts of the "Golden Age" of porn in the 1970s, I also imagined film sets to be an updated version of *Boogie Nights*, where playful orgiastic sex ensued between people who really didn't care much if the camera was rolling. Instead I found no single story for the women that enter the porn business. While some admitted coming from abusive or neglectful family backgrounds, others spoke about having grounded and loving single or dual-parent households. Where I expected to see unmitigated eroticism I found work sites that were decidedly desexualized, where cast and crew moved about with workmanlike focus to get their movies made on time and, ideally, under budget.

It is only by talking to those involved in the production of pornography that we can move past some of the myths and categorical generalizations about the business and its controversial products. As a historian, I wanted to know more about how black women became part of pornography, and what the changing regulatory, technological, and social contexts of porn's development over the past century or more meant for black women's representations, working conditions, identities, and aspirations. In hunting down long-lost

vintage pornographic images in libraries and private collections, I soon realized that there was a vast missing archive of black pornography and erotica,
and that black women performing in pornography prior to its deregulation
would unfortunately have to remain unknown and, to an extent, unknowable.

As a feminist, I wanted to understand how mainstream pornography,
which appears to be so extremely focused on addressing white heterosexual
male pleasure, is actually experienced by the women involved in making it.
While it was not possible to track down black adult film actresses who worked
prior to the 1980s, I discovered that the women I did contact were willing, if
not eager, to talk about their experiences and to be understood. Like Jeannie
Pepper, they knew that even to speak about their lives and work would challenge the stigma and silence around these issues for black women. Yet my
informants fiercely desired to be seen and heard, to tell their stories and explain their performances, especially to another black woman. I had no choice
but to see and hear them. This book is my attempt to recover and redress an
untold dimension of black women's sexual lives, by letting them speak for
themselves.

# Sepia Sex Scenes

*Spectacles of Difference in Race Porn*

The same unknown actress appears in two 16 mm stag films projected onto the wall of a private collector's apartment located just down the block from Harvard University. The collector, an expert in film restoration with a soft spot for vintage erotic film, explains that it is not unusual to find footage from one pornographic film used in another because, from the 1920s to the 1960s, films were constantly edited and duplicated to make new material. The actress is an attractive black woman in her twenties, with a light-skinned complexion, pressed hair set in waves almost to her shoulders, a dancer's perfectly toned body, and bright, captivating eyes. In the first film, which like most 16 mm stags of the period was only about ten minutes long and lacked a soundtrack, the unnamed actress plays a maid. The film is titled *The Golden Shower* because the mistress of the home, Miss Park Avenue, apparently gets urinated on while having sex with her butler in the bath.[1] Following this, the intertitle claims, "desire lingers on"; Miss Park Avenue, still naked in the bath, calls for the maid to bring her robe. Dressed in a maid's uniform, the black actress arrives after she, too, has had a romp with the butler in the living room. As she begins to fulfill the sexual demands of the mistress by kissing, caressing, and providing oral sex, an intertitle announces, "No Depression here. Stock Market's down and so is the maid." Shot in the 1930s, this stag film uses humor about the financial crisis to narrate the heightened tension of the times about sex across race and class, between a black woman and a white woman, a domestic worker and a wealthy employer.

In the next film the collector screens for me, *The Hypnotist*, the same actress appears once more. This time she is Madam Cyprian, a hypnotist for hire in what appears to be her own home. A rather matronly white woman arrives with her better-dressed husband, and from the few intertitles in this

FIGURE 1.1. *Golden Shower*, 1930s. Collection of Albert Steg.

film, we can deduce that they are looking for help in their sex life from a skilled hypnotherapist. Madam Cyprian first begins a "séance" with the wife. The camera focuses on her entranced face and especially on her mesmerizing eyes, framed by gesticulating hands. Madam Cyprian leads the transfixed wife to her bedroom to have sex, returning later to enact the same "séance" with the husband, having sex with him as well. Once satisfied that she has instructed him, Madam Cyprian leads the husband to the bedroom to meet the naked, now-aroused wife. There the hypnotist directs the entranced spouses in how to have (presumably improved) sex. Finally, Madam Cyprian joins in, and the three possessed bodies form a spellbound ménage à trois. Through the black woman's exotic, sexual, supernatural abilities, the white family is magically restored. The white man, whose gaze this film was assuredly designed to address, realizes his fantasy of having both women, one domestic and the other exotic. Yet in both films, though the black actress performs two kinds of sexual labor in the service of white women and men, there are powerful moments in which the camera focuses on her mesmeric face and we find her smiling back at us, mischievously winking, comically rolling her eyes, mugging for the camera, and playfully sticking out her tongue. In these animated facial performances—what I call "facial stunting"[2]—stag-film

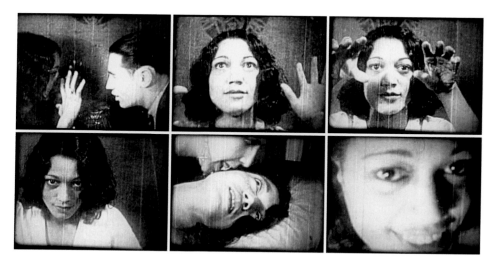

FIGURE 1.2. *The Hypnotist*, 1930s. Collection of Albert Steg.

actresses inserted a complex performance of black subjectivity into the film text. These gestures are important because they highlight how black women's performances in pornography simultaneously conformed to and challenged the representational and physical conditions of their labor.

In these gestural interventions, I argue, there are clues as to how black women in early pornographies experienced their sex work and deployed creative, embodied repertoires of performance to negotiate the representations they were called to inhabit. Imagining that actresses like the unknown woman in *The Golden Shower* and *The Hypnotist* may have intervened in these films' racialized fantasies about black womanhood, at a time when modern commercial pornography was just beginning to take shape, helps us to consider the strategies of black erotic performers more than eighty years later. If we acknowledge that black sex workers in porn are not only victims of bad representations, but sexual agents and complex social actors who work on, within, and against problematic tropes about blackness in today's pornography, we might imagine that early performers, under rather different conditions of sexual commerce, technological innovation, and racial oppression, may have done the same thing.

Stag films, or early pornographic movies, offer a rare lens through which to observe gendered sexuality, unauthorized fantasy, and racial fetishism as they were imagined, performed, captured, and circulated in the early twentieth century. This early pornography helps to historicize erotic fantasies as objects open to study. Because pornographic media were illegal in the United States during the stag-film era, we can now view only what was rescued from, or catalogued and archived by censors charged with eliminating these films. Because so much early pornography was deliberately destroyed or unintentionally lost, the remaining materials are even more remarkable for those of us hoping to trace the performances of the anonymous actors and models therein. The rarity of surviving stag films also means that it is extremely difficult to evaluate the nature of their representational codes, the labor conditions and experiences of stag performers, or the precise nature of the production and consumption of these materials. Moreover, because early pornography was both illicit and stigmatized, it is difficult to find former actors who acknowledge a role in making it. If these actors are still living, there is no simple way to track down people who worked under aliases in what was truly an underground enterprise. No one has collected their stories, no libraries keep their records, and no grandchildren, assuming they even knew about it, are proudly stepping forward to share knowledge about their grandmother's porn career during the Depression. Despite these difficulties in researching stag films it is essential to understand how black women came to be objects of interest in pornography. Although much of the evidence available in the latter part of this book—including the voices of the actors—has been lost, the stag period provides a crucial background to the story of how black women shape pornography and how they are shaped by it.

To study black women in stag films one must first reconstruct an archive of the presence of black people in this popular though underground media form. I have been involved in a process of excavation and interpretation of this lost archive of black women's images throughout this project, digging for rare photographs in bins in the street markets of Paris, culling materials from the secret vaults of institutional research centers, and screening the private collections of film buffs trading in vintage erotica. My own work has been akin to the methodology discussed by Giuliana Bruno in her book *Streetwalking on a Ruined Map*, in which she illuminates what it is like to move through an "archeological site of textual absences and voids" of a cultural production that has "not only been forgotten but lost to the historical archive."[3] Like Bruno, I am interested in exploring a "territory of subjugated popular knowledge," and, like an archeologist, I want to "mine the field" to "reveal discontinuous, diverse, and disqualified areas."[4] In mapping a genealogy of black women in pornography, this project necessarily navigates a terrain of knowledge that is incomplete, inaccessible, devalued, and dying—much of the material I found is literally disintegrating! Researchers that have been able to excise and examine the extant materials tend to focus on genre and spectatorship, rather than on the production of early pornography as a site of racial erotics, racial drama, and race relations.[5] By mining the landscape of forgotten and lost pornography I want to illuminate how pornographic images are firmly embedded in economic, social, and cultural systems that create and circulate meanings about racial difference and blackness in the West.

## A Competing Gaze

The concept of the gaze, for many feminist scholars, serves as a paradigm for asymmetrical power relations: the domination of the slave by the master, the colonized by the colonizer, and woman by man. That the spectacle of the enslaved or colonized black body was presented for a dominating "imperial gaze" is an important starting point for thinking about how black bodies have historically been imbued with sexual meanings that come to be reiterated in pornography and to have powerful legacies in U.S. media culture today.[6] That spectacle is separate from the spectacle of black people in early pornography, which was a specific genre of representation created to excite arousal and circulated to extract profit. Yet both types of spectacle—the imperial gaze and the spectacle of black bodies in stag film—are intertwined. If the function of slavery was to guarantee the use of enslaved black bodies for the needs of the master, part of the power of the master's imperial gaze was the assurance of visual pleasure, and of owning the right to look. This voyeuristic pleasure in the imperial gaze shaped black women's representations and labors, and at the same time rendered them objects of this gaze, as other and obscene, through forces of the market, law, science, art, invention, and ideology. This pornographic gaze extracted pleasure from the eroticized, fetishized creature it created. It fabricated black women as illicit erotic objects.

Imagine the abjection and pain endured by black women experiencing the sexualized nature of spectacularized vision: their very sense of self attached to the look of others, the profound forces of social control they experienced daily linked to the exposing imagery of their bodies. Yet despite these very real material constraints black women faced as spectacles, we must not forget their subjectivity.

I propose that the spectacle of racial and sexual fetishism in early pornography can be reread to include moments of subjectivity, consensual expression, and sometimes, resistance alongside histories of sexual subordination. Since the 1970s many scholars have challenged gaze theory, arguing that the spectator/spectacle relationship is not merely one of social control, but is full of contradictions and reversals.[7] What I am suggesting here is that, although the pornographic gaze—the visual culture around black women's sexuality that gives rise to the formal industry of pornography in the late-twentieth century—has, at its roots, a racial and sexual fetishism obsessed with the fascinations and horrors of black women's difference, this relationship of power can be, and has been, refused, deflected, and appropriated by black women themselves.

The idea that black women could insert subjectivity, agency, or even resistance into oppressive and alienating representations like pornography may seem unthinkable. This unthinkability is especially the case for the period under discussion in this chapter, spanning slavery to Jim Crow, when African Americans embraced conservative moral values to counter discourses of black sexual deviance. Because historians have often allied the narrative of black resistance with conservative sexual morality to counter sexual appropriation and abuse, my choice to center the pornographic may seem to risk reasserting the dominant perception of black sexual pathology and inferiority. Yet, to see black women only as spectacles fixes them in a passive role that denies them any chance of articulating their own desires, pleasures, and needs.[8]

Discussions of how black women operate on the sexual margins continue to produce anxiety among blacks about how all black people might be seen by whites, and about the purported romanticization of rogue actors, who, in accommodating racist and sexist images, fail to present a favorable view of the black community. As many scholars have argued, black subjects on the margins call into question the logic upholding bourgeois gender and sexual norms within black communities, which have been used as a bid to achieve civil and human rights.[9] These marginals expose gender and sexuality as disciplinary regimes which when embraced by black communities, all too often, propel the very regimes of racist, biopolitical control of black populations that black people are attempting to resist. Black gender and sexual outsiders—sex workers, queers, gender nonconformists, and others—offer a lens through which to view how racial power is always bound to gender and sexuality, and how those persisting under these intersecting oppressions labor to negotiate and shape the forces of race, gender, and sexuality in their lives.

This book attempts to conceptualize how black women's historical subordination operates in chorus with their always-present insurgency against the unbearable weight of oppression in their lives. Using a mobile conceptual framework that I term "black feminist pornographics," this chapter launches a reading practice that strategically speculates on the evidence missing from this incomplete archive. Inspired by my research on living performers in the adult industry (see chapters 3–6), this methodology argues that attempts to assert a competing vision of value and desire—a competing gaze—are embedded in the most egregious and mundane representations. These moves toward a competing gaze may not always be successful, or progressive, but they are always contestatory of existing looking relations.[10]

For black women, representation is a contest of wills. This understanding leads me to what might be considered an anachronistic and even risky scholarly practice of reading backward, recovering black women performers' subjectivity through taking seriously chance moments like the self-aware facial performance of the unnamed actress who opens this chapter. To read backward is to revise history. Beyond recounting black women's appearance in early pornography and the kinds of representational fetishes they were called upon to embody in their performances, this recovery of the archive involves speculating on how they might have experienced and made use of pornography as a site of erotic labor and expression, while holding in tension the ways that they must have also experienced it as a space of exploitation and constraint. While we cannot know the intent of these unknown and unknowable actors, I argue that we must consider their possible resistant uses of pornography despite the probable conditions that existed for them under particular and shifting historical circumstances. To imagine a space for black women's resistance in early pornography, we can plumb the ambivalent performances found in this dying archive. This is a necessary risk for the project of centering the subjectivity of marginal black woman actors.

## Black Feminist Pornographics: A Brief History

Black sexual history is not merely a story of expropriation and regulation, but one that involves black people's sustained battle for sexual subjectivity, agency, and autonomy. A wide range of expressive forms have given voice to black Americans' aspirations for erotic sovereignty. Following the demise of slavery in the United States, sexuality, Angela Davis writes, became an essential domain for black women to activate subjectivity, agency, and autonomy: "For the first time in the history of the African presence in North America, masses of black women and men were in a position to make autonomous decisions regarding the sexual partnerships into which they entered. Sexuality was thus one of the most tangible domains in which emancipation was acted upon and through which its meanings were expressed. Sovereignty in sexual matters marked an important divide between life during slavery and life after emancipation."[11] Though songstresses like Gertrude "Ma" Rainey,

Bessie Smith, and Billie Holiday were not always the authors of their lyrics, their performance of blues songs still expressed a complex sexual experience and consciousness that would have been impossible under slavery. Davis reads chance moments in blues performances as evidence of black women articulating their longings for love, intimacy, and sexual pleasure alongside critiques of their racist lynching, exploitative wage labor, systemic abuse, and grinding poverty. These "blues women" show that within expressions of sexual subjectivity there can exist critiques of sexual and other kinds of oppression and injustice.

Like the blues, early photographic and film pornography featuring black women functioned as a tangible domain for sexual subjectivity and sociality. Black women's dynamic pornographic performances provide sites to imagine where, even when they do not control the means or modes of production, black women could potentially express a visual poetics of erotic being and relation. In addition, like blues women, black women in pornography confronted both forces of structural oppression and expectations from the African American community to live up to middle-class respectability.

I continue Davis's method of reading subjectivity in performance in order to discover black performers' own longings for visual pleasure and erotic sovereignty in the pornographic archive. Because early pornography lacked sound, I do not attend to the lyrical revisions or to the grain of the voice of the performer articulating feeling or meaning, as Davis does with the audible texts of blues women.[12] Nevertheless, these silent performances do contain sonorous looks and gestures. It is in these embodied expressions that I find evidence of how black performers launched critiques about the pornographic project and even gained pleasure through this performance. I also follow Hortense Spillers who argues that black womanhood is socially constructed in complex ways that render black women as both belonging to and alien to what it means to be black and a woman, and as simultaneously insiders and outsiders to these fraught and policed categories.[13] I read representations, performances, and labors of black women in pornography in ways that maintain these important complexities while imaginatively recovering their subjectivity from the erasure of history. Given the complicated meanings attributed to the black female body and black women's subjectivity, the challenge of reading stag film lies in learning to read how they activate themselves in the overdetermined realm of pornography as more than objects or bodies, but as performing and laboring subjects with their own ideas about sexual expression and autonomy.

For example, the engaging, unnamed black actress in the two stag films discussed above was called upon to represent black women's sexuality in ways that affirmed ideas about black women's *differentness* from whites, in their ultimately obscene and grotesque interiority. Yet her playful, self-aware performance suggests alternative readings are possible, including ones that account for the actress's labor in employing sexual, gender, and racial meanings and then revising them. By making an unruly spectacle of herself,[14] our maid/Madam Cyprian shows black women's potential, sometimes volatile, investment in their own spectacularization through performances I analyze later in the chapter. But first, I provide a brief narrative of how nineteenth- and early twentieth-century meanings about black female sexuality have been mobilized in pornography. Next I examine how black women might have used these meanings for multiple ends. From the fractured gestures left to us in the incomplete archive of stag film, my own speculating gaze seeks to recover black women's negotiations at the emergence of modern commercial pornography.

*Spectacles*

To understand black women's representations and labors in modern commercial pornography we must begin with the understanding that their sale as slaves on the auction block was an explicitly sexual, even pornographic process of exhibition, performance, and psychosocial trauma. The representations found in pornography today have their roots in the meanings created about black women's bodies during slavery, and later, post-emancipation in the United States and colonialism in Africa. Contemporary spectacles of black female sexuality in porn emerge not only from these earlier knowledges and visual regimes; they are embedded in a political economy of sexualized labor that also has its genesis in slavery. The "spectacle of the slave market" sometimes included a coffle, a coerced performance of a jovial song by slaves as they were led to sale.[15] The spectacle of the chained black bodies of women, men, and children moving and singing as they were led to sale in the public market provides a stunning example of how, for enslaved Africans, the "exercise of power was inseparable from its display."[16] This exhibition made visible the difference between enslaved and free, and the differentness of blacks, a category of persons equated with enslavement. An image of haunting despair, the coffle functioned to attract potential buyers and to fascinate observers, who then imagined those black bodies to absorb the projection of their desires and identities. Within the captive, suffering body, Saidiya Hartman observes, blackness provided an "imaginative surface" for the power relationship between master and slave.[17] This imaginative surface became a site for the projection of a "nexus of race, subjection, and spectacle," as well as for "forms of racial and race(d) pleasure, enactments of white dominance and power, and the reiteration and/or rearticulation of the conditions of enslavement."[18] Linking blackness to the display or spectacle of trauma upon and mastery over the enslaved, the slave economy enacted the ritual subjection of the black body as a visual regime, one in which the holders of the gaze took voyeuristic pleasure.

Historian Walter Johnson suggests that there was a pornographic element to the sexual economy of slavery. He depicts the auction block as a visual event, where buyers became intimately involved with and aroused by "reading bodies" of slaves in the inspection process at market. Johnson writes about the story of a female slave who was brought into the "inner room" of the marketplace and, according to one witness, was then "indecently '*examined*' in the presence of a dozen or fifteen brutal men."[19] Although slave buyers legitimated such "examinations" as necessary to confirm the reproductive abilities of slaves expected to produce more profit-generating slaves, Johnson argues that such a claim actually "served as public cover for a much more general interest in her naked body."[20] The rationalizations of slave buyers were "careful stories" that masked "something everybody knew: that for white men, examining slaves, searching out hidden body parts, running hands over limbs, massaging abdomens and articulating pelvic joints, probing wounds and scars with fingers, was erotic."[21] This corporeal intimacy of power enacted on the bodies of enslaved blacks reflected a ritualistic, private eroticism at the heart of domination. These ritualistic examinations in the slave pen resemble the imaginative, titillating, and consumptive practices of pornography. "Gazing, touching, stripping, and analyzing aloud," Johnson tells us, "the buyers read the slaves' bodies as if they were coded versions of their own imagined needs."[22] The process of "reading bodies" at the slave market vitalizes our understanding of the deep, intimate, tactile, and scopophilic gaze that made black female bodies legible for economic, political, and social relations. Their blackness and femaleness served as objects upon which to animate desire and capital. Black women's fecund, firm breasts signified their capacity to create wealth for the plantation economy, to perform sexual labor, and to suckle the children of their owners, thereby reproducing the white family and its inheritance through gendered labor.

In addition to being sites of visual pleasure, enslaved black women's bodies were loci for a variety of mechanisms of domination in the antebellum sexual political economy. The exclusion of blacks from legal rights codified their subordination through laws that ensured that "children inherited their status as enslaved or free from their mothers," and that sanctioned sexual violence against enslaved women.[23] Adrienne Davis explains that in the antebellum sexual economy of slavery "enslaved women's reproductive capacity" was converted into "market capital to serve economic interests. In the United States it was enslaved women who reproduced the workforce."[24] The transference of enslavement and inheritance of inferior status through the coerced reproductive use of black women's bodies was a particularly egregious formation of violence—normatively ensured in law and custom—that Hortense Spillers terms "high crimes against the flesh."[25] This political economy of sexuality not only maximized profits for the slaveholding class, it also institutionalized access to black women's bodies, compelling them to perform sexual labor for the purposes of pleasure and punishment.[26] The overt market for mixed-race, quadroon, and octoroon "sex slaves" was especially profitable: so-called fancy girls were usually sold at auction where "anxious buyers bid up the price many times that of a good field hand."[27] White men, the endowed rulers of this racist and sexist heteropatriarchal system, justified their sexual coercion of black women by arguing that not only did black women's lascivious ontology and "relaxed morals" make them willing participants, but the degraded and "casual" nature of sex with them protected white female chastity.[28] Pleasure, masked by rationalizations, denials, and "careful stories,"[29] enabled the creation of "economies of the flesh,"[30] markets for the use and abuse of black female bodies for a range of economic, political, medical, scientific, and entertainment purposes.

Another grievous dimension to the formation of black female bodies as objects of a probing, pornographic gaze, even before the emergence of pornography as a commercial visual form, can be traced to the voyeuristic, penetrative discourses and practices of "racial science." The legendary 1810–15 London and Paris exhibition of Sara Baartman, a South African woman of the Khoi-San tribes, was only one part of a broader entertainment custom of exhibiting human curiosities as "freaks" of nature, and specifically African women as Hottentot Venuses. Baartman's "freakishness" was seen as empirical evidence of both her pathological racial biology and her sexual degeneracy, and as iconic of black racial inferiority. As the "central image of the black female" during the nineteenth century,[31] Baartman's most famous Hottentot Venus embodied the "living evidence—the proof, the Truth" of her "absolute 'otherness' and therefore of an irreversible difference between the 'races.'"[32] The evidence for this difference was located in her supposedly primitive genitalia, including her protruding buttocks, which scientists designated a pathology termed "steatopygia." Even more fascinating for scientists, like the leading French anatomist and zoologist Georges Cuvier who later dissected Baartman's body upon her untimely death, was the "Hottentot Apron"—an elongation of the labia minora. Although it was later found to be a customary manipulation practiced by some African women to achieve sexual desirability in their communities, early nineteenth-century scientists in Europe believed the "remarkable development of the labia minora" was an inherited trait that, along with the steatopygia, tellingly "distinguish[ed] these parts at once from those of any of the ordinary varieties of the human species."[33] Examined through laboratory tests and dissection following death, the sexual parts of black women appeared to provide physiognomic evidence for the ascendant polygenic view that people of African descent emerged from a separate and inferior race. African women's assumed "primitive" genitalia confirmed their "'primitive' sexual appetite, and vice versa."[34] This categorization of black females as innately sexually different and deviant pervaded understandings of black people as the "nearest approximation of the lower animals."[35] In fact, European observers of African women had long circulated their suppositions that black women's simian-like animality lay in their inability "to guide or controll [sic] lust."[36] Their alleged desire to copulate with apes and practices of bestiality were imagined by writers like Edward Long, who in 1770 wrote that "an oran-outang husband would [not] be any dishonour to an Hottentot female; for what are these Hottentots?"[37]

Through scientists' intimate examination and, finally, dissection of Sara Baartman, she became the "master text on black female sexuality for Europe's scientific community."[38] Yet this medical scientific gaze was also "tempered with eroticism."[39] In Cuvier's notes we find an arousing interest that counters the supposed repulsion to Baartman's alleged deviance found elsewhere: her shoulders, back, and the top of her chest were "graceful," her arms "well made," her hand "charming," and her foot "alluring."[40] This simultaneous fascination and fear shaped how Baartman and other women like her became "eroticized/exoticized" black venuses in the European imagination, important figures whose public display titillated white spectators.[41] Following Baartman's dissection under Cuvier's direction, a pornographic gaze continued to orient her display: Baartman's genitals and a cast of her body, including her famous protruding buttocks, were exhibited in the Musée de l'Homme in Paris for many years, and lithographic drawings of her nude body in frontal and profile view were widely circulated. The practice of fetishistically displaying African bodies in museums and in "living exhibitions" for world's fairs and shows continued during the nineteenth and early twentieth centuries all over Europe and the United States. These displays operated as extensions of the voyeuristic taxonomic project of scientific racism. The frontal and profile views established during the investigations of the Hottentot Venus also gave rise to visual practices of capturing and indexing "mug shots" of criminals, racial others, and the mentally ill and the disabled for years to come.

Technologies of looking, categorizing, and dissecting that produced the alluring stigmata of the black woman's body became associated with the emerging discourses on gendered deviance. As Sander Gilman argues, this included prostitutes as an "atavistic subclass" that, along with black women, were considered "outsiders."[42] The figures of the black woman and prostitute were both important to the development of the Western nineteenth-century medical-scientific sexual apparatus. The supposed sexual perversion and degeneracy of black women, prostitutes, and queers instantiated hierarchies of sexual and racial difference, but also generated systems of surveillance to manage the line between the normal and the deviant.[43] As such, the sexual labor of the black female body included not only coerced work as a scientific object, but the burden of defining the terms and mechanisms of normativity, citizenship, and belonging. The circulation of theories about black women's nonnormative racial, gender, and sexual nature operated in a transatlantic framework; discourses and practices of the emerging sciences of race and sexuality traveled between Europe and the United States, just as pornography soon would.

### Early Studio Photographic Pornography

Although written pornography had been circulating in Europe for centuries, the new technology of photography made it a commercial visual form.[44] Modern pornography developed among European elites in the fraught politics of the age between the Renaissance and the French Revolution.[45] The consequent repression by religious and political authorities drove pornography, in both its literary and visual forms, underground. Photography revolutionized how pornography was consumed and prompted its mass-market industrialization, but this technology also transformed its content. Pornography became less concerned with political critique and more interested in the process of visualizing the body, particularly women's bodies, as the essential and natural locus of sexuality. From the mid- to the late nineteenth century, thousands of pornographic photographs were made and sold as *académies* or studies of nude models that were intended for use by professional and student artists, but were also purchased by elite consumers. These académies then morphed into the more lucrative and intentionally titillating form of boudoir images.[46] Académies and early boudoir photographs are some of the earliest pornography depicting black women outside of the hybrid form of ethnopornography, which included the scientific documentation of African women as part of the European colonial project in Africa.[47]

Black women often appeared in académies and boudoir images as hand-maids and attendants to white women. In these images, black women bathe, dress, brush the hair, or otherwise attend to the needs of their white mis-tresses. Reflective of Orientalist Western art traditions of presenting the reclining white nude accompanied by black women, children, or eunuchs, boudoir images usually portrayed sumptuously decorated rooms with the intricate fabrics and feminine accouterments reminiscent of a harem.[48] The presence of the black figure in these images suggests the sexual availability and consciousness of the white female nude. The contrast between white and black feminized bodies also asserts the symbolic power of white, feminine, idealized beauty. Edouard Manet's *Olympia* (1865) is the best-known example of this sexualized black-white duo in Western art. Olympia's maid, presenting flowers from an inferred suitor, marks the white woman's status as a prosti-tute and, by virtue of her blackness, confirms the illicit quality of the scene. The white female is sexualized through the lascivious and always-already-a-prostitute symbol of black womanhood. As in the fine arts, the emerging low form of boudoir images used black servants to mark the sexual availability of the white female and the illicitness of the imminent act of sex. Through contrast, they also highlight the beauty of the central figure.[49] Black women's bodies in this context force a distinction between the nude and the naked woman: "The 'nude' body is an aesthetically pleasing, idealized rendering, while the 'naked' is a more realistic, less flattering depiction."[50] Whereas white women's bodies signify seduction and a normative aesthetic of beauty, the black woman is figured as having a separate and subordinate sexuality marked by the unaesthetic weight of her black skin.

Nineteenth-century boudoir photographs of black women alone were rare. One circa-1850s daguerreotype of an anonymous black woman by an unknown photographer in the United States that is held in the special collec-tions library of the Getty Institute suggests an alluring sexual awareness that signifies black women's status as concubines and prostitutes in the antebellum Fancy Trade. Discussed in Willis and William's *The Black Female Body*, the daguerreotype depicts this woman presenting herself for the male observer on a lace-covered sofa that evokes the hyper-feminine but cheap decorative sen-sibilities of the brothel.[51] In exposing her genitals and raising her arm to draw attention to the line of her breasts, the photographer manufactures an image of an available woman. The woman's hand touches her genitals at the center of the frame, suggesting the exchange value of this visual economy, while the

FIGURE 1.3. Boudoir photograph, likely French origin, late nineteenth century.
Collection Archives D'Éros by Éditions Astarté © http://www.archivesderos.com.

lack of focus around her lower body underscores the fantasy of her sexuality. Contemplative, the young woman seems to be looking at a far-off dreamy place. If this image conflates black women's sexuality with concubinage and prostitution, as Willis and Williams assert, then, I argue, it simultaneously underscores how their sexual labor intersects with pornography. Indeed, because images of black women's sex work in the antebellum United States are so rare, this image illuminates a moment in the history of black women's sex work, during which, in the years leading up to and following the Civil War, black women were battling between the forces of coercion and the desire for consent in their labor.[52]

Photographs of black couples during this era are also rare, and most extant images of interracial couples appear to feature black men and white women, especially in Europe where the smaller population of black people perhaps allowed for less policing of the sexual boundaries between races during this period. In light of the fact that the grouping of black women and white men was not common then, I was excited to find at least three series, likely of French origin from the 1890s to 1910s, and all printed in sepia tones, in the collections of the Kinsey Institute and Éditions Astarté. Located in Bloomington, Indiana, and Paris, France, the broad dispersal of pictures from each series reveals at least two vectors in the transnational circulation of these images. In one series, a plump, brown-skinned woman gives a dynamic performance in a sequence of poses opposite her young, white male co-model. While he performs an ecstasy-filled climax by tilting back his head, eyes closed, with a slight mustached smile, she, on her hands and knees, performs a kind of comedic bewilderment. Leaning on one elbow and turning toward the camera, she scrunches up her face in a droll grimace, as if to play off the almost serene pleasure expressed by her partner. This unknown model's facial expressions, which move alternately from devilish to guileless to teasing, seem to tap into the trend for some pornographic photographs and postcards coming out of fin de siècle Europe to use comedic play and double meanings to poke fun at social proprieties and the privileged.[53]

Given the gulf between the status of white men and black women in the context of the French empire, another series stood out because the texture of the couple's interaction was noticeably familiar and gentle. The photographs feature a voluptuous, dark-skinned black woman and a stout white man. In several of the images the youthful interracial couple embrace in a sensual kiss, and in others they engage in hardcore—that is, penetrative and explicit—sex acts that also take on the grain of tenderness. The images are charged by the eroticism of the interracial pairing and a palatable mutual attraction between

FIGURE 1.4. French origin series, late nineteenth to early twentieth century.
Collection Archives D'Éros by Éditions Astarté © www.archivesderos.com.

the models. This sexual performance conveys gentleness, sensuality, and a sense of fair exchange and equality between subjects. In one photograph he sits on her lap and in another they stand and embrace; in both they kiss, revealing a surprising intimacy. While it is important not to reify intimacy as the only mode of displaying sexual equity and progressive erotic relation, given the taboo of presenting interracial couplings as mutually interested, almost romantic couples, this series stands out as subversive for its time.

This moment of intimacy between a black woman and white man in fin de siècle French erotic photography was not replicated in the United States, however. It is not until later, during the 1920s and '30s, that black women or men appear in any great number in erotic studio pornography in America, and many of those images are stills taken during film shoots rather than images found in the independent circulation of erotic photography. This notable absence is curious. It could relate to the fact that so many early images were confiscated and destroyed by censors. Photographs of black women and men in sensual situations, be they alone, together, or with whites, would have been seen as especially obscene and deserving of confiscation and destruction. The absence could also speak to the powerful prohibitions around interracial mixing and fears of miscegenation specific to the U.S. context. During a period of wholesale vigilantism against black men, women, and children, at the turn of the century, the charged energies around racialized sexualities seem to have been directed toward other sites such as violent public spectacles like lynching or the comedic parodies of blackface minstrelsy. The surviving erotic photographs of black women that circulated during this period are fascinating because they show the primacy of racialized and gendered aesthetics of beauty in erotic studio photographs as they became increasingly manufactured. In this early period, women seem to have been older, more voluptuous, and darker skinned than later, when feminine, lithe bodies and light skin tone—reflective of the normative ideal of women's beauty—became dominant.

One photograph taken some time before World War I shows a corpulent, dark-skinned black woman posing in front of a shabby doorway. Standing directly facing the camera with her hands to her sides, she is naked except for her stockings and shoes, which we can see have holes. The model's dress is crumpled on the ground at her feet as if she had removed it in a hurry. It is as if the amateurish photographer wanted to quickly capture a black woman as a sort of pseudoscientific study of racial types. The lack of adornment and care of her body by the photographer and her apparent poverty and frozen stance heightens the voyeuristic quality of the image. Yet there is something unavailable about this woman: her gaze seems to push back against the probing looks of the photographer and the viewer. Her expectant stance underscores the fact that the image was taken as part of monetary sexual exchange.

A second photograph, this time from the 1930s–1940s, presents a smiling black woman standing in front of a blanket used as a backdrop and posing with her hands behind her head. This pose functions to accentuate the lift of the model's breasts and the curvature of her waistline. Captured about twenty years after the previous photography, this image possesses a very different quality. The patterned blanket in the background offers some adornment, while two lights illuminate this woman's body much more clearly than in the earlier image. The model is notably more light skinned than the first woman, and her long wave-set hair parted in the middle and slim body adhere to standards of beauty in the African American community at the time. Aside from the clear technical development that occurred between the creation of the first and second photographs, what stands out most is the contrasting embodiment of the women. The woman in the second image smiles coquettishly for the camera in a way that expresses a visceral sense of eroticism. Wearing makeup and carefully arched eyebrows like popular film stars, she expresses a prettiness and confidence. Communicating this potent self-awareness, she seems to self-consciously display her body. Her exhibitionism separates this image from the first one, and connects it to many photographs I have found of African American women from the 1930s forward that present black women as erotic agents.

Another image likewise displays the model's understanding of pornography's scopic practice. This model also fully engages the camera. Looking directly at the photographer/viewer and holding her hand on her hip as she stands fully nude, we see she has adorned herself with makeup and a large flower in her hair in the style of Billie Holiday. With confronting gazes, practiced poses, and knowing expressions, these models convey an erotic subjectivity that marks a turning point in the evolution of pornographic images of black women. Although it remained publicly censored, by the 1930s pornography had become widespread. Black women's involvement in pornographic media was linked to their larger relationship to the commodification of black performance and black sexual economies.

## Hustling Women

We know little about who the women in early pornographic photography were, and the same goes for pornographic film actresses in this era. What did they experience, and what might they have said about their performances and

FIGURES 1.5–1.6. French origin series, late nineteenth to early twentieth century. Courtesy of the Kinsey Institute for Research in Sex, Gender, and Reproduction.

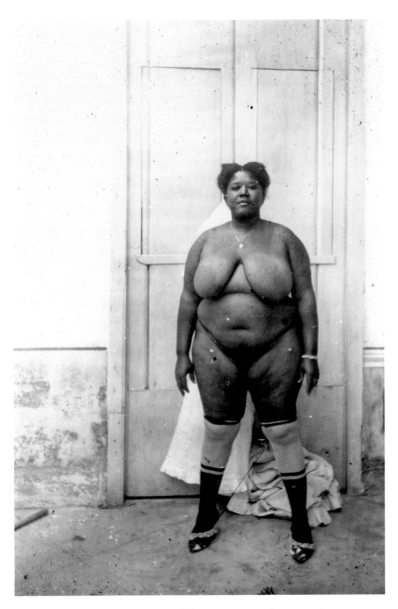

FIGURE 1.7. An unavailable gaze. Likely U.S. origin, early twentieth century. Courtesy of the Kinsey Institute for Research in Sex, Gender, and Reproduction.

FIGURE 1.8. Expressing prettiness and confidence. Untitled, U.S. origin, 1930s–40s. Courtesy of the Kinsey Institute for Research in Sex, Gender, and Reproduction.

work? We do know that because pornography was illegal before the 1970s, these early actresses were part of a clandestine sexual underworld and many were prostitutes.[54] During the proliferation of photographic and moving image pornography in the United States before and after World War I and following World War II, major social transformations occurred that changed the lives of millions of African Americans. The Great Migration of African Americans from the rural South to northern urban centers such as New York,

FIGURE 1.9. Conveying an erotic subjectivity. Untitled, U.S. origin, 1930s–40s. Courtesy of the Kinsey Institute for Research in Sex, Gender, and Reproduction.

Chicago, Detroit, Cleveland, and Philadelphia gave rise to their massive segregation in urban enclaves.[55] These ghettos contained a vibrant nightlife where blues and jazz music and theatrical performance were not only important modes of expression but also some of the few forms of capital African Americans had.

As African Americans reached a new level of visibility, a kind of "Negrophilia" emerged, giving rise to appropriations of African "primitivism" and

African American vernacular traditions in modern art, the surrealist movement, and popular culture. With the rise of a new "black aesthetic," northern
whites were introduced to black culture in the clubs, dance halls, and cabarets, which they consumed with voyeuristic and hedonistic pleasure.[56] Black
women migrants, regarded as "sexually degenerate, and therefore, morally
dangerous," became innovators in musical theater, cabaret, and burlesque
performance, and actors in the sexual economy linked to these leisure and
entertainment worlds.[57] Josephine Baker was an iconic figure for modern
black female performance culture as it circulated in the United States and
Europe. Baker's skillful nude performances, which built upon a long tradition
of black burlesque, invited white spectators to take pleasure in black women's
sexuality, to see them as newly desirable, and to explore their own erotic identification with blacks.[58]

The 1920s ushered in a sexual revolution, a vast transformation of gendered and racialized sexual mores informed by the profound influence of
black performance culture of the Jazz Age. These performances were saturated with illicitness linked to the specific charge of black sexuality in a segregated and quickly modernizing society.[59] In the shadows of a divided nation,
blacks and whites met in public and private sites of contact and exchange, in
what Kevin Mumford terms "interzones."[60] These spaces were circumscribed
by eugenic, middle-class Progressive Reform campaigns against commercial
vice, "white slavery," sexual degeneracy and disease—campaigns aimed at
saving white women and children from the contagion of the racialized urban
landscape. Even as they offered forums for forbidden, cross-racial, and often,
same-sex sociality, interzones were an arena for racial and sexual control.
"Prohibition contributed an aura of criminality to some of the proceedings
as white-controlled organized crime infiltrated the environment," write John
D'Emilio and Estelle Freedman of the Jazz Age sex industry. "Law enforcement agencies looked the other way, caring less about some forms of black
behavior than they would if it were white."[61] Campaigns to eradicate red-
light districts only drove these contact zones into the margins, and much to
the chagrin of the black middle class, to black neighborhoods.[62] These districts functioned to spatialize the sex industry in ways that specifically affected black women. White prostitution operated indoors, while black women
were forced to work the streets.[63] Although vulnerable to police harassment
and arrest, many black working-class women during the period chose prostitution over the main alternative for black women's work: grueling and exploitative domestic labor. Domestic labor exposed black women to sexualized

violence; it isolated them in white households and made them vulnerable to extortion from their bosses. This fact, in combination with low wages and punishing working conditions, led many black women to turn to the illicit economy of sex work.[64]

University of Chicago sociologists St. Clair Drake and Horace R. Cayton's landmark study of African American migration and community formation discusses "Hustling Women" among lower-working-class urban denizens in Chicago's Bronzeville section.[65] The study provides rare accounts of commercialized prostitution in black neighborhoods from black community members, the governmental and policing apparatus, and prostitutes themselves. During the hard economic times of the Great Depression, black "streetwalkers" became more prevalent, increasing the reputation of Bronzeville as a "vice area."[66] One resident complained, "Honey, this place is full of whores. They are the cheapest, nastiest set in Chicago. If I could get me another place I wouldn't be here."[67] An official from the Chicago Vice Squad admitted: "The Depression has caused a lot more hardship among the Negroes than it has among the whites. Since the Depression prostitution has increased about 20 per cent. Recently our 12 p.m.-to-8 a.m. shift has picked up an average of a hundred girls a month."[68] A Social Service Department of Morals Court member agreed: "The question of vice in the Negro district is mostly streetwalking. . . . Police arrest street-walkers rather than prostitutes in the higher-class vice resorts."[69] Across the United States, growing numbers of black women turned to prostitution, while increasing numbers of black women working as prostitutes were criminalized. In New York City during the 1930s, black women accounted for more than 50 percent of the arrests for prostitution, which amounted to an arrest rate ten times that of whites. In Harlem, 80 percent of the black women arrested in 1935 were charged with "immoral sex behavior."[70]

Unemployed or underemployed in traditional labor sectors, black women lacked access to other areas of work reserved for men and white women. These mainly poor women in Bronzeville were simply trying to eke out a living: "If they could just get a job scrubbing floors you wouldn't see them trying to be whores very long," said one police captain.[71] But most black women did not want to scrub floors. Even educated women saw prostitution as an alternative to the poorly paid, menial work they too were destined to perform. A judge at the Morals Court admitted: "We have Negro girls come in here who are high school girls. I ask them why they are prostitutes and they tell me that the only work they can get is housework, waitresses, and in hotels. It is true that many of these girls cannot get employment because of their race. The Negro girls who have better education want the better things of life. They are not satisfied to work for these small wages."[72]

"I didn't want to do housework," one former white-collar worker reported. "Here I had been in some kind of office since I was fourteen years old. Now why should I start scrubbing floors at this late date in life? I tried first one thing and then another, and I couldn't make a hit of it, so . . ."[73] Another "young woman in a buffet flat" expressed her extreme disgust with what she identified as the much more exploitative labor of domestic work when she said: "When I see the work maid—why, girl, let me tell you, it just runs through me! I think I'd sooner starve."[74] Revealing the deep extent to which domestic work was reviled, these testimonies underscore the salience of sex work as a labor option for many black women in the urban context. While both trades involved a dimension of sexual exploitation, the fact that so many women turned to sex work instead of domestic work reveals that they identified the former as an area in which they could assert greater control over their bodies. "Black prostitutes and vice workers," writes Kali N. Gross about early twentieth-century Philadelphia, "seemed to use sex as a transformative vehicle, possibly embracing the illicit in an attempt to dismantle sex as a potential instrument of violation."[75]

Black actresses and models involved with early pornography were likely actors in these sexual markets and, using sex work as a form of survival, may have also embraced illicit sex to dismantle their prevailing sexual exploitation. If they were not involved in street hustling or brothel work, these performers traded sex informally as a supplement to their work in other sectors, including the entertainment and leisure industries, and underground circuits of vice such as gambling, theft, and counterfeiting. Some might have been among the black women who worked as madams, or those who ran income generating sex parties in private apartments known as "buffet flats." Conceivably, some of these sex workers may have been approached to come to a photo or film shoot by purveyors in the black communities in which they lived and worked.

For whites, black women symbolized the ultimate sexual deviance, and white men were known to be black sex workers' most eager (and affluent) customers. Patterns of the commercial sex industry were closely linked to the trade and orientation of pornography, and both served the desires and preferences of white male managers and clientele. Discussing one client's unusual erotic tastes, one black prostitute at the time contended: "They seem to feel that, because some of us have remote ancestors who lived in Africa once, we are primitives at heart when it comes to sex."[76] This element of sex tourism, which operated at the interzones where white and black people met for social and commercial purposes, was mentioned by another commentator in 1934: "I have seen colored girls galore, catering to a white clientele who are satisfied to pay high prices for novelties offered."[77] This account of black sexual labor for a plurality of white sexual fantasies was also confirmed by Malcolm X, who was himself a steerer (a transporter of clients to prostitutes) in the 1940s: "Negroes catered to monied white people's weird sexual tastes. . . . Harlem was their sin-den, their fleshpot. . . . I wouldn't tell all the things I've seen."[78]

As Malcolm X and the prostitutes quoted above reveal, black sex workers had a sophisticated awareness about the nature of the sexual marketplace as it was organized according to hierarchies of racial value and realms of racial fetishism, and a sense about how to navigate them—to hustle—in their own interests. For historians Cynthia Blair, Tera Hunter, Victoria Wolcott, Kali N. Gross, and Cheryl Hicks, black women's sex work from the late nineteenth century to the Depression era and World War II provided an arena for black women to exhibit economic self-reliance and individual self-respect, make choices about their labor, contest prevailing black middle-class sexual and gender values, and struggle against the meanings and modes of control that disciplined black female sexuality at every turn.[79] As we consider black women's sex work, and as we think about their performances in pornographic texts, we must continue to hold in tension the understanding that the exploitative conditions of economic disenfranchisement, discriminatory segregation, and abusive criminalization were met by black women's own labors to survive, to assert themselves, and to move within and against sexual expropriation in ways that suited them. Hustling is a tool of survival for the dispossessed. Yet in putting their sexualities to work, these women may have seen this tactic as open to revision, mediation, and other worlds of imagination.[80]

*Race Porn*

If black prostitution offered white clientele the ability to enact racial sexual fantasy and blacks an economy in which to exploit these fantasies for their own economic and personal needs, illicit pornographic film production provided another arena for these conflicting desires to operate. Moving-image pornography from 1908 to the late 1960s, known in America as "stags" or "blue movies," was generally commercially produced and distributed to clandestine male audiences.[81] To call these films stags is to refer to the intended male spectator: screenings of stags were "instructional and communal" functions that offered sites of ritualistic socialization and initiation in homosocial spaces like fraternal societies and men's clubs.[82] These gatherings were also known as "smokers" for all the cigar or cigarette smoke that would fill the room. Because the films were silent, "both inter-titles and the audience repartee articulated an oral culture of masculine sexuality, drawing on both the folk tradition of vulgar humor and the personal bravado of individual spectators competing with each other."[83] An itinerant distributor was contracted to provide the film reels and projection equipment for these events. Although stag films were illegal thanks to the vice campaigns of moral reformers, the state largely condoned their clandestine circulation because they inhabited a strictly male milieu. In fact, despite its prohibition, pornography became so customary for male sociality that "policemen, in particular, often having access to confiscated prints, shared in the stag rituals."[84] With little capital investment required to produce stag films—they were usually shot on a single 16 mm or, later, 8 mm film reel—thousands were sold in an underground pornography marketplace with production centers in the United States, Britain, France, Italy, Germany, and Latin America. According to film historian Thomas Waugh, at least two thousand stags were made before the theatrical explosion of porn film in the 1970s, and three-quarters of those were made during the 1960s with the expansion of film technologies like small cameras and projectors as consumer products.[85] Other scholars argue that around seventeen hundred stags were made prior to the 1970s, with the United States being the chief producer after the 1930s, responsible for creating more than half of all the films made.[86]

While the illicit, underground spaces of erotic film spectatorship encouraged homosociality for men, racial and class segregation maintained a divided audience. It is not clear to what extent black men's fraternal societies and clubs were able to access stag films and stage their own smokers. It is certainly plausible that black men's fraternal organizations would have been able to afford the costly fee to hire a projectionist. Later, when projection equipment became more affordable and stags were increasingly made and distributed among amateurs, working-class or lower-income black men might have gained access to the materials, perhaps also sharing in the masculine, voyeuristic, social practice of viewing "dirty pictures." Moreover, during the early twentieth century a black cinema movement emerged in response to black desires for entertainment of their own, and though fledgling, it could have produced stag films aimed for a black cinephile audience.[87] Yet it is not clear how male audiences consumed racial fetishism in stag film, and to what extent early film pornography with black performers was desired, enjoyed, ridiculed, or rejected by these racially and class-segregated male audiences. According to one study, interracial sex between black women and white men was depicted in 6.8 percent of the films during the decades spanning the 1920s to the 1960s. The study also showed that while the rate of black women–white men sex films stayed the same during this period, the demand for black men and white women, while significantly less than for black women and white men, increased by over four times, from under 1 percent in the 1920s to 4.4 percent during the 1960s.[88]

That white American male viewers wanted to see films depicting sex between black women and white men more than they wanted to see those with black men and white women is not surprising given the fierce panic at the time about the perceived sexual threat black men posed to white men's sexual property, white women. But stags existed as part of a wider world of specifically sexualized entertainment in which black women and men performed for white audiences. Burlesque concerts, dance halls, and cabarets featuring erotic performances proliferated in the first decades of the twentieth century, particularly in urban areas. Reflecting the complexities of racial segregation in both public and private entertainment spaces during the era, much of this sexual culture was segregated but also defined by cross-racial, black-white mixing, especially as whites came to encounter and intermingle with blacks in the intimate nightlife settings in places like Harlem.[89] In depicting the crossing of the sexual color line, race porn was very much concerned with the visual pleasures of racial/sexual encounters. It became much like the interzones of subcultural racial intimacy created within entertainment and nightlife spaces.[90] But just as those interzones operated as sites for cross-racial encounter and desire, they were also sites for sexual racism.

In relationship to the emerging Hollywood film system and the outsider, alternative circuits of Exploitation Cinema, stags both reflected and confronted similar anxieties over racial desire and disgust. For example, as Eric Schaefer argues, colonial-themed exploitation films created during the 1930s used the conventions of educational travelogues to show naked black bodies on-screen. Employing African American actors to play African "savages" in films like *Angkor* (1937), these "exploitation exotics" played up the "myth of unbridled black sexuality"—in *Angkor*, for example, the women are shown as having sex with apes (men in ape suits).[91] If these films were pleasurable pursuits, Schaefer argues that exotic exploitation movies also played a specific role in addressing the racial anxieties of white audiences: they simultaneously affirmed white racial superiority and capitalist supremacy for the white working class *and* authorized fear of interracial sexuality and miscegenation as precursors to "the decline of the [white] population."[92] Like the exotic exploitation film that aroused feelings of desire and disgust, the early pornographic film sanctioned a voyeuristic, desirous white gaze upon primitive, black sexuality, and in the process, constituted white bodies as superior to and separate from black bodies.

As products of racial fetishism, race porn displayed contemporary processes of racialization, and ideas of racial difference and segregation played out in an explicitly sexual field.[93] Race porn featured all-black casts, as well as interracial casts, and was made, as far as we know, primarily by and for white male audiences. Sometimes regressive, posing blackness as the object of denigrating, anachronistic fantasies; sometimes transgressive, allowing a venue for socially critical or racial and gender nonconforming intimacies; and sometimes neither; race porn used emergent moving-image technology to commercialize and make newly visible black sexuality. For black women who had long been models in erotic still photography and had also been active in the broader erotic entertainment culture described above, the stag form opened up a space to perform on film as porn actresses. While little is known about who these women were and why they worked in stag film, what the conditions were on set, or how they negotiated issues of production in the context of pornography's illegality, their compelling performances saturate the archive that remains.

Reviewing many of the extant stags, I found that black performers did not appear significantly in the films until the late 1920s and '30s. *Darkie Rhythm* (1932–35), *Doc Black* (1932–35), *Saturday Night in Harlem* (1936–41), *Negroes at Play* (1930s–1940s), and *Black Lovers* (1940s) are all black-cast stag films, but they appear to have been produced by white directors. Not only do white hands and body parts enter the shot at times to direct the sex between black performers, but the means and modes of production of stags during this period were highly specialized and largely dominated by white men working in the underground networks of a prohibited vice trade. Although many of these black-cast films did not treat racial difference in ways that were particularly denigrating and exploitative, they did not ignore race or elide blackness either. Indeed many of their titles and intertitles highlight race and racial difference. There is often little difference in the plot or scene of sex between black-cast and white-cast films, as they employ many of the same conventions of narrative or gender play. The primary interest of these films seems to be in exposing illicit sex—like all-white-cast stags—but black-cast stags expose these risqué themes through embodied racial and gender difference.

*Negroes at Play* is an example of a stag in which there are no characters listed, no intertitles or plot; the film's title marks the scene of difference by highlighting blackness as its central thematic. *Negroes at Play* presents sex be-

FIGURE 1.10. *Negroes at Play*, 1930s–1940s. Courtesy of the Kinsey Institute for Research in Sex, Gender, and Reproduction.

tween three black women and a black man, in alternating combinations. The group performs a variety of sex acts including cunnilingus, fellatio, vaginal and anal penetration, and two women have sex with a double-ended dildo. During the latter scene a white man's hand suddenly emerges from behind the camera, scene left, to move the woman's knee out of the shot. This gesture not only confirms that the cameraman (and likely the director) was white, it serves as a powerful metaphor for the ways in which white fantasy manipulated black sexuality in early pornography. Created by white men for a presumably white male audience, *Negroes at Play* illuminates how black actors performed sexual labor for the dominant gaze. Yet, drawing on what we know about black sexual labor and black sexual expression, from the blues to burlesque, the scene of sex between these three black actors also forces us to consider the possibility that they may have performed for their own, unknown purposes and desires.

*Darkie Rhythm* is an example of a stag film that, though neither particularly denigrating nor subversive, exposes how racial fetishism marked black sexuality in pornographic cinema. "Rhythm" of course references the imagined embodied sexual rhythm of the black characters, Mable and Rastus, played by "Iona Hotbox" and "Will B. Hard." The eight-minute, 16mm film plays with gender, employing the then-popular trope of illicit sex between a woman and a plumber or handyman. It begins with a black woman in a lovely floral dress who, after arriving home to her studio apartment, relaxes in a chair reading and later touches herself erotically. When she takes a break to use the sink she finds it broken and calls a repairman on a wall-mounted phone. A well-dressed black man in a suit, fedora, and briefcase—a bit too well dressed for a plumber—arrives to fix the drain. A dildo-like object falls out of his briefcase, which the woman picks up, curiously inspects, and then sits down to masturbate with. The not-so-shocked plumber takes his cue. A playful sex scene ensues and, in between shots of penetration, the couple caress, hug, and kiss. She spanks him as he moves on top of her, she smiles as he kisses her ear, and she rolls her eyes comically as if to suggest that he is a superb lover—or not. After sex they sit side by side on the bed. She wipes her sweat with a towel, then picks up the dildo-like object, and, smiling, places it next to his penis as if to evaluate whether the real thing measures up to the fantasy. This gesture suggests a lighthearted, humorous exploration of gender difference and sexuality common to other stag pornography of the period. Constance Penley argues that humor structures the production and reception of early stags, "and not just any kind of humor, but bawdiness, humorously lewd and obscene language and situations."[94] While it is difficult to glean exactly what is intended in this silent, grainy black-and-white film (which lacks intertitles), the actress's dynamic and performative use of bawdy humor in the closing moments of *Darkie Rhythm* might be read as a "fleeting moment" of comedy used by the woman as an equalizer against her coactor and against the likely all-male audience of "the smoker."[95] If the man in the film really does not measure up to the dildo, as the actress suggests in her Rabelaisian performance—which includes eye rolling, exaggerated pleasure shown in her facial expressions, and flailing limbs, spanking, and postcoital jokes—then what does that say about the (white) men who are the known spectators of black sex in stag film?

The repairman as ruse for sex was common in all stag films at the time, but *Darkie Rhythm*'s title and characters also play on stereotypical representations of black people that a white audience might have found pleasingly humorous. Darkie/darky was a popular derogatory name for African Americans at the turn of the century, and the idea that all African Americans possessed a unique and superior sense of natural rhythm was also in circulation, as is evidenced in the short film *Dancing Darkies* (1896). Rastus, the plumber's name, was also a stock black male character in minstrel shows and in early film, including a series of short films from 1910–17 with titles like *How Rastus Gets His Turkey* (1910), *Rastus in Zululand* (1910), and *Rastus Runs Amuck* (1917). These early films played up the figure of Rastus, the simpleminded black man who, as film historian Donald Bogle writes, "presents the Negro as amusement object."[96] It is impossible to know if the title and the character names were original or added to edits that were sold later, but they nevertheless show that racial fetishism was a constituent aspect of *Darkie Rhythm*'s production and reproduction. This kind of racial fetishism sought to mark the difference of black sexuality by placing it, through stereotype, at a safe and comedic distance. In the process, presumably white male spectators could observe and take pleasure in consuming black sexuality as an object without feeling overly implicated in its construction.

Because, as Constance Penley contends, a great many American stag films were "structured like a joke," particularly "really bad jokes, ranging from terrible puns to every form of dirty joke," *Darkie Rhythm* may have been making a multifaceted joke.[97] On the one hand, the joke is *on* African Americans—a send-up of their renowned and completely constructed sexual virility, including their tireless, rhythmic sexual natures as performed by the characters of Rastus and Mable. This joke, which Freud would term a "hostile joke" because it is aggressive, satirical, and defensive, structures the film and establishes a set of expectations marked out by the title.[98] Meanwhile, the plot and performance suggest that in following a standard theme or fantasy in all pornography, from stags to the present, the other joke, what Freud called the "obscene joke,"[99] is on men. While this joke also accesses the more common narrative of the housewife who cheats on her husband, the send up of the man here still operates as a critique of male sexual prowess more generally. Focusing on the apparently single woman who first seeks to pleasure herself, then initiates sex with the man that she has hired, and still later pokes fun at his penis by measuring it against a large dildo, *Darkie Rhythm* draws upon sexual anxiety about the transformation of gendered relationships and women's increasing sexual autonomy in the early twentieth century. In this dirty joke, the woman's sexual agency can be read as more than a come-on or compensatory lead up to sex. Instead, the film opens up the possibility that men do not know all that women desire or what they fantasize about, or even what women do, when men are absent. These anxious sentiments may have been laughed at and dismissed in the all-male spaces of stag viewing, and such readings of gendered upheaval may have been read quite differently depending on whether the men in the audience were white or black. Black male spectators might have understood that they were the butt of both jokes—one hostile and one bawdy. Yet the playful, seemingly off-the-cuff performance by the black actress references a long tradition of black women in black popular culture as trickster figures.[100]

Another area of subversion is in the facial stunting used by the actress who plays Iona Hotbox in *Darkie Rhythm*. A popular technique in black musical theater and cinematic performances during the period, which was also mimicked in white actors' performances, eye rolling conferred comedic and sometimes satirical meanings. Josephine Baker was widely known as an expert eye roller, having also excelled at crossing her eyes in severely funny expressions during her live and movie dance routines.[101] The *Darkie Rhythm* actress most likely parodied the eye-rolling gestures of musical theater to distinguish her performance. Like a silent film star taking advantage of her close up, the actress adroitly rolls her eyes during the penetration scene, back and forth, up and down, expressing teasing amusement. In this way, her performance directs viewers' gaze to her talented facial stunting and pokes playful fun at the sexual skills of her co-performer. Another maneuver this actress employs to direct the gaze is to raise her leg high in the air, artfully bending her knee to show off her shiny patent leather high-heeled shoe. The gleam of the elegant shoe in the center of the shot again refocuses viewers' attention to the actress and infuses the character with a quality of high-class taste through sartorial expression. The actress also points to her character's desire by using her hands: she strokes and grips the actor's buttocks when the camera closes in on the penetrative action as they lay in "missionary position," her lighter complexioned hands standing out against the dark skin of the actor. When the actor kisses her cheek, the actress breaks into a smile—a moment of perhaps genuine sweetness and kinship between the performers. Similarly, in *Negroes at Play*, the actors kiss with notable and probably unscripted tenderness while at the same time the actress uses prettiness in her pose and a relaxed facial expression to present desirability to the camera.

The films that opened this chapter, *The Golden Shower* and *The Hypnotist*, also allow a reading of black women's complicated performances in the early stag-film genre of race porn. Their compelling bodily techniques produce alternative meanings in the texts. By seductively engaging with the camera—directly gazing back at the spectator in close-ups or purposefully drawing the gaze toward her—the actress makes a spectacle of herself.[102] In this actress's performances we see playful and dramatic gestures: she giggles and petulantly sticks out her tongue; widens, rolls, and bats her mesmeric eyes; contorts and wiggles her fingers like a soothsayer culling secrets from a crystal ball; and flashes first a naughty and then a pretty smile. She becomes a disruptive force who manipulates her construction as an illicit erotic object in the imagination of the viewer. She seems to take up the stag film for its radical possibilities of exhibition, not just voyeurism.[103]

Although in *The Golden Shower* she plays a maid, again subjected to the fetish for black female servitude in pornography, the camera is forced to linger in a close-up of her expressive face, unflinching and seductive stare, and her lips as she speaks in this silent-film recording. It is as if she vociferously refuses to be diminished by a narrow, stereotypical subservient role

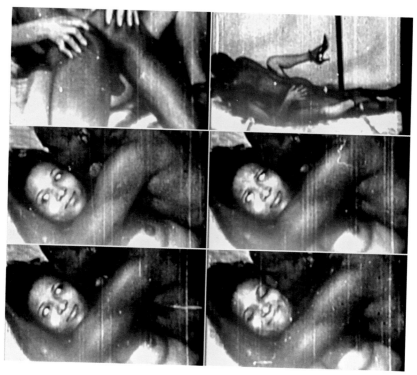

FIGURE 1.11. *Darkie Rhythm*, 1930s–1940s. Courtesy of the Kinsey Institute for Research in Sex, Gender, and Reproduction.

and imagines herself as another kind of surface and depth upon which the viewer projects his fantasy. In *The Hypnotist* her character, Madam Cyprian, is an Orientalist trope rather than a typical African American one, perhaps offering more space to maneuver within exoticism than the confined, domesticated role of the maid. Like Jeannie Pepper's desire to play the "voodoo girl" rather than the maid (see chapter 3), this actress seems to take extra pleasure in the space allowed for robust, creative expression in the Madam Cyprian role. Perhaps a result of her extremely fair complexion, wavy hair, and athletic, dancer-like figure, this black actress could "pass" in a role not designed for the racial and gender fetishism of black womanhood, though clearly marked by some kind of racial Otherness. Her racial and gender crossing could have been fueled by a broader interest in light-skinned black women's performances in popular culture, including black chorus girls known as "Creole Queens" in burlesque, "dusky belles" in Broadway musicals, and "tragic mulattas" in Hollywood films, like Fredi Washington's Peola in *Imitation of*

*Life* (1934).[104] Light-skinned black women represented the obscene sexuality of black women, but their proximity to whiteness also marked them as feminine, beautiful, desirable, and classy, and therefore comfortably consumable for white audiences.[105] They also represented the pleasure and threat associated with miscegenation and interracial sex; their bodies formed a limit, border, and convergence zone between black-white intimacies. Hence, this actress embodied a specific sexual economy of desire and contempt that both allowed her to access agency and denied her autonomy from the constraints of racialized sexuality. Her complex performances in these two films demonstrate how black women sexual actors could put black female sexuality to use in ways that were both confined by and exceeded the limits of race, gender, and sexuality in Jim Crow America.

### Negotiating Violent Fantasies

Stags that presented the extreme taboo of interracial sex in the context of Jim Crow race relations were extremely charged scenes that tended to denigrate black sexualities and performances even as they portrayed them as pleasurable and exciting. These films also tended to cast black men and women as domestic figures, rather than exotic characters, within fantasies firmly situated in intimate and historically charged spaces of racial interaction, like the white home. Black men played the milkman, mechanic, or deliveryman who happens to visit when a white housewife is home alone. She seduces the black man into bed—that is until the husband arrives to catch and displace him by having sex with the wife instead, as was the case in the stag film *Leaky Sink* (1966). Usually, no violence ensues and the husband either just kicks the black male usurper out of the house, or simply pushes him aside so that he can take his place. This is an interesting displacement on multiple levels, as outside of pornographic fantasy these situations would probably have led to violent, punishing attacks on black men, resulting in either imprisonment or mutilation and even murder. Films like *The Black Bandit* (1962) show black men entering white women's rooms uninvited and forcing sex, sometimes violently. These films expose white male anxiety about being cuckolded by sexually superior black men, whom they fear their wives secretly prefer. The charged fantasy of these interracial films relied upon the knowledge that sex across these specific racial and gender lines was in real life violently guarded.

Black women stag performers often played sexually passive domestic servants in interracial encounters with white men in films like *The Maid* (1937), *Baby Sitter* (1948–55), and *Cleaning Woman* (1950). In *Cleaning Woman* a black actress is cast as a maid to a white man. As she is sweeping the living room, the white man, sitting on the couch, pats her buttocks and pulls up her housedress to reveal her naked body underneath. He soon stands to push her down on the couch, but she resists, struggling as he holds her wrists. I should note this is not a *real* struggle, but performed, and not that intensely. The scene cuts to and then repeats (as if reedited to make it longer, a common practice in stag production) the scene of both performers on the couch naked, she no longer struggling but compliantly performing fellatio, he stroking her genitals. The roughly edited and nonlinear twelve-minute reel shows the pair having intercourse, and then, in a quite ordinary fashion, washing themselves at the bathroom sink. Two similar films, *Making the Maid* (1965–66) and *Her Maid Raped* (1966), produced in England, both feature a black maid being forced to have sex with one or more white men. In *Making the Maid* a white man is lying in bed when a black maid enters the room with a tray of coffee. As she sets the tray down he pulls her to bed, holds her down as she resists, and has sex with her. In *Her Maid Raped*, a black maid in a sexy French maid's uniform is "raped" by two white perpetrators posing as repairmen. When the mistress of the house returns to find her maid tied to a ladder, the men "rape" her too.

In all three films, coercive sex, and the woman's performed resistance, is part of the fantasy. The black actresses in these films enact fear and distress just as they act out the subservience, attentiveness, and labors of maids. These roles as domestic workers provide a familiar rationale for proximity across race, gender, and class difference between black women and white men. Just as domestic work was the main form of employment for black women during the first part of the century, it was also a mainstay Hollywood representation of black women. Moreover, the sexual expropriation of black maids was a commonplace occurrence that not only made clear the synonymousness of sex work and other kinds of work in the lives of black women, but defined the ways in which black women at the time sought to cope with and master a complex sexual terrain.

While these domestic rape fantasies are more commonplace, KKK *Night Riders* (1939) stands out as a particularly egregious violent fantasy of black female sexual availability and rape for the pleasure of white male spectators. Yet this disturbing film also provides an opportunity to consider black women's sexual subjectivity and how they negotiated their sexual labor within even the most abusive fantasies presented in race porn. The film begins with a black woman alone in a humble shack, lying in bed reading a newspaper. A man enters from screen right wearing an inexpertly crafted Ku Klux Klan robe and hood made out of what looks to be bedsheets, and carrying what appears to be a long blade or knife sharpener. Walking up to the bed, the man points the weapon at the woman's throat, pulls back the covers to expose her nakedness, and begins to fondle her breasts. Visibly shaken, the woman says to him—via intertitle—"Oh Lordy, don't hurt me! I'll give you my all." The film cuts to the black woman, her hands shaking, as the man points the weapon at her belly and then her genitals. Another intertitle says: "Here I am Mr. Klansman. I'm all yours." A medium shot depicts the woman, still naked, entering through the door, sitting on the edge of the bed, and then standing and leaning on the bed. Another intertitle: "All night riders must have their fun." The man enters the room once again, this time weaponless and naked except for his hood. He wears the hood throughout the sex scene, a fact that seems to irritate the actress because she puts her arm over her face or looks away as to avoid looking at him. Finally he says, "Your [sic] sure hot, I'll re-move my white mask." When he removes the white-hooded mask, however, we see that his disguise remains because he wears yet another mask, a dark stocking. "Does you all feel good now Mr. Klansman?" the woman asks, as she uncovers her face and seems to relax. They perform oral sex, genital touching, and penetration until the encounter ends with the man ejaculating twice. That is, at the end of the version of the film that I screened at the Kinsey Institute there are two ejaculation scenes: one that appears as if someone poured a batch of heavy cream from above the frame, and a second in which the actor ejaculates (or perhaps more cream is added) on the woman's breasts as he straddles her.

The film KKK *Night Riders* references the symbolic power of the white southern male, a power inextricably linked to historical, racial, and sexual violence against black women. Yet multiple interpretations are possible of both the film and the performances. In one view, the film presents the history of slavery, Reconstruction, and post-Reconstruction, and through a nostalgic lens, presents an unmitigated white male ascendancy empowered by an accommodating and inexhaustible black female sexuality. In another view, if the film employs the paradigm of the joke, its humor might be directed against white men. Rather than a sentimental view of white southern patriarchal prowess, the film could be poking fun at the Night Riders. In particular, the makeshift costume of the klansman—which features a KKK insignia that looks nothing like the true logo of the organization as it was made widely popular in the poster art and the film *Birth of a Nation* (1915)—suggests that the creators of KKK *Night Riders* were not attempting to accurately represent the group. Instead of protecting white womanhood and white communities from the threat of black assault, the film suggests, the underlying reason for

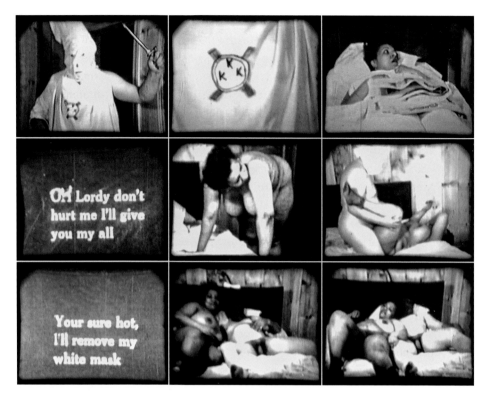

FIGURE 1.12. *KKK Night Riders* (1939). Courtesy of the Kinsey Institute for Research in Sex, Gender, and Reproduction.

KKK night rides was actually to have illicit sex with black women. In both interpretations of the film, the representation of one black woman's willful submission masks the penetrating realities of the violence against black women more generally. The black character's consensual participation in the affair conceals the history of white male rape of black women and mobilizes the myth that black women's seductive, hypersexual nature made them complicit partners in these nighttime trysts.

Revealing how racial fetishism enacted regressive fantasies of white illicit erotic desire for black bodies, the film also exposes the coercive context of sex work for black women in stag filmmaking. As Linda Williams argues, black women's lack of agency as workers and performers on stag-film sets, especially in comparison to white women, is vital to consider.[106] However, Williams contends that describing these women as "sexworkers" is both anachronistic and euphemistic, that the framework of sex work elicits a politics of consent and choice that black women in these spaces lacked. Within this framework Williams argues that KKK *Night Riders* is essentially a rape caught on film. I disagree. To identify these early black pornographic actresses as performing sex work, I argue, helps scholars to conceptualize their active negotiation of racialized sexuality within historical conditions of constraint and appropriation, as well as to think about black female porn performers' self-determined choices about how and when to deploy their sexual labor. Their performances and participation in pornography tell us something about their tactics of negotiation as well as their labors of consent.

First, if we understand that hustling women, as discussed above, negotiated between one form of exploitative work and another, choosing illegal, stigmatized, and dangerous sex work over menial domestic work, we can conclude that black women in early pornography were capable of evaluating the conditions of their work. If porn work meant signing up for a filmed rape, they may have chosen to remain in domestic work. The explicitness of sexual risk in porn work makes the work categorically different from domestic labor, in which the risk of sexual assault was also endemic. Therefore porn work may have offered black women more opportunities to negotiate the conditions of their sexual labor. Next, in KKK *Night Riders* we are confronted with a black woman working to perform a fantasy that is presumably not her own, in which she is playing the role of someone allowed no power other than to submit. Her performance shows that the actress understands what it means to play submission, and that this performance of submission may involve a play of sensuality and transgressive erotic relation. If the performer were simply abjected by her performance labor, we might expect her to just lie there, passively, or to emote an understandable distress. Instead, her performance is much more ambivalent and deserves a deeper look.

While this may have been scripted, at times the actress seems so bothered by the KKK hood that she looks away and then appears to reach up as if to take it off the man. The intertitle suggests it is the man's decision to take it off: "Your [*sic*] sure hot, I'll remove my hood." However, this removal could have been one of several interventions that the actress made to change the conditions of her work on set. Her performance appears more actively sensual than would be surmised if we only see the actress as utterly circumscribed by the oppressive setting.[107] Her frightful surprise and trembling hands—which are quite well done—are quickly replaced by aroused self-caresses, sultry breast jiggling and hip swaying, and active sexual exchange with the actor. At one point in the scene she snuggles next to the man and caresses him; at another point she moves her hips up and down as he caresses her genitals so as to heighten or at least suggest her own arousal. At around five minutes into the scene the actress, lying side by side with and tenderly caressing the actor, looks directly at the camera and smiles.

While these gestures may seem small, especially compared to the enormity of the text's fetishistic narrative of coercion and of the context's inequalities and exploitations along lines of race, gender, and class, I am arguing that they should be taken seriously as representing the actress's attempts to deconstruct or disidentify with the dominating gaze. Rather than allowing the scene to build a fantasy of black female subjection, the actress's gestures, eroticism, and confrontational look back at the camera suggest her desire to challenge this fantasy by asserting some agency in her performance. While looking at the camera itself is not necessarily a claim for agency, or even unique to black actresses (white actresses did it too), in this context the look interrupts the narrative by acknowledging the "fourth wall" of the viewer and the construct-edness of the gaze and its object, and thus inserts subjectivity into the "scene of subjection."[108] One of the most significant gestural acts that demonstrate this black actress's labor in negotiating exploitation and agency occurs at the very close of the film. Following the actor's ejaculation on her breasts (the second one), he dips his finger in the ejaculate and brings it to her mouth for her to lick. She refuses it by averting her face. In this instance the actress asserts the limits of her labor; she makes clear what she is not willing to do in the performance: eating the actor's ejaculate was not labor she would take on.[109] Conceptualizing this performance within a black feminist pornographic gaze means looking closely at what this black actress did to navigate appropriation and assert some agency, however circumscribed. It means imagining how this performer might have recognized the fantasy disguised beneath the layers of the Klan hood and black mask as a combination of anxious threat and illicit pleasure. Her gestures to tear the mask off, to expose the myth of prohibition that is constitutive of white male desire for and control over black female bodies, are important symbolic subversions and actual strategic acts within specific labor conditions. To argue that KKK Night Riders represents a filmed rape is to ignore these moments, denying the skillful negotiation employed by the performer to control the conditions or her labor.

I argue that, like Hollywood actors Bert Williams, Stepin Fetchit, Hattie McDaniel, Louise Beavers, and Butterfly McQueen, who repeatedly play against racial stereotypes they perform, endowing their performances with nuance, skill, and individualism, this early pornography actress attempts to play against expectations. If we consider Angela Davis's assertion that black women's erotic sovereignty was one of the most important domains of their lives, and Cynthia Blair's contention that black women's sexual labors were one key part of their strategic negotiations for survival and autonomy, these stag films exit the realm of pure exploitation, instead offering scholars the opportunity to read black women's labor in cocreating pornographic images. Perhaps the actress's performance was also invested in the joke, in exposing white disgust as lust? By appreciating that black actresses were performing in complex ways in these complex spaces, we can avoid overvaluing and perpetuating the process by which they are objectified. We can instead acknowledge black women's gestures to assert erotic subjectivity, complex personhood, and forceful social critiques within their erotic performances.

Unlike earlier black women who were exhibited without their control or consent at slave markets or in scientific studies, black women in early stag pornography are performers, workers who seem to have an interest or a stake in exhibitionism. This kind of self-display shows an unruly desire to cross boundaries and to transgress social rules. By refusing the call by black social reformers and political activists to make themselves into images of moral and respectable womanhood as a counter to black women's stigmatized, hypervisible sexuality, some black pornographic actresses might have exhibited their sexualities on different terms—terms that underscored their refusal to veil their expressive sexuality or forgo their sex work.

The pornographic gaze has been obsessed with black women's difference, but it is a relationship of power that black women have refused, deflected, and appropriated. Using pornography as a site of labor, performance, and, sometimes, pleasure, black actresses throughout the twentieth century continued to confront powerful constraints. Impacted by vast technological and social developments around pornography's production and circulation, the sex industries, and sexual culture, and by transformations in racial relations and representations, they faced shifting terrains of danger and desire. As stag films gave way to a boom in magazine production, pay peep show arcades, and theatrical release films in the post–World War II period, black women found that while they could win new roles current with the times, the old meanings attached to their embodiments remained.

As this study shows, the negotiation between what stories are available about black women and what they strive for and attempt to enact for themselves is more than difficult. Although it is not possible to recover the voices of the actresses in this early period, and the pre-1980s video era of pornography in general, we can infer that when today's actresses give voice to their experiences and critical knowledges about what it means to be a black woman in a sexual field like pornography, they speak to a history that they perhaps unknowingly inherited. Showing that slavery was in fact pornographic, and that pornography relied on racial ideologies, fantasies, and political economies, this chapter has laid out a foundation for black women's porn work by acknowledging the vital need to address black women's interventions, however compromised, as cocreators of a powerful and enduring sexual culture. In the next chapter I describe how, during the sexual revolution of the 1960s and '70s, black people's own new ways of thinking about sex and politics came face to face with the interests of an expanding and newly visible porn industry, and how black actresses exposed the productive power of these cataclysmic forces in their performances.

# Sexy Soul Sisters

## Black Women in the Golden Era

*Sex with Soul*, a DVD featuring a compilation of hardcore interracial sex scenes from the 1960s and '70s, advertises screen-scorching "sepia smoker celluloid" to savvy collectors of vintage erotica. "If you have a taste for brown sugar," the description reads, "both male and female, then you can't afford to pass up this classic example of cinema SEX WITH SOUL."[1] A new aesthetic of black eroticism emerged during the 1960s and '70s, an aesthetic I term "soul porn." Unlike stag films from the 1920s through the 1950s, soul porn featured a new kind of intimacy with and interaction between white and black Americans. Changing legal frameworks and social attitudes ushered in a fresh willingness to display and view black sexuality and black-white sexual relationships. Pornography, like other media, reflected broad social advances in racial integration and interracial relations. Whereas once black sexuality seemed to be held at a comfortable distance for white consumers, white viewers now saw blacks as militant sexual agents. Yet the genre of soul porn is not only defined by the desirability of black sexual aesthetics for white audiences, and whites' appropriation and imitation of what they saw as black "soul" during the era. Soul porn is also constituted by black people's deployment of their own racialized eroticism into sexual media. This confrontation between white desire for blacks and black desire for themselves is embedded in soul porn, and inscribed in black pornographic performances of the time.

As I discussed in the last chapter, pornography has depicted black-white interracial sex since its emergence as an underground photographic and film form. It was not until the 1960s, however, that black erotic models and performers gained significant visibility. Magazines displaying black nudes popped up everywhere, black women began to be featured in *Playboy*, black sexual ephemera were traded widely, and black women and men were often

seen in 16 mm and 8 mm loops, and increasingly in 35 mm theatrically released pornographic films. These media were part of the greater viability of
pornography in a time when the social strictures and legal barriers to the
production of explicit sexual culture began to collapse. Black pornography
during the era was one manifestation of a more widespread and amplified
black-authored erotic expression occurring in music, literature, art, film,
mass communications, and popular culture. The black body, especially for
African Americans, now represented a new image of self-determined and
dynamic erotic force. African Americans seemed to be more interested than
ever in participating in, and making their own, erotic media.

In the 1960s and '70s, largely white pornographers slowly began to realize the lucrative potential of playing up black racial difference, although it
was not until the 1980s that interracial and black-cast porn would be recognized as a commercially viable and specialized niche market. Beginning in
the 1960s, black actors were increasingly integrated into largely white-cast
pornographic films, and interracial and black-cast 8 mm loops were produced to a greater degree than the previous stag-porn era. Pornography created during this period—often called porno, which I will use here in the spirit
of that context—was particularly focused on exposing and exploring sexual
taboos in a time when attitudes toward sex were being revolutionized. A central sexual taboo was the crossing of racial borders through new intimacies
between blacks and whites.

A sense of agentive black subjectivity flourished during the civil rights and
black power era, arousing interest and anxiety among white Americans. Even
with a growing base of black porno consumers, the white male gaze continued
to determine the fantasies represented in most pornographic media. Thus,
porno during this period betrays the powerful ways in which the white fetishization of black sexuality—marked by both titillation and fear—grappled
with black people's changing social status and the progressively resistive politics asserted by African Americans. The production of soul porn emerges
from the historical and social sexual politics of the civil rights era, where the
objectification of black bodies confronts a newly radicalized black subjectivity.[2]

I use the term "soul porn" to describe the assertive aspect of black sexuality
that appears in pornography's representational economy during this period.
Soul porn describes both how black people interacted with and performed in
porn through the uses of soul, as well as how whites' fascination with black
sexuality is represented in porn through the iconography of soul. Whites certainly appropriated and commodified black sexuality in their production of

soul porn as they comprised porno's major producers and audience. However, black people were also interested in launching and viewing their own sexualities in explicit media, as evidenced by the tremendous outpouring of erotic materials, music, and performance during this period, including raunchy stand-up comedy, drag balls, risqué pinup spreads in magazines like *Jet* and *Hue*, and "shake dance" shows by well-known black burlesque dancers such as Lottie the Body and Jean Idelle. Black sexual identities were shaped differently along lines of gender. Black men's desires had a visible impact in shaping the direction of some porn media, including magazines, loops, and feature films. It is important to consider how the new visibility and erotic agency of black sexuality mobilized in soul porn responded to black men's previously unaddressed fantasies. Black women, though also seeking to explore their fantasies, still lacked the power to decisively shape the marketing of their sexuality in pornography. Nevertheless, as in the stag era, black women intervened in their representation as performers in powerful and important ways.

Most of the black porn actresses during this period, though visible, went nameless, and are today lost to memory. An exception to this rule was Desiree West. The first African American porn actress to gain name recognition and remarkable roles in popular sex films, Desiree West is well known among fans, adult industry movie critics, and avid collectors in online communities like *Vintage Erotica Forums*. Desiree gained a somewhat renewed notoriety as porno and exploitation films from the 1960s and '70s were re-released on DVD and recirculated to both popular and academic audiences during the 1990s and 2000s. Known for her "vaguely Asian" exotic looks, "curvaceous body with huge, firm, naturally hanging breasts," curly-styled Afro, and sassy attitude, Desiree West becomes an icon of black women performers in the era of soul porn, and hence images of Desiree reach beyond her reputation as a figure in the porn industry.[3] Not only was Desiree a standout performer, she was also one of the few black women to work consistently through the 1970s and share scenes in feature-length porno films with leading white actors. In 2010 a fan created a YouTube video tribute to Desiree, in which other fans posted comments about her beauty, sex appeal, energetic erotic performances, and unfortunate second-billing status.[4] These observations are reflected in one online biography:

> Desiree West was one of the first black porn starlets. . . . Desiree West's voluptuous good looks set the stage for the sexual fireworks that she invariably provided to each film she appeared in. Desiree West was one of the first "wild women" of porn, always ready to push the sexual en-

velope with her nymphomaniacal need for raw, passionate sex action. Desiree West . . . soon had established herself as the black starlet to call on if you wanted some spicy, sensual sexing. She was a very good actress who could handle any sort of part, from down-and-dirty to high-class. Desiree West never got too many starring roles, though, and was relegated to heating up scenes from a strictly supporting level. She never let her lack of top-flight fame affect her performances, however. Desiree West could always be counted on for a hip-grinding, teeth-chattering good time.[5]

Desiree West is remembered as a passionate and versatile sexual performer who helped usher a fan culture around particular porn actresses as movie stars, rather than as nameless bodies. Although Desiree delivered the high-powered eroticism so valued by consumers and critics of adult media, she was relegated to supporting roles behind white actors. Though this fan biography lauds her eroticism, it does not explain how Desiree's secondary status was part of a commonplace lack of recognition for black actresses. Not only did black actresses confront marginalization and occupy a lesser status in porn, the industry's racialization of their sexuality rendered their powerful performances mere fodder for a growing market of interracial and black-cast porn films. By examining black women's performances from the 1960s and '70s, I argue that performers like Desiree West embodied erotic subjectivity, even as they were deployed as props in other people's fantasies. The social context for race and gender relations was transforming, and with it, black women's place in pornography and the wider sexual culture. As so-called sexy soul sisters, black women porn performers were on the front lines of a major cultural revolution in which black desires became newly articulated, and desires for black bodies became newly evident.


## Putting the Soul in Soul Porn

The concept of "soul" in black life is important, if difficult to define. As Lerone Bennett argues, "Soul is a metaphorical evocation of Negro being as expressed in the Negro tradition."[6] Or as the "Queen of Soul" Aretha Franklin defines it, "Soul is black."[7] Soul is a concept that, in fact, "exceeds the power of language to recapture."[8] Nonetheless, many have used the word "soul" to capture the melding of the cultural and the political, the sacred and the profane, the collective and the individual, the psychic and the aesthetic, and the dialectic of memory and transformation in black life. It is most often discussed as the expression of black culture, especially through music, that is lived in a particular kind of embodiment that marks blackness. Although soul is a force that emerges from the African roots of African American culture, circulates throughout the worldwide African diaspora, and continues to define black life today, many critics cite the 1960s and '70s as the generative period, and perhaps demise, of soul.[9] For African Americans, soul emerges out of the traumas of enslavement, the indignities of segregation and disenfranchisement, and the struggles of the "long" civil rights movement that began in the 1920s, accelerated during World War II, and was ferociously fought during the 1960s and '70s.[10] But it was the interaction between the activist, artistic, and intellectual arms of black nationalism (not that these are discrete forms), and the cultural lives of everyday black people who were coming to understand themselves in the revolutionary terms, epitomized by the phrase "Black is Beautiful," that made the soul aesthetic of the 1960s and '70s so unique. Soul is understood to capture the oppositional energy of a time when being black, and pro-black, was bound up with defiance and celebration.

While icons of the "soul era," like the Afro, are now regularly taken up as shallow symbols of black fashion, in the 1960s and '70s they marked a stylistic militancy. Black people asserted themselves by styling their bodies in ways that seemed so dangerous they became targeted for repression by the state and dominant culture.[11] Yet the stylistics of soul, based on these radical embodiments, were also about pleasure—the transgressive enjoyment of a much-maligned blackness. Hence, soul presented a "certain way of feeling, a certain way of expressing oneself, a certain way of being,"[12] that reflected an embodied recuperation of blackness as well as a "desire for a distinctive unassimilable style."[13] Soul also had a representational economy that was used as a marketing mechanism and commodity interest at the time.[14] A range of industries, including pornography, sought to capitalize on soul. Little scholarship exists on the intersection of soul with sexual media as it was created or consumed by blacks or whites during the 1960s and '70s. Moreover, because soul is such a tricky term to undress, it is difficult to say how sexual media took up soul or the appearance of soul, or how these two registers—soul and its simulation—might have worked as one.

## From Underworld to the Golden Age

The intersection of white and black interest in black sexuality produces embedded tensions in the makeshift category of soul porn and provokes important questions about desire, pleasure, and representation. *Sex World* (dir.

Anthony Spinelli, 1977), a key example of soul porn that I discuss later in this chapter, uses notions of black sexuality as militant, transformative, and stylistic to shape its racial fetishism. In depicting the coupling of a black woman with a racist white man, *Sex World* both capitalizes upon and flouts the taboo nature of interracial sex. By addressing both interracial sex and racism at the same time, *Sex World* presents itself as both a subversive and politically charged text. Adult filmmakers at the time believed pornography was the epitome of the transgressive energy of the sexual revolution, and had the power to revise sexual norms. These filmmakers saw pornography as a vanguard cultural movement within a new American sexual liberalism because it explicitly confronted the legal and social frameworks that policed sexual expression in film, literature, performance, and political speech. Since the Comstock Law of 1873, all materials depicting sexual matters (including contraception and birth control information) were broadly defined as indecent, immoral, lewd, or lascivious, and forcefully prosecuted. Under pressure from regulators and purity campaigns like the Catholic Legion of Decency, Hollywood enacted its own self-censorship. Pornographers maneuvered around the "smut-hounds" in clandestine networks, but some, often unwittingly, stood up against censorship.[15] A series of Supreme Court rulings beginning in the 1950s narrowed definitions of obscenity and opened up opportunities for pornographers to ply their trade. *United States v. Roth* (1957) upheld the conviction of a pornographic book dealer, but also declared that "sex and obscenity are not synonymous"; only material "appealing to prurient interest" could be prosecuted as obscenity.[16] In 1966 the court determined that obscene materials had to be "*utterly* without redeeming social value" to be deemed "patently offensive."[17] Because "utterly" left a lot of room for interpretation, this ruling had a huge impact on the proliferation of pornographic materials and also brought about more liberal values in mainstream media.

The old "Comstockery" was further undermined in 1970, when the President's Commission on Obscenity and Pornography recommended the "repeal of all laws prohibiting the distribution of sexually explicit material to consenting adults."[18] However, a more conservative Nixon administration suppressed the report. In 1973, in the case of *Miller v. California*, Chief Justice Burger ignored the President's Commission report and sided in favor of making it easier for authorities to prosecute for obscenity. The new requirements stated that obscene materials must lack "serious" artistic or social value, be designed to feed "prurient interests," and be judged by "local community standards."[19] Therefore, while the *Miller* ruling created opportunities for law enforcement to go after pornographers on the state and local level (and they did, focusing on adult movie theaters, bookstores, and video rental outlets as well as porn producers and distributors), the ruling was also vague enough that pornographers could advance their industry unconcealed. Consequently, porno producers began to view themselves as producing legitimate entertainment for responsible adults. Maneuvering around liberal but indefinite obscenity statutes and within a social framework of sexual permissiveness and constraint proved tricky. Nevertheless, porn manufacturers seized the chance to test the waters of public values and prurient interests. The culture was changing, and they wanted to play a role (and of course, make a buck).

"One of the most visible components of the sexual revolution of the 1960s," Robert Nye argues, "was the explosion of pornographic literature, films, videos, sex toy emporiums, and live sex shows, in short the commercialization and mass production of items formerly reserved for a few cognoscenti."[20] No longer confined to private all-male gatherings in frat houses and Legion halls, during the 1960s porn films could be seen in adult arcades with their coin-operated peep booths, or projected on the walls of private homes with the newly portable and affordable 8 mm projectors sold to middle-class consumers.[21] Those same middle-class consumers could buy Super 8 cameras and make their own kinky home movies. Exploitation films and softcore pseudo-documentaries of nudist colonies shown in art house and grind house theaters competed with a declining Hollywood by showing ever more nudity and violence, and both competed with television.[22] Even in Hollywood, both nudity and sexual themes became commonplace. Meanwhile, relatively tame but artful burlesque performances were replaced by raunchier topless and nude strip shows. Times Square in New York, like many other city centers, became a veritable red-light district, populated by denizens of the underworld: prostitutes, pimps, johns, hustlers, cruisers, dealers, gangsters, and vice cops. Sparkling night and day, marquees announced X-rated fare to gay and straight audiences. Smut was everywhere.[23]

As pornographic media became available to a broader audience, a "widespread fascination" ensued. According to Estelle Freedman and John D'Emilio, in the 1960s, "sex was put on display" in all forms of cultural expression and in daily life.[24] During what became known as the Golden Age of pornography, pornographers in San Francisco and New York City developed feature-length productions for exhibition in theaters. Taking advantage of a cultural and legal opening, and a financially troubled Hollywood, makers of adult movies innovated a new way to put sex on display. Since it was necessary to prove explicit media had "redeeming social importance," pornographers responded to regulation by innovating full-length movies with plots, scripts, and characters. Rather than splice together a series of sex acts loosely based on a theme or particular fetish, as had been done in previous dirty pictures, pornographers of the 1970s appropriated the narrative style of the Hollywood feature film as a focus for hardcore media. "The pornographic feature is a hybrid of the classic stag and the movie industry's staple melodrama," writes pornography historian Joseph Slade. "It takes the sex from one and the length from the other."[25] In this "most public of the contemporary pornographic formats,"[26] feature porn films exploited prurient interests but were registered as "legitimate" artistic expression. This hybrid form allowed pornographers to operate in legal and lucrative realms of distribution. Some even imagined an eventual integration of hard core into Hollywood, and turned their aspirations for mainstream media acceptance into creative productions, which captured a more sexually liberal, young, and urban audience.

   *Deep Throat* was the first feature-length hardcore film to attract a mainstream audience.[27] The film, which starred Linda Lovelace and Harry Reems and was directed by Gerard Damiano, opened in June 1972 at the New World Theater on Forty-Ninth Street in New York City. The first porno to bring hardcore into the arena of popular culture, *Deep Throat* marked what Camille Paglia has called an "epochal shift" in American sexuality.[28] Although prosecuted for obscenity in thirty-two cities and banned in twenty-three states, it was watched by millions of Americans including women, who had been excluded from porn spectatorship in the past. Even respected TV journalist Barbara Walters reflected in her autobiography on watching *Deep Throat* when porno was suddenly cool.[29] The film garnered so much attention from the upper and middle classes, celebrities, and the press that Ralph Blumenthal of the *New York Times* referred to the trend as "porno chic."[30] Made on a budget of $25,000, the film was said to have made somewhere between $100 million and $600 million in revenue.[31] Other pornographers quickly took notice of the lucrative potential of the feature-film medium. Between 1973 and 1975, one hundred hardcore features were produced in America each year, while less than four hundred films per year were coming out of the declining Hollywood film industry.[32] Although they continued to produce loops for public screening and private distribution, porn purveyors saw feature-length movies as a bankable complement to their businesses.

   Opening just months after *Deep Throat*, *Behind the Green Door* (1972), produced by the Mitchell Brothers, was the first pornographic feature film to be widely released across the nation. It is also likely the first 35 mm film to depict a hardcore interracial sex scene.[33] Ivory Snow soap model Marilyn Chambers plays Gloria, a woman who is kidnapped and made to surrender to a series of sexual acts in a bizarre show. "Ladies and gentlemen, you are about to witness the ravishment of a woman who has been abducted," a voice announces to a private audience of men, women, and transvestites, all wearing masks, as the show begins. They watch, spellbound, as Chambers is penetrated by a black man, actor Johnnie Keyes. A former boxer, Keyes created an iconic performance of muscular black masculinity overpowering fragile white womanhood in *Behind the Green Door* at a time when interracial sex, especially between black men and white women, remained hugely taboo. The spectacle of a white woman being ravished by a black man was intensified by knowledge of Chambers's previous role as a squeaky-clean soap model. On the Ivory Snow box, Chambers smiles down at a white baby swaddled in a white cloth. Ads with her image (recalled by Procter and Gamble when *Behind the Green Door* came out) announced that Ivory Soap was "99 and 44/100% pure." The white, motherly figure of Chambers connoted femininity, domesticity, and racial purity. Moreover, the trope of soap has historically been associated with the capacity to cleanse and purify the (racial) body—in nineteenth-century advertisements, African babies bathed in Pears soap miraculously emerged white.[34] In *Behind the Green Door*, the symbolism of soap and cleanliness underscores Chambers's pure white womanhood, which becomes subsumed to the "polluting" force of blackness vis-à-vis interracial sex. The film pushes the symbolic registers of racial desire and disgust, using Johnnie Keyes's erotic labor to embody the sexual danger and excitement black bodies represented for whites at the time.

Though *Behind the Green Door* was the first feature-length porno to show a black man and white woman subvert racial-sexual norms by coupling, it was not alone in doing so. Eight-millimeter loops (stag films without the stag parties) continued to circulate during this period, and a number were devoted to this very forbidden fantasy. Stag films during the 1960s and '70s consistently prioritized black male sexuality over that of black women because the idea of black men being intimate with white women was so much more taboo. From a number of 1960s and '70s catalogues for mail-order 8 mm reels, it appears that many more films depicted black male–white female sex than black female–white male or black male–black female sex. For instance, in the Diamond Collection catalogue for films 1–96, 31 of the 96 films include black actors, but only 6 of those 31 feature black women. Hence, black men were the focus of 25 out of 31 films with blacks, and more than a quarter of all the films advertised in the catalogue. Attention was focused on their penises: "huge 12 inch cock," "big black dong," and "black weapon" are described in ads for couplings between black men and white women, as well as between black men and Asian women and black women.

"Black stud" was a term consistently used in marketing materials to describe scenes where black men appeared. In Swedish Erotica reel #85, *Coed in the Van* (1978) featuring Dashiel (Desiree West's purported boyfriend) and renowned Asian American adult actress Linda Wong, the description tells us that "a good looking black stud spies a gorgeous Oriental girl standing beside her bicycle." He invites her back to his camper and then "plunges his long black manhood faster and faster to satisfy her panting climax." Cast as "exotic" ingénue minus the exotic location, Linda Wong's "Oriental girl" fulfilled a fantasy held by white and nonwhite American men rooted in a long history of sexual exploitation around U.S. military bases in east Asia and embedded in Asian immigration to the United States.[35] Not quite as idealized as white women, and not as disparaged as black women, Asian porn actresses occupied a middle ground of objectification in porno. In this integrationist moment, there was a major fascination for images of interracial sex visualizing the powerful collision between the embodied "weapon" of the black stud and the imagined submissive sexuality of Asian women.

Loops formed an alternative and parallel economy of smut at a time when feature films were getting all the attention.[36] Most black actors worked in the stag market more often than in major feature-length pornos. Dashiel, King Paul, Jonathan Younger, Mick Jones, Smokey, and Bob White worked in these film shorts, often sold by mail order and in adult stores. Black actresses Shauna Evans, Flower, Kelly Stewart, Nancy Edwards, Trinket Fowler, and many other unknown women also worked in 8 mm format films.[37] Like black Hollywood actors, these performers faced a lot of stereotyping.[38] But sometimes the films eschewed racial tropes and just focused on the sex. *Bubble Gum Honey* (reel #68), a stag film featuring unidentified black male and female performers, portrays black heterosexuality unadorned with explicit stereotype. It begins with a pretty young woman in the park listening to music on a portable radio. A man flirts with her, they go get ice cream, and they have sex. In focusing on their smiling faces and relaxed intimacy, the film's eroticism is not drawn from the same dramatic collision of opposing forces fetishized in interracial porn; rather the film reveals a kind of relaxed sweetness, equality, and intimacy. Films like *Bubble Gum Honey* show black sexual subjectivity differently as they hint toward an alternative black erotic imagination and labor.

## Blaxploitation and the Politics of Black Eroticism

*Lialeh* (dir. Barron Bercovichy, 1974) is advertised as "the first black XXX film ever made," but that is not true. *Black Is Beautiful* (1970), also known as *Africanus Sexualis*, is the first 35 mm black-cast sexploitation film that I have uncovered, and it is an utter schlockfest. Purporting to educate its audience on "the sexual drives of the black man," *Black Is Beautiful* is a fake documentary on African sex practices that touts black nationalist and Afrocentric politics. As a "white coater,"[39] *Black Is Beautiful* actually went further than most softcore sexploitation films by showing some explicit shots, but because it depicted simulated sex the film was not quite hardcore. *Black Is Beautiful* is narrated by an African American man playing the role of an expert on African sexual customs and performed by African American actors dressed as rural West Africans. Like classic exploitation "exotics" from the 1930s (e.g., *Ingagi*), *Black Is Beautiful* presents a kind of "ethnological" exhibition of "African" people for popular consumption.[40] Whereas 1930s exploitation exotics sought to capture a white working-class audience fearful (and desirous) of "unbridled black lust" in the figure of "negro as beast,"[41] *Black Is Beautiful* seems directed at harnessing the interest of African Americans at a time when they were deeply concerned with (and active in supporting) Marxist anticolonial struggles exploding all over the African continent, as well as in embracing African aesthetics in black American cultural expression.

The smirking narrator shows how the film, in a completely didactic way, attempts to counter stereotypes for white audiences while also promoting them for black audiences. While purporting to dismantle the myth of the hypersexual black stud, the film actually instantiates it by using supposed African sex practices and gender dynamics as a model for African American couples. While it shows that the myth of the stud was actually a concept that black men (and women) could possibly identify with or take pleasure in, *Black Is Beautiful* uses heterosexist ideas circulating in black cultural nationalist discourses at the time to present a regressive view of black gendered relationships. Although it is completely fabricated, the film's documentary framing makes the claims of the black sex expert about "marriage customs" and "the family system of Africa" *seem* empirical. For instance, the narrator describes supposed African sex positions with Afrocentric names like the *wazi grip*, the *abuba arrow*, the *kwango*, and the *mongun och*, as if they really exist, and as if there is one common language in all of Africa. More problematically, when the expert argues that homosexuality in Africa is "relatively rare" save in a few tribes and asserts that African women "take care of their odor so that it

FIGURE 2.1. *Black Is Beautiful, aka Africanus Sexualis* (1970).

does not offend," viewers may begin to understand that this Afrocentric view of black sexuality is firmly set on privileging the desires of heterosexual black men over black women or black gay men. The narrator continues:

> The African male is considered the dominant partner and the central force in the marriage. A woman is usually taught by her mother that it is her duty to please her husband whenever he wishes to be pleased. . . . Woman is considered the property and primary possession of her man. Our ancestors felt that the man was master and the woman his slave. Even though we no longer carry to this extent [*sic*], we will not abide a dominant woman. You might say we consider both partners equal. One is just more equal than the other.

In constructing black men as dominant partners in heteronormative, patriarchal relationships, *Black Is Beautiful* echoes the arguments of actual Afrocentric critics like Molefi Asante and Frances Cress Welsing who assert that homosexuality "doesn't represent an Afro-centric way of life" or amount to a form of genocide imposed by whites.[42] The film represents how black erotica at the time reflected black nationalist concerns about developing black families based on heteronormative gender and sexual behavior. In focusing on black male control of marriage, the film articulates a disciplinary fantasy of black eroticism, rather than a liberatory one. As L. H. Stallings reflects, "Sadly, a model of rhetoric created to liberate one faction of people often time lapses into a type of policing of the same group."[43] This confining vision of gendered power was extremely contested in black nationalist discourses, particularly by black feminist and queer critics, yet it animated much of black erotic production. Ironically, black erotica seemed as interested in promoting heteronormative respectability as it was in subverting it.

Movies like *Black Is Beautiful* exploited a "rising black box office" hungry for films that depicted black actors as something other than passive sidekicks and sexually neutered leads, especially as agents in images of sex and violence.[44] In 1971, Melvin Van Peebles's "maverick breakthrough movie" *Sweet Sweetback's Baadasssss Song* set the mold for the black exploitation film genre, otherwise known as Blaxploitation.[45] Exploitation films had long explored taboo subjects of sex and violence, but rarely from a black perspective.[46] Intensely controversial, *Sweetback* established many of the features for Hollywood's production of similar black-focused films of the period. Reflecting black cultural nationalist sensibilities, the eponymous film's (anti) hero both defies the racist power structure and dominates black gendered relationships in the quest for survival, autonomy, and justice.

The figure of black-man-as-revolutionary-hero that dominates the film's narrative employs courage and quick thinking along with ineffable style and sexual prowess. *Sweetback* provoked debates about the logic and validity of this "revolutionary" portrayal of the protagonist's heroic and glamorous defiance of state power. The representation of black sexuality in *Sweetback* was also debated, with questions about the portrayal of explicit sex and the exploitation of black women by the protagonist. Some saw Peebles's decision to make Sweetback a hustler who gets paid to sleep with women in sex shows as perpetuating stereotypes of black men as super spades and black women as whores. Yet *Sweetback* and later films of the genre of black exploitation provided a "more aggressive affirmation of black cultural identity" than was the norm in Hollywood.[47] These films incorporated stereotypes of black violence and hypersexuality but also reappropriated them in order to create new images that many saw as resistive.[48] According to Stuart Hall, "In the ways [these] heroes deal with whites, there is a remarkable absence, indeed a conscious reversal of, the old deference or childlike dependency. In many ways, these are 'revenge' films—audiences relishing the black heroes' triumphs over 'Whitey,' loving the fact that they are getting away with it! What we may call the moral playing field is leveled."[49] While black men took on white power in this defiant cinema, they also asserted symbolic control over black women.

Gordon Parks Jr.'s *Superfly* (1972) was another controversial Blaxploitation film that prioritized black masculinity at the expense of black women in its glamorization of the black-man-as-outlaw. Like *Sweetback*, *Superfly* captured "a new kind of Black social realism."[50] It artfully presented the seductions of criminal life through the figure of the black gangster in a narrative that spoke to the insurgent desires of an urban, young black audience in the anxious aftermath of the civil rights movement. *Superfly* tells the story of Priest (Ron O'Neal), a stylish Harlem cocaine dealer who wants to get out of the drug game. But first he must do a final big deal to afford an escape and stick it to the mob boss who controls him. Although the film does not develop the female characters, Priest's black girlfriend, Georgia (Sheila Frazier), and white Park Avenue mistress, Cynthia (Polly Niles), are important figures. While Cynthia establishes that Priest is so successful that he could exceed the confines of the ghetto and access the forbidden fruit of white womanhood, Georgia gives him the quality of being "of the people." While Priest is impatient and domineering with Cynthia, he is patient and loving with Georgia, who unconditionally supports him and shares his vision of freedom from "the man."

Despite *Superfly*'s adherence to representational codes of black male sexual dominance it is critical to acknowledge that the film's famous bathtub scene was the most significant and explicit representation of intimacy between a black couple on-screen up to that point. The scene thus presents a foundation for the assertive and defiant black sexuality found in soul porn. Unlike the sexual scenes in *Sweetback*, which played upon the commodified, masculinist spectacle of black sexuality through the uncompromising, workmanlike talents of the black stud, the couple in *Superfly* seem to be propelled by their own erotic energy.

Beautifully shot by Parks, the bathtub scene captures an autonomous black sensuality based on equity. Priest and Georgia kiss, caress, and have sex in the soapy water. Both partners are equally passionate, and both act with a sense of urgency made all the more intense because Priest's life is in danger. Parks's careful attention to lighting allowed the actors' wet brown skin to appear warm and luminous rather than flat and gray, as in many other films depicting the skin of people of color.[51] This love scene is graphic without being exploitative or tacky; it achieves a sense of realism and beauty in black sexuality as no other Blaxploitation film has. It has been mimicked in many other films, such as *Lialeh* (discussed below), but was never equaled in execution or sentiment during the Blaxploitation era.

As a result of the Blaxploitation boom, Hollywood studios began "scrambling for black acting talent."[52] This phenomenon allowed for the entry of black female actors in leading roles, adding another dimension to the mainly crime-based Blaxploitation genre. Black female characters became more prominent narrative figures, not just girlfriends or attendant prostitutes. Their roles combined sex, violence, and action, as they played the femme fatale who always manages to display her stunning black figure in compromising situations. Pam Grier became best known for portraying vampish protagonists. She had a potent "propensity to disrobe" and a "not-to-be messed-with independence and active sexuality."[53] In films such as *Coffy* (1973), *Foxy Brown* (1974), and *Sheba, Baby* (1975), Grier not only kicked the asses of the powerful and corrupt while seducing the audience with her stunning physicality and undeniable eroticism, but she also became an important box office commodity. According to the *Washington Post*, in 1977 she was one of the top-three most "bankable female stars in Hollywood,"[54] along with Barbra Streisand and Liza Minnelli. For Grier, the sexual liberalness of her films was reflective of her personal belief in exploring sexual expression and independence despite the concerns of some in the black community that the films were exploitative. Revealing this sense of ownership over her sexuality and choices at the time, Grier explained: "Just because we were black cinema artists, we weren't going to deny that we were sexual also."[55]

According to Cedric Robinson, Blaxploitation depoliticized and caricatured black communities.[56] A degraded cinema, Blaxploitation transformed the energy of black political resistance into commodified eye candy to be fed back to black audiences. Audiences were seduced by images of black revenge and the titillating body of the "Bad Black Woman" vigilante. For Robinson, that Bad Black Woman represented "Hollywood's fabrication of Black society, all the libidinal desire and social pathology of America's urban classes."[57] Moreover, her mimicking of revolutionary political figures such as Angela Davis and Kathleen Cleaver "eviscerat[ed] the original's intellectual sophistication, political and organizational context, doctrinal commitments, and most tellingly, her critique of capitalist society and its employment of gender, race and class."[58] As a "false Angela Davis," Pam Grier's performance of black woman as cinematic ghetto revolutionary impregnated the exaggerated fantasy of Blaxploitation with authenticity. Grier's image reinforced black women's role as objects of sexual voyeurism on a new, more explicit level and portrayed revolutionary women as destroyers and avengers rather than as creators and sustainers of community.[59]

However, Grier's characters, and those of other leading black actresses of the genre such as Tamara Dodson, also presented a forceful image of black women as sexual agents. They offered counterexamples to stereotypes of black women in cinema as solely fit to occupy menial, subservient roles as maids and companions. Just as black male figures pushed against a subordinated masculinity, black female figures in Blaxploitation resisted sexual colonization. Although designed to provide titillation, these black female characters use their sexuality to their own advantage, and in the end triumph over the "bad guys." Often their triumph was politically subversive for the black community; they destroyed the drug traffickers, pimps, and corrupt cops that hurt their communities. Moreover, because these films were based on a genre of action-oriented crime stories, their goal was not to reflect reality but to reference it. In comparison to their male counterparts, these women were never promiscuous—their sexualities were confined to a single lover or were used as tools for the cause.

For Grier, expressing her sexuality through her performances was important rather than gratuitous. It meant *not* denying that as a black woman she *had* sexual desires. Unfortunately, Grier's articulation of such sexual desires did not translate into longevity in her film career: for many of the black actors, directors, and film technicians of the period, when the fad for Blaxploitation ended, so did their jobs. Nor did such films give rise to more complicated renderings of black women's sexual politics in later mainstream cinema. Ultimately, the representation of black women in Blaxploitation film was highly ambivalent, reflecting the "double-sided nature" of representation and stereotyping. The roles of black women in Blaxploitation framed them simultaneously as sexual objects and sexual agents.[60] Despite its conflicts, however, the popularity of the Blaxploitation genre showed that black people were hungry for their own defiant sexual images in media.

### Players in Print

While the effacement of black political articulations in the Blaxploitation genre occluded the possibility of a truly "revolutionary" black radical sexual culture in film, the representation of black sexuality for black people remained important. Many blacks, men and women, became more open and public about sexual mores and desires and expressed them in a range of formats— from the highly eroticized album covers of the Ohio Players to pornographic softcore magazines—during the soul porn era. Impacted by the sexual revolution happening in black communities, they sought out sexual media, hardcore and softcore. While they had participated in pornography as models, performers, and consumers in the past, there was a veritable explosion of black erotica in the 1960s and '70s. Pam Grier appeared in both *Playboy* and *Players*, while Blaxploitation actors Fred Williamson and Jim Brown both appeared in *Playgirl* magazine in the mid-1970s, showing that purportedly straight black men also participated as models in erotic images. In addition, an industry of black gay erotic images by photographers like Sierra Domino provided other images of black male desirability. Unlike the male leading actors who appeared in *Playgirl*, Grier posed nude. By engaging in the commercial sexual culture of print erotica, Grier expanded her noted role as a sexual icon. Joining black *Playboy* models Jeannie Bell, Gina Byrams, Lola Falana, and Azizi Johari, Grier embodied the desire of many in the black community to see black women as national figures of beauty and desirability. Grier represented a version of black women's sexual agency in a period dominated by a masculinist black politics that subordinated black women's sexual identities to the needs of black men.

Players was the first widely circulated men's magazine exclusively focused on capturing a black market. Published beginning in 1973 by the America Distribution Corporation, *Players* was more than a nudie magazine.[61] Before its decline in quality in the early 1980s, *Players* was a sort of black *Playboy* in that it presented the seductive image of an affluent consumer lifestyle for men. Unlike *Playboy*, *Players* marketed sex and commodities within a black cultural orientation. Black Arts Movement writer Wanda Coleman was the first editor; her vision of a smart, relevant, black sexual lifestyle magazine infused *Players* with a progressive tone that made the dual focus on political discourse and sexy centerfolds of the magazine a defiant cultural statement.

Players, like *Playboy*, featured regular columns about trends in music, movies, and technology, focused on capturing the interests of male readers. Unlike *Playboy*, or any mainstream black lifestyle magazines at the time, *Players* published articles by eminent black writers, critics, and cultural workers and consistently focused on black cultural and political themes. Contributors included Amiri Baraka, Alex Haley, Julian Bond, Huey Newton, and Stanley Crouch. The magazine featured a range of salient articles on Africa, Haiti, and Maoist China, and an exposé on the prison industrial complex alongside news from African American communities in New York, Philadelphia, Los Angeles, Miami, and Washington, D.C. Features on leading activists, entertainers, actors, and athletes focused on Dick Gregory, Paul Mooney, Richard Roundtree, Yaphet Kotto, Sammy Davis Jr., Quincy Jones, Vivian Reed, George Benson, and Arthur Ashe. Arts were also a major feature of *Players*, with exposés on black artists such as renowned sculptor Nathaniel Bustion and designer

Jim McDade. Psychedelic drawings by Bob Smith illustrated short stories by writers such as Donald Goines, Iceberg Slim, and Chester Himes. Finally, *Players* emphasized the exciting contemporary cultural productions of jazz, funk, and soul coming out of black communities, as well as the black film boom of the mid-1970s. Reflecting black stylistic trends, *Players* featured the incredible fashions of the period, from Afrocentric versions of bubas, caftans, and agbadas to outrageous polyester suits, platform shoes, and fur-trimmed ensembles. These fashions expressed soul as an urban, vernacular aesthetic that many found to be culturally affirming and innovative.[62]

The magazine's monthly feature spreads of models—usually in three-to-four-page spreads, including one centerfold—presented a range of black women's looks and styles. The models' backgrounds were multinational and multiethnic, as evidenced by the premiere issue's cover girl, Ethiopian-born model Zeudi Araya. Cuban-born Judit was highlighted alongside African American models including Kimberly, Spice, and Tatum. These women— whether their monikers were real or constructed by the magazine editors— represented a range of skin tones, from deep cocoa brown to light cream, and hair types from straight processes, to wigs, to short natural Afros, to braids. Their bodies differed as well: some women were more voluptuous with large breasts, while others were very petite with smaller busts. None of the models would be considered "fat," with, for example, large bellies and thighs, and they were decidedly young—their youth was accentuated with coy poses, lace, ribbons, and playful lingerie. The models' figures were all within gender norms for desirably sized embodied femininity, though some were curvier, reflecting the embrace of alternative aesthetics for women's bodies in black and Latino communities. The range of beauty found among these women of color models rejected the dominant racialized ideals exhibited in white pornographic magazines. By both spotlighting diverse beauty images and policing the boundaries of what constituted desirable feminine bodies for readers, *Players* simultaneously expanded and delimited the roles of black women in softcore sexual media.

Readers celebrated this focus on black sexuality in their letters to the magazine. As one letter to the editor read:

> Dear *Players*, I just got hip to your black *Playboy* magazine known as *Players*. And I have a lot of skin books or magazines in my household. But this is the best I've ever had and me being black and to see these tender bronze women getting funky . . . man! It was really a sight to behold! This magazine really did something to let the black woman ex-

press herself to the world in this manner. You can believe me, whenever I get the money, I will get your year thing.
—Charles D. Lewis, Los Angeles, California.[63]

As this letter demonstrates, black male consumers of *Players* enjoyed the magazine's focus on black women and regarded these women not simply as tender bronze objects, but as women expressing themselves. These men were also a previously untapped market that advertisers could now target. In the back of the magazine, beyond the cigarette and liquor ads, devices and drugs for penis enlargement and sexual enhancement were advertised, acknowledging black men's anxieties that sharply diverged from myths of their super-sexual prowess.

*Players* provided a unique forum for sexual culture and information about sexuality not only to black men, but also to black women. Black female consumers could potentially enjoy the magazine's sexual discourse. Although it was not the intention of the magazine, heterosexual, bisexual, and gay women of color could potentially appropriate the erotic presentations of the women of color centerfolds as a venue for identification and sexual fantasy, and they could use the sexual culture and information for their own needs. Importantly, *Players* also provided a space for black women models to be seen and to work. Pam Grier's layout in the magazine's third issue (March 1974) helped establish *Players* as a venue for aspiring models and actresses. Unlike other pornographic magazines focusing on black women during the 1960s, '70s, and early '80s, such as *Terrific N' Tanned*, *Black Girl*, *Blackbirds*, *Chocolate Candy*, *Chocolate Pussy*, *350*, and *Soul*; and white hardcore magazines that featured some black women, like *Blue Climax* and *Ero De Luxe: The Swedish Sex Magazine*; *Players* exhibited many more models of color and benefited from a wider, international distribution. The preeminent symbol of soul porn during the 1970s, *Players* was a vital forum where black consumers could locate images that prioritized black sexual subjectivity in a time when cultural politics and sexual politics were deeply intertwined and transforming.

## Lialeh's Tease

"Sweet, sweet, sexy, Lialeh," sings renowned rock and soul drummer Bernard "Pretty" Purdie over the funk grooves his band lays down in the opening scene of the film *Lialeh*. A woman with a long straight-haired wig, wearing only red thong panties, glides and shimmies between the saxophone, clarinet, congas, guitars, bass, and piano players, lingering around Purdie's drum set. The film cuts back and forth between the dancer's smiling face and lithe body twisting to the beat, and Purdie's face as he croons the honeyed lyrics. This opening scene of *Lialeh* sets it apart from the rest of Golden Age porno. By referencing Curtis Mayfield's performance of "Pusher Man" in *Superfly*, *Lialeh* signals its emergence from the black film movement of the 1970s. Directed by Barron Bercovichy and starring Jennifer Leigh and Lawrence Pertillar, *Lialeh* expresses the cultural sensibility of black performance and aesthetics of the soul era, including the interface of music with black politics and black eroticism. By linking these, *Lialeh* references the energy and interests of the soul aesthetic and the black power cultural milieu. Yet, like much of black exploitation cinema, the film is not only technically shoddy and narratively incoherent, it seems to have been created by white filmmakers for the sole purpose of capitalizing on black people's desires to see their own sexuality on screen. As an example of soul porn, the film reflects an attempt to portray the sexual agency of black people and the erotic potential of relationships between blacks and whites. But like much of soul porn, as well as much of black exploitation cinema, black women are not only objectified, they are marginalized in favor of black men. Here, even the title character Lialeh is sidelined. How does Jennifer Leigh's Lialeh perform within, and perhaps against, the limits of the black woman's role? I begin to answer this question with a description of the film.

Purdie's soulful soundtrack continues to play as the scene shifts to show the introductory credits over the lights of New York's Times Square. Enter Arlo (Pertillar): a black man wearing a flashy zebra coat and a red fedora walking the square, surveying the cityscape, his strut in time with the funky score. The next scene introduces Lialeh (Leigh) as she, wearing a rather demure powder-blue trench coat, rides a bicycle through the city. Arriving at a theater dressing room, she sits at a mirror and gazes at her reflection. She soon begins to apply makeup and puts on a fashionably large Afro wig. Arlo is auditioning women for a sex revue. Frustrated that the auditions are going nowhere, he tells all the women waiting in the wings to leave. Lialeh won't accept his dismissal; she insists that he listen to her song by pushing him down into a chair. As she begins to sing, she sways her thin, sinuous body, and lifts her short red skirt. In a nod to the "casting couch,"[64] she kneels down to give Arlo a blow job. Needless to say, Lialeh gets the job.

The narrative strays from here, following the exploits of Arlo rather than the title character, Lialeh. For instance, the next scene shows Arlo kissing a different black woman as they ride in a chauffeur-driven Rolls-Royce through the city. After clearly establishing that Arlo is both fashionable and a ladies man, the film then shows that he is also political. He gets to "stick it to Whitey" when he goes to meet with the slumlord who owns the theater where he wants to put on his sex show. The secretary, a white woman (Diane Miller) who is eating a hot dog at her desk, looks both disgusted and afraid of Arlo, asking, "Are you going to rape me?" "Is that what you want?!" Arlo angrily quips. When Arlo tries to force his way into the office, the secretary jumps in front of him and takes a martial arts stance, warning that she has a "brown belt." They circle each other as if they are going to break into a kung fu fight.[65] Wrestling the secretary to the ground, Arlo begins to seduce her with kisses and caresses instead. As she begins to moan, in delight rather than fear, Arlo enacts his revenge. He has "stuck it to her" by putting her hot dog in her vagina. "So long, bitch! Enjoy your lunch!" he says as he leaves her enraged and embarrassed on the floor of the office. By humiliating the racist secretary, Arlo is cast as a defiant hero, even if the act was in fact a form of sexist forced penetration or rape.

Strangely, Arlo, the ladies man, never seduces Lialeh—at least not in person. They have a tepid phone sex scene instead. During a call Lialeh masturbates while Arlo simply walks around his stylish apartment. Arlo even hangs up on Lialeh when another black woman arrives at the door (she is conducting a survey on soul food), and soon they have sex in a rather sensual bubble bath in a direct reference to Park's famous *Superfly* scene. Instead of hooking up with Arlo in person again, Lialeh has two hardcore scenes of her own. First, Lialeh has a sex scene with a minister following gospel choir practice at a run down, storefront church. Given the sexual conservatism within the black church, Lialeh's sex scene with the black minister is quite remarkable. Although other hardcore films have used gospel music and religious symbolism in sex scenes, I have not encountered another in which a minister performs a sex scene, or which depicts the sex actually happening between the pews on the floor of a black church. Set to quite well-arranged blues-inflected music, the scene presents Lialeh as the sexual aggressor who seduces the minister. Lialeh's second sex scene is with the hapless production assistant. They have sex on the dressing room floor just before the big show, which viewers may have forgotten is the plot device, because of the narrative's incoherent twists and turns. Lialeh again is the aggressor in the scene, but she also shows tenderness, assuaging the PA's low self-esteem about the small size of his penis.

Finally, the revue begins. Purdie's band performs and we discover that the song "Lialeh" is actually part of the show. Lialeh's solo performance is next. Wearing a stylish red strapless gown, a white feather boa, and white gloves, Lialeh begins to sing a low-voiced sultry song. In a low angle shot with the

FIGURE 2.2. Lialeh's solo dance, *Lialeh* (1974).

stage lights positioned behind her, Lialeh slowly moves her hips and flutters her arms as she begins to remove her clothes in style of a burlesque dancer. A glaring red stage light heightens the drama of Lialeh's performance, underscoring its "red light" nature as it glistens on her brown skin. As the tempo of her song picks up, Lialeh's striptease gains fervor. She dances fiercely, dropping down to the floor and pushing her body in forceful, thrusting, push-up like motions as the song climaxes. Lialeh's performance is impressive, sensual, and even beautiful. At the end of her number, having removed most of her costume, Lialeh descends to the audience and presents her G-string for cash contributions. She shimmies up to a white man, but then petulantly rejects his tip. "That's a fiver not a c-note," Lialeh says as she sticks the folded bill in his mouth and defiantly walks away. This final move by Lialeh to establish her desires—to be valued as a performer who deserves at least $100 tips—undermines the white male consumptive gaze. Like Arlo's reprisal against the slumlord's secretary, Lialeh's uncompromising rejection of the spectator's cheap tip establishes her as a valuable sexual agent as well as a political agent in her use of sexuality. This is the only time in the film we get a sense of Lialeh's underlying motivations as a political actor, however.

*Lialeh* ends on an unusual note. In its final scene, two other black women

dancers and three black male dancers join Lialeh on stage. Wearing gold sequin evening gowns, the women dance and sing in a line facing the men.
Surprisingly, the men are dressed like Johnnie Keyes's "African" in *Behind the
Green Door*: they wear bodysuits with a hole cut to expose their crotch, bone
necklaces, and face paint. The performers seem to have fun as they sing and
playfully perform a collective striptease. Just as the performance gets going,
Arlo appears in the audience asking to see tickets. When he comes to a con-
servatively dressed white couple, he insists that the white woman (Amy Math-
ieu) come on stage. When she resists, Arlo actually picks her up, throws her
over his shoulder, and carries her up to the stage. There, he forces oral sex on
her. The entire group of black male dancers joins in.

The film ends without fully exploring the intriguing and sexy secrets of
the main female character, sacrificing her development to the conquests of
the black male characters. Lialeh's role is limited, and her sex acts seem more
compensatory gestures than important scenes for her character or the plot.
The other black actresses (all uncredited) are used solely to help develop Arlo's
role. At the end of the stage performance they disappear altogether. Although
problematic, *Lialeh* is highly significant to the history of black sexual culture
and pornographic feature film. It brings the two forms together in what one
critic called a "sophisticated, sensual, fast-moving, and entertaining . . . blaks-
ploitation [*sic*] sexploitation treat."[66]

Yet black film critic Donald Bogle had reservations about the film: "Like
most pornographic films," Bogle argues, "*Lialeh* obviously exploits female
characters and is often too graphic for its own good."[67] Bogle's prudishness
aside, although the female performers mostly serve to support the interests
of the men — a common feature of pornographic film — it is also important to
consider how these women performers might have exceeded their limited and
exploiting roles. The film is ultimately redeemed by Lialeh's engaging Revue
Nègre performance, which references a historical musical tradition around
black sexuality, but is placed in a black cultural nationalist moment. Jennifer
Leigh brings charisma and an otherwise unseen grace to the burlesque scene.
Her performance allows the film to exceed any other contemporary film in the
black, Hollywood, exploitation, or porno film traditions by advancing a space
for the articulation of the hardcore sexuality of black actresses. By capturing
Jennifer Leigh's use of sexualized performance, the film creates an important
rupture in the silencing of black female sexual desire in American popular
culture. This staging of her climactic performance before an audience — black
and white, men and women — reflects the performativity of racialized sexuality and underscores its relationship to manipulation and voyeurism. It in-

sists on voyeurism's malleability and on black women's ability to mediate the meanings of their own sexualities. Lialeh's striptease references a long tradition of black women's erotic and burlesque performance. Even her classy red dress and feather boa acknowledge the privileging of images of elegant white women in Hollywood and Broadway, and how black women can in fact appropriate them. Hence, her erotic performance pushes against the historic dichotomy between glamorized white femininity in Hollywood and Broadway and the forced unglamour of black actresses' parts. Her performance represented black women's roles in taking ownership in their sexuality and using it for their own desires for eroticism, visibility, and opportunity.

As a porno, *Lialeh* is not so much "too graphic," as Bogle asserts, but often too awkward and tedious. This is in part due to the below-average quality of the film's production, surely stemming from the constraints of time and money intrinsic to an underground shoot. For example, Arlo's bathtub scene ends up being rather tepid. The lighting and not-so-sudsy water do not capture the sexiness of the exchange in the way Gordon Parks Jr. was able to in *Superfly*. Additionally, poor lighting and sound in Lialeh's dressing room scene add a shoddy and gratuitous quality to the exchange, as if the director realized at the last minute that another hardcore scene was needed to carry the film and decided to cut it in. At the same time, a lot of time and care was put into the score, costumes—including choir robes and elaborate performance outfits—and staging the scenes.

Bogle may not have been open to the graphic nature of the production, but he did acknowledge the camp intentions of this "funny enough" film. Like much of vintage and Golden Age film pornography, humor was one vehicle used to manage the tensions around displaying the hardcore sexual scenario.[68] Here humor serves a political purpose as well, as in the "hot dog scene" in which Arlo's comical yet sexist revenge on the white secretary functions to critique the historic caricature of black men as rapists. Lialeh's snipe at the white male tipper in the audience of the revue serves to destabilize the power of white patriarchal supremacy and upset the notion that black women's sexuality is always available on the cheap. These filmic reversals of power relations address the largely black, urban population who were most likely the intended audience.

## Black Girl in a Sex World

Desiree West's role in Anthony Spinelli's *Sex World* best exemplifies how black actresses performed in porno that mobilized racial conflicts in order to heighten the erotic charge of—and therefore, interest in—soul porn.[69] *Sex World* is like the setting of the TV show *Fantasy Island*, an exclusive weekend retreat where visitors learn that they can forget all their problems, knowing that "every fantasy will be fulfilled," as one of the Sex World guides promises. During the orientation, the guide describes to arriving guests how they should submit to counselors who will probe their erotic predilections, while behind the scenes, technicians use surveillance cameras, computers, and communication systems to arrange sexual scenarios that enact the guests' deepest fantasies. Desiree West plays Jill, a guest who is paired with Roger (John Leslie), a rather pompous white guest who is cynical about the whole enterprise. As her scene reveals, Roger is also a bigot. Jill and Roger have an intense exchange in which Jill aggressively convinces Roger to put his bigotry aside and have sex with her. The Sex World technicians have put them together because they believe the key to solving Roger's sexual problem is to, in fact, pair him with "someone he hates."

The opening of the scene shows Roger in a bathrobe picking up the phone. He asks for the manager, but is instead connected to one of the technicians who is watching him on a surveillance monitor. She asks, "What's the problem?" Roger complains that the room is not to his taste: it features burgundy and black zebra-print paint, large tropical plants, and woven rattan screens. "You gonna have some Zulu race come out and dance for me?" Roger says in a thick New York accent, "Come on! What's going on?" The technician cuts him off just as there is a knock at the door. Roger turns to see Jill standing in a white terry-cloth bathrobe, her hand on one hip, smiling. "What do you want? You here to clean up the room?" Angry, he hangs up the phone, turns to Jill and says, seething with frustration, "Well, if you're going to clean up, clean up!"

Jill responds, "I'll clean your wet cock when we're done, son." She smiles and kisses the air as Roger looks at her with the sudden realization that she is not the maid, "Oh no! You can't be my trick!" "Surprise, honey!" says Jill as she approaches the bed. "There goes the fucking neighborhood," Roger mumbles. Sultrily moving to the bed, Jill reaches toward Roger, but he pulls back. "Now look, fat lips, you got the wrong room, and the wrong boy!" Keeping her cool, Jill wryly responds to Roger's abusive words by saying, "Oh, well they told me to go find that honkey boy. Ain't that you?"

Roger is getting nervous. As Jill moves closer he moves back. "Uh uh, but I'll tell you a secret," he announces. "At Thanksgiving, I went for the white meat—I said give me the breast. Period." Jill rejoins: "Don't say breast, say *titty*. Live a little." She smirks with satisfaction as she can see Roger beginning to freak out. He picks up the phone again but the line is dead. "It's just you and me," she provokes, "Come on, you ain't never had no *black* pussy before?" "Not yet," he jumps up; "Not now," he bounds across the bed; "Not ever!" he declares from a chair on the other side of the room. "You don't know what you've been missing," she breathes, kittenishly stroking the bedspread. "Haven't you ever heard? The *darker* the meat, the *sweeter* the juice." Jill sits up to face Roger. "Don't you want to see my juice, honey?" she asks. Looking away, Roger stubbornly declares, "I don't want to see nothing from you." Jill stands up and seductively opens her robe. "Now, this *ain't* too shabby, is it?"

The film cuts from Roger's awe-stricken face to Jill's bust—she wears a white lace bustier—and then slowly pans down her body, stopping at Jill's exposed crotch white framed by a garter belt. The film cuts back to Roger's stunned face, his mouth now hanging open. Suddenly he bolts from the chair to the other side of the room. Jill turns to Roger and stares. "Well," she pauses, cocking her head to the side, "if I ain't got me a first class honkey bigot here. Ooohweee!" "Now, wait a minute!" Roger declares. "You can't call—I am not prejudiced! I just don't happen to *like* you people." "Okay, white boy, I'll prove your *spigot* ain't no bigot," Jill teases as she lets her robe fall to the floor, "Let's get your *foster* out, and see if we can get it *flowing*, huh?" The film cuts to a close-up of Jill's genitals from Roger's point of view. It pans up her body to her breasts then quickly cuts away to Roger's face before jumping back to Jill's face. This shot-reverse-shot structure suggests that Roger cannot take his eyes off Jill's body; he is spellbound. "You are built kinda nice. I'll say that," Roger almost mumbles to himself, as if ashamed to admit it. "Fucking A, I am Caesar!" Jill says in a louder, more confident voice. Still smiling, undaunted by the cat-and-mouse game, Jill cups her breasts. "These jugs are filled with *honey*. And down here," she touches her genitals, "is my honeypot. Just for *you*." The camera pulls in on her face as she speaks in a slow drawl, "This is home, Jerome."

Finally moving to face Jill, Roger says, "All right, I'll give you the benefit of the doubt. But what are you supposed to do for me?" "Me? *I's* provides the entertainment, *suh*." "All right, entertain me. You're supposed to have such rhythm, do a little dance." In a soft, sweet voice Jill replies, "The rhythm I got ain't in my *feet*!" Placing her hand close to her pelvis Jill coos, "It's about three or four feet *higher*. Between my *thighs* is where my rhythm *lies*." Jill kneels

FIGURE 2.3. John Leslie as Roger in *Sex World* (1977).

FIGURE 2.4.
Desiree West as
Jill in *Sex World*
(1977).

FIGURE 2.5. Desiree West and John Leslie in *Sex World* (1977).

on the bed and slides next to Roger, her voice almost singing, "*Fine* as wine, so *divine*." Jill begins to wear down Roger's resolve, and she encourages him: "Now that's the way!" She exposes her breasts. "Ain't these 'bout the finest tits you ever seen?" She strokes her thigh, "And these *thighs*, tell me, don't these thighs make your peter *rise*?" Kneeling in front of him, she caresses her butt. "And this *ass*, ain't this a *class ass*? Tell me this ain't the *finest* ass you ever had stuck in your *face*?" "You people do have nice asses," Roger admits. Jill keeps pushing: "Go ahead, put your hand on it. *Feel* it. Bet you never felt one." Roger reaches out, tentatively, to touch her. "There you go! Oooh, you got nice hands too. There you go, dip into the *valley*. *Dally* into the *valley* for a while." Roger rather awkwardly touches Jill between her buttocks cheeks and then smells his fingers. "Hmmm, you don't *smell* funny. I thought you people smell funny." "Not this ass! It just smells like *ass*," Jill says, touching his shoulder and pulling Roger in. "Go on, smell it! Yeah, come on, stick your nose down there!" Shaking his head and pulling away, Roger whines, "I'll touch it but I don't want to smell it." Jill then turns around to face Roger. "Don't be *mad*. Let's be *glad*."

"Come on," she says, pushing down her bustier to expose her breasts more, "I seen you sneaking a peek at these titties a long time ago. They're yours. Ain't nobody gonna know. It's just for *you*." Jill finally grabs Roger and pulls him down on the bed.

Throughout the scene, shots cut back to Jill and Roger enthusiastically having sex, culminating in Roger ejaculating on Jill's chest. Roger is transformed by this sexual encounter with a black woman. In the end, when the rest of the guests are boarding the bus, we see him attempting to bribe a Sex World porter to let him remain at the fantasy retreat, ostensibly with Jill. "I just want to go through again, that's all," he pleads. "See, there's this girl—it might turn out to be serious! Look, cash. If that's the problem, I got cash!" Jill looks over her shoulder to see Roger's negotiations with the porter, shakes her head bemusedly, and boards the bus.

This captivating scene plays out the tensions of interracial desire through the trope of the aggressive black woman who seduces the unwilling, aloof white man. It propels what I have called the "myth of prohibition," whereby white men's desire for black women is made visible, instead projected onto the figure of the hypersexual black woman. As the myth goes, white men do not willingly cross racial borders to have sex with black women. Rather, they are compelled to engage in interracial sex by black women who, because their very natures are defined by sex, demand it of them. When white men do become intimate with black women, this discourse asserts, it is because black women tempted them. Saturated with this cultural myth, representations of interracial sex between white men and black women evoke the ways in which black women trouble the mechanisms of denial, concealment, and projection white men have used to legitimate and deflect their race and gender privilege and sexual domination. A colonial fantasy and legacy of American slavery, the myth of prohibition is central to the unconscious tapestry of racialized desire at work in porno like *Sex World*.[70]

Even though Jill is a paying guest at the retreat who is entitled to realize her own fantasy, she is used to fulfill the desires—unacknowledged and disavowed—of another guest, a white man. White characters, including white women, experience Sex World as a sexual utopia. They emerge at the end of the film satiated and personally transformed. One white woman desires sex with women outside of her marriage, while another secretly longs for sex with a black man. Both become agents of their own sexual needs through their encounters with the objects of their desire at the resort. Yet Jill, the sole black female character, is not only subject to the only abusive scenario in the film, her true desires and motivations are left unaddressed. Just as Roger confuses her for the maid, Jill is used to perform a kind of service for him—that is, she helps him realize that his bigotry is actually unrealized desire. In this way, *Sex World* rehearses a scenario that dates back to the plantation sexual economy, in which black women's sexuality was made available to white patriarchy, objectified and imagined as desirous of the (white man's) civilizing mission.

In many ways, *Sex World* reflects pornography's attempt to fabricate a world of fantasy free of limits, a "pornotopia" where it is "always bedtime."[71] But as theorist Frantz Fanon has shown, racism is inevitably sutured to the modern unconscious.[72] Racism defines the very terrain of our imaginations and dreams. It weds black bodies in particular to physical torment, psychic violence, and emotional trauma, which black people in turn internalize and build identities from. In American culture, porn is a stimulus of a popular imagination stratified and, indeed, haunted, by race.[73] And race is itself defined by sexuality.[74] The racial drama that Desiree West and John Leslie so expertly perform is embedded in the idea that interracial erotic sociality invites conflict. This conflict pervades the scene and marks it with intensity, just as it shows that racialized sexuality can never be untangled from the haunting history of violence against and exploitation of racialized minorities.[75] Spinelli relies on this notion of interracial conflict to mirror the fantasy structure of pornographic film: a conflict exists between the characters, sex takes place, and the conflict between characters is resolved. Aimed at creating a fantasy text from the still illicit nature of cross-racial encounters in 1977, *Sex World* uses Desiree West's performance of the character Jill to articulate desire for interracial sex, though Jill's own desires remain invisible.

Central to the abuse Jill receives in her seduction of the character of the bigot, Roger, is his angry and fearful repulsion of her body. Roger calls Jill "fat lips" and says that, at Thanksgiving, he prefers white meat to dark meat. He continuously moves about the room to escape any kind of intimacy with her. The violence Roger projects onto Jill's body is a function of his sense of identity and control, which when confronted with the exposure of his concealed desires is thrown into question. Despite this violent context, Jill uses her body as the very mechanism to undo Roger's power. Not only does she force him to confront her body by moving close to him, using her body to intrude into his space and revealing ever more skin, Jill uses language to describe her body as a desirable landscape for Roger's exploration. Jill's words seduce Roger, force him to confess a desire kept silent, and expose the lie of his disgust. In the process, Jill recuperates her body from abjection. As the italicized words in the dialogue suggest, Jill uses some words with particular emphasis, and the cadence and rhyme of her speech is a key aspect of Jill's seductive labor in the scene. Utilizing sexual slang and black vernacular speech, Jill portrays a critical facet of the soul porn aesthetic: soul.

Jill's speech is key to the mechanism of this racial-sexual trespass discussed above. The employment of black vernacular speech for the scene's "dirty talk" necessarily references the concept of soul, as it deploys the spoken word. "Spoken soul," contends Claude Brown, is embedded in the "lyrical quality" of African American everyday life.[76] A source of inspiration of many black writers, the language or "lingua franca" of the black vernacular, Toni Morrison explains, "is the thing that black people love so much—the saying of words, holding them on the tongue, experimenting with them, playing with them. It's a love, a passion."[77] Desiree West's performance captures this play and passion for spoken soul, despite their likely origin in a white imitation of black speech. The words were scripted by the filmmaker, Spinelli, and they are so extremely rhymed it is likely that a white writer attempting to ape 1970s black vernacular speech conceived them. Nevertheless, Desiree's performance powerfully animates this appropriation of spoken soul and also deconstructs it. "Between my *thighs* is where my rhythm *lies*," she says, holding "thighs" and "lies" on the tongue. This seductive lyricism entices John Leslie's fearful Roger to "abandon" his racism—which actually be-*lies* his desire—and discover the "open secret" of black women's desirability hidden between Jill's thighs. We see in close-up Roger's face move from disgust to curiosity to unbarred lust thanks to Jill's lyrical and gestural provocations. Desiree West's exquisite performance of the black woman as sexual instigator employs speech and embodiment to show how stereotypes once used to police the racial border come to eroticize its transgression.[78] Desiree's animated and transgressive performance of her scripted lines shows how black female hypersexuality, too, is a confining script that might be used in dynamic ways. If *Sex World's* script painfully shows how white titillation relied upon often demeaning representations and treatment of black actresses like Desiree West, it also shows how black women find ways to work within and against these powerful and limiting roles.

The sexual aggressiveness projected onto black women in soul porn is not confined to the myth of prohibition or sexual stereotypes in popular culture. Instead these popular ideologies were reflected in policy discourses and state interventions concerning black women during this period. According to the Moynihan Report of 1965, black women's roles as heads of households— wrongly defined as a "black matriarchy"—were "at the heart of the deterioration of the fabric of the Negro society" and the "deterioration of the Negro family."[79] The Moynihan Report constructed poor, black, single mothers as the cornerstone of the black American family's instability and social displacement because they supposedly displaced and demoralized black men.[80] Moreover, black women were described as bad mothers who transmitted degenerate patterns of behavior to their children, raising them to become a class of fatherless criminals. Instead of exposing the structural impoverishment and isolation of the black family and community, or theorizing black women heads of households as assets to the black family structure, the Moynihan Report portrayed black women as the cause of their own victimization. In the minds of American liberals and conservatives alike, following the report, young black men were the victims not of institutional racism but of emasculating black women who had too many children and exploited taxpayers' money through their endless consumption of welfare.

Whereas during slavery black women's bodies were reproductive commodities manipulated for private and state interests, in the 1960s and '70s black women's fertility created a problematic surplus workforce for the capitalist economy.[81] Black women's sexuality was framed as a drain on social resources, an economic liability.[82] Black matriarchy discourse deflected attention from the state's role in sustaining black poverty just as black women workers began to fight for greater access to War on Poverty programs such as job training, and to demand more labor options in the postindustrial U.S. economy.[83] Employing sexual stereotypes of black women as aggressively matriarchal and irresponsibly hypersexual, black matriarchy discourses functioned to legitimate multiple forms of surveillance and social control over black life. Sexual scripts likening black female sexuality to social pathology facilitated the intervention of social workers, the police, and others into African American communities. The popularity of these discourses among liberals and conservatives made projecting the state's failure to stop widespread social unrest, massive inequality, and urban decay onto black women easy.[84]

Black women's sexuality was a useful target for whites' concerns about a black political insurgency. As African Americans pushed back against institutional racism, sexism, classism, and homophobia at home and against American imperialism abroad, they inspired a range of groups to launch powerful political movements to claim civil and human rights and demand a more just national politics. These new political alliances showed that cross-racial, black-white collaboration and intimacy were not only possible but desired. The collapse of de jure and de facto racial segregation across the states was a result of this new interracial sociality, which had important sexual implications. Racial segregation, the legal norm since *Plessy v. Ferguson* in 1896, had in fact "rested on the deep seated fear that social mixing would lead to sexual mixing."[85] While segregation did not prevent white men from gaining access, often violently, to black women's bodies, or black and white couples from risking arrest to be together, it did function to normalize fears of sexual mixing across the color line. Additionally, antimiscegenation laws criminalized marriage and sex between whites and people of color. Alongside the horrific practices of lynching, vigilantism, and intimidation, laws against interracial marriage and sex operated to minimize potential threats to white racial purity, property, and political power. In the 1967 case *Loving v. Virginia*, the U.S. Supreme Court found that these laws violated the equal protection and due process clauses of the Fourteenth Amendment. According to the court they were clearly "designed to maintain White Supremacy" and therefore were "unsupportable."[86]

However, though interracial sex and relationships became legal for black women and white men during the 1960s, cross-racial intimacy still registered as a forceful moral concern. Indeed, sexuality on the racial border was still coded in many representations as a perversion that needed to be avoided at all costs. Interracial eroticism was bound to an ineluctable fear linked to a long history of proscription and punishment. It also provoked a powerful disgust projected onto the racial Other, or for black people, onto the racial Oppressor. For black women, fear of racial betrayal also shaped the taboo of interracial eroticism. While black men like black power activist Eldridge Cleaver could claim sex with white women was an opportunity to display their superior virility to dominant white men—he even called rape of white women "an insurrectionary act"[87]—for black women, pursuing sexual relationships with white men was much more fraught. It meant betraying black men, their families, and the entire black struggle.

Unfortunately, Desiree West was not willing to discuss her career, which approximately spanned the years 1976–79, or her performance in *Sex World* for this book. Nor did I uncover interviews with her during or after her time as an actress and model in the adult industry. However, it is fascinating to note that rumors abound about her, one being that she was actually a member of the Black Panther Party. Fan blogs say that because the police were after her due to her illicit work with the Panthers, Desiree used various pseudonyms to protect her identity: Rayha Teresee, Dee Dee Willing, Patty Lester, Pat Lee, Patricia Lee, Pat Desado, and Susie Sung Lee, though it was common for actors to use multiple pseudonyms or for directors to make them up for specific films.[88] In the tell-all *Skinflicks*, then active director David Jennings recalls a story in which Desiree, whom he called "the Black Panther porn star," showed up to a shoot with her boyfriend Dashiel, a black man who performed in some loops during the 1970s, sometimes with Desiree. Desiree was in a rage because poor directions had caused the couple to get lost coming from Oakland to San Francisco.

Although it is unlikely that Desiree was actually a Panther, the Black Panther Party first emerged in Oakland in 1966 and had a very strong presence there through the 1970s. Deemed "the greatest threat to the internal security of the country" by J. Edgar Hoover, its national network was infiltrated and dismantled by the FBI's counterintelligence program (COINTELPRO) in a matter of years.[89] From 1974 to 1977, during the height of Desiree West's career in porn, Elaine Brown became chairwoman of the Black Panther Party. Having run for Oakland City Council in 1973 and 1975, Brown was widely known throughout the city. She was a powerful symbol of black women's leadership in the face of the institutionalized racism that depressed the Oakland ghetto.[90] Brown also symbolized black women's resistance against entrenched sexism in the black community, including in the Black Panther Party. She was part of a larger movement of black women who were standing up to the "militant 'brothers'" of the black liberation movement. According to Linda La Rue, many black men bought into the "myth of matriarchy" and enacted a form of "sexist colonialism" in the lives of black women.[91] An emergent black feminist consciousness proliferated among black women across the nation that was deeply critical of "white supremacist capitalist patriarchy" as well as black men's sexism.[92] Thus, while it is unlikely that rumors about Desiree West being a Black Panther are true, it is more accurate to say that she was located in a social context where radical antisexist, antiracist, and anticapitalist black nationalist and black feminist politics were very much in the air. For whites, particularly those that lived in San Francisco like Jennings, or who, like Jennings, seemed to lament interacting with blacks, the image of strong and self-defined black women like Desiree West was certainly perceived as a threat.

As Jennings's comments convey, Desiree must have experienced racism as part of her labor in the porn world. Given the known masculinist leanings of black power discourses at the time which were so prominent in black communities like Oakland, she may have experienced sexism and patriarchal attitudes from within her own community as well. These dual constraints of racism and intracommunity sexism, alongside the continued economic marginalization and exploitation of black women's labor during the period, most likely shaped the way in which Desiree West negotiated the porn industry as a black woman, even as one of the few black actors with notoriety during the era. Desiree might have known that for a black woman to use her sexuality for her own profit (and possibly pleasure) at that time, particularly in inter-racial sex scenes with white men, was a dangerous act. Performing, in addition to being a form of economic survival, could have been one way for Desiree to resist racial militancy, or to even express a critical perspective about how black women should be portrayed. Despite Desiree's likely experience, she comes off as an attitudinal black woman rather than a sexual rebel in Jennings's story. The director describes how he had to work around Desiree's demand that Dashiel not ejaculate on her face at the climax of the scene. This seems like a reasonable request from a woman who not only knows what she is comfortable with, but feels that she can speak up to control, to an extent, her performance and her labor. Viewing her as a complainer, however, Jennings employs a lens that many whites used to interpret black people—outspoken women in particular—who embraced radical politics.

Some years ago, I had the chance to chat with John Leslie during the annual Adult Video News Convention in Las Vegas. Leslie, who remained active in the adult industry as an actor, director, and producer from 1975 until his passing in 2010, is widely respected as one of the most significant players in adult film over the past forty years. I asked Leslie, not on tape, about what it was like to perform in that famous, and to my mind highly racist, scene in *Sex World* with Desiree West in 1977. He laughed, saying that it was all in fun. The scene, to him, was a playful parody of sorts, and Desiree was down with the joke. For Leslie the scene was part of an exciting time in adult film, and Desiree was a consummate performer. If she was uncomfortable with the script, he was not aware of it. Yet, we could ask, would Leslie have been aware of Desiree's feelings, or even sensitive to them? The film required a black actress to be the object of his joke, to turn the bigot into a lover of blacks and thus underscore a supposed lack of white culpability in racism, because after all they really do like "you people." Without Desiree's voice it is impossible to know just how she did feel on set and about Leslie. She could have been wary about his intentions and his politics, suspicious about the nature of his and Spinelli's joke, indifferent, or altogether enchanted with her character's meaty role as the savvy challenger to Leslie's arrogant and abusive Roger. Nevertheless, Desiree's fluent performance of soul-porn aesthetics is remarkable given the racist industrial context of 1970s porno, and the extreme racist dynamics of the scene.

Because Desiree West performed extensively and worked with many well-known white actors like John Leslie, John Holmes, and Paul Thomas, producers must have seen her as bankable and her costars may have viewed her as easy to work with. It is possible to imagine that Desiree might have tried to explore her sexuality through her work as an actress in porno. She appeared in girl-on-girl sex scenes with several popular white actresses such as Annette Haven and Sharon Thorpe. In *The Egyptian Princess* (a 16 mm reel), Desiree plays a slave to Annette Haven's princess, but the sex between them is recipro-cal. The idea of playing the slave to a white actress portraying African royalty might have been a bit hard to swallow, but Desiree brings a sensuality of the exchange that shows that adhering to a black cultural politics of representa-tion was perhaps not always her core political issue. Always forcefully erotic in her performances, Desiree used pornographic performance to portray herself as comfortable circulating in both black and white sexual worlds despite their real-world entrapments. Even if she might have worked in the adult industry solely for the money, as many performers did and, according to my interviews with women performing since the 1980s, continue to do, this does not exclude Desiree from mobilizing her own desire for mobility and transgression in her work. Desiree's desires on set may have also included minimizing abuse, pushing back against offensive roles, and finding a way to avoid criminaliza-tion at a time when it was legal to watch but not to film pornography. Whether it was to pursue the pleasures of sex, of performance, of mobility, or of earning an income and protecting herself from other far-worse forms of exploitation, Desiree West's role in both black-cast and interracial porno was to portray the aggressively sexual black woman, a role that she clearly understood how to execute. Her performances of this role communicated undeniable agency, complexity, and subjective intensity—even if her personal narrative of these experiences remains less attainable than fan narratives circulating around her.

With the emergence of soul porn, black audiences had unprecedented ac-cess to black erotic images. These images reflected the desires of black people to see themselves as self-determined and sovereign erotic subjects, rather than servants for white fantasies. Nevertheless, soul porn, especially when created by white directors, did precisely that—it showed the newly asser-tive and politically situated black sexuality through a white male gaze of fear, anxiety, pleasure, and titillation. In this way soul porn shows the continuity of racial fetishism in pornographic production, from its emergence to the present period. Yet the new social and political contexts of civil rights and black power necessarily fostered an altered image of black sexual difference, one that reflected black people's own dynamic performances of eroticism and desire for a black gaze. As the period of social and political eruption and in-vention began to shift and give way to a backlash of sexual and moral conservatism in the 1980s, VHS emerged as a new force in the adult film industry. The rise of this technology, in the midst of accelerated state and social reactions against pornography, fostered a new interest in black sexuality evacuated of the agency expressed by black performers in the 1970s. Unlike soul porn, black porn of the 1980s was a creation of pure market interest.

# 3

## Black Chicks
### *Marketing Black Women in the Video Era*

In January 2007 Angel Kelly and I traveled to Las Vegas together for the Adult Video News (AVN) Adult Entertainment Expo. When we met in 2003 in Memphis, Tennessee, Angel, the first black "contract girl" during the 1980s, was surprised that anyone remembered her so many years later, let alone would be interested in interviewing her for a book about black women in the adult film industry. Following that interview, Angel experienced something of a personal renaissance. Since retiring from the business in 1990, she had, for the most part, been working to support her family and live a "normal" life outside of the public eye. Suddenly inspired by my visit, she started her own music, talent, and event promotion business and began looking for ways to capitalize on her former fame. Angel's teenage daughter started a MySpace page for Angel Kelly Productions and helped Angel learn to use the Internet for social networking and shop for the latest stylish clothes. Angel started to put on rap music events and garnered thousands of contacts on MySpace and Facebook. Laughing with excitement, she talked about writing a memoir: the story of the first black contract girl and her exciting adventures and mysterious affairs with celebrities. It could even be a TV movie. Angel Kelly was reborn.

This new Angel was thrilled to attend AVN, to see how the industry she had helped to grow had changed, as much as to let the industry see the new her. Soon after we arrived, however, increasing frustration met by an acute attack of laryngitis created a sense of dislocation that she could not articulate. Walking the floor of the convention, an event many times larger than it had been in the 1980s, I could see Angel quietly turning inward. Not only was the industry so much larger, sleeker, and more corporate and impersonal, but it was dominated by multitudes of young women in platform heels and schoolgirl miniskirts, followed by even greater numbers of almost-fanatical fans. The new business model for porn and the template for porn stars were so different than they had been in the 1980s.

We sought out the veteran actors, saying hello to Jeannie Pepper, Nina Hartley, Porsche Lynn, John Leslie, Randy West, and Bill Margold. Angel felt happy for a while to connect with those former colleagues and those memories of a time when the industry was, as Angel said, "like a family." But the combination of feeling mostly ignored, insignificant, and unremembered, along with being groped by random men and propositioned by a couple of sleazy producers to make a low-rent "comeback video," wore her down. When we went to the AVN Awards Show, the capstone event of the annual gathering, Angel seemed even more uncomfortable. Given tickets in the nosebleed seats by the publisher of AVN magazine—who hours earlier did not take the time to greet Angel on the convention floor—Angel sat looking down at the show in silence. Staring at the decorated round tables on the floor of the massive theater with the porn industry decked out in its glittering finest, she remembered how she had once been in the spotlight. What had happened to the industry she knew? What new world was this that had forgotten one of its biggest black stars?

To understand Angel Kelly's story it is essential to look at the context in which she became a star. Angel became the first black actress to gain an exclusive contract from a production company during the video era of the 1980s, a formative period for the U.S. pornography industry. If the Golden Age of the 1970s presented an increasingly popular pornographic film industry, the Silver Age of the 1980s moved porn into the mainstream, making it more accessible to consumers, would-be porn stars, and even critics. Home video produced black sexuality as a specialized market for private consumption. It transformed Golden Age porn with black casts into a recognizable subgenre focused on racial difference. With this manufacture of adult video for specified markets based on racial preference, black actors gained access to an industry that was growing exponentially. Unlike soul porn of the 1970s, which ultimately focused on black male sexuality, the porn of the 1980s turned to black women as potential, if somewhat second-class, porn stars. Although marginalized in many ways, black porn actresses were critical to the awesome growth of the adult entertainment industry in the 1980s. Their work in creating and selling X-rated videos helped to make the industry a financial success story that continues to this day.

The "video revolution" of the early 1980s to the mid-1990s prompted vast changes in the production and distribution of pornographic films, transforming the consumption of racialized sexuality in America. These technological developments changed the adult industry's engagement with black women as sex objects and sex workers. As highly charged racial fantasies became newly accessible to a growing consumer audience, previously illicit desires were brought to light. The explosion of a specialized market for black-cast and interracial (usually black/white) cast videos was due to white men consumers, and the media was designed around their purchasing preferences and sexual fantasies. Video technology offered new ways to circulate black pornography to viewers and new opportunities for black women as actresses.

On the surface, black women's participation in video pornography of the 1980s was not socially transgressive. They were represented in problematic and stereotypical roles including possessed "voodoo queens," lazy maids, and urban hookers, while black men often portrayed hustlers and pimps. Porno-graphic video mobilized these tropes of black women as hypersexual and hyper-available, reflecting a legacy of visual figurations of black womanhood in pornography and other media. Yet black women were also performers with their own ideas about their roles and how they would participate in adult entertainment. Sometimes performers took on problematic roles as a neces-sary part of their erotic labor in the sex industry. At other times they attempted to fashion performances that embodied their personal desires and fantasies. Black women's representations both maintained and transgressed dominant views about black female sexuality in the 1980s. Actresses of the video-porn era told me how they perceived their roles and sought to intervene in them. Although most of the roles on offer were problematic, performers like Angel Kelly and Jeannie Pepper created self-fashioned performances that attempted to work within and against stereotypes. This chapter untangles the threads of representation, performance, and labor of black adult video actresses in a time when the adult entertainment industry was expanding, evolving, and changing itself as well as the sexual politics of America.


## The Video Revolution

Even before mainstream Hollywood caught on to video as a distribution technology, the porn business recognized the cost-cutting potential of VHS by transferring its popular film productions to videocassette. Pornography, Laurence O'Toole argues, "was performing its regular duty as a key driver for the economic emergence of a new technology."[1] Just as pornographers had exploited early technologies of photography and 8, 16, and 35 mm film as lucrative and interactive media technologies, they were visionaries of video's potential for expanding the porn market. In 1979 videocassette recorders (VCRs), a specialty item for the tech savvy professional class, were found in less than 1 percent of American homes. Ten years later, more than half of American homes had VCRs. Because the "majority of early [video] cassettes were pornographic," the adult video business had played a primary role in the success of this new technology in the United States.[2] "The thing that changed everything was the development of the home video industry," says late adult industry historian and critic Jim Holliday. "A whole new market was open to sexploitation films."[3]

At the forefront of the video revolution, pornographers saw the vast possibilities for distribution inherent to the medium. Video transformed the viewer's relationship with pornography, allowing it to become more accessible to a broader audience. Rather than join the "raincoaters" in the XXX cinema and peep shows of the nation's red-light districts, Americans could watch hardcore movies in the private spaces of their own homes. The gendered impact of this technological transformation was profound, as women became an important, growing sector of the hardcore-video consumer audience. Whether alone, with friends, or with their male or female sexual partners, female pornography consumers enjoyed unprecedented access to material that had previously been available only within the men's-only spaces of fraternal clubs and uninviting adult showplaces. Women, who might have had limited access to hardcore cinemas and peep shows, could now rent or purchase videos from local retailers or from mail-order catalogues. According to industry estimates, by the end of the 1980s women made up nearly half of all adult video renters.[4]

Some adult filmmakers bucked the transition from film to video; they saw the new technology as a threat to the craft of filmmaking, and its cheapness and lower quality of image production as a sell out. "We didn't want to recognize video," recalls director Ron Sullivan (also known as Henri Pachard), "We didn't want to lose our work."[5] The director and founder of Catalina Home Video, Bill Higgins, echoed Sullivan's ambivalence toward video as the new visual medium for porn: "I don't think anyone wanted to shoot on video. We all resisted." According to Higgins, video not only cheapened the profession of filmmaking, it also made recording moving flesh difficult because the quality of video's image was clearly inferior to film. The gritty and stark aesthetic of video revealed blemishes on the actors' skin. "It changed everything for the worse once we got into video," Higgins added.[6] Even so, the development of the handheld video camcorder by RCA in 1985 meant that beyond transferring classic films to video for increased distribution for home viewers, producers could shoot movies directly on video. Ultimately, video was faster and cheaper to produce because video production crews could be smaller. Jim Holliday asserted, "The decision to shoot on tape [was] one of economics. In a shrinking theatrical market, a producer could shoot five $20,000 videos and turn his money faster than he could with one $100,000 feature film."[7] Virtually anyone who could operate a camcorder could potentially become a porn director. In this way, video thoroughly transformed pornography's economy.

By the late 1980s, porn filmmakers' initial reluctance to embrace video technology had dissolved into an all-out video-making frenzy. In 1983, only four hundred X-rated videos were produced, with 92 percent of these videos being transfers from film. Five years later, nearly fourteen hundred tapes were released, and 96 percent were shot on video.[8] "The truth is that video is better for pornography than film ever was," Bill Higgins conceded. "None of us ever wanted to admit that because we would think we were giving up too much of our craft."[9] So much "product" was manufactured that a significant crisis developed within the adult industry: "market competition for that desired 'piece of the pie' [became] more and more intense."[10] Dozens of small manufacturers and distributors emerged on the scene and began flooding the market with scores of cheaply made videos each month. These new manufacturers were accused by more established companies of "price whoring"—lowering their wholesale prices so as to win a share of distribution and retail sales—and as a result, the "video glut" became a major focus of the adult industry trade journal *Adult Video News*, which warned: "The glut is here. The glut is real."[11] As more manufacturers became "hooked by the bait of inexpensive shot-on-video production and the lure of big profits," industry journalist John Paone argued, manufacturers, distributors, and retailers would now be forced to "fight hard against the current to weather the storm and keep their businesses afloat."[12]

Poor-quality productions in expensive packaging became the norm as companies churned out dozens of videos every year. Consumers complained of "poorly produced," "unprofessional" tapes with "little or no story-line," "shaky camerawork," "poor lighting," "wasted footage," "bad acting," and "boring" settings.[13] Industry experts bemoaned the rise of quantity over quality in productions, which undercut the wholesale prices for all tapes—including well-made features—and they warned manufacturers to rethink their approach to supply-and-demand economics in the new "sexvid wasteland."[14] Even though women were involved in nearly a half to two-thirds of adult rental decisions, too few videos addressed the "women's market," let alone, as one writer put it, "romance, passion, realism, build-up, foreplay, intelligence . . . all part of real life eroticism."[15] Instead, production focused on the same facile formula: "the same old five-sex-scene-75-minute-bare-plot-cheap-set-one-day-wonder."[16]

The simultaneous cheapening of and investment in video pornography affected participants in every sector of the business. Marketing became one of the most significant issues during the decade as industry experts emphasized the importance of generating moneymaking strategies and ways to professionalize within pornography's new industrial framework. One strategy was to target audiences with niche materials, as adult bookstores had done for years. The subsequent creation of subgenres included the manufacturing and marketing of "all-black and interracial tapes" during the mid-1980s and illustrates how racial difference was commodified in the business of sexual commerce. A second strategy was to foster a star system, through which companies would market materials based on one porn actress's notoriety rather than the director's filmic concept. These two innovations produced a unique set of circumstances for black porn stars like Angel Kelly during the Silver Age's video revolution.

## Marketing Black Porn

Because of video, the pornography market expanded, bringing in millions of consumers, but it also developed specializations, or niches, catering to every conceivable desire, fantasy, and sexual taste. The industrialization of racial types as consumer sexual preferences became one set of niches. Video pornography made images of black sexuality more accessible than they had been during the stag era or the Golden Age of adult film in theaters or peep shows. Seeing how consumers enjoyed black-cast and interracial video, manufacturers, distributors, retailers, and industry experts became captivated with the development of black pornography as a lucrative arm of the porn marketplace. According to one AVN survey of one hundred video stores that carried adult video in 1985–1986, ninety-three carried "all black and interracial tapes," the largest subgenre reported, compared to sixty-nine carrying "gay tapes and/or bisexual tapes" and "lesbian tapes," fifty-nine with "old loop tapes (pre-1970s)," forty-eight with "bondage tapes," twenty-nine with "fat people tapes," and eleven with "old people tapes."[17] In a survey of fifteen hundred consumers and readers of AVN, "all-black and interracial tapes" came in as the second favorite subgenre at 16 percent, just behind "lesbian tapes" at 21 percent.[18] Despite the demand for black and interracial porn from consumers, and the subgenre's presence in a major proportion of adult video retail outlets, black and interracial porn of the 1980s was shaped by the powerful forces of the adult video industry glut's trend toward poor quality and cheap production standards. In fact, black and interracial video, though acknowledged as strategically lucrative, was seen by many experts to be treated with even less care than the already problematic videos that manufacturers rushed to produce in the hundreds each year.[19]

Beginning in 1984, adult companies began to produce black and interracial pornography as a niche market in earnest. Perhaps not coincidentally, during the same year, Vanessa Williams, the first black Miss America pageant winner, made headlines when she was forced to abdicate her title. In July 1984 *Penthouse Magazine* publisher Bob Guccione announced to the major television news networks that in the September issue, he would print sexually explicit pictures of Williams in simulated lesbian sex poses with a white woman. Williams had done the photo shoot a couple of years prior to the pageant, when she worked as a studio assistant for fashion photographer Tom Chiapel. For Guccione, the projected sales of $5 million for the scandalous issue made it "a simple business choice; whether I get Vanessa into a rift with the pageant people versus the desirability of these photographs in the eyes of my readers. Of course I went with my readers."[20] Beyond the obviously self-serving business interests of this pornographer, and the hypocritical conservatism of the similarly sexually exploiting Miss America pageant, the media event had profound resonance. As Jackie Goldsby writes, "Williams was in no position to overturn the forces of consumerism that had been stimulated by Guccione's appropriation of the pictures. Nor could she revise the racial symbolism of film and the acts depicted in the images, precisely because the historical construction of black sexuality is always already pornographic."[21] The Vanessa Williams incident proved that the far-reaching fascination in, and mass marketability of, black female sexuality was ripe for pornographers to fashion for profit.

Just as *Penthouse Magazine* appropriated Vanessa Williams's erotic pictures, white-male-owned companies manufactured, distributed, and sold black pornography for a mainly white male consumer base. White director, actor, screenwriter, and adult industry historian Bill Margold, in speaking about this subgenre, admitted: "When I make a movie about black people, I project my fantasies, not theirs."[22] Both black-cast and black-white interracial heterosexual productions presented fantasies manufactured by and designed to appeal to white men.[23] The videos represent an erotic economy that expanded beyond the formations of pornography to the wider sexual culture's investment in black bodies and racialized sexualities. The subgenre eroticized the racial border, but usually in ways that upheld established sociocultural boundaries rather than transgressing them.

Black pornography in the video era reflected anxieties about the perceived threat of black-white sexuality to the dominant social order at a time when interracial sex was still taboo, but also as African Americans occupied a new polarized visibility. In popular culture and political discourse black Americans were portrayed as highly successful—as if they had finally reaped the benefits of the civil rights movement—such as in the image of the affluent Cosbys on the highly rated sitcom or the unparalleled celebrity of Michael Jackson. Simultaneously, African Americans, especially black women, were presented as social failures, an urban underclass pathologically dependent on welfare and drugs. Unlike previous eras, and the production of race porn and soul porn, black video porn presented this dual perception of African American exceptionalism and conformity to the basest stereotypes of racial deficit.

Eroticizing black bodies and cultural practices often included the desire to ridicule those bodies and practices. This "love and theft" of black culture in black pornography in some ways resembled the racial performances of nineteenth-century minstrel shows.[24] For example, historian Eric Lott writes about minstrel performance as a "mixed erotic economy of celebration and exploitation"; for whites, minstrel performance served "less as a sign of absolute power and control than panic, anxiety, terror, and pleasure."[25] Black video pornography exposed an ambivalent attraction to black sexuality, one of terror and pleasure combined. Like minstrel performances, in which blackface was a prominent feature (for white performers and later, also for blacks), black video pornography was "less a repetition of power relations than a signifier for them."[26] In other words, while black pornography was in many instances a racist form, it was, perhaps more importantly, a racial creation. Racialism is not the same as racism, according to Michael Omi and Howard Winant, but racialism creates the opportunity for, and enables, racism.[27]

Black-oriented pornography reflected power relations between races, but it mostly explored the erotic celebration and exploitation of racial relations across historical fantasies, taboos, anxieties, and desires. Sometimes black pornography veered into the clearly racist, but to simply call all pornography that commodified images of black and interracial sexual relations "racist" would be to miss the complexities of desire within these forms, to reduce racial fantasy to mere racist domination, and to ignore how performers also intervened in their own sexualities for their own purposes of desire and fantasy. In racialized pornography, race serves to expose and amplify how black sexuality invokes both desire and disgust on the part of the producers and consumers. Racial fetishism, along with the production of black female and male bodies as illicit erotic objects of desire, is the key framework for understanding the simultaneous celebration and exploitation of black sexuality in the emergent subgenre of black adult video. Black women and men were also participants in both racist and racialist fantasies of pornography. They often saw themselves not just as objects, but as subjects who contributed to, undermined, or otherwise reworked the meanings of the images in their performances and labor.[28]

The manufacture and strategic marketing of black pornography exposes the coinciding forces of desire for and shame about sex and sexual fantasy across racial borders. It exposes the prominence of racialized sexuality in the U.S. national obsession with these forbidden, outlaw, and obscene aspects of sex. Despite or perhaps because of these anxieties along racial borders, industry experts saw black pornography as easily exploitable. These experts understood that the new visibility of black sexuality would attract white audiences and, although potentially profitable, it would also pose a threat to consumers invested in keeping this taboo desire a secret fetish. After only one year on the market, the subgenre of black-cast and interracial video garnered substantial attention. In a review of *Black Bun Busters*, the first commercial black-cast anal sex videotape, AVN declared, "The genre of all-black tapes is extremely popular."[29] One month later, Paul Fishbein, then editor at AVN, was so impressed with the trend that he formulated an action plan for manufacturers, distributors, and retailers, presenting it in an article titled "How to Sell Adult Tapes: Marketing All-Black or Interracial Cassettes":

> Let's start by saying that the all-black and interracial adult videotapes that are currently on the market are among the easiest sell-through items. Because they are considered a specialty item, they are very saleable. Adult is not unlike the regular movie market: a surprisingly small number of cassettes starring black actresses and actors is available. However, what has flooded the market are average-quality tapes, produced solely to exploit a new genre. Very few of these tapes have received high ratings in *Adult Video News*. However, that hasn't prevented the manufacturers from selling big numbers. The market is definitely there and exploitable. The very nature that the tapes feature black performers opens up that market.[30]

This adult trade article from 1985 lays out the key concerns for black-cast and interracial video marketing at a time when the genre was emergent. First, black pornography is popular, but because it is a specialty, consumers will spend money to buy the videos ("sell-throughs"), rather than just rent them, which makes fast and easy money for manufacturers. Next, while in demand, black sexuality remains taboo. As in Hollywood, films starring African Americans are marginalized rather than mainstream, but in pornography the limited or specialty nature of black video also adds to its profitability. Moreover, the market is overrun by low-value productions, which mainly function to exploit black sexuality to consumers hungry for black performers.

Paul Fishbein goes on to assert that urban black male consumers were seen as a promising market to exploit with the marketing of black sexuality in addition to the usual white male clientele. During the 1980s, the adult industry, like other consumer industries such as apparel and fast food, recognized the highly profitable nature of urban black and Latino communities as consumer markets, despite their relative economic disenfranchisement. Blacks constituted 25 percent of mainstream cinema audiences, and as video became more accessible to middle- and working-class buyers of all stripes, pornographers assumed the black and Latino adult video shares would rise.[31] The majority of profit gained by producers of black pornography would not come from urban minority communities, however. White consumers drove the rising demand for interracial sex, primarily featuring black men and white women, while urban black men were imagined as the likely consumers for black-cast video. Fishbein, addressing retailers, wrote:

> Fortunately, white audiences also find black actresses and actors appealing, so you can make money selling these tapes in areas where you have no black clientele. However, in urban areas or neighborhoods with a dense black population these tapes will be sure winners. In addition, when dealing in areas with a predominantly white clientele, you might want to emphasize interracial tapes, rather than all black tapes. . . . Keep all these tapes in one section and if possible, at one sale price. . . . Remember that with any specialty adult item, a customer may be hesitant to ask for tapes with black performers. However, if they are all together, he can pick and choose discreetly. . . . These titles will sell themselves. . . . There is such a *need* for this type of material that just by stocking up on these tapes, you're creating a new market for yourself. . . . You'll be surprised and pleased with the results.[32]

Fishbein advises retailers to set one sale price for black and interracial videos, and to segregate the subgenre within one section of retail stores. This marketing strategy sought to facilitate discretion for timid shoppers, presumably white consumers who found this product so "appealing." Yet it also ensured that all black pornography products, despite differences in quality, were treated the same in order to promote sales. The notion that racial fetish products were all the same may have encouraged a speedy, smooth sale to embarrassed white customers, and hence easy profits for manufacturers, distributors, and retailers. However, it also allowed pornographers to avoid caring about the quality of the movies they produced and sold because products, regardless of production value, would have the same market value. Writing four years later about the black pornography market, Fishbein noted that this tendency contributed to the utter "disregard for minorities," and the cheapening of the pornography business as a whole. He seemed to regret his previous advice; instead, Fishbein complained that manufacturers and retailers shared the blame for their failure to market films to a "real-live minority audience," including the "huge black audience who rents adult videos on a regular basis and who does not share the same fantasies as the white audience."[33]

The production of the specialty black pornography market was motivated by the display of white fantasies about black sexuality and the empowerment of an invisible white male consumer. An article titled "Displaying Adult Tapes" in 1986 recommended that retailers group "tapes with black stars" together because "many would be afraid to ask for recommendations" for "interracial films" even though "we all know these specialties are very popular." "This way," the article advised, "the consumer can browse and pick his rentals, without having to ask questions."[34] Gene Marino, spokesman for Essex Video, argued that the interracial videos were produced to appeal to a white male and increasingly black male market: "Black tapes aren't a fad. They've appealed to a white audience, and they've created a black market awareness where there wasn't one before. We can look at our sales in Detroit and the Southeast to see this."[35] Notwithstanding this trouble-free profitability, there was an element of shame surrounding black video in the porn business. Joe Arnone, president of Arrow Home Video, lamented that despite its growing significance to the market, black pornography consistently suffered from a lack of investment from the adult industry: "Everyone is afraid of [black videos]. For the few companies that have the guts to make them, black tapes have always done well. But no one will put any money into it."[36] Part of the underinvestment in black products went beyond a simple fear of bringing sexual taboos to market. It seems that the legal environment of the 1980s could have partially shaped manufacturers' overwhelming reluctance to take on interracial video as a major earning opportunity.

During Ronald Reagan's reelection campaign, Reagan, hoping to appease key supporters in the Christian Right, promised that he would fight three evils: abortion, homosexuality, and pornography. With the failure to outlaw the first two, Reagan was under pressure to assail the latter. In 1985 he appointed Attorney General Edwin Meese to organize an investigation into the operations of the national adult industry at all levels, with the mandate to "determine the nature, extent, and impact on society of pornography in the United States," and to propose "effective ways in which the spread of pornography could be contained, consistent with constitutional guarantees."[37] The yearlong public hearings by the Meese Commission on Obscenity and Pornography were thus part of Reagan's attack on the adult industry.[38] In this conservative legal environment, retailers across the country, particularly in the South, were arrested and their inventories confiscated by the FBI.[39]

As a result of this enhanced policing, a culture of self-policing arose, with industry professionals arguing that it was important for manufacturers to avoid "extreme" fetishes that might attract the attention of federal investigators. Interracial sex was not considered as extreme as porn featuring bondage, but it was close—especially for distributors concerned about its reception in the southern states. While many in the industry began to galvanize around the free speech issues, few saw interracial sexuality as a cause to fight for. Even though interracial videos were selling in the South, the idea that they might expose an already-embattled adult business to public ire and government harassment became accepted logic. The bottom line for the adult industry lay in trying to make money and survive government repression.[40] The interest in fostering niche markets, including black and interracial video, was defined by this focused concern on profitability and survival. The industry would choose from a trite menu of particularly exploitable stereotypes for black performers to enact, precisely because they were easy to produce and sell. The practice of repeating facile and tested tropes for an increasingly profitable market became the paradigm for how black performers in pornography would be incorporated and used for the next two decades.

## A Mockery

Many of the cheaply produced adult videos during this period lacked coherent plots, and had tawdrily designed sets with shabby couches and garish interior décor. Most videos depicted actors entering a scene, saying a few words of dialogue, and then initiating intercourse. This, cut together with four other similar scenes, was called a finished product. In this sense, videos featuring black actors were much like those that did not include them. However, many adult industry experts and commentators at the time noted a clear difference in both the quality of black-cast videos and in the kinds of roles black actors were called upon to perform. Feminist writer Susie Bright's exposé "The Image of the Black in Adult Video" (1987) criticized black pornography producers for their carelessness in wasting the valuable talent of black actors: "Obviously interracial tapes are not a labor of love, and it shows in the quality. Few have received critical acclaim, and the ability of some of the black performers often seems wasted in the typical script environment."[41] Bright chides adult producers for being trapped in an "X-rated time warp," deploying backward "Sambo and Delilah" tropes reminiscent of minstrelsy. Along with their anachronistic cultural ideologies of black sexuality, the cheapness of the productions showed a disregard for black audiences: "Black audiences will continue to have a special loyalty to black performers, and this mandate will allow producers to go on spending next to nothing, care even less and still make a bundle."[42]

Most black characters in these films were constructed as the racialized Other; they appeared speaking in "dialect," as maids, bartenders, prostitutes, pimps, sidekicks, and in other recognizable servile roles. With little care for the imagination of the black consumer, producers sought to ensure that white audiences would be contented that their fetishes of black sexuality remained familiar and accessible. "Confining people of color to stereotypical parts," argues Donald Suggs, "was the strategy for making white audiences comfortable with interracial lust."[43] Pornographers assumed that these representations were exactly what consumers wanted, since after all, they bought the tapes. In a typical review of an all-black video, writer Alvin Zbryski gave *Black Dynasty* (1985), a parody of the mainstream television hit *Dynasty*, a "Below Average" rating for story content and only a "Fair" rating for sexual content.

> I've seen all these all-black or nearly all-black video features and I've yet to be impressed. Obviously, there's a big audience for this material, as these tapes always seem to sell in decent numbers. But the producers and directors of these tapes seem to think that all you have to do is throw a bunch of black actors on the set, give them a few dumb lines and shoot a few sex scenes. If you want to have a huge hit, you have to do something with this talent. . . . *Black Dynasty* will definitely appeal to those looking for this kind of tape. However, that's a big audience, one that deserves something a little better.[44]

It is apparent from this review that several people within the adult industry were critical of how low production quality and stereotypical roles combined to make substandard productions. In a review of *More Chocolate Candy* and

*Chocolate Bon Bons* published in 1986, Paul Fishbein lamented, "The state of affairs for black actors and actresses in adult films borders on dreadful. If adult films can be accused of not representing reality or normal sexual values (a lot of them can), then the current rash of all-black and interracial video features should be brandished for their lack of intelligence in dealing with black life-styles." As for *More Chocolate Candy* and *Chocolate Bon Bons*: "Thankfully, the latest two examples of black exploitation videos cannot be called racist. They are just poorly made tapes. . . . Each production contains extremely straightforward and repetitive sex, bad scripts, stiff acting and sloppy editing. . . . Both tapes have echoing sound. . . . I wonder when producers and directors are going to give blacks the same opportunities in adult cinema that they're finally getting in mainstream cinema."[45]

Racial stereotyping along with poor production quality were the driving forces behind the growing black and interracial genres, and these forces pushed black adult actors into substandard conditions at a time when mainstream black actors were on the rise in Hollywood, including Whoopi Goldberg in *The Color Purple* and *Jumpin' Jack Flash* and Eddie Murphy in *Beverly Hills Cop*. In addition to the pitiable depiction of black actors as "little more than sexual slaves," Fishbein complains about the lousy filmmaking and post-production work of the manufacturers. Many black-cast videos were made by amateurs, including entrepreneurial distributors-turned-video-producers that lacked technical skill and experience.[46] Problematic scriptwriting and direction gave rise to the inordinate mediocrity of black-cast video, and this was emphasized by the fact that most videos centered on ill-conceived sexual and racial comedic scenarios. These comedies heightened black pornography's minstrel-like economy of pleasure and terror in interracial intimacies. Comedy became the forum for many of the auteurs of black pornography to display a fundamentally conflicted relationship with black people and their culture.

Bill Margold wrote the scripts and assisted in the production of some of the first black-cast hardcore videos of the period: *Hot Chocolate* (1984), *Black Taboo* (1984), and *Hotter Chocolate* (1986). Margold's libertarian irreverence for all forms of political correctness and censorship included racial mores. "We were all making a mockery of each other," he argued. "We always wanted to make a mockery of the business itself."[47] Despite growing up in a family with progressive views about racial politics, and enjoying his relationships with black actors in the adult business during his career performing and producing in the 1970s and '80s,[48] Margold, a white man, described his involvement in creating black pornography with a mixture of pride and dis-

dain. In discussing the impact of his films and his own contribution to innovating black pornography as a market in adult video of the 1980s, Margold
noted: "I'm very proud of *Hot Chocolate* and its tremendous success reaching a nationwide market. We came up with a real story, sports and sex in
the case of *Hot Chocolate*, and real characters. Everyone has copied us. . . . I
don't get turned on by it. Nobody wants to do these black tapes. They're hard
to light, they don't create enough heat. . . . But I think under the shoddiness
of tapes like *Hot* and *Hotter Chocolate* there's a little tiny soul."[49] If there is
a soul in these films it would be due to the remarkable work of the actors.
They infused Margold's caricatures with sensuality and fun, despite the films'
shoddy quality and offensive humor. *Hot Chocolate* centers on the exploits of

FIGURE 3.1. Bill Margold goes over the script for *Hot Chocolate* with actors Tina Davis, Jack Baker, Alexander James, and Silver Satine (Los Angeles, 1984). Courtesy of Bill Margold.

a black male basketball player and includes a bizarre scene in which the actors fight one another with barbecue spare ribs. In the sequel, *Hotter Chocolate*, watermelon and chicken are on the menu, a point that Angel Kelly, who performed in the film, later recalled as representative of the ways black actors face ridicule through disparaging portrayals. *Adult Video News* editor Paul Fishbein called out white screenwriters like Bill Margold for "making racist references to basketball or fried chicken, depicting blacks as little more than sexual slaves."[50] "But this is still a business," Fishbein lamented, "that caters to *white men* and that's a shame."[51] According to Margold, "Blacks can denigrate blacks and get away with it. It's entertainment."[52] For him this amounted to a double standard, which seemed unfair.

Margold's video *Black Taboo* (1984) plays up the idea of the dysfunctional black family and incest wrapped in racial comedy. Sonny Boy (Tony El-Ay) is finally about to return home from a POW camp in Vietnam years after the war. When he arrives, the family is so happy to see him—especially his mother (Tina Davis) and sisters (Sahara and Jeannie Pepper)—that they all fall into incestuous sexual play with him, until it is finally revealed in a climactic scene with his mother that he is not her son. "Well I guess we all look alike!" she says. Margold explained this comment as a sardonic device to communicate that the sexual escapades between mother and son, and sisters and brother, did not constitute incest after all.[53] Yet the joke establishes what is already understood: it functions as a prejudicial overstatement about black people as an interchangeable, homogeneous group, and repeats outdated, racist humor that is not really that funny.

However, the representation of African Americans in adult videos also included an even darker current than silly sex comedies like *Black Taboo*. The most racist and absurd portrayals of black people during the video era were produced by the white male production duo known as the Dark Brothers. Former New York University film student Gregory Hippolyte, also known as Greg Dark, directed, while Walter Gernert, who became Walter Dark, acted as executive producer. Greg Dark, whom one reviewer described as the "Salvador Dali of Porn," explained his interest in making black genre films from his unique perspective: "When I decided to make a black tape, I wanted to approach it as a street movie, black street culture."[54] While living in Oakland, California, Dark played tennis at the local courts, where he met black men from the predominantly working-class, black neighborhood who "had a lot of stories to tell."[55] Almost all of the black men in the Dark Brothers' films appear as pimps and hustlers.

According to Greg Dark, these brief encounters with black men in Oakland informed his perspective on how to represent them in hardcore video. "I put black people in my films as caricatures," Dark explained, "like street graffiti, almost." He continued, "I got into [the porn business] because I was interested in the elements of street life. . . . Middle America has a fantasy of seeing a freak show. What the Dark Brothers have done is make porno into bizarre stage plays with music and situations that become outrageous. . . . We try to push things as far as they can go in an outrageous fashion."[56] That Dark described his black characters as "caricatures" and as "street graffiti" is actually profoundly illuminating of the issues around spectatorship, appropriation, and consumption of black culture in hard core. The caricatures Dark produced of blacks attempted to imitate an imagined blackness in figurations that were true to the definition of "caricature": distorted, inferior, and ludicrous.

Laura Kipnis argues that all porn deals in caricature, the fantastical and allegorical that tickle the underbelly of our social mores, the "roots of our culture at the deepest corners of the self."[57] Indeed, the spectacle of black people as sexual freaks reaches into the deepest corners of the American self.[58] Blacks define the cultural boundaries of normality and deviance, pleasure and danger in U.S. society. The long history of exhibiting black people as abnormally sexualized objects for consumption informs pornography's racialized characterizations. Mobilizing shame and desire, the Dark Brothers' films delve into these mythical and hyperbolic representations of black sexuality and exploit anxious fantasies of racial domination and subordination in black-white sex acts.

Greg Dark fashioned himself a pioneer of black pornography: "I think many distributors are old fashioned. They didn't think they could sell to middle or lower class people or blacks. . . . I guess I was one of the first to use whites and blacks in the same film . . . that area was left alone for a long time."[59] While Greg Dark understood himself as a trailblazer in bringing blacks to pornographic film, the adult industry saw him, and the Dark Brothers team, as innovators in hardcore filmmaking. Compared to the vast crop of cheap, rote, and unimaginative videos produced during the period, the Dark Brothers' films stood out for their creative use of bizarre, over-the-top themes and slick production values. They were known for producing scenes of taboo, charged, strange, and extreme sexual scenarios, and doing it with joyful abandon. In an advertising blitz in adult magazines during the mid-1980s, the Dark Brothers presented themselves as bringing about the resurrection of a "stagnant porn industry" with the "most extreme porn epics known to man."[60] In one ad, Anthony Petkovich writes, they "portrayed themselves as garishly dressed white pimps sitting in extravagant wicker chairs, surrounded by stuffed iguanas and rubber snakes, while casually restraining sexy young black women by collar and chain."[61] The Dark Brothers fashioned themselves as white pimps on safari; they were reaping the bounty of a pornographic landscape based on taming, manipulating, and exploiting black women's bodies.

In 1985 the Dark Brothers produced their first foray into bizarre racial comedic porn with *Let Me Tell Ya 'Bout White Chicks*. Advertised as "The Original Interracial Classic," *White Chicks* mobilized stereotypes of black men's insatiable desires for white women. In the video, a group of black male urban hustlers, including a pimp (Jack Baker), sit around recounting their sexual exploits with white women. One man (Tony El-Ay) emphatically resists

FIGURE 3.2. A Dark Brothers advertisement, circa 1986.

the group's suggestions that sex with white women is better than with black women. The characters describe posing as service workers who use their black masculine charm to persuade white women to invite them into their homes, or acting as burglars and breaking in uninvited. They engage in sex with the all-too-willing white women left home alone, in domestic spaces such as the kitchen and the bedroom. In *White Chicks*, black men are like foxes in the henhouse, but the hens have invited them in. If black men are giddy about their seduction of white women, white women are shown to be equally enthusiastic about engaging in taboo sex. The one black man who resists the pressure to lionize white women is eventually convinced of his delusion when the canny pimp magically produces a white woman and sex ensues.

While the black characters in *White Chicks* are figured as good-for-nothing criminals who feloniously seduce white patriarchy's most prized possession—white womanhood—they actually do a great deal of labor for white manhood. Titillated by the illicit eroticism of black male sexuality and the sexual charge of proscribed, interracial sex, the white male gaze takes pleasure in the fetishistic construction of sexual danger in a fantasy world of transgressions without denial, shame, or consequence. Authored by and for a white male gaze, this fantasy of boundary crossing fetishizes the black penis, seeing it as a symbol of power, ecstasy, and threat. Again and again, this representational script is conjured in interracial pornography—a form that celebrates the "theatrical performance of sexual risk, ritually staging pleasure and danger under remote control."[62] This ritual staging ultimately empowers white men as arbiters of the gaze. While white men may be aroused by images of sexual threat, this performance is firmly in their control and catered to their imagination. These fantasies were also designed by a white male imaginary: the Dark Brothers fashioned themselves as the ultimate white pimps, after all.

Even in light of how *White Chicks* powerfully reiterates problematic stereotypes about black male lascivious behavior and exploits the cultural proscription against interracial sex for white men, however, the film makes two important interventions that clarify how we can understand the participation of black actors in black and interracial adult video during this period. First, the script for this film is actually believed to have been written by Jack Baker, the actor who played the pimp.[63] If so, a black man's authorship of this staged fantasy shows that black actors were actively involved in the production of pornography during this period. In ways large (writing scripts) and small (performing a character or scene in a particular way), black actors were associated with and preoccupied by the stories, characters, contexts, and conditions in which they performed and labored. Even by producing scenes that satisfy a white male gaze, or by enacting characters that stereotypically represented black gender and sexuality, black actors were participants in the construction of illicit eroticism and saw themselves as innovators in the incorporation of black people into pornography.

For example, Jack Baker's alleged script for *White Chicks* not only reveals a recognition that white spectators would find titillation in such sexually charged scenes between black men and white women, but that black actors had the chops to narrate and perform this fantasy in a major adult feature video production. Second, in *White Chicks* black male characters have more dialogue than in any black-cast or interracial video to date, especially for a scene in which black men are shown together, speaking to one another and performing in character, rather than being thrown into sex in films with little to no characterization or dialogue. In this way, though the videos of the 1980s featured problematic themes, this does not exclude an analysis of how black actors might have viewed their roles and participation in these videos, and taken opportunities to create more complex readings or better conditions. These tactics of self-representation and performance also define how black actresses of the 1980s, like Angel Kelly, Jeannie Pepper, and others, navigated the shifting terrain of hardcore media.

## A Bizarre Fantasy

The same dialectics between the pleasure and threat of white fantasy for black sexuality, and between the calculated maneuverings of racial fetishism and sexual performance, are illustrated in the Dark Brothers' next video *Let Me Tell Ya 'Bout Black Chicks* (1985), a sequel to *Let Me Tell Ya 'Bout White Chicks*. In the video, also rumored to have been scripted by Jack Baker, four black maids sit around a hotel room they are supposed to be cleaning, enjoying a colorful conversation about their taboo sexual encounters with white men. Unlike the format of *White Chicks*, which focuses on black men's passion for white women, *Black Chicks* is organized around black women's narratives of desire for white men. Each scene is composed around a flashback, as the black female characters reminisce about their lustful experiences with white men. In this film, it is black women who are the instigators of socially pro-scribed and illicit erotic encounters, and, as in the myth of prohibition, they are presented as the instigators of sex with white men. Black women in this video affirm white patriarchy because their sexuality remains at its service and beholden to its power. Underscoring this dynamic, the black women are depicted in service-worker roles as maids, nannies, and bathroom attendants.

The maids, played by Sahara, Lady Stephanie, Purple Passion, and Cherry Layme, each wear lingerie-like "French Maid" uniforms and feather-trimmed, high-heeled shoes. Although viewers do not learn all of their names, they each are marked by a different color: their feather dusters, hair clips, and ankle socks coordinate in hot pink (Lady Stephanie), aqua blue (Purple Passion), bright yellow (Sahara), or lime green (Cherry Layme). Each costume's vibrant accent colors are complemented by the neon colors of the set décor, including the graffiti-strewn walls of a men's public bathroom, and by the outrageous props, such as an oversize rocking chair in a child's playroom. Like other Dark Brothers' films, *Black Chicks* celebrates the extreme, bizarre, and carnivalesque.

The maids' conversation begins with one commenting on the mess left in the room by a presumably white guest. Another maid, conveniently named Sapphire (Lady Stephanie) for her aggressive demeanor, says she thinks the slovenly guest must have been a black man. A conversation about the merits of black men versus white men ensues, with the other three maids teasing Sapphire about her disgust-filled reluctance to have sex with white men. One maid suggests that sex with white men even offers an employment option: "You know you don't have to be no maid cause you can *always* be a ho' because whitey *loves* us for that dick food." Sapphire scoffs, "I'd rather be collecting whitey's welfare!" "What's wrong with you, Sapphire?" her colleague rejoins. "Don't you know the good Lord gave us the ability to be maids *or* whores? It's a sin for you to be sitting on your ass all day collecting welfare." As Sapphire questions the size of white men's penises in comparison to "our fine black brotherhood," another maid asserts that she would "rather be sitting on a white boy's dick all day long." The first maid continues to goad Sapphire: "Hush up, Negro! What *you* know about white boys? Have you ever let one eat your cunt or stick his alabaster pole in your hole?"

The maids sit around, talking about sex instead of working. Unlike the black male pimps and hustlers who must break into white homes in *White Chicks*, here the black maids exist as workers already present in white intimate spaces. Because the black female body is always already a laboring body, we do not need to see her work to understand labor as her fundamental role. Yet in *Black Chicks*, the maids' conversation about work prompts questions about the kinds of labor black women prefer. Do they prefer working-class jobs, welfare, or sex work? It seems that the filmmaker believed black women are only fit to be servants or whores for white men. In both capacities they are service workers fulfilling menial labor normalized as "women's work" and represented historically as "black women's work." Their roles as maids or potential whores symbolize their established sexual availability.

Not only are these black women portrayed as apt service workers for the needs and desires of white men, but they *want* to be so because of their insatiable desire for white men's bodies. Sapphire is the one exception who attempts to remain loyal to black men. What is most striking about this opening scene in *Black Chicks* is the reference to "whitey's welfare," a discourse that certainly seems out of place in a porn video. This is most likely due to the 1980s conservative political backlash against entitlement programs, which circulated the image of black women as "welfare queens" in the public imagination.[64] When Cherry Layme's[65] maid tells Lady Stephanie's Sapphire that "it's a sin" for her to sit on her ass and collect welfare, the video implies that it was black women's laziness and greed that has propelled their condition of poverty and need. "Whitey's welfare" is depicted as something belonging to white people that these black women, as welfare queens, constantly threaten to exploit.

Sahara's maid character insists that she prefers hustling sex from white men over collecting welfare or working her menial job as a maid.[66] In Greg Dark's warped imagination, black women have few options outside of being maids or whores for white men, and the two roles are in fact intertwined; in the video the maids make themselves sexually available to white men, just as they were believed to do in real life in a discourse that masked the sexual harassment endemic to black women's domestic labor. True to the Dark Brothers style, these women are bizarre caricatures, but they reflect a powerful ambivalence, pulling between fascination for and fear of interracial sex. The discourse on black women's labor shown in the film underscores the formidable force of racial, gender, and sexual anxiety in defining the kinds of fantasies Americans generate. Why use such reductive stereotypes of black women to capture a convincing narrative for interracial desire? "When systems of representation are used to structure the projections of our anxiety," Sander Gilman explains, "they are necessarily reductive."[67] The Dark Brothers' stereotypical images reflect the ways in which many white male producers remained obsessed with exploiting powerful anxieties about taboo interracial intimacies to heighten the contrast between the actors and to make the sex seem more erotically charged. In the search for compelling scenarios, they reproduced reductive racist fantasies as well as oppressive discourses about black women.

But the most arresting part of *Black Chicks* is the scene in which one black

FIGURE 3.3. Scenes from *Let Me Tell Ya 'Bout Black Chicks*, directed by the Dark Brothers (1985).

maid (played by Sahara) recalls willingly having sex with two men dressed as Ku Klux Klan members, who even wear their frightening hoods during the scene. Introducing the sequence, she says to the other maids, "Listen, I gotta tell ya 'bout the time I let these two whiteys do me at the same time. Mmm hmmm! It was too good!" The sex scene opens with Sahara masturbating on a bed in what appears to be a young woman's bedroom. She wears an aqua top and shorts pulled to the side to reveal her genitals. Large earrings and aqua eye shadow adorn her face. The sound of a black woman's voice singing a gospel-inflected song plays in the background: "I feel good! It's all right. Wooo hoooo, yeah." Suddenly, two Klansmen appear from behind the wall where the headboard is located. Simultaneously, an ominous red light shines from behind the wall. They wear characteristic white hoods, but their white robes are more like makeshift capes that open in the front to reveal their naked bodies. Sahara looks disturbed for a moment when she looks up at their hooded faces, but then looks down at their penises and smiles. She touches herself as the men address one another. In a deep, raspy, southern-accented voice, the first Klansman, named Lester, says, "Well, looky here Grand Dragon, a hot, dark kitty cat, just waiting for us to give it some milk." In an even thicker southern accent, but a higher-pitched voice, the Grand Dragon responds, "Well shit, Lester, let's fuck the shit out of this darky.

You know my great, great, grand pappy used to say that in the old days, this shit was *fine*!" "I don't believe that!" Sahara retorts in taunting defiance. "You guys can go ahead and try if you want to, but I don't think you can do *anything* down there!" Put off by this obvious challenge to his masculinity, the Grand Dragon orders Lester, "Shut her fucking mouth with your dick!" Sahara continues to challenge and provoke them: "You're going to have to prove it to me. I ain't afraid of no ghosts!"

In this scene of *Black Chicks*, which remarkably recalls the stag film KKK *Night Riders* (1939), the vulnerability of a black woman's body to the most extreme historical symbol of racial and sexual terror for black communities is directed toward a presumed white gaze. The undoing of the myth of prohibition of sex between white men and black women, the black woman's supposed lack of power in relation to the white vigilantes, and the heavy threat of coercion and resistance saturates this fantasy scenario. Calling Sahara's character "hot, dark kitty cat" frames her vulnerability; she is small, animal-like, and yearning. The fantasy relies upon a disavowed, but nonetheless collective, national memory of the long history of sexual violence against black women at the height of KKK vigilantism during the post-emancipation era. The presumed white male viewer is prompted to acknowledge and erotically invoke this denied memory, creating an obsessive, fetishistic replaying of racial trauma as sexual pleasure and shame.

Sahara's character attempts to subvert the Klansmen's sense of manhood and ability to control her sexuality by questioning their genital size and sexual prowess ("I don't think you can do *anything* down there!"). By attacking their sexual abilities in a mean, taunting manner, the black woman character threatens white men's understanding of power and causes potent feelings of anxiety and shame, which, set alongside titillation, erotically charge the scene. The men respond with the threat of violence: "Shut her fucking mouth with your dick!" Yet Sahara's maid continues to undermine and provoke the men by intentionally refusing to see them as dangerous. In confidently asserting that she "ain't afraid of no ghosts," Sapphire denies their power and points to the hollowness of their threat. Declaring them ghosts, she mocks the Klansmen's attempt to disguise themselves in their ridiculous white sheet costumes.[68] Through her performance of Sapphire, Sahara renders the men shadows at the service of her character's fantasy and undermines the official construction of the fantasy as one of coerced sex.

In the sex that ensues between the three performers, including double penetration, the black woman would seem to be doubly exploited by an ugly fantasy that recalls a history of black women's abuse at the hands of white men. This interracial sex fantasy appears to be authored (and directed by Greg Dark) so as to arouse feelings of nostalgia for the erotic force of white supremacy. Sahara's complicity does not condone white supremacy, and she does not take up a pure victim status either. Instead, in this scene—which is one of the most extreme scenes I have viewed in my research, and certainly the most explicitly racist I have observed from the 1980s—Sahara's performance goes beyond representing and submitting to black women's abuse. Her sex performance is full of vocalizations, expressions of pleasure, and gestures that affirm she is in control of the scene. This is not a filmed rape. Sahara's representational labor is more complex: she provides a potential disruption in the eroticism of white supremacy by articulating an agentive sexual performance that presents the possibility of black women's own fantasies of racial-sexual domination. This scene exposes the ways in which fantasies of interracial sex, by white men or black women, that are necessarily informed by our collective history of racial and sexualized violence, are potential fields for a dynamic economy of desire.

## Just a Movie

*Let Me Tell Ya 'Bout Black Chicks* posed challenges for the black actresses involved, perhaps more so than most of the other black-focused movies of the genre, because of its extremeness.[69] While it offered the actresses involved an opportunity to perform on a feature adult video set and engage in acting and improvisation from a much more extensive script than the generic light comedies and sex-based films they normally worked in, *Black Chicks* forced the actresses to negotiate a minefield of racial and gender stereotypes. In the process, the film compelled the actresses to make decisions about how they wanted to participate and perform. Rather than play a maid, adult actress Jeannie Pepper insisted on playing the "voodoo woman" in a scene that is presented as a story told by one of the maids about how a black woman enjoyed hot sex with white men. In the scene, donning a grass skirt, brightly colored makeup, jewelry, and headscarves, Jeannie moves around a hut-like room dancing and chanting as if she were possessed. Jeannie found the role to be a valuable opportunity to work and to feel glamorous and beautiful, and it was certainly preferable to performing the role of the maid. "I wanted the part," she explained to me:

> I was glad to have that [role]. You know two white guys [the Dark Brothers], they don't care. I loved the way they dressed me up, with the

costume. You know they made me look very exotic with all the makeup and feathers. . . . I didn't want to play [one of] the maids. Those other girls were playing the maids. And they had Sahara doing the scene with the KKK guys with hoods on. People had a fit when that came out, but it sold like hot cakes. I liked [the video]. I didn't know the KKK thing was going to be in the film. But then I just paid attention to my scene, and was like "Well, you all are doing *that*."[70]

When I asked her if she felt at all uncomfortable being associated with the *Black Chicks* because of its overt racist and sexist imagery Jeannie Pepper responded:

No. Because it was a *movie*. If [Sahara] chose to do [a scene with actors performing as members of the KKK], it was on her, but it wouldn't have been me. No way! I was like, "Are you out of your mind?" You know, my parents grew up in the South. In Georgia, and [racism] was all we talked about back in the day. And they are still around. Whoa! They were like, "Oh, it's just a film." But if I had done that scene I would have gotten all the flack. If someone else does it, it's okay. . . . I had a feeling that my career was going to go somewhere. I would have caught hell, and that would have just followed me through my career. . . . I didn't want it to come back to haunt me.[71]

It is unclear what Sahara's experience performing the scene in *Black Chicks* may have been, but it did seem to impact her career, which lasted for five years, from 1984 to 1989. In 1985, the year *Let Me Tell Ya 'Bout Black Chicks* was released, Sahara performed in close to twenty feature videos. However, she began to work less: in 1986 she acted in about twelve feature videos, and in 1987 she appeared in only nine feature videos. By 1989 Sahara had left the business, reportedly moving to Europe with her husband.

It is not possible to know if the criticism Sahara received for performing in *Black Chicks* haunted her, or ultimately inspired her to quit the adult entertainment business. It is feasible that Sahara felt that her performance in *Black Chicks* was misunderstood or undervalued, and that, as Jeannie Pepper describes for herself, Sahara may have seen the racist video as simply "a movie." It was meant to portray a fantasy, not to reenact horrific sexual violence by white supremacists against black women. It is also feasible that Sahara felt frustrated by the lack of opportunity to pursue quality roles not mired in offensive themes. Like Jeannie Pepper, Sahara played a possessed "Voodoo Woman" in another Dark Brothers video, *Black Throat* (1985). However, whereas we have Jeannie's commentary, we do not have Sahara's voice to understand her labor choices. We do not know whether Sahara felt a sense of control over, or pleasure in, her performance of the maid with a passion for sex with white supremacist men.

*Let Me Tell Ya 'Bout Black Chicks* emphatically exploited extreme myths about black women's sexuality, creating black women as illicit erotic objects in a white supremacist fantasy. Black adult video actresses had to contend with the representational, industrial, and personal dimensions of this regulatory discourse not only in this video, but throughout the video era. As I have described, performers use various tactics to engage their fetishistic representation in pornography on their own terms, and this process of negotiation impacts them emotionally and psychically. They also use tactics to control, or attempt to control, their labor by designating which roles to take on, what changes to the role they could effect, how much they were paid, and the conditions under which they worked. Yet black porn workers' power to control these industrial factors was limited: until 1987 pornography in California—the mecca for the adult entertainment industry—was legal to consume but not to produce. Because their labor was largely criminalized and few actors had the means to create their own production companies, black women adult video actresses lacked the power to create the kind of pornography and work experience that they would have liked.

Jeannie Pepper saw *Black Chicks* as an important opportunity for black actresses like herself, and for consumers to see black sexuality on screen, even if contrived. In our interview, Jeannie asserted that a number of the films offering roles to black actors during the video era "were kind of racist." In this video, she made a tactical choice—based on her personal values, the expectations of family, and her hopes of a long-term career in adult film—to play the voodoo sorceress. Jeannie perceived the character as glamorous and beautiful because she was able to wear a fun costume and makeup, infusing it with her own creative styling. She also viewed the character as a more empowering role than that of the maid because the sorceress controls men with her dark, sumptuous magic, exotic beauty, and forceful eroticism. Jeannie felt that she could make the part her own and inject it with alternative meanings, while the other roles were much more limited. Her tactical choice illuminates how black actresses sought to negotiate their roles, whenever possible, and infuse them with an understanding of their own agency.

At the same time, Jeannie viewed *Black Chicks* as "just a movie"; she and many other black actresses were often less concerned with the political implications of particular representations than they were with their own experiences as actors working in the adult business. They focused on the availability of work and its rewards and opportunities. Jeannie hoped that a successful *Black Chicks* would serve as an important stepping-stone for other roles. For Jeannie, who had been a secretary struggling to take care of her daughter before entering the industry, and who aspired to become a major porn star, playing the voodoo seductress was an important professional choice. "I thought I could go somewhere with [my career], and carry the torch for all the black women," she said.[72] Jeannie saw herself as representing black women's ability to become stars in a white-dominated industry, and she took seriously the task of projecting an image of black women's powerful eroticism and sensuality. She felt it was important to work collaboratively with other black actresses. For her, *Black Chicks* offered that rare chance to work with other black women in a feature film that involved dialogue, costumes, and elaborate sets. *Black Chicks* gave these performers the space to play with aesthetics and characterization and to just spend time together on set: "We had a great time working together," Jeannie recalled.[73]

Jeannie also acknowledged the structural nature of race and gender discrimination in the casting of black women in subservient and deviant roles: "You won't find me in any of the family sagas: I can't play Ginger Lynn's mother or Amber Lynn's sister."[74] The adult video industry's resistance to casting blacks alongside whites in leading roles as mothers, sisters, daughters, and wives—despite the fact that most of the scenarios and pairings defy logic anyway—amounted to a failure of the imagination for both the industry and its consumers. It was clear to Jeannie that the audience "will always praise the blonde."[75] Yet in spite of the subordination of black women's roles to the blonde, white female ideal—and their forced subservience to white women in the role of maid—Jeannie pointed to the importance of transgression: "It's not just playing the maids, it's what the maid gets to do [that matters]."[76] In *Guess Who Came at Dinner?* (1987) Jeannie plays a sycophantic servant to a wealthy, white, racist family, but she and another black servant (Billie Dee) get to laugh at them when the brother comes home with his new black wife (Angel Kelly). The format of the satirical film gave the actors the chance to play with power relations and make racism look ridiculous.

Vanessa Del Rio, one of the most celebrated adult film actresses of all time for black and Latino consumers, had similar experiences: as a woman of color working in the late 1970s and '80s, Vanessa was often cast as the maid—an exotic, Latina version—rather than the wealthy heiress, wife, or businesswoman: "I've had my share of maid's roles and fruit on my head—you know, the Carmen Miranda thing," she explained. Nevertheless, Vanessa Del Rio found ways to subvert her subordinate role: "They wouldn't hire me as the star, but I always ended up on the video cover, because I always wound up stealing the show."[77] For Vanessa Del Rio, the act of outperforming the other actors, and "stealing the show" was an articulation of her power within the confining boundaries of porn's racist and sexist economy of desire and value. In *Vanessa . . . Maid in Manhattan* (1984) Vanessa appears in only two scenes as Juanita, the seductive maid, but she appears in both the title and video box cover ahead of the purported white female lead, Brooke Fields. As Angel Kelly affirms, "The point was to get the movie, get the cover. If you are on the cover that meant your face sold that movie."[78]

## Glamour Girl

In an interview in 1990 on the Black Entertainment Television show *Our Voices*, Angel pushed back against talk show host Bev Smith when Smith questioned Sahara's role in the KKK scene in *Black Chicks*: "But isn't it playing to all of the stereotypes that white men have about black women?" Angel deftly responds: "Back then, all black actresses only could get parts as maids or whores. OK? And the people that produced this particular video were the biggest people to work for, so I'm sure when they approached her and [said], like, 'Hey, we want to use you,' it's like [she thought to herself], 'Do I work or not?'" In the moments prior to this exchange, Smith accuses Angel of wrongly desiring "respect" for her work when she was, in a scene in another movie, in an orgy with three white men: "But you use the word 'respect.' You were having sex with three [white] men in every imaginable position." "I don't feel ashamed of anything that I've done," Angel rejoins. "OK. What I mean by respect is, if you look back about, um, let's say six or seven years ago with the adult industry, when they were making 35 mm films, they were shot in a professional manner, with big budgets, and good stories, with good acting. That's what I mean by respect. It's gone down, down, down, down, down." Angel powerfully illuminates the decline in conditions for actors due to the shift from theatrical film production to mass-produced video tapes, while also "checking" Smith for her presumption that respect and sexual labor are mutually exclusive. For Angel, respect means being treated with regard, decency, and value as a worker who is only trying to hone her craft. So, too, when black women in porn are seen as representing a politics of disrespect for African Americans, Angel shows that this perception harms an already marginalized class of black sex workers. Angel resists Smith's assumption that she does not deserve to use the word "respect." Instead Angel states that she

FIGURE 3.4. Angel Kelly as Sadie in *The Call Girl* (1986).

does not feel shameful about her work even though she has strong criticisms of the labor conditions that women like herself face in the adult entertainment industry.[79]

Angel spoke to me about how she attempted to assert control over the limiting roles open to women of color actresses, even the dreaded caricature of the maid: "If they wanted the maid, I was going to look good! I was not going to be the run-down, Aunt Jemima–looking maid. I wasn't going to be the sleazy prostitute. . . . I'd take the role, but why do I have to look *that* way? You can still be the maid, the conniving maid that slept with the mother, the father, the brother. (*Laughing*) You know what I'm saying?"[80] Angel Kelly saw herself as redefining the servant role by inserting a subversive sensibility into it. She wanted to project an attitude of control, mischief, and even classiness. In the film *The Call Girl* (1986), Angel plays Sadie, a housekeeper working for a wealthy white family. In the opening scene, as the parents (John Leslie and Nikki Knights) discuss going away for the weekend and leaving their college-aged adopted daughter, Utopia (Porsche Lynn), home alone, Angel enters, playing up the racial stereotypes associated with her role as much as possible. She emphasizes her subservience by assuming a stooped, obsequious posture and speaking in exaggerated southern black speech. Angel performs the "Aunt Jemima" cliché so well that she not only steals the show, she infuses the role with disidentificatory complexity by over inhabiting it. Angel's shuffling characterization is so over the top that her performance serves to lampoon the caricature of the black maid, and ridicule the feigned airs of the upper-class white family.

FIGURE 3.5. Angel Kelly (as Sadie) becomes a glamorous exotic dancer in *The Call Girl* (1986).

As Angel describes above, she relished the role of the "conniving maid" and played it up through the character of Sadie, whose performance of subservience is soon revealed as disingenuous. Beneath her oversize clothes, homely head wrap, and downtrodden demeanor, she is a savvy, gorgeous woman. Instead of depending on the meager income of a domestic servant, she works on the side as an exotic dancer who earns a great deal of money from tips. In a scene in which Sadie performs a seductive striptease for two patrons, we see that her exaggerated use of black vernacular dialect is an act, and so too is her hunched, arthritic carriage. In the last scene, Sadie finally reveals her duplicity to her employers: she had pretended to be afflicted with painful arthritis when in truth she was only sore from all the pleasurable sex she was having with her boyfriend, Jackson (Billy Dee)! The culminating sex scene between Sadie, Jackson, and Utopia—which Sadie arranges at Utopia's insistence—demonstrates the affected quality of racial performance. Sadie and Jackson move in and out of their caricatures as they seduce "Miss Utopia." They alternate between stereotypical black speech to seduce Utopia and plainspoken sensual declarations to address their own sexual pleasure during the scene.

In an interview with Susie Bright in 1986, Angel revealed that it was her idea to make Sadie more than a shuffling maid. "I was this slow, slave-type maid who suddenly becomes a glamour girl in bed. I wanted to show my transformation, but it wasn't originally in the script. I talked to the director about it and we worked it out, and now, in the tape you can see the process where I change."[81] Angel discloses the ways in which actors were sometimes able to push against the constraints of stereotypical and problematic roles in

1980s video porn. By insisting that the character should shift from subservient maid to glamour girl, and by performing this transformation, Angel offered a critical image of black women's sexuality in the film. By contrast she saw little opportunity for such self-fashioning in *Black Chicks*, seeing *The Call Girl* as "light humor" but *Black Chicks* as simply "horrific."[82] Angel's intervention reveals that some black actresses fought the terms of their representation in 1980s video porn but that their tactics of resistance depended on the industrial context as well as their own sensibilities. These actresses desired to be seen as beautiful, talented performers who were good at their jobs. The figure of the glamour girl offered a site to create a persona that transcended the prevailing discourse of black women as poor, dependent, and pathological.

Angel started out as an exotic dancer in Lansing, Michigan, and entered pornography to become a headlining dancer in the national gentlemen's club circuit. "I thought if I became a famous [porn] star then I could make more money dancing," she explained. She did, and she also opened doors and crossed racial barriers: "Every place I went," Angel mused, "I was the first black feature."[83] Having taken college courses in dance, Angel enjoyed performing on stage and inhabiting the erotic dimensions of movement. In the adult film business, Angel's stunning physique and dancing, acting, and erotic performance skills garnered attention in 1986 and 1987. Her fame opened up starring roles in black and interracial films and allowed her to cross over into predominantly white films.

Earning a contract from Perry Ross's Fantasy Home Video, Angel became the first and one of the few black actresses to become a "contract girl" in the adult industry. Her model looks, powerful eroticism, and strong acting chops earned Angel a lot of attention, both nationally and internationally. Like Jeannie Pepper, she toured countries including Italy, France, Germany, and Sweden, and participated in films, photo shoots, adult conventions, and exotic dance shows. As *Adam Film World* describes Angel: "Angel Kelly could be the model for the perfect black woman. Sweet as cherry wine, pretty as a porcelain figure, sexy as a new bride, with an exquisite body, Angel is the prettiest black woman in porn. Her obvious love of sex and playfully seductive nature, coupled with her natural ability with dialogue, make her a welcome addition to any adult video she appears in."[84] Angel was amazed at her newfound celebrity as an A-List porn star, and she enjoyed the limelight. In describing her first visit to the annual AVN convention in Las Vegas, she said, "I remember [the hotel] had lost our reservation and [Perry Ross] said, 'You know who this is? This is *Angel Kelly*!' And all of a sudden I had a suite. I was in awe! I remember that was my first reality check."[85] Realizing her growing fame and crossover appeal, Angel used her contract girl status to demand up to $5,000 per film, far more than the $500 to $1,000 that she made before landing a contract.

As a contract girl, Angel was able to influence the roles, scripts, and titles of her films, perhaps more than any other black actresses at the time. Angel described one of her early films, *Hotter Chocolate* (1986), a comedy directed by Drea and written by Bill Margold, which included the scenes of the black actors eating watermelon and chicken, to be typical of the demeaning roles she hoped to avoid as a star.[86] "I wanted to be portrayed better," she recalled. "I wanted to be recognized better." Discussing the problematic and marginalized roles black actors were called upon to perform, Angel said, "Seeing my movies and the other [black] movies and actors helped me to actually recognize that [racial stereotyping] was actually going on and that I'm not going down that road. I didn't want that."[87] Angel soon found herself maneuvering around roles that she found compromising, and when she took them, as she did in *The Call Girl*, she attempted to infuse the characters with sensuality, intelligence, and above all, self-determination.

The persona she created for herself as a star worked to reimagine and reconfigure Angel's roles and infuse them with beauty, value, and complexity. Angel said of this persona: "She was fun. She was free. She was not a whore. She was not a slut. She loved classy things. She made herself a classy person, you know, by her attire. In the shows I would have these nice dresses and the jewels and stuff, versus the girl who had the iddie biddiest tiny piece of bikini. I always had a good makeup artist. The hair I did myself, and the clothes that I wore I chose."[88] It is important to point out Angel's deliberate self-fashioning as classy, against the tendencies to view porn actresses, and especially black porn actresses, as trashy, whorish women. While "classy" is a loaded term that presupposes that people constructed as lower class lack decorum or proper values of respectability, here I see the term "classy" as reflecting a value important to marginalized people—to resist alienation and disenfranchisement. In films like *Alice in Whiteland* (1988) and *Alice in Blackland* (1988), Angel's costumes include beautiful satin dresses, silk lingerie, trendy and playful outfits, high-fashion heels, and sparkling, diamond-like jewels. Angel saw her self-styled costumes as infusing her character and persona with prestige and worth in the face of an adult video industry that consistently devalued black women. Even as a prized contract star, Angel felt disregarded in comparison to white porn stars, some of whom received cars and other luxuries as part of their contracts. "The [white] girls on contract had someone assigned to get their clothes and this and that, but I never had that," she pointed out, "They just told me what my character was and I got the script and I'd read it and say 'This is how I see this person.'"[89]

Angel demonstrated her interest in reconfiguring roles for black women in her performance *The Boss* (1987) as a bar owner obsessed with counseling her patrons to pursue their sexual fantasies. She organizes patron hookups and even joins in when she advises a married white couple on how to recapture their lust for one another. Angel, dressed in her trademark beautiful dresses and jewelry, crafted a character that expressed sexual agency, confidence, and power. She enjoyed the film and was hungry for more dynamic roles. In *Angel Kelly Raw* (1988) she plays herself, a porn star who sets up sexy encounters with her fans, helping them to realize their sexual fantasies. Filmed at the height of her contract with Fantasy Home Video, and with a mainly white cast, the film peaked in the top twenty of national video sales, showing that Angel's name and star power could prompt significant profits. Angel held her own in a major feature film entitled *Sorority Pink* (1989), in which she costarred and appeared on the box cover with all of the renowned white actresses of the time: Nina Hartley, Porsche Lynn, Barbara Dare, and Sharon Kane. Not only did Angel perform with the top white actresses of the day—she was close friends with many of them and they created a (short-lived) proto-union and support group called the Pink Ladies Social Club—but she also participated in the film's production by helping to organize the cast, crew, costumes, and location.[90] Working alongside leading white actresses increased Angel's status in the industry but also allowed her to forge many important friendships and connections.

Although many adult industry workers and experts are not aware of her directorial work, Angel was the first recorded black woman to direct a porn film. Two of the last films that Angel performed in she also wrote, codirected, and coproduced: *Little Miss Dangerous* (1989) and the sequel *Even More Dangerous* (1991).[91] She was also the first black woman to be on an AVN cover. To promote Angel's directorial debut, the *Adult Video News Buyer's Guide* for 1990 featured her on the cover dressed in a sexy classic 1950s mobster costume: she wore a double-breasted jacket and fedora and nothing else. Holding a machine gun across her body, she looks directly in the camera, a slight smile on her face. While these films were not big hits (and have not been transferred to DVD or VOD), they show that Angel was invested in reimagining and reformulating roles for black women in porn. Angel's celebrity also enhanced her

sense of pleasure in sexual performance. "I made movies because I enjoyed it," she recalled. "I didn't do anything that I didn't enjoy. There was nothing that I did that was demeaning or uncomfortable."[92]

During our first interview in 2003, when I asked Angel if she felt recognized for her work or was aware of her accomplishment in knocking down important doors for black women in adult film, she stated that she was "never recognized." Angel explained, "Well, all those awards shows. I never got nominated. The [AVN] Hall of Fame, no. And I know that every year that they go back and all these people, they look them up and bring them back to honor them. I kind of felt that they just wrote me off. [Like] I was dead and poor and homeless."[93] The lack of formal recognition for her pioneering role in the adult film industry was disappointing. Although she asserted that she never felt demeaned or uncomfortable working in the industry, not only do Angel's previous comments about stereotypical racial roles belie these statements, but her increased withdrawal from pornography while still at the apex of her career shows that she had ambivalent feelings.

Following the tragic suicide of one of her fellow actresses and Pink Ladies Social Club members, Megan Leigh, Angel, still grieving, began to focus more on dancing. Aside from a couple of brief returns, she mainly pulled out of filming, to the disappointment of many of her colleagues and producers. In interviews at the time, Angel seemed increasingly critical of exploitative practices in the industry. "I've been swallowed up by the adult video industry. I feel used and cheated," she had said in an *Essence Magazine* interview.[94] At the time, Angel was becoming increasingly frustrated with production companies that wanted to underpay her but still use her image for video box covers and advertising. Angel received some criticism from her colleagues for speaking out. In addition, new black actresses like Heather Hunter were beginning to grab the limelight. Focusing on stripping allowed Angel to get back to what she saw as a "normal life": "I didn't have to answer to anybody, I could just go there and work my schedule . . . make my money, pay my bills, and I didn't have to see any of those people in the business. I didn't have to kiss up to anybody. I didn't have to explain myself or be somebody I'm not. It just seemed to get to that point."[95]

Eventually Angel escaped the pressures of the fight for stardom in the porn industry. She moved to the South in 1992, started a family, and got a "straight" job. Few people recognized her, so she was able to live, for the most part, in anonymity. But her significance to black and white fans of adult film lingered; fans wrote about Angel in online message boards, private collectors saved and exchanged her videos, and many of her films, once transferred to DVD and rereleased, sold. She returned to Hollywood in 1996 to appear in rapper Tupac Shakur's sexually explicit and censored version of the music video for the song "How Do You Want It?" The video featured the artist partying with legendary porn stars of the 1980s and '90s like Angel Kelly, Heather Hunter, and Nina Hartley. Excited by the renewed attention, Angel considered a comeback but became disenchanted again by what she felt were lowball offers. A couple of years after our interview, during which she expressed frustration about being "written off," Angel at long last received her first award. She imprinted her hands and carved her signature into a cement block as part of the ritual for her induction into the Legends of Erotica Hall of Fame, an honor organized by a humbled and proud Bill Margold and celebrated in a ceremony by porn fans and veteran actors.

In 2008, one year after we attended the Adult Entertainment Expo in Las Vegas, Angel was finally inducted into the Adult Video News Hall of Fame. At last Angel was recognized for contributing so greatly to the adult film industry. Even so, the industry still does not acknowledge how Angel Kelly and her contemporaries—Jeannie Pepper, Sahara, Lady Stephanie, Cherry Layme, Purple Passion, Ebony Ayes, Nina DePonca, Mauvais DeNoir, and others—provided the pornography business with the critical human capital and erotic talent it needed to fully expand its specialized market of black and interracial video. Working largely in black-oriented video pornography, black adult actresses ignited a new market and consumer base for emerging adult companies. Although seen as marginal to the overall adult film economy, black-oriented pornography relied on the diligent labor, forceful erotic performances, and consumer appeal of black porn stars like Angel Kelly.

Despite the fact that many of their roles were stereotypical and problematic, their films underdeveloped and technically shoddy, and their working conditions and benefits inferior to that of their white counterparts, some black actresses fashioned themselves in ways that attempted to reconfigure racialist and racist productions. Actresses like Jeannie Pepper and Angel Kelly had their own ideas about their film roles, their sexual fantasies, and about how to reinterpret racial and gendered scripts. As the video era faded into the digital era of the 1990s and 2000s, black actresses would face even greater challenges of even more racism and sexism, as well as competition from new actresses and declining pay. The industry would transform from small businesses trying to make use of video technology to a globalized, corporate behemoth. Black sexuality would move from the margins of a small subgenre to the center of an expanding, hip hop-influenced niche marketplace. With new

opportunities to work in pornography, many more black women would enter the industry. Yet few of them would know about the first black contract star, and the important work she and others of her generation did to repurpose pornography's problematic representations and labor practices in favor of black women's greater visibility and autonomy.

# Ho Theory

*Black Female Sexuality at the Convergence*
*of Hip Hop and Pornography*

When Larry Flynt's Hustler Productions collaborated with popular West Coast hip hop artist Snoop Doggy Dogg to produce *Snoop Dogg's Doggystyle* it became the highest-selling hardcore video of 2001.[1] "*Snoop Dogg's Doggystyle* is a prime example of how adult oriented erotic entertainment is crossing over into the mainstream," boasted Scott Schalin, president of the now defunct adult Internet company Interactive Gallery.[2] Snoop's first video sold "in the hundreds of thousands" of copies, outstanding in the adult film industry where two thousand copies sold is considered a success.[3] His second video, *Hustlaz: Diary of a Pimp* (2002), nearly matched that sales figure.[4] Both won best-selling video awards from *Adult Video News*, a remarkable feat as few so-called ethnic-themed videos win AVN awards in nonethnic categories. *Doggystyle* and *Hustlaz* signaled a triumph for hip hop-themed pornography. In some ways, pornographers and rappers had more in common than mutual financial interest. *Hustler* founder and publisher Larry Flynt, a longtime activist for free speech and against obscenity laws, appreciated the outlaw orientation of hip hop and the pluck of its celebrity rappers: "The rappers have this 'don't give a damn' attitude which is great. They don't care who criticizes them for what. So it's been a pleasure working for Snoop and it's been a successful relationship for both of us."[5] "Hip hop and porn are a natural marriage," one adult industry critic argued, "From underground traditions and celebrating outlaw lifestyles, they have both become the source of eye-popping profits for savvy investors."[6] Together, pornographers and rap artists orchestrated the convergence of two controversial media forces: pornography and hip hop. Observing the surging popularity of pornography in mainstream media, and the widening market for hip hop pornography, these two industries began to work together with the glee of robber barons. Within a year of *Doggystyle*'s release, rap celebrities Ice-T, 50 Cent, and Lil Jon came out with their own hip hop porn videos.

Hip hop has influenced the production of pornography since at least the early 1990s, but celebrity-rapper-oriented pornography in the early 2000s made this influence visible and more marketable than ever. This synthesis brought more fans of rap music to pornography. Adult film producers have long understood that hip hop opened up markets for their "ethnic product" beyond the primarily white male buyers who fueled the growth of an interracial and black-oriented adult video market in 1980s. Although companies such as Vivid, Metro, Elegant Angel, and VCA Pictures had previously invested little in black-cast and interracial videos, following the enormous success of the Snoop Dogg and Hustler Video collaboration, they jumped on the bandwagon. For commercial hip hop artists, pornography was another gainful venture that mobilized their stardom for profit. It also allowed them to have a kind of creative freedom to showcase sexuality that was impossible in more censored formats, like music videos and live performances. These videos often revolve around the fantastical lifestyle of famous rappers as they go on concert tours or have orgiastic house parties in multimillion-dollar estates with a harem of sex workers—mostly played by real-life black exotic dancers and porn stars. Snoop's *Doggystyle* was filmed at his home, which lent a feeling of authenticity to his claims of authoritative "player" status. Shock G/ Humpty Hump of Digital Underground performs the role of comedic host at a house party in a palatial mansion filled with porn stars, strippers, and rappers, in which sex and a game of "Sex Olympics" ensues for the documentary-style video *Sex and the Studio* (2003). The rappers 50 Cent and Lloyd Banks star in the interactive video *Groupie Love* (2004), inviting the viewer to imagine themselves as wealthy celebrities partying with porn stars on a G4 private jet and in a Hummer limo. In this way, porn produced by famous rappers follows the same recipe as their often nearly softcore music videos. Even before rappers entered the porn market, rap music videos often reflected a fantastical and pornographic sensibility, with images of rappers living flashy and fun lifestyles, surrounded by gorgeous, perpetually aroused women, being used to sell records. Music videos—commercials-to-a-beat for hip hop artists—have also been key vehicles for the corporations invested in hip hop markets, such as television and lifestyle brands, in addition to the corporate music industry. Commercial hip hop's presentation of abundant consumption and sexual permissiveness thus creates a fantasy world and real-life sexual economy that parallels the adult entertainment industry.

As in the pornography business, sexual labor, such as that of the video model or "video vixen," produces the tremendous wealth earned by rap artists and the corporations attached to them. Like the porn star, the video vixen is the eye candy that, with every wiggle of her body, sway of her hips, and glisten of her skin, sells the rapper, the products of his supposed lifestyle, and finally, the song. She is crucial to the economy of profit and pleasure in hip hop, and her seductive, erotic performance infuses hip hop videos with a palatable sexual energy and sense of erotic fantasy.[7] "Many hip hop videos are very nearly softcore porn," one hip hop critic argues, and "they wouldn't be the same without the everpresent [sic] background of rump-shakin,' booty-quakin' honeys."[8] Celebrity hip hop porn propels the conventions of the nearly softcore hip hop video to a newly explicit level. It does so by replacing the video vixen with the porn star, continuing to use black sex workers' bodies as the hard currency of a thriving exchange.[9]

Not only has the interface between a certain kind of commercial hip hop and pornography been marked by a critical change in the representation of black women's sexuality in pornography and the public sphere, it has also transformed the nature of black women's sexual labor. The "ho," the updated black vernacular hip hop version of the super-sexual Jezebel or whorish "naughty woman," is a slur that has become almost synonymous with black working-class or sexual nonconformist womanhood since the early 1990s. The trope of the ho is so ubiquitous in popular culture, pornography, and commercial hip hop discourse, including in song lyrics and visual imagery used in videos, concerts, and marketing, that other representations—Desiree West's militant diva or Angel Kelly's glamour girl, for instance—have become even harder for black porn actresses to access. Not only does the ghetto-fied image of the ho become an inescapable text for all African American women, but the entrenched, demeaning sentiments attached to the ho mean that many black women find it difficult to escape the ho's pernicious influence. For black sex workers this influence has been particularly negative, as their erotic capital in the sexual labor market is undermined by the ho's low-value status. Even though black women's sexuality has a high market value, selling both porn videos and hip hop records, it is forcefully diminished by the discourse of the ho.

This compromised position of black sex workers under ho discourse tracks with the broader vulnerabilities black women have faced since the neoliberal social austerity of the 1980s and '90s, which included the cutback of entitlements and benefits, diminished employment opportunities outside of poorly paid service and retail work, and exponential increases in criminalization and incarceration.[10] These forces impact black women in ways that increase the importance of sexual labor as a viable choice (see chapter 5). Since the 1990s there has been a major rise in the number of black women working in the commercial sexual economy, specifically in the porn industry. Young, working-class black women turn to work in entertainment-oriented industries as video vixens, strippers, and porn stars because erotic performance is seen to offer opportunities not available in other kinds of sex or non-sex work. When they enter these industries, however, they are overwhelmingly assigned the distinction of ho, because the discourses and structural forces that surround black women and shape their experiences are increasingly bound up with this trope. Although these performers are regularly portrayed as hoes in popular culture, hip hop, and pornography, they do not identify with the low-status attributes ascribed to hoes. Instead, like the performers of the 1980s, they actively revalue their images and work.

While many critics see black women who perform sexual labor in commercial rap culture and hip hop pornography as problematically reinstantiating a negative stereotype, these critics fail to address just how embedded and powerful the trope of the ho is as a social reality.[11] It is not so easy to escape hegemonic terms and neoliberal politics that define most black women's lives, and which black women themselves have not created. Moreover, representations are not so simply reversed; no single positive representation can undo structural stereotypes like that of the ho. Nor can critics pretend that the rising significance of class, poverty, and labor exploitation under advanced capitalism does not impact the ways we think about or choose to use our sexualities. My interest here is in how these vastly powerful discourses suture black women to a socially constructed idea, and to a sexual economy, that often runs counter to their interests. As I have argued throughout this book, black women in the sex industries are not simply victims or puppets manipulated by overriding forces of economic and sexual exploitation. Rather, they can be viewed as actors working within and against larger structural and discursive constraints. Not only does the study of sex work illuminate what some black women *do* under advanced capitalism, it also sheds light upon how the erotic labor of working-class black women, encapsulated by the ho image, provides a site for their contestation of their oppression and even for the assertion of power. Still, the ways in which their race, class, and sexuality intersect to define the terms of representation and labor politics in the adult entertainment industry exposes the position of deficit and insolvency from which black porn actresses thus negotiate their work. This is because the primary lens to view (or even fantasize about) black women has emerged as a figure of moral corruption, social deviance, and economic drain, especially in the field of hip hop influenced sexual media. Given that pornographers and rappers are so indebted to black women's sexuality for their profits, this inequity is particularly striking.

Within the cultural and economic confluence of hip hop and pornography, black porn actresses have made crucial interventions that attempt to exceed the limits of their narrow role. They thus expose the complicated tensions between black women's sexual images and sex work. While black women may be characterized as valueless hoes, in fact both white and black men benefit a great deal from commodifying black women's sexualities. The desire to impose a fetishistic, devalued image upon black women is met by black women's own desires to employ, repel, or rework those images, reshaping representation. The text of the ho is not static but historical and evolving, and is infused with the meanings that black women create out of their own contestatory actions to negotiate race, class, and sexual politics. Exercising illicit eroticism, black women in porn provide more fluid and complex meanings for black female sexualities both inside and outside the sexual marketplace. Using their sexualities strategically, they aspire to material survival and security, but also to define their own sexual needs and desires outside of everyday exploitation.

Hip hop porn has been, since the 1990s, the principal force in setting the terms of blackness in popular culture and the public sphere, and pornography, during the same period, has come to have an overwhelming impact on how we think about sexual representations and relationships in our society. Because blackness is thought of as always already pornographic, hip hop porn presents a spectacle in which black people's assumed sexual deviance becomes consolidated by the hydraulic force of pornography's socially transgressive, yet economically orthodox, dispensation. The convergence of hip hop and pornography raises important questions about much more than the porn business's appropriation of hip hop aesthetics and markets, or hip hop's appropriation of porn's aesthetics and business networks. It raises fundamental questions about black women's negotiation of their sexual images and sexual lives.

By focusing on how black sex workers use hip hop porn as a site of labor, I show how their performances take place as part of a complex negotiation. In addition to looking at how these performances work within and possibly against the grain, it is vital to address how performers voice their own analyses of the forces shaping their performances. By examining hip hop's influence on pornography, I want to show hip hop's critical impact on black women's sexual representation in the 1990s and 2000s. I do this by looking at the particular representational conventions of the subgenre as well as the historical context from which it emerges and within which it continues to act. I employ what I term "ho theory" as an analytic for black illicit erotic performance aesthetics, identity formations, and labor tactics from the point of view of the *purported* ho. I thus seek to highlight how black porn actresses maneuver in the genre of hip hop pornography and in the convergence of hip hop and porn cultures more broadly.

## Hip Hop's Influence

During the late 1980s and early 1990s, pornography began to infiltrate mainstream media representations and sexual culture, and so did hip hop. Popular media-industry appropriations of hip hop music in fact inspired the adult industry to seize upon the currency of what was then a largely urban, black and Latino, youth-oriented cultural movement. Video Team, one of the most successful black and interracial production companies, was the first to capitalize on the mainstreaming of hip hop with *In Loving Color* (1990) an interracial porn film that borrowed the name but not the format of the popular Wayans Brothers' hip hop-influenced sketch comedy show *In Living Color* (FOX, 1990–94). Video Team followed *In Living Color*'s success with the black-cast series for their Afro-Centrix line titled *My Baby Got Back* (1992–2010), titled after the controversial Sir Mix-a-Lot rap party song "Baby Got Back" (1991).

Sir Mix-a-Lot's rap exposes his own desires and comments on those of other black men:

> I like big butts and I can not lie
>
> . . .
>
> I'm tired of magazines
> Sayin' flat butts are the thing
> Take the average black man and ask him that
> She gotta pack much back
> So, fellas! (Yeah!), fellas! (Yeah!)
> Has your girlfriend got the butt? (Hell yeah!)
> Tell 'em to shake it! (Shake it!) Shake it! (Shake it!)
> Shake that healthy butt!
> Baby got back![12]

The lyrics celebrated black women's purported voluptuous buttocks and offered a revision of their association with Hottentot Venus–like deviance. In the video, which was widely screened on MTV, the shapely posteriors of black female dancers—situated around enormous sculptures of round brown butts—are shown to trump idealized images of white feminine beauty.[13] While the song mocks white women's disdain for black female bodies, with two white female commentators at the beginning of the song being used to make fun of this attitude, it shows a clear preference for black women's bodies by comparing them favorably to white women's bodies. "I ain't talking bout *Playboy* / Cause silicone parts are made for toys," Sir Mix-a-Lot raps. "I want 'em real thick and juicy." Long seen as ugly and animalistic, black women's rear ends, in this instance, became newly fetishized, or counterfetishized, by hip hop music. In ways, by objectifying black women's bodies, hip hop has sought to reclaim them for black desire.

Although this element of the song is rarely acknowledged, Sir Mix-a-Lot asserts respect for black women at the same that time he sexualizes them: "A word to the thick soul sistas / I want to get with ya, I won't cuss or hit ya." Here, Sir Mix-a-Lot acknowledges the overriding violence projected onto black women, and black men's specific need to take responsibility in stopping abuse. Sir Mix-a-Lot also addresses the transactional use of black women's sexualities, speaking to how some black women may exploit the desire for their bodies to access material benefits, even as they gain pleasure from the music's discourse of black feminine beauty and sex appeal. For instance, he raps, "If you wanna roll in my Mercedes / Then turn around! Stick it out!" The "Baby Got Back" music video makes visible this mapping of the black female body and some of the complex issues surrounding black men's relationships with black women. Like E.U.'s "Da Butt" (1988) and Wreckx-n-Effect's "Rump Shaker" (1992–93), the song marked a disruptive moment of reclamation for the sensual possibilities of black female embodiment. "Baby Got Back" provided a site of pleasure and pride for many black women (though not all). Played as an anthem of sorts at black house parties and in black dance clubs across the nation, the song gave black women the opportunity to sing and dance in celebration of their own bodies. They followed Sir Mix-a-Lot's call to "shake it" by doing "booty shake" dances—and they did so not simply for black men's pleasure but for themselves and for, or in alliance with, other women.

"Baby Got Back" was part of a larger movement within hip hop that focused on playfully representing black sexuality, including the use of explicit language about sexual desire and monetary exchange. A subgenre of hip hop called Dirty Rap was very popular at the time, and rappers like Sir Mix-a-Lot, though not technically Dirty Rappers—Dirty Rap made Sir Mix-a-Lot look like Nat King Cole—frequently borrowed from it to enhance the appeal of particular Party Rap or Gangsta Rap songs. While immensely diverse and constantly morphing into new forms that picked up on changing stylistic, socioeconomic, and political contexts, hip hop music as a whole began to be criticized for problematically subverting codes of decency as well as racial, gender, and sexual norms. Consequently, rap music, increasingly visible in the public sphere, also became a target for surveillance and normalization. Hip hop's growing appeal was due in part to its perceived transgressive interventions in culture. As many critics have noted, since the late 1970s, hip hop's political critiques of state power, economic divestment, and police brutality gave a vital voice to disenfranchised black urban youth during a time of real economic and social crisis.[14] This music, and its related cultural forms of graffiti art, dance, and fashion, was a direct response to the white supremacist and neoliberal conditions urban youth experienced daily, yet the political radicality of their cultural production was often less understood by fans in hip hop's increasingly mainstream circulation. It was also hip hop's complex sexual politics—and particularly its discourses of sexual pleasure and fantasy—that attracted pornographers interested in expanding their markets for black pornography.

Christian Mann, former president of Video Team, explained how his company came to use hip hop to market black pornography in the early 1990s. Dominique Simone, one of the actresses featured in *In Loving Color*, went to audition for the role of a Fly Girl on the then-popular FOX television show *In Living Color*. Fly Girls were dancers that did numbers between the skits; they performed energetic and sexy routines to popular hip hop tracks, giving the show an urban, hip, youth culture sensibility as well as sex appeal. Viewers tuned in to see the outrageous comedic sketches by the likes of not-yet-Hollywood stars Jim Carrey and Jamie Foxx, but also to see the Fly Girls—particularly a standout dancer named Jennifer Lopez. In the audition for the role of Fly Girl, Dominique Simone (as Mann tells it) was told by producers: "With all due respect, you cannot be a Fly Girl. *Baby ain't got back!*" Mann describes how Dominique's painful rejection at the *In Living Color* dancer audition got his attention. He made a point to watch MTV and see what it was about the hip hop song that made it, and the celebration of black women's butts, so popular.

A simultaneous trend in porn filmmaking, gonzo, also caught Mann's attention. In 1991, director John Stagliano, known by the name Buttman, after a character he played, gained notoriety for shooting a kind of first person, "porn verité" version of hardcore, which also focused on women's butts. Stagliano's gonzo featured the cameraman as narrator and pursuer of ostensibly unsuspecting women (actresses) who would then expose themselves, masturbate, or perform sex on camera. This reality style of porn moviemaking became widely popular with consumers and was soon adopted by almost every other production company. Gonzo's ready-made style picked up on the aesthetics of amateur porn, which, thanks to the greater accessibility of camcorders, was starting to infringe on the market dominance of professional productions. Though it is not clear how much he was influenced by hip hop, Stagliano's work also brought new attention to women's buttocks in porn films. Christian Mann pointed to Stagliano's innovative approach to "butt worship": "It's a new view of the female ideal!" "Something told me then, especially looking at the *Baby Got Back* [music] video," he explained, "if this marketing is doing well with white customers, imagine what a similar marketing would do with black customers!"[15]

Copying Stagliano's marketing, but not his gonzo style, Mann created the *My Baby Got Back* series as a way to capture an audience for black-cast porn that borrowed from hip hop aesthetics. "I came up with a video called *My Baby Got Back* [that was] just a slight variation on the [original Sir Mix-a-Lot song] title. It was going to be about butt worship! And the video went through the roof! We had a front box cover that was similar to the photograph that 2 Live Crew used for their *As Nasty as They Wanna Be* CD. It was really the first intersection of hip hop marketing and pornography, I believe."[16] It is not surprising that Video Team's *My Baby Got Back* video series (1992–2010) was inspired by the likes of rappers Sir Mix-a-Lot and 2 Live Crew, with their lucrative expositions on black women's derrières, given the widespread attention these rappers received at the time. Mann was keen to use the sexual culture emerging from black communities, not only because it was obviously already a commercial success, but also because it captured a new potential market: "I believed this interest in black women with large butts was something that was being fueled by black men's interest and was about black men wanting to see black women."[17]

For the video box cover, Mann employed imagery from 2 Live Crew, a controversial Miami bass Dirty Rap group.[18] The group ignited a firestorm when their live performances and album, *As Nasty as They Wanna Be*, became the focus of social conservative groups like the American Family Association. Prosecuted for obscenity in 1990, 2 Live Crew sparked a heated national debate about the nature of explicit sexual representations in popular culture and the free speech rights of recording artists. The group also incited powerful disagreements among African American critics, who like many in the black community, were becoming increasingly concerned about the explicit sexual lyrics and images presented in hip hop. Black feminists like UCLA law professor Kimberlé Crenshaw charged that the music constituted unadulterated misogyny against black women. Black literary scholar Henry Louis Gates Jr., on the other hand, argued that 2 Live Crew's bawdy music was part of a long tradition of humorous black vernacular performance culture and risqué social critique.[19]

Both scholars were right, of course. The group's use of demeaning lyrics reached beyond dirty to become offensive and harmful to black women. Yet 2 Live Crew's music was also a form of artistic expression that said something about young black people's desire to enact a playful and irreverent sexual politics. Both arguments, however, neglected to address how 2 Live Crew was unfairly singled out by social conservatives who used black music as a scapegoat to launch wider attacks on black communities, LGBTQ persons, sexual dissent, and free speech. Meanwhile, corporate music companies and media conglomerates took advantage of this controversy by quickly moving to commodify the most sexist and sexually explicit (thus attention-grabbing) forms of hip hop.

The album cover for *As Nasty as They Wanna Be* showed four black women in thong bikinis standing shoulder to shoulder, their backs and nearly bare butts to the camera, with Miami Beach gleaming in the background and the warm glow of a setting sun falling upon their brown bodies. Lying between each of their open legs was one of four members of the band, each wearing a black T-shirt, baseball cap, and numerous gold braid necklaces. Mann copied the album cover almost exactly for his video box cover, though he featured three instead of four models (Dominique Simone, Janet Jacme, and Lorna Dee) and the rappers were missing. By directly referencing a popular black music group, a national controversy, and a new trend in "butt worship," Mann discovered that black-cast porn could prove hugely successful if marketed correctly. In all subsequent volumes of the series *My Baby Got Back*, Christian Mann designed the video box covers to present black women's backsides first: whether they are sitting or standing, the models always have their backs to the camera in order to highlight their posteriors, and they look over their shoulders, gazing desirously at the camera and the imagined black-women's-butt-loving consumer.

During the 1990s, with the enormous popularity of artists like N.W.A, Ice-T, Dr. Dre, and Snoop Doggy Dogg, commercial hip hop came under the influence of West Coast Gangsta Rap. The adult entertainment industry was located just miles from the black working-class district of South Central Los Angeles, the center of Gangsta Rap production.[20] Porn companies capital-

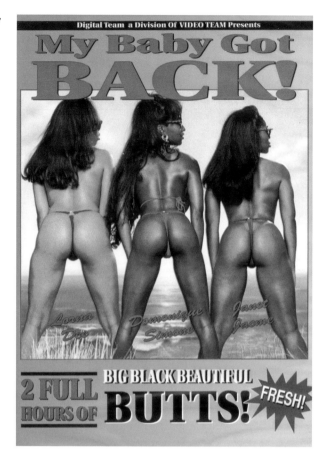

FIGURE 4.1. *My Baby Got Back* box cover (1992). Courtesy of Christian S. Mann / Video Team.

ized on the gangster trend to market black-cast porn videos and the specific sub-subgenre often referred to as "ghetto porn." Ghetto porn was hip hop-influenced gonzo, narrative, or wall-to-wall porn that used representations of the inner city, poverty, violence, gangstas, pimping, and prostitutes in its themes and marketing materials.[21] These videos, including the series *South Central Hookers* (1997–2002), were markedly different than the high fashion and upscale look Mann hoped to promote in Video Team's line of stunning women of color contract stars. Instead ghetto porn videos posed black actresses as prostitutes and constructed sets to depict the "hood," with bars on windows, graffiti walls, trash-strewn concrete floors, and garbage cans. Although the sex acts are similar to those in other types of porn movies—they do not depict violence, as the advertising suggests—the quality of the sexual exchange between black actresses and black actors or white actors is often depicted as solely exploitative.

FIGURE 4.2. Christian Mann shows off his leading actresses for Video Team's Afro-Centric Line (clockwise from his left): Naomi, Crystal Knight, Monique, Midori, and Dee. Courtesy of Christian S. Mann / Video Team.

For gonzo-styled ghetto porn like the vignettes on ExploitedBlackTeens .com, viewers are invited to watch "real ghetto girls" (played by actresses) get hit on by white men, taken to seemly motel rooms, and "fucked." A series of stills that advertise the streaming videos available on the website show the progression of exploitation that the website promises; by the end each ghetto girl looks like she's been put through the wringer, her hair and makeup in disarray and ejaculate all over her face. Similarly, HoodHunter.com presents sex scenes in which thuggish black men "find dem hood bitches, fuck em and leave em." The website features a collage of images to create the scene of sex in the hood: police tape, chain-link fence, a gun, a Cadillac with bullet holes in the windshield and shining rims, and pictures of black women being penetrated by black penises. Although the photos are of known professional actresses such as Lacey Duvalle and Vanessa Blue, they are presented as anonymous representations of ghetto hoes. Although Lacey worked as a contract star for Mann's Video Team during the early 2000s, her opportunities to be shown as glamorous, beautiful, and valuable were certainly limited outside of that contract. A speech bubble above Lacey's head reads "ENTER OUR HOOD PIMP!" Black actor L.T., dressed in a HoodHunter.com T-shirt and skullcap, grimaces at the viewer, and a speech bubble next to his mouth says "LET'S GET IT ON BITCH!" Next to an image of a gun that is superimposed on the photographs of the actresses so that it points directly at Lacey's genitals, a graffiti-styled description reads "SLAP DAT BIG ASS WHORE AND CUM ON HER FACE IF YOU ARE DA MAN!"

This fantasy of the ghetto, the result of white-run production companies' attempts to authenticate black sexuality with seeming emblems of the ghetto, was so influential that by the early 2000s it had become the norm for low-budget black-cast and interracial porn. Black men in these movies (sold as DVDs or streaming on websites) are usually portrayed as gangsters or pimps, and white men are often sadistic businessmen or adventurous slummers. Occasionally conflict or violence is invoked to charge the scene and mark the fantasy as authentic and "ghetto."[22] The image of violent men and degraded, victimized women in hip hop porn is instilled with a mimetic and voyeuristic quality. It is a poor (even comedic at times) imitation of black life portrayed in shoddy, unconvincing scenarios. These scenarios imagine "the 'ghetto' [as] a place of adventure, unbridled violence, erotic fantasy, and/or an imaginary alternative to suburban boredom."[23] Given the long history of how white people have projected these kinds of fantasies onto black spaces, it is difficult to imagine that the only market for ghetto porn is black men. Since hip hop's popularization by scandal and specific tactics of music-industry marketing, the majority of its audience is white teens and young adults who live in the suburbs. Thus, we might conclude that hip hop porn shares the same dynamic.[24] These productions not only benefit white producers but also present desirable fantasies for white consumers.

If the ghetto becomes the terrain for a voyeuristic imagination of black sexual pathology, it is also a contested landscape of structural marginalization, discrimination, inequality, and abuse, and of the agentive desires of the oppressed as they find avenues to negotiate power and desire. Although black working-class lives exceed the confines of the ghetto, for African Americans it occupies an important symbolic register for meanings attached to family and community, economic and political disenfranchisement, nostalgia and progress, and pleasure and pain. The ghetto—in addition to being socially stigmatized, spatially segregated, and economically divested—constitutes a venue for black sexual economy, in which black people are shaped by and enact forms of sexual exchange and expression for economic, social, and psychic survival. Yet there are other locations for the thriving black sexual marketplace of the 1990s and 2000s, such as the strip club.

As a space for labor, consumption, networking, leisure, and sociality, the strip club has become a particularly significant site of late. This has been reflected in hip hop music and music videos, and in hip hop pornography.[25] Moreover, the strip club has become a particular symbolic cultural practice that exists beyond its physical location; strip clubs are symbolically mobile and we find them employed as tropes that bridge hip hop-influenced men's sexual consumption cultures and pornography. The rapper Nelly's controversial music video for "Tip Drill" (2003)—which was so explicit one of the few places it could be seen was at 3:00 A.M. on the Black Entertainment Television (BET) music video program UNCUT—portrays the intimacy between strip-club culture and pornography as it is presented in a lot of contemporary commercial rap music. Set in a sprawling mansion and filled with more than twenty bikini-clad black women performing as exotic dancers, the video proffers a sense of luxury, abundance, and sexual possibility consciously figured within a sexual marketplace. The tremendous talent of the exotic dancers—indeed some of their moves belong to the province of acrobats—is valued for how it elevates men's status as sexual managers, as pimps.

Effaced from the scene is the black male sex worker, and invisible in the image are the market and labor relations that produced the image and the context in which it is consumed. As Nelly playfully swipes a credit card through the crack of a dancer's buttocks and smiles into the camera, he shows how some black men aspire to gain control over commerce, sexual and otherwise. In this gesture, black women are figured as both the currency and the mechanism of exchange in the strip club's flow of capital and masculinity. As hoes, they are simultaneously property and a device for procuring power, which some black men seek to use and others never attain. This symbolic act of commodification shows the importance of hip hop's deployment of black women's sexual labor to address black and other men's pleasure. The fantasy of abundant and available black female sexuality shared by commercial hip hop video and celebrity-oriented hip hop pornography offers a sense of boundless erotic possibility, unlimited economic mobility, and pleasure in what may be seen as outlaw or deviant sexual play. The "Tip Drill" music video, along with much of pornographic hip hop and celebrity hip hop pornography, eschews the ghetto that confounds black aspirations and warps black images even while it continues to cite the ghetto as a key symbolic marker of authentic black experience. Yet, like so much of hip hop that speaks about sex, the video ignores the structural reality of sex as a mobilizer of economic exploitation, even as it depends on the labor of sex workers. In the following two sections I discuss these structural relations through black male and black female sex work.

### The Pimp and the Stud

As hip hop became the main form of legibility for black culture to white Americans, it also became a primary lens for black people to see themselves. What many saw in the most popularly circulated commercial hip hop images diverged sharply from the "Old School" socially conscious or fun, party-oriented rap productions by groups like Run-DMC, Public Enemy, De La Soul, or Kid 'n Play. Popular rap music in the late 1990s and 2000s fixated on images of heterosexual commerce and entertainment. Incorporated into pop culture, mainstream hip hop kept its outlaw aesthetics but sidelined a lot of the antiestablishment political critique, innovation, and playful sensuality that defined the Old School. Instead, record companies and artists focused on a new rap style that was fun to dance to, but empty of social defiance.[26] This brand of rap prioritized a form of black male machismo defined by individualism and commodity consumption, and expressed it with a huge degree of misogyny in its "bitches and hoes" lyrics.

In spite of the rampant sexism and sexualization of female artists and women in the commercial hip hop community, the compelling sound and virtuoso lyricism of particular rappers were also enjoyable and important to forming black sociality and an explicit sexual consciousness. This popular form of hip hop, which so clearly used sexuality as a mode of expression, prompted porn companies to go further than merely referencing the form. Noticing the increased sexualization of hip hop music and videos and a rising discourse of black male pleasure in pornographic culture during the 1990s, porn producers set their sights on acquiring actual rappers for a new subgenre: celebrity rap porn. Of course, rappers were also looking to hardcore for an opportunity to expand their own entrepreneurial interests and illicit erotic desires.

The assumption of hip hop performers' "celebrity lifestyles" as always already hardcore porn organizes the celebrity rap porn genre. The form is invested in the repetition of symbols and practices that reflect a kind of self-rendering by the rappers (coproducers of the videos) that promotes hypersexuality, hypermasculinity, and heterosexism. At the same time, the rappers' performance is fraught with the impossibility of this fantasy; generally what they are presenting is not real life, but a fantasy and a performance.[27]

The emphasis on sexual bacchanalia—as seen in the opening party scene in *Doggystyle*, in the final orgy scene in *Hustlaz: Diary of a Pimp*, and in the "Sex Olympics" scene in Digital Underground's *Sex and the Studio* (2003)—shows the significance of hypersexuality for black men. While I have focused on the sexual images that present a certain view of black women in pornography, and how those images have changed over time, it is also important to acknowledge how pornography engages black men's sexuality, and the relationship that it sets up between black women and men.

In most of the celebrity hip hop porn, the rappers conduct the show by playing the "host." They function to organize the narrative and manage the sexual labor, but they do not perform sex acts in the films. The rappers perform as pimps who oversee the interaction between sex workers (their hoes) and black male porn actors. Therefore, the rappers in hip hop porn also objectify the bodies of black men in their self-representations of black masculine authority. These performances allow these men to valorize themselves and resist dominant discourses that render black men powerless in relation to white patriarchy.[28] The performance of rapper-as-pimp is a self-articulation that makes use of black men's outsider status and reframes it as an oppositional and autonomous masculinity that is defined by a consciously chosen and managed hypersexuality. This complicated process of subject formation mobilizes the historical use of the pimp, player, hustler, and badman figures as vernacular sites of identification and legibility for African American men.[29] As black men negotiate how to respond to the multiple ways in which they have been "objectified, catalogued, and exploited" by racist patriarchal and capitalist systems of social control, these kinds of performances of the illicit, underground, uncontained, and deviant take on greater importance.[30]

Snoop Dogg's porn work mobilizes an iconography of pimps as sexual managers in the genre of celebrity hip hop porn. The opening house party scene of *Doggystyle* shows Snoop's entourage of male friends and associates, known as the Dog Pound, standing around a patio as several sex workers dance to the song "Let's Roll" by Goldie Loc Dancers, including Sinnamon Love and Caramel, booty quake bottomless and in the nude as Snoop joins in the rap with the chorus: "Now I have fucked one million hoes / And I have done bout a million shows / I gotta bout a million dollars in gold / While I'm dippin' with the homie Goldie Loc let's roll."[31] Smoking blunts, cheering, and sometimes groping the dancers' bodies, the collective of black men as house party revelers echoes scenes, also interspersed in the film, of black men as customers in strip clubs. In addition to presenting a space for sociality between men and male voyeurism of black women's sexual performance, Snoop and

FIGURE 4.3. Goldie Loc and Snoop Dogg perform "Let's Roll" as Caramel and Sinnamon Love dance in the background in Snoop Dogg's *Doggystyle* (2000).

his rapper colleagues, members of his group Tha Eastsidaz, also mark themselves as possessing control beyond that ostensibly held by the lady's man, or "player." Snoop's rap references his enormous wealth and excessive number of sexual conquests, emphasizing his exceptional status among the men.

Later in the video a member of the entourage tours the street outside Snoop Dogg's Claremont, California, estate where the film was shot, pointing out the luxury cars lining the street—"Muthafuckas got Benzs that you need binoculars to look in the back seat, you need to page the muthafuckin' passengers"—and the high-end security system, electronic gates, and pit bulls that protect and isolate the estate. Inside, a bevy of exotic dancers perform for the entourage as rappers Tray Deee and Sugar Free join Snoop in the song "Pussy Sells." Crip gangster Tray Deee's rap begins the song and establishes the sexual economy of the film set as vitally linked to the logics of pimping known as Pimpology:

> A bitch main purpose is to service a mac
> In a skirt till her feet hurt workin the track
> No breaks, ho break mine or she don't sleep
> Pussy just a piece of meat another means to eat
> ("Pussy Sells," The Eastsidaz, RapGenius.com)

The scene's editing cuts back and forth between the rappers and the performers stripping, representing the lyrics as narration for the world Snoop seeks to create. This world of women as pussies, and pussies as meat and a means to eat, specifically references black cultural production around the pimp figure and the aesthetics that emerged out of the 1970s celebration of this trope in cultural products such as Iceberg Slim's autobiographical novel *Pimp* and a number of Blaxploitation films. These tropes were taken up again in the late 1990s and early 2000s in black-produced films and documentaries such as *The Player's Club* (dir. Ice Cube, 1998), *American Pimp* (dir. Albert Hughes/Allen Hughes, 1999), *Pimps Up, Ho's Down* (dir. Brent Owens, 1999), *Hookers at the Point* (dir. Brent Owens, 2002), and *Pimpin' 101* (dir. Tony Diablo, 2002). In the 1973 Blaxploitation film *The Mack* (dir. Michael Campus), starring Max Julien and Richard Pryor, an older pimp named Pretty Tony (Dick Anthony Williams) philosophically conveys the rules of the profession to a fresh-out-of-jail Goldie (Julien): "Remember, a pimp is only as good as his product. And his product is women. Now you've got to go out there and get the best ones you can find." Leaning on a cane that doubles as a sword, Pretty Tony continues, "And you've got to work them broads like nobody's ever worked them before. And never forget: anybody can control a woman's body, you see, but the key is to control her mind." Pretty Tony goes on: "You see, pimpin' is big business. It's been going on since the beginning of time. It's going to continue straight ahead until somebody turns out the lights on this small planet. Can you dig it?" "Yeah," says Goldie, "I can dig it."

According to Eithne Quinn, the pimp's super-sexual lifestyle is very much concerned with image. Quinn suggests that in addition to the "commodification of women," the "affluent 'pimp daddy' is preoccupied with the conspicuous display of material wealth," which serves to lend him recognition and a kind of respect.[32] In hip hop porn, rappers are invested in "conspicuous display" as a mode of self-making and social legibility, and as a tool of charisma, used to hypnotize those brought under their influence. These rappers define their sexual agency in ways that disidentify from the traditional black middle-class adherence to respectability as the only path to access, opportunity, and citizenship. As black capitalists, rappers identify with the kind of conspicuous wealth, privilege, and mobility garnered by white male corporate elites.[33] As a source of self-making, they draw on the pimp's over-the-top sexual charisma and prowess, and his embedded critique that the system itself is ruthless and requires ruthlessness to survive. Yet this sense of autonomy is based on the rapper's power over women, as well as over other men. Describing his *Lil Jon and the Eastside Boyz World Wide Sex Tour* (2005), Lil Jon reveals how the performance of rapper-as-pimp becomes a way to assert that the fantasy of sexual management and erotic excess is just like rappers' real lives: "Our shit is different because it's kind of like our lifestyle, like you are hanging out with us for the duration of the tape. You are hanging out with us, partying, wiling out, doing crazy shit. It's funny. And you got some good sex on the tape. . . . I mean sex is a part of every man's lifestyle nowadays. I'm just happy to be an entertainer. So I get more sex thrown at me than the average [man]."[34] Lil Jon performs a version of hypersexual black manhood that recalls the figure of the pimp in order to position himself within the culture and to mark his exceptional status as someone who has made millions of dollars as an entertainer. In our interview, Lil Jon flirtatiously flashed his jeweled teeth, necklaces, and rings in a display of wealth and easygoing sex appeal that marked him as a pimp figure. As his attempt to flirt with me and brazenly touch my breasts during our interview might illustrate,[35] Lil Jon's reliance on the pimp trope is seen to authorize him to have unfettered access to, and reign over, women's bodies and their sexual labor.

In some ways, rappers seem frustrated that they cannot move from the role of pimp to the role of the stud, even though the stud is ostensibly just another sex worker. The stud or Mandingo figure, which emerges during U.S. slavery, is a black man that is used for sex; he is known for hypersexual performance.[36] Although the stud was exploited and demeaned by white men, the representation has been somewhat recuperated as a symbol of resistance in black cultural production by figures like Melvin Van Peebles's Sweetback, as discussed in chapter 2. Rappers cannot really perform as studs, however. There is a danger in exposing their bodies in porn in the way that a stud must. In performing as a stud, rappers show that they actually do not fulfill the stud fantasy. Because black male bodies are powerfully fetishized through the image of their exceptionally large penises—and in most porn since the 1990s black men are virtually required to have at least ten-to-twelve-inch-long penises— the stud must be "hung." Performing the stud would open rappers up to critique and vulnerability, especially in terms of their reliance on mainstream corporate sponsorships and endorsements. The rapper cannot be undressed, moreover, because compulsory heterosexuality, fear of homoeroticism, and homophobia do not allow the rapper's desire to be gauged on their bodies and thus exposed. Further, exposing themselves would show that despite their attainment of wealth, mobility, and status and their performance of hypermasculine authority, their sexualization as studs invokes a feminization process, whereby, as sex workers, black male rappers-turned-studs are rendered vulnerable to both the gaze and socioeconomic power of consumers. In order to maintain their control of/in the image, they remain detached observers of the sexual economy within which they are actually participants.[37]

Because hip hop porn rappers prefer not to perform sex on scene, they call upon black male sex workers to fill the role of stud in their movies. Black men working in the pornography industry must navigate the popular fetishization of their sexuality as well as the demand for their sexual labor in hardcore.[38] Whereas black men were treated as marginal and mildly threatening to white masculine dominance in the porn of the 1980s (this was the case for performers such as Johnny Keyes, Ray Victory, Jack Baker, and Billie Dee), the popularization of black and interracial genres and the appropriation of hip hop themes in the 1990s and 2000s has meant increased opportunities for work for black porn actors. Defying the old adage that actresses make more in porn, black actors who perform the stud sometimes have greater erotic capital than black actresses. The growing demand for extreme sex acts, cheaply made gonzo productions, and interracial performances (primarily black men with white women) has also centralized the roles of the most popular black male performers of the last fifteen years such as Sean Michaels, Lexington Steele, Mr. Marcus, Tyler Knight, Julian St. Jox, Jake Steed, Byron Long, Prince Yahshua, Mandingo, Jack Napier, and Justin Long. Since the early 2000s the popularity of black actors has also opened up a low market of lesser-known and casual black male sex workers from nearby South Los Angeles. It is this two-tiered economy of black male sex work upon which hip hop pornography relies, for as necessary as the video vixen and porn actress are, black male porn actors are vital to the fantasy of unfettered sexual excess and deviance that the genres of black and interracial pornography elicit in their texts.

Justin Long comments on how his blackness and masculinity became signifiers for his professional persona in the business. The surname "Long" references the "hung," Mandingo-like mandate applied to black actors. According to Long, this requirement was exposed during his first interview with World Modeling agent Jim South. Justin described being taken to a room and told, "Take off all your clothes, here's some magazines, just get some wood." He was instructed to get an erection for the Polaroids South would use to evaluate potential talent. Although Justin had taken a bus across country, from Atlanta to Los Angeles, for this opportunity, his nerves were a challenge for the task of providing the evidence of his employability. "I'm just becoming flaccid by the second," Justin recalls. His nerves mounted as, after the photo session, he watched Jim South evaluate the Polaroid:

> Jim's an old cowboy, you know, and he wears his reading glasses and he's on the phone and [his assistant] puts down the Polaroids and Jim is continuing with the conversation on the phone and is sorta flapping the Polaroids, getting them to dry. And then he sorta looks at the Polaroids, and he sets them down, and he pulls his glasses half way over his

eyes, then looks at me, puts them back up, then looks at the Polaroid again, and he gets off the phone and his first words are: "Well, I guess we'll just have to call you 'Horse'!" (pers. comm. 2012)

Equating the bodies of black men with those of horses, mules, gorillas, and other creatures has a long history and is part of the discourse that facilitated and legitimized their use as "studs" in the slave economy, and their sexualized torture and punishment in its wake. While the Polaroid is a standard technique used by adult industry agents and producers to evaluate actors, Jim South's invocation of Justin's purported animality is a particular sorcery that functions to conjure a sex economy based on the alchemy of black men's sex work and sexual myth.

Despite this, black actors appropriate the figure of the hung-as-a-horse hypersexual stud as they mobilize their sexualities for their own purposes of labor and pleasure. Taking advantage of being in demand within the adult industry—and they are, sometimes more popular than less-hung leading white male performers like Rocco Siffredi, Evan Stone, and James Deen—black male sex workers in porn counterfetishize the representation of black men as sexual beasts through their performances and creations of hardcore productions. More successful at gaining investors and distribution contracts than black women sex workers, many of these actors direct their own videos and start production companies, which address the desires of black male consumers and white male voyeurs of the interracial video genre. Jake Steed's series *Little White Chicks and Big Black Monster Dicks* (1999–2003) is one example of how some of these men fetishize their own sexualities while exploiting the market's demand for certain types of performances by black men, especially that of interracial sex with white women. They also use their importance in the industry to acknowledge and critique the confining script of stud work. Sean Michaels directs many of his own films in which he portrays professional and suave 007-type characters, while Tyler Knight uses his performance in the porn parody genre, such as of Tiger Woods in *Tiger's Wood*, to aim for expanded opportunities outside of the typical work open to black men sex workers. Justin Long is another actor who attempted to push back against the limits of representation for black men and their lack of control over their labor at the work site: he penned an opinion piece defying the industry's silence about racial discrimination and the privileging of white actors. In the controversial essay, Justin claims he will refuse to perform in interracial scenes with white women from then on because so many refuse to work with black men. Having been told by agents and producers that these scenes will lower their overall erotic capital and opportunities in the business, white women, Justin argues, are complicit with an unjust system of white privilege in the adult entertainment business. In the aftermath of the piece, which was extremely controversial among adult industry workers and producers, Justin articulated to me the desire to focus his labor in ways that made him feel less like an object and more like an agent. Having worked in a number of films with titles like *Big Black Beef Stretches Little Pink Meat 6*, *Big Black Dicks in Little White Slits 4*, and *Dark Meat White Treat 4*, Justin gave up a lucrative part of his job to protest conditions that, he felt, compromised his integrity. Pushing against the disrespect of black men's bodies by white actresses and production companies in this case meant choosing to work exclusively with black women and other women of color for the remainder of his career. Even in the absence of a black-white dynamic that references the psychic threat of the black male phallus and entrenched power of the racial sexual border, the black male body, as it is deployed in black porn (or black-Asian, black-Latino porn) retains the stud trope. Like the ho, it is an all-encompassing, inescapable text.

## Can the Ho Speak?

In his essay "Can the Queen Speak?" Dwight A. McBride explains how black racial essentialism "legitimates and qualifies certain racial subjects to speak for (represent) 'the race' and excludes others from that very possibility."[39] Similar to African American gays and lesbians who are, according to McBride, so often written out of discourses about "the black community," sex workers are marginalized within the discursive construction of black communal belonging. The ho and her dysfunctional siblings—freak, skeezer, chickenhead, hoochie, hoodrat, and golddigger—are figures that trouble the notion of black collectivity that rests on ideologies of racial uplift and moral citizenship. As public women who use sex for their own interests (be they profit or pleasure) rather than for the reproduction of the racial community, hoes are not only outside of black respectability politics, they are utterly loathed. The slur is used to describe a class of women who are perceived to represent multiple legitimacy crises—the "disappearing" black family, epidemics of teen pregnancy, HIV/AIDS, and even the materialism and consumerism of black youth culture. Hoes exist as outcasts—part victim, part threatening force. Because, as a subaltern figure, the ho troubles black heterosexist attempts to put her in her proper place in the home, in the church, or alongside a breadwinning husband, the violent disciplining and erasure of her role in black communities is legitimated. As a figure, the ho symbolizes the construction of an African American "underclass" that is shaped by cultural deficit, moral debt, and economic disenfranchisement.

In the wake of neoliberal policies like the Personal Responsibility and Work Opportunity Act of 1996, otherwise known as Welfare Reform, the structural divestment in black women during the 1990s not only opened up new modes of criminalization and dimensions to poverty, it fostered an environment within which black women were scapegoated as agents of cultural deficiency to an even greater degree than ever before. The ho, a social grotesque, became a figure to represent black working-class women's hypersexuality and their failure to uphold personal responsibility. Not only was the legislation designed to discipline black women on public assistance by forcing them to take positions in minimum wage service jobs and limiting benefits to a five-year lifetime maximum, it mobilized new criminal justice technologies to capture poor women making money in gray or black markets and through various sex work contexts by indicting them with fraud and filtering them into debtor's prisons.

But what if the ho, like her maligned ancestress the Jezebel, does insurgent work? As members of the community's most marginalized laborers, black sex workers possess unique insight into the stakes of advanced capitalism and color-blind discourse that, as T. Denean Sharpley-Whiting argues, render black women "fair game for rape and sexual assault."[40] Looking deeply into the ways in which some sex workers mobilize the disciplined and disciplining force of the ho might allow scholars to understand how some black people make sense of their bodies' interpenetration by neoliberal policies and their popular cultural ideologies. Porn's racialized economy and its exploitation of independent contracted workers in a vast array of subgenres like "ghetto porn" provide one way to appreciate this interpenetration. As performer Candice Nicole states, the adult industry's interest in maintaining black women as "ignorant and out of shape" and marketing "that ghetto shit" is motivated by profit.[41] Porn's use of hip hop to market "ethnic products" has had important implications for black performers, because of its appropriation of African American youth culture in its most heterosexist and masculinist forms. Even though this crossover brought about increased work opportunities for black porn actresses, it has often done this through perpetuating the racially exploitative and sexist roles available to black women since pornography's inception. Black women's appearance in a variety of medium- and low-budget porn films with ghetto culture themes shows how their representations are also tied to their general ghettoization within the political economy of the adult industry, and to the silencing of their voices.

I have found that black porn actresses, like rappers who use the pimp figure or black porn actors who engage the stud image, seek recognition by employing the terms that are available to them. Their everyday negotiations of porn work are punctuated both by moments of defiance and by a degree of complicity with the limits of the representational economy.[42] Through illicit eroticism some black porn actresses mobilize the figure of the ho for their own needs, while also trying to put other images and meanings to work in their performances. In the process, these performers shape the terms of representation in black pornographies. Their work is complex, weaving between contestation of and consent to damaging images that constantly evolve and take on a life of their own. In addition to these representational tactics within illicit eroticism, black porn actresses engage tactics of labor, which allow them to navigate the economic terrain of sex work that employs the representations to reproduce its logics of inequality and exploitation. Furthermore, along with representational tactics and tactics of labor, black women in pornography, whether they explicitly engage the figure of the ho or not, utilize psychic tactics to understand their own resilience, to believe against the grain, and to *imagine otherwise*.

It is important to note that these performers are not critical of the ho image simply because it objectifies black women's bodies, as many feminist critics would argue. The real problem with the ho, according to black porn actresses, is that it devalues their labor, hence diminishing their worth in an economy in which erotic capital is key. One of the strategies actresses use to deal with this problematic devaluation and intensely unequal set of labor relations is to avoid hip hop-oriented films altogether. Sasha Brabuster chooses to avoid working in hip hop-oriented pornography, preferring to appear mainly in the BBW (Big Beautiful Women) and Busty genres. Identifying hip hop porn as problematic through its narrow racial and gender stereotyping, Sasha told me that she mainly works in interracial BBW videos in order to protect herself from the kinds of limited representations that narrowly define black women in the hip hop genre. "I choose movies that put me in a positive light," she says, "that will market me in all positive ways."[43] Big Beautiful Women and Busty porn, Sasha believed, offered opportunities to be portrayed in what she saw as a more respectful manner than did hip hop porn.

Sierra, a former professional exotic dancer and porn star from Atlanta, shared Sasha's concerns about misogyny in hip hop, including music videos and adult videos. Sierra turned down many opportunities to work in both: "It's sickening. It is sickening! That's why I won't do [music] video work. People have tried to get me to do rap videos. No, sorry, I'm not going to sit there and let you call me a bitch. I'm not having it. . . . I just refuse to be called that and smile. Sorry, someone has to put their foot down. Why can't it be: 'See this pretty girl over here? Watch her do this.' . . . Sex is a beautiful thing. It's not something you should use to degrade people with."[44] Sierra was critical of how hip hop porn abused black women by attacking them as "bitches." She also saw hip hop misogyny having a growing influence in the porn industry. This presented a double bind: while hip hop encouraged the porn industry to produce even more films highlighting black and interracial sex—and thus provided more opportunities for black women to work in the videos—the roles hip hop porn offered were often compromised. These roles tended to lower actresses' value and undermine their ability to cross over into other kinds of porn. Although she was critical of the style, Sierra had worked in several hip hop porn videos, which highlights how difficult it is for black women working in hardcore to escape the genre.

Because companies know that ghetto themes may be offensive to black performers, they sometimes avoid telling them about the films in advance of the shoot. India, a popular performer during her career spanning more than a decade, from 1997 to 2008, and former Video Team contract girl, described to me one particularly upsetting experience on a film set. The set was constructed as an alley where black actresses were to portray hookers attempting to pick up johns. Her narrative of the event illustrates some of the discriminatory schemes porn producers use:

> You have the right to ask [about titles], but they are not going to tell you. If you are a smart girl you will ask, but they are not going to tell you unless you ask. . . . I was on set. I got called for the job, and the rate was great [but] they didn't tell me the title. So I asked for the title when I got there because I had never worked with that company before. He [a member of the production company] said, "Well, we don't have a title yet." But I'm like "That's a lie!" Hello? Here's a girl in an alley having sex with a guy, they made up an alley with an old, beat up car, and she's got a forty-ounce [bottle of malt liquor] sitting right there! I said, "If I don't get a title on my model release then I'm not completing the model release, and I'm not doing the movie." They said, "We agreed to pay you your rate." I said, "That doesn't matter. My rate is one part of the business. But me knowing (because [it] is my right to know). I need this

filled out, where it says 'Title of Movie,' I need all this filled out!" I see the girls [on set] are looking at me like "Damn!" Finally they tell me the title of the movie is called *South Central Hookers*, and I'm like damn! I'm sitting there like I don't think so! I am from Compton. I grew up in like South Central [Los Angeles] and that is offending me! You are offending me as a woman, a black woman, and where I'm from! It's not like that where I am from. I don't remember that! I said, "I don't want to be a part of this." And you know what? That took a lot. I walked off set and actually tried to pull some of the other girls with me, but they wouldn't go. They were all black. I was telling them: "You guys don't have to do that! They are degrading you!" But they didn't leave. I am the only one that left.[45]

India's testimony exposes how racial and gender stereotyping produces discrimination at the workplace as both a structural problem and an intensely emotional and bitter experience. She expresses a powerful contempt for the coercive tactics of the production company to mask the title of an obviously derogatory film and to persuade her that she did not have any power to alter the terms of her work. Angry that the film's depiction of her as a ho would misrepresent her, distort her community, and provide warped images of black women, India walked off the set. Rejecting the exploitive intentions of the porn company by refusing to perform the role of a "South Central Hooker," India also attempted to influence other actresses to resist the roles created for them by joining her protest. Her hope was to take a collective stand against images that she saw as degrading. To India's disappointment, the women did not leave. Even though they may have had misgivings about their roles, they chose to continue the work—perhaps in the interest of keeping their jobs, or perhaps because they thought the trope of the ho was something they could work with.

India also asserts a distinction between her performance in a previous film playing an upper-class call girl and the degrading role of the ghetto ho:

[The director] said: "You did a movie with such and such company"— where we did this big feature where I was a call girl, and the way they had me was really glamorous and I lived in this big house and I was really doing it! So, I'm like *big difference*! Because if I was a prostitute I would be a call girl, and I would be making $20,000 to $50,000 a guy! I would never be a hooker, where I'm on the street putting myself in danger. It would be organized if I did do it. There was a difference, where I was more like a princess, than just like . . . nothing.[46]

For India, the economic power and sexual autonomy of a call girl is preferable to the dangers and exploitations of street prostitution. The director's conflation of street-based prostitutes with high-end private escorts ignores an important stratification in the sex industry and the ways in which many sex workers attempt to position themselves in higher-status work. Many use class distinctions to do so. Rejecting the figure of the ghetto ho, and identifying with the glamorous, high-status call girl, India revalues her work. In mobilizing class difference, she claims more autonomy than hoes are allowed.

Sinnamon Love, a savvy performer, model, dominatrix, and businesswoman with nearly twenty years in the adult entertainment industry, exposes the complexity of this issue. Although during her film career (which spanned the years 1993–2011) Sinnamon had appeared in numerous videos with hip hop themes, including *Snoop Dogg's Doggystyle*, she is critical of the problematic representation of black women's sexuality in films such as these. In addition, in our first (2002) of many interviews over a decade of conversations and collaborations, Sinnamon described how the schema of representation for black women in porn in the late 1990s and early 2000s left black actresses few choices and no middle ground.

> It's almost as if companies are saying that men of color, or white men, [want to see] black women who either look extremely ghetto or are assimilative to their own [white race]. It's gotta be one or the other, there is no in-between. The girl has to be either in a La Perla knock off and in a mansion setting, or she has to be [in] *Ghetto Bitches in the Hood Volume 17*! It's as if the [production] companies think or feel that there is no middle-class market [that wants] to see just an average black girl [who] has a nice body, is pretty, and also likes to have down and dirty and nasty sex.

Sinnamon, who fashioned herself as an adroit crosser of boundaries and keen observer of the economic, technological, legal, and health and work-policy aspects of the adult entertainment industry, really wanted to have the freedom to have down, dirty, and nasty sex without the limiting pressures of regressive representation.

Nevertheless, to fulfill her needs and survive in the business, Sinnamon often used her sexuality in ways that conformed to the expectations of black female performance. When I asked her how she felt about acting in both non-stereotypical films and hip hop-themed ghetto porn, Sinnamon said this:

I've done both because that's all there is. You either do one or the other. I've dealt with it because I understand that it is the nature of the business. The industry really only cares about—when it comes down to the girls, the guys [are] a different story—the companies really only care about the last movie she spread her ass in. Because this is a male-run industry. I recognize that my power in the business comes from the core. The core being your center [*presses her two hands down toward genitals*] and women don't realize how much power they have between their legs. I feel like if I have to continue to present myself in a way that they (company owners) will deem acceptable in order to get what I want, then that's what I'm going to do, because I'm gonna get what I want. I'm not gonna bitch about it and complain that there is nothing out there for me, I'm gonna continue to do what I need to do in order to be able to maintain, all the while using that money to fund my own project. So I can do something that I can feel good about.[47]

"A project that you would create yourself?" I asked. Sinnamon replied, "That I'd create myself! And I won't have to worry about [the fact that] this is all there is." Sinnamon then revealed a bit more about her motivations to put up with racist and sexist roles: "I'm not afraid to be in, you know, *Black Street Hookers*. Whatever, I don't care. The title is a title is a title. But because that is all that there is, and this is what I want to do. That's a choice I have to make. It funds my other projects. It allows me to continue." Sinnamon highlights the complicated negotiations that are part of the everyday strategies of survival and mobility for black women in adult entertainment. She makes a compelling argument that sex workers need to understand their sexual labor power as they navigate an industry that does not necessarily have their best interests in mind. She is clear about her desire to mobilize her sexuality in order to access opportunity, mobility, and fame.[48] Sinnamon's fluid dance between a desire to legitimate her choices and a critique of the limits of those choices exposes how these negotiations are indeed complicated, because each of these roles appears exclusive of the other. In addition, she wrestles with her desire to find pleasure in sex work, while the industry insists on the importance of markets over the needs of its workers.

During her film career, Sinnamon Love was a compelling performer who communicated joy in the erotic performances and took pleasure in knowing that she could present her talents no matter what role she was cast in. She is proud to be inducted into both the AVN Hall of Fame and Urban X Hall of Fame for her outstanding performance work, which is like winning both the

Oscars and BET Awards in mainstream entertainment. Though Sinnamon often consented to the dictates of the market, where diminished and subordinated roles for black women are the norm, like Sasha, Sierra, and India, she found ways to resist those roles by setting her own terms.

Sinnamon became involved in BDSM fetish modeling and dominatrix work many years ago when she noticed that the opportunities in mainstream porn acting were sorely limited for black women. The fetish world offered the high-end glamour that hip hop-oriented gonzo sets lacked. She explored the kink world and found opportunity and enjoyment in the seemingly oppressive role of the submissive, or "sub." Being tied up with ropes and seemingly tortured, many people told her, was "setting black people back 200 years."[49] Sinnamon disagrees; she argues that what she does is about sexual pleasure, and her performance helps uncover black people's forbidden desires to be freer to explore sex without the constant burden of representation. One of her proudest moments, she asserts, was winning the Audience Choice Award of the CineKink festival for her performance in *Tristan Taormino's Rough Sex 2* (2010). Sinnamon sees herself as transcending the confines imposed on black female sexuality, including the ways in which pornographic hip hop culture and hip hop-oriented pornography limit black women to objects for someone else's fantasy and profit. In her PowerPoint presentation in a colleague's class at the University of California, Santa Barbara (UCSB), her first slide described herself as a: "Sex Worker, Porn Star, Fetish Model, Webcam Girl, Phone Sex Operator, Dominatrix, Writer, Mother, Daughter, Sister, Lover, Friend."[50] This self-fashioning speaks to how she sees herself playing multiple roles, exceeding the trope of the ho, roles often denied to sex workers in the popular imagination. It also illuminates how Sinnamon has had to be quite savvy about working outside of the confines of porn in order to make a living while pursuing the kinds of erotic performance she wants to do. Unapologetic about her commitment to sex work, Sinnamon has appeared on talk shows such as *Tyra*, *Jerry Springer*, and *Jenny Jones* and on dozens of conference panels and university lecture stages to give voice to black women's employment in and of sex work. Sinnamon also took on the role of sex educator and activist within the hip hop community by performing on stage with the Punany Poets, a traveling troupe of hip hop-generation performers who stage erotic poetry with HIV/AIDS outreach, and has been involved with Take Back the Night, and a working group on sexual-health issues in the porn industry.

Although her career has sought to expand black women's representations in the porn industry beyond the hip hop stereotype, Sinnamon also saw hip hop's convergence with porn as a career opportunity, as well as a space for

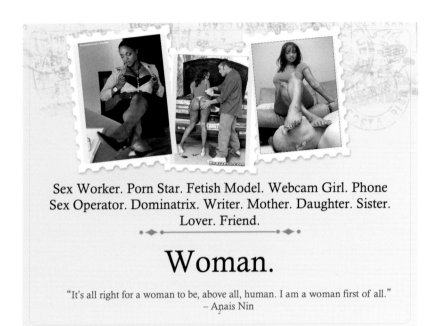

Sex Worker. Porn Star. Fetish Model. Webcam Girl. Phone
Sex Operator. Dominatrix. Writer. Mother. Daughter. Sister.
Lover. Friend.

# Woman.

"It's all right for a woman to be, above all, human. I am a woman first of all."
– Anais Nin

FIGURE 4.4. Slide from Sinnamon Love's presentation to students at University of
California, Santa Barbara (2011). Courtesy of Sinnamon Love.

pleasure and expression. Sinnamon sought to place herself in strategic positions to garner the advantages offered in hip hop porn's popularity. She not
only appeared on the cover of *Fish N' Grits* magazine with popular rapper
Redman, she wrote magazine articles and blogged about her contact with
notable rappers like Dead Prez and Talib Kweli. Leveraging her contacts to
famous rappers, Sinnamon gained an opportunity to perform in the opening
music-video scene of the best-selling *Snoop Dogg's Doggystyle*.

While most of my informants decisively rejected the construction of the
ho, and employed various strategies and tactics to navigate away from this
role, there were some exceptions to this rule, and lots of complexity in how
these illicit erotic workers understand and use perceptions of black female
hypersexuality. Some sex workers appear to take up the ho image for her strategic know-how, working-class recognizability, and appeal. The ghetto ho is
transformed into a savvy and stylish girl next door (in the hood, not the suburbs), someone who in her perceived authentic performance of working-class
black womanhood garners a sense of autonomy and resilience.

Pinky is a porn actress and exotic dancer who not only has her own adult video series (*Pinky's Tons of Buns, Pinky's Bitches and Whips* for Black Market Entertainment), but also has regularly toured the nation to feature dance and take on celebrity appearances at hip hop clubs. She may present one example of a performer who employs the ho trope to her advantage. An underground rapper from Oakland who often uses her appearances in strip and hip hop clubs to promote her independently distributed music, Pinky has a significant online presence: tracking her work to broadcast her own image is one way to see that her performances influence, and are influenced by, a wider culture currently circulating around representations of black women's sexual performance. Pinky is known for her striking hot-pink hair, voluptuous, petite body, and strong acting chops. But her real claim to fame and source of leverage is her shapely buttocks, and what she can do with them. She is famous for boldly presenting her talents with her butt—she often is seen pulling up her dress in random settings to show off her skills. This partly explains her immense web presence. Not only are pirated copies of her films all over sites like xtube and YouPorn, but hundreds or more videos of everyday, working-class black women (including strippers, aspiring strippers, porn actresses and others) are fashioning performances on YouTube that reference, or surpass, Pinky's renowned buttocks-centered dance moves, or what I term "booty antics" because of the highly outrageous, amusing, and playful nature of the movement. Referencing stripper performance aesthetics and strip-club culture, booty-centric performance is also an essential tool for online video performers including Twerk Team (YouTube), Caramel Kitten (YouTube), Sultry Simone (World Star Hip Hop), and Mz. Peachtree (members-only pay site). Although "twerking" has become popular as a mainstream dance craze, especially following pop star Miley Cyrus's performance at the MTV Video Music Awards in 2013, its appropriation by white performers means that black women's innovations in booty antics, and their use of their bodies in the sexualized economy of music, dance, and strip-club cultures, are less celebrated or understood.

The butt, or "booty," is the key marker of a particular image of working-class black womanhood. Hence, the booty is a key site where these women work upon their bodies, to discipline them to conform to the most desirable kind of fleshy black feminine embodiment. Pinky and others present their butts for view in ways that acknowledge the gaze fixed upon them. Oiled booties peeking out of string bikinis and thongs and shown in close-up, low-angle shots are pervasive in this image landscape. Unlike the frontal and profile images that emerged out of nineteenth-century racial science—Georges Cuvier's dissecting look of the Hottentot Venus—this new taxonomy presents the black female body in a low-angle close-up of the butt from the vantage point of the Peeping Tom–like gonzo consumer. Many black women take care to apply body oil to their skin, producing what Kobena Mercer and Isaac Julien have noted as a kind of sheen of blackness, where the skin itself, its shine and glow, becomes another layer of fetishism.[51]

The booty is not just a marker of the ho's difference, it is both a site of control and of possibility. If a performer can master bootyfulness, they can come into visibility in ways otherwise foreclosed. The video *Big Ass Boot Camp* (Score, 2008) shows how this visual regime acts as both disciplining force and opportunity for pride and self-fashioning for bodies normatively seen as deviant and degraded. Pinky whips her recruits into shape, showing them how to become properly skilled booty warriors. Sharing her expertise, Pinky becomes the authority on a coveted technique that garners erotic capital in the sexual marketplace. As the drill sergeant, Pinky trains and disciplines the other women, dressed in matching camouflage hot pants and tank tops, to work hard and use their butts as weapons of survival and mobility. Although this militaristic image conjures the systemic predominance of people of color in the U.S. military and how soldiers of color are trained to fight in wars that risk their lives and the lives and social wealth of their communities, it more closely references the body boot camps popular in fitness culture. In this film the booty—the very maker of black women's *unfitness* as human species according to eugenic theory, and as citizen-subject according to the cultural deficiency theory that deem the matriarch and welfare queen as exemplars of black pathology and social waste—becomes the site where these performers work to assert their *fitness*. Thus, women whose bodies are read as black and female and working-class reclaim their fitness, using it as a mechanism to gain visibility and assert value at the sight/site of black flesh.

Movement is part of the fetishistic spectacle of the ho's performance. The "booty clap" is a dance move that forms an important part of the modern black stripper's repertoire. This move is not limited to strip clubs, however. It is related to other Afrodiasporic dances like the whine (hip rolling) popular in Caribbean dance hall or the bounce out of New Orleans. The booty clap involves a kind of knee-knocking bend-and-butt-shaking move to the rhythm that, when one's buttocks cheeks are adequately fleshy, produces a clapping sound. The dance move is valued for how difficult it is to accomplish and do well. That only women with properly fleshy bottoms can achieve it means that the booty clap is a significant way that racial aesthetics that valorize curviness often run counter to the dominant norms of thinness occupied by white women in the sex and media industries.

Like other moves in the black exotic dancer's repertoire, such as the pussy pop, the booty clap is challenging, high-intensity work. It is part of a set of important skills needed for their craft, including flexibility, athleticism, stamina, and novel acrobatics. For dancers that make it to music or porn video the ability to use these skills before the camera, often for hours on end, is important. These performers must also evince beauty, style, charisma, and sex appeal in order to get screen time. For black porn actresses drawing on the hypersexual ho's desired booty, the booty clap can be taken further by using it as a sex act. By performing the booty clap during sex, the move's appeal lies in its reference to vigorous and voluptuous sex. Along with other sexual skills, like the aggressive, deep-throated blow job, hip and leg flexibility, and fast-pounding topping, black porn actresses, drawing on ho aesthetics, must work hard to perform booty antics. Yet their skillful dance is defined by the perception that such embodiments are damaging representations that exacerbate black female exploitation. Indeed, when a dancer named Monique Ford, aka Whyte Chocolate, performed the booty clap in "Tip Drill," the Nelly video mentioned above, as he slid a credit card down her butt crack, Monique came to represent a lewdness and disdain for black women critiqued by many black feminists, who felt that Nelly profited from Monique's abjection.[52] Because they are so often singled out for critique, I believe those employing the corporeal spectacle of booty antics understand that they are using their bodies as sites of defiance and as erotic capital in a political economy of pleasure.[53]

Does the ho do insurgent work? Some women of color are engaging the iconic force of the ho, with its inescapable, panoptic, and destabilizing presence in black women's lives, by using it as an aesthetic or symbolic site from which to operate. Employing what I term "ho theory" we can see how this inescapable image compels and incites women to begin to think about their booties as potentially commodifiable sites of fascination and desire. Ho theory opens up ways to think about the ho figure's overall work of survival and recuperation as a public woman. In light of the performative labors of sex workers who draw on the iconicity of the ho—with her "'round the way" authenticity, working-class roots, thick desirable body, and unique set of corporeal craftwork—it is important to think about the other ways in which the ho can "speak."

Pinky's video for her song "Bad Bitch" places her amid the Oakland black motorcyclist scene: a large group of bikers cheer her on as she claims to be a "bad bitch" and "hustler." Underscoring how important ho'ing is to survival for some black working-class women, and how key the performance

FIGURE 4.5. Pinky promotes her music via social networking sites like MySpace.

of sexual autonomy and control is for those women who use sex to make a living, Pinky raps,

> I'm a hustler, my mind focused on getting paid
> Would you believe I made all this paper off sex?
> I'm in the zone. Why you depend on a nigga? I buy my own shit.

Here, Pinky aggressively equates the work of the ho to that of hustling and the underground, illicit labor normally associated with working-class men. If the hustler is validated as an autonomous figure of black masculinity in rebellion against the exploitations of capital, and in pursuit of capital's benefits, the ho might likewise be seen as a savvy survivor who uses the conditions she lives within for her own benefit.

Unlike the quasi-masculine, aggressive tone she uses in "Bad Bitch," Pinky employs a playful sing-songy rap tone in the upbeat song "Trick Off," a kind of celebratory anthem for her "money-making girls" released on MySpace and iTunes. The sex workers she pays tribute to are exotic dancers, and the song matches the kind of beat and energy that dancers would use in their numbers. Pinky raps about her own dance abilities and instructs other dancers how to use their sex appeal to make money. To "trick off" is slang for the act of men spending money on illicit pleasures—prostitutes, liquor, drugs—"on the side." However, the phrase also has a mobile, changing use: "tricks" are women who sell sex, but also, in a similarly derisive spirit, the clients or johns of those women. In contemporary hip hop culture "trick off" describes men spending money, sometimes surreptitiously, on prostitutes, strippers, and girlfriends. Hence, in this usage, trick off also indirectly references the labor women do to get men to spend money on them. Pinky deploys the term to show how women can control their sexuality and use it for profit by manipulating men to spend money on them.

Pinky's version of the trick-off game is remarkably like the "badger game," which Kali N. Gross explains was used by black sex workers and other marginal women at the turn of the twentieth century to rob clients of their money. They would lure men into thinking they would get sex and then take their money with or without delivering the goods, sometimes through simple extortion, and sometimes by beating the clients up or pulling a knife. Like the badger game, the trick off is a game for survival.[54] But also like the badger game, women in the trick off must evaluate the "dynamics of power and vulnerability" between them and their "tricks," and using "slurs as armament," transform "themes contributing to black female victimization into offensive tactical maneuvers."[55]

For the sex workers central to hip hop culture, such as porn stars, video vixens, strippers, and call girls, the song "Trick Off" delineates the ways in which they might put sexuality to work in their own interests, and "trick the tricks."[56] As a form of illicit eroticism, to manipulate the trick off is to play with power by maneuvering in the sexual economy in ways that expose and capitalize on myths about black female sexual deviance. In this way, black sex workers might tactically appropriate the image of the ho, but do so under specific terms that draw upon the repertoire of skills the ho uses to survive within sexual exploitation and to enhance her living. Successfully tricking off the trick, then, would mean dexterously honing and revaluing one's sexuality within a complex and shifting economy of desire. This maneuver is not unfamiliar in marginalized black communities: "crafting" in the black queer ballroom community, as Marlon M. Bailey explains, is a form of illicit activity that includes credit card and identity theft that black queer and transgender ballroom community members use to live, to afford the necessary tools to make their costumes, and even to put on the balls.[57] Crafting is, like the badger game and the trick off, a stealthy reappropriation of exploitation launched by marginalized subjects who are essentially divorced of power.

The trick off is the "game" that some women use to capitalize on their sexual performances, but ho theory allows us to see how the labor involved in this hustle is part of the ho figure's overall work for survival and recuperation as a public woman. In this way, we might read the maneuvers that black sex workers use under the panoptic force of the ho under assumptions about their always already ho-ness or ho-ity, and within conditions that produce sexual economy as hegemonic. In this way, the ho's deviance might offer a potential utility. Her symbolic transgressions are part of an effort to shape an identity and constitute the self under conditions of dominance and regulation in ways that do not ignore the ethics of intersubjectivity, desire, and pleasure.[58] There is a notable pleasure in the power that such sexuality wields. Pinky sings in the chorus of "Trick Off":

> When I drop my ass low
> Watch my stock roll up
> When I drop it to the floor
> Watch these niggas go nuts
> sliding down the pole for bucks . . .
> All my thugs in the club showing love tricking off
> If you got it go ahead and trick it off . . .
> To my ladies and my homies go ahead and stuff that money in your bra.

In the chorus Pinky sings as men chant in the background. She raps:

> Trick Off, Trick Off, Trick Off, Trick Off!
> Now this goes out to my money-making girls,
> Tell the DJ this your song let it twirl
> Go on get it girl, it's your stage, it's your world . . .
> Go on spend that money, nigga, go, go get your money girl.

Rapping to the moneymaking girls, the strippers in the club, Pinky instructs them to trick the tricks—that is, to expose and manipulate men's desire for their purported hypersexuality. She encourages these women to capitalize on what is essentially an exploitative situation—to *exploit the exploiters*. She ridicules men who ineffectually perform the pimp and act like they have both affluence and power over the ho. "If your pocket's on E [empty], take your broke ass home," Pinky sings, with women's voices chanting behind her.

"Trick Off" powerfully shows how the sexual economy of adult entertainment intersects with hip hop and exposes how black female sex workers attempt to revalue their work, sometimes by using hip hop as a mode of self-fashioning, articulation, and critique. Moreover, these sex workers appear to take pleasure in portraying a sense of their erotic sovereignty that stages a set of autonomous and affiliation-based relationships. By prioritizing an expression of erotic capital and by relating to other women who are fighting to earn erotic capital in the sexual economy, sex workers who draw on ho aesthetics are also speaking about the ways in which they want to be visible and valued. In "Trick Off" Pinky demands respect for her own and other women's sexual labor, and celebrates this labor as a form of accomplishment and erotic expression. Despite the fact that sexual pleasure and curiosity are important motivating factors for many young black women to enter the sex industry, the policing of black women's sexuality within the black community means that it remains taboo. Additionally, that black women may take pride in sex work also proves unspeakable outside of the ho framework. My formulation of ho theory is an important first step toward understanding how sex workers conceptualize and interact with the demand for their labor, and how black women in particular use the image of hypersexuality for a variety of purposes.

The fact that black women are putting hypersexuality to work in their performances and labor movements in imaginative and strategic ways may seem paradoxical. Because self-commodification is equated with objectification rather than subjectivity in many feminist frameworks, sex workers are not allowed the complexity given to other kinds of workers, performers, and artists.[59] To many feminists, therefore, it seems impossible that black women would want to launch their sexuality for personal profit *and* pleasure, or would take up sexual deviance, as Cathy Cohen explains, as a possible site of resistance.[60] Discussing the strippers and models that populate hip hop music videos, Joan Morgan points out that "very, very, very few women make any money."[61] While pleasure may be an important drive, it is not divorced from the material realities of the sexual economy or black women's lives under advanced capitalism. I argue that pleasure both resists and cements the power of capital in black women's lives.

I have found that black sex workers in porn grapple with the politics of pleasure in their sex work. These workers are attempting to carve out more fluid and complex meanings for black female sexualities both inside and outside the sexual marketplace—to find pleasure in moments of autonomy from exploitation and within exploitative conditions. They face huge obstacles to do so, showing in the process how deeply implicated pleasure is with our sense of how we are valued, and how much work in general produces an *absence of pleasure*. Looking at how some performers like Pinky actually use the most reviled image of black women—the ho—in order to expose the architecture of exploitation that occurs in the sex industry, in hip hop, and between black men and women in this particular moment, it becomes clear that the ho does queer work. She destabilizes forces of race, gender, and class even as she constitutes them.

The figure of the ho may assert a politics of pleasure in commercial sex or an attraction to alternative forms of work, but it is also one of the only images working-class black women occupy in the public sphere. Given the explosion of self-produced and distributed images of working-class black women's sexual performance in online social media, as well as their sustained presence in popular culture, the meanings and circulations attached to the ho figure are ever dynamic and ever powerful. Indeed the ho has defined many black women's legibility, even for themselves. In the context of the neoliberal sexualization of black culture, and the feminization of poverty and low-wage service labor, the question of how agency and pleasure factor into questions of labor, sex, and visibility become ever more crucial to explore.

# 5

## (Black) Porn Star
### Aspirations and Realities in Porn Work

In the summer of 2010, Montana Fishburne, the eighteen-year-old daughter of award-winning theater, film, and television actor Laurence Fishburne, shocked the nation when she announced that she was releasing a porn video and entering the adult film business. "I wanted to do porn," she said in an interview with *Adult Video News*, "and that is the way I wanted to come into the entertainment industry."[1] In the media frenzy about Montana's decision to become a porn actress, many questioned her logic. She compared her first film to the fashionable sex tapes of celebrities like Kim Kardashian, saying in a press release, "I watched how successful Kim Kardashian became and I think a lot of it was due to the release of her sex tape by Vivid. I'm hoping the same magic will work for me. I'm impatient about getting well-known and having more opportunities and this seemed like a great way to get started on it."[2] Although Montana was highly articulate in interviews about how she sought to explore her own sexual fantasies by performing them on camera, most critics believed her choice to perform in pornography was a major miscalculation for someone who intended to become a mainstream entertainment star.

American media institutions, including the pornography industry, profit from circulating the mythology that anyone can in fact become a star. Consumption-oriented and leisure-like work is idealized in exposés of the rich and famous and reality television featuring celebrity lifestyles. Reality TV stars like Kim Kardashian and Paris Hilton have profited from celebrity sex tapes, using their sexuality by transforming it into a consumable product.[3] These "carefully contrived publicity stunts" are purportedly sold against the stars' wishes, but routinely to their financial benefit.[4] Kardashian, for instance, denied a role in releasing her film, but nonetheless received $5 million in a settlement with Vivid Entertainment.[5] Montana Fishburne saw the celebrity sex tape as a device to assert her eroticism and to create opportunities. "It wasn't a goal," she said of her foray into porn, "but it's a step . . . in a direction."[6] Employing illicit eroticism, then, Montana chose to mobilize her sexuality for some gain—in this case, instant fame. With notoriety based on her celebrity pedigree, but also in her eyes on her own accomplishments, Montana could then parlay her stardom into her real interests—modeling and acting. Instead of creating a sex tape and then denying a role in its release and sale, she brazenly decided to go straight to pornography, reversing the formula and at the same time exchanging the performance of feminine guilelessness with one of aggressive showmanship.

Montana made an undisclosed sum from the sale of her Vivid tape, which sold out in its first printing of twenty-five thousand DVDs, drawing blockbuster revenues of more than $1 million in the first weeks of sale.[7] Yet some said she made a mistake. She could have made much more if she had first garnered fame outside of the adult business, which is, although increasingly mainstream, still regarded with harsh public disapproval. Women who begin in porn, like Montana's idols Jenna Jameson and Sasha Grey, may cross over, but they are extremely rare. And they are white. When we consider the fact that Montana Fishburne is African American, though from a wealthy family, we see that this discourse about her cheapened erotic capital is informed by the diminished value of her black womanhood in the cultural marketplace. As a publicly sexual black woman, Montana is already seen as a devalued commodity, and her strategic efforts to take up pornography for a bid at celebrity and even pleasure are compromised by that fact.[8] What Montana was perhaps unaware of is that black women have struggled on the margins of porn stardom for three decades, trying with all their power to transform a taste of notoriety in pornography into other kinds of cultural capital and social access. For the most part, they have not succeeded due to the hugely complex forces of racism and sexism that define their mobility and value.

Montana's stunning choice of pornography for her first foray into the entertainment world reveals much about the politics of strategic sexual labor. With the shame around sexuality in our culture, porn stars rarely transgress the stigma attached to sex work to become national symbols of success or glamour. Yet their desire remains. Thousands of other, unknown Montanas are drawn to pornography precisely for the same reasons as the daughter of an A-List Hollywood actor.[9] This chapter focuses on black women's motivations for entering the porn business. It considers how, driven and constrained by the particular vulnerabilities that shape their lives, they endeavor to try on porn stardom for themselves, and to see what opportunities it provides. In light of these forceful aspirations, what are the realities and barriers that black women confront as they mobilize their sexualities for profit and pleasure?

## Employing Sex Work

While sex work has been a historical facet of black women's labor in the United States, the growing global sexual marketplace is becoming more significant today.[10] During the last twenty years, the globalizing economy has offered few other avenues for African American women to achieve financial independence or access to the middle class. These women have sought out alternate paths to economic mobility by putting their sexualities to work in illicit economies of sex.[11] Historically, African American women have used informal, illegal, and quasi-legal income-generating activities, including prostitution, pimping, drug dealing, bet running, music and movie pirating, running dice, card and chess games, and smuggling.[12] These underground practices of economic survival, mobility, and independence show how African Americans, marginalized in the formal U.S. labor market, have traditionally found work in or around the sexual economy. Still on the socioeconomic margins and in the midst of a changing political economy that is developing ever more levels of vulnerability and exploitation to women of color's work transnationally, African American women continue to employ their erotic capital, knowledge, and skills for survival, mobility, and the care of their communities.

I use the term "illicit eroticism" to describe how black women use, manipulate, and deploy their sexualities in the economy. Commodifying one's own sexuality is part of the strategic and tactical labor black women use in advanced capitalist economies. Oppressed by their gender as well as their race and class, African American women in particular have mobilized illicit eroticism in ways that show what it means to navigate a sexist, racist, and classist society by using their embodied, or corporeal, resources for material survival. In the context of declining economic opportunities and a shrinking social welfare state, young, working-class black women recognize the value of profiting from the global appetite for black cultural production and black sexualization. These women are not just passive victims of the transforming socioeconomic relations that rely on their marginalization and abjection: they are active social agents, striving to use alternative economies to access upward social mobility.[13] Catalyzing a "new black body politics," these women expose how black women who deploy illicit eroticism become what Patricia Hill Collins calls "new commodities."[14] Through a range of sex-for-work arrangements, their bodies are deeply implicated in relations of value and exchange, which tie them to and enhance the very structures they seek to escape. In the process of commoditizing black female sexuality for a burgeoning consumer demand, and their objectified bodies for sexual labor, black women sex workers confront a complex set of challenges that define the landscape of sexual commerce, racial politics, and globalized, neoliberal capitalism. Unlike Collins's formulation, however, I argue that those taking up the politics of illicit eroticism are constantly aware of and adapting to the politics of their sexualized, self-commodification.

For African American women, sex itself has been its own prohibited terrain—a no-go zone profoundly attached to exploitation, abuse, and trauma, but also shaped by community-born regulations of gendered sexual behavior. Encountering these prohibitions and anxieties around sex, black women's sexual commodification, and the traumas of racialized sexuality, black women become illicit erotic workers who negotiate a set of powerful and intersecting forces and interdictions. One aspect of being an *illicit erotic worker* is recognizing the consumer demand for one's sexuality, including (but not limited to) the unspeakable, taboo desire for racialized erotic fantasy that dominates most markets for black-oriented adult entertainment. Another is the knowledge that you are seen as a sexual deviant for doing this work. Lastly, this means the laborious mobilization of sex, sexuality, and eroticism in ways that promote one's human capital, survival, and self-care in the face of enormous impediments.

Black women find sex work, and its relative flexibility and high income, attractive because it offers increased opportunities for what Michel Foucault terms "care of the self."[15] That is, while porn work allows an array of embodied problematics, it simultaneously induces illicit erotic workers to perform practices, techniques, and moral philosophies to constitute themselves in the social world. These technologies of self-care produce illicit erotic workers as actors reaching toward subjectivity, opportunity, and erotic sovereignty, even as they seek to promote their own livelihoods and happiness in a setting that regulates, polices, and diminishes the value of their lives. With trends in African American unemployment and underemployment, and the rise of feminized poverty and subordinate work, increasing numbers of young, working-class black women in America identify the sex industries as preferred spaces to make a living for themselves and their families.[16] Participating in a range of sex-work oriented jobs—streetwalking, private escorting, modeling, exotic dancing, phone sex, webcamming, s/m domination, or performing in sex films—black sex workers maneuver in the context of neoliberal transformations in production, consumption, and labor organization, and are subject to new and different stresses and disciplinary regimes.[17]

Given that only 61 percent of black women in the United States are employed in the formal wage economy,[18] and that sexuality has been refigured as a "sign to energize, in effect to sexualize, late-capitalist consumption,"[19] we might guess there are significant numbers of black women who might use sex for some sort of monetary or resource exchange to supplement their underemployment.[20] Compared to other sectors of the U.S. economy, where black women are overrepresented at the bottom of the labor force, particularly in low-wage, less secure, contingent, subcontracted, temporary, and peripheral work, it is easy to understand how workers might consider the adult industry a promising employment option where they could potentially earn more money for fewer hours of work.[21] The seeming advantages of sexual labor are compromised by the dangers: criminalization (in most fields of sex work, though not always in porn performance), social stigma, violence, harassment, disease, and exploitation. Yet these concerns are not unique to sex work, and porn work is not always more risky than other jobs black women find themselves in. Black women in the formal economy are also faced with systemic inequality, prejudice, violence, harm, and exploitation.[22]

Many scholars have noted African American women workers' experiences of racial bias in employment, and their traditional concentration in the dirtiest, most dangerous, and vulnerable jobs.[23] Black women workers have been maltreated in legitimate labor arenas—in blue-, pink-, and white-collar work—and continue to be subjected to occupational segregation, limited employment mobility, debilitating health risks, and major resource inequities. Concentrated in lower-level service work, from McDonald's to Walmart and from nursing homes to domestic work and child care, black women, Evelyn Nakano Glenn suggests, have gone from servitude as slaves to being deemed "particularly suited for service" in the new wage economy.[24] Even workers in higher-status jobs like nursing and teaching face job insecurity, and black women graduating with college degrees confront troubles in the job market.[25] African American women who are employed grapple with discrimination and disadvantage, and the black median household income remains only 63 percent of whites,' while white families possess five times the net assets or wealth of African American families.[26] It should not be surprising then, given these overwhelming socioeconomic factors and employment conditions, that some black women decide to pursue another kind of service labor: sex work.[27]

Some critics have asked me if money could be, in itself, the primary drive for people to enter porn work—assuming that there must be some other factor that enables individuals to choose sex work. My answer is that money is the mobilizer of all workers' labor, across industries. To assume that porn workers do porn simply for the sex, as opposed to the money, is similar to believing that supermarket workers choose employment in food retail because they like food.[28] Nevertheless, my research shows that sex and performance are aspects of porn work that workers think about, invest in, and perceive as both attractive and destabilizing features of the job. More than other venues of sexual labor, pornography attracts those keen to put their sexualities to work on camera. Because pornography is a desire industry more aligned with film acting than streetwalking, porn work carries a certain level of legitimacy and esteem that other forms of sex work lack.[29] Porn work is legal, at least since the late 1980s in California, the node of U.S. porn production, and hence it offers a space where workers can avoid the vast apparatus of criminalization that intrudes upon the lives of many sex workers. I conceptualize porn work as a tactical negotiation of the changing political economy, in order to uncover how black women take up pornographic performance for a complex set of drives that overlap with financial need. One of these drives is the desire to stage and experiment with eroticism, or to be seen as a desirable and acknowledged star.

As discussed in previous chapters, black women's interventions and recuperations of explicit sexuality in media show that pornography offers a compelling site for the performance of a range of aspirations and attractions intimately tied to black women's socioeconomic and sexual lives. In this chapter, I want to question more deeply how black women have articulated the appeal of working in pornography, and how they understand the opportunities and obstacles their choice presents. Women approach work in porn from a diversity of perspectives and experiences. It is impossible to make a simple definitive statement about who black porn actresses are, what type of families they are from, or how their backgrounds have influenced their decisions to enter the porn and sex industries. Some performers in my sample grew up working-class, while others were from middle-class families. Some have only high school diplomas, and others have college or advanced degrees. A number were raised in homes where sexuality was strictly guarded, but a few grew up with looser reins allowing them to explore sex. Several are single mothers, and most help support their parents, siblings, or extended family. A number of women came from Los Angeles and the area surrounding San Fernando's "Porn Valley," but many were from small towns or big cities in Michigan, Illinois, Georgia, Iowa, Hawaii, Florida, New York, and Nevada. The one thing almost all women I interviewed shared in common was that they viewed porn performance as work.[30] When I asked a performer named Dee why women get into the porn business, she responded: "Money, sex, and fame, all in that order."[31] "Not money, fame, and sex?" I asked. We were sitting together at the Video Team booth at the AVN Adult Expo in Las Vegas, shouting over the din in the large convention hall into my voice recorder. "No, money, sex, and fame!" Dee then turned to a fan that was lurking nearby, watching us. "Why do you think girls get into the business?" she asked. "Because they can't get laid anywhere else?" he offered. Laughing, Dee turned back to me and said: "That's *not* the reason."

## Money

Whether their interest was short-term, to pay the bills, or long-term, to make a career for themselves, my informants stated that their main motivation for entering the adult industry was money. As Lexi expressed, "It was a labor choice of saying [to myself] 'How am I going to make more and more money?' It happens to be in the adult industry."[32] Many performers described the pay rates of $300 to $2,000 or more per movie scene as "rent money." That they could pay their rent or mortgage from one day's work, or could earn as much in one day as they could make in one week or month in a "normal" job was a compelling force in workers' decision to enter pornography. Getting paid more money and receiving their pay faster meant that they could afford immediate expenses as well as save for the future, perhaps moving on to pursue other career aspirations. Crystal, who began acting in adult films after her eighteenth birthday, said: "I'm doing this because I need to go to school, get a car, and a house. I really want to be a nurse."[33] Sandi Beach had only been in the industry for one week when we met. "I'm not planning on pursuing this as a career," the twenty-year-old Latina New Yorker explained. "I just want to [do this] because I'm going to school now too. My major is pre-law and my minor is computer programming. So, I'm going to school and supporting myself. It's just an easy way for me not to stress too much and accomplish my goals at the same time. I'm building for my future."[34]

Considering the high cost of a college education in the United States and the lack of financial resources many women of color have, it is not surprising that they would be attracted to high-paying jobs with adaptable schedules that require no prior experience such as those in the adult industry. My informants use porn to support themselves while in school, to save up for expensive degree programs, or just to earn money while they figured out what studies they really wanted to pursue. The porn industry focuses on hiring young women in the eighteen-to-twenty-three age range for the majority of acting work during which many women are looking for short-term career options. Young women like Crystal and Sandi are somewhat ideal workers for this industry because they want to come in, make money, and leave without becoming overly invested in transforming labor conditions or challenging the status quo. These women show that rather than falling into pornography because they have a bad life, or other popular discourses of how women come to be exploited by the pornography industry, a major sector of women working in porn are very clear about their intentions and what they want to get out of the labor. When I asked Angel Eyes about her motivations for working in the industry, she responded: "Honestly, the money. I'm used to making anywhere from $500 to $2,500 a day. Most people are like, 'I'm not going back to a regular nine to five.' I definitely will go back, but right now this is what's taking care of me. What I enjoy doing. . . . I want to either go into the fiber optics field or go back to school for accounting to be a CPA [certified public accountant]. Right now I'm just doing this to have fun and make money."[35]

"It allows me to work two days out of the week and have the same amount of money for working the whole week," Lola Lane explained. Women like Lola seek employment in pornography because they need to supplement their incomes in order to pay their bills and take care of their families. "I have a child. I like staying at home and helping him with his homework. I can go to his games on Saturdays. I was working retail and you never have a Saturday off."[36] Like Lola Lane, Sinnamon Love worked full-time in retail while raising her children. Sinnamon was enrolled in a nursing program at a Los Angeles–area university and spent most of her day shuttling between work, school, and home with her kids. She was exhausted and having trouble making ends meet when she decided to answer an ad for nude modeling in *LA Weekly*. After making some money as a nude model, she soon realized that she could support her family by acting in pornographic films just two to four days a week. In addition, because of the money she was making she would no longer have to take out school loans and would be able to pay back her debt even more quickly than in a nursing job. Soon Sinnamon decided to devote herself full-time to building a career in porn. In an essay she wrote for a lifestyle blog, Sinnamon describes the life pressures that compelled her to investigate such a career: "I'd never watched porn or stepped foot in a strip club, but with 2 toddlers under two years of age, a husband I decided I could do better without, 2 jobs and 13 units, I found my way into porn so I could cut back on my work hours and actually raise my children instead of letting day care do it for me. I wasn't looking to be famous. I was looking to supplement my income to support my family and not have to forego [*sic*] my dream of finishing college. And I did."[37]

Almost twenty years later, Sinnamon remains active in speaking and writing publicly about her life, career, and the pornography business. She is a single mother to three teenagers, and she talks openly about enjoying her dual roles as mother and porn actress. "I revel in the duality of my life," she asserts. "Some days I feel like a superhero; making dinner and leaving the sitter with instructions before rushing to pack my luggage to fly cross-country in my cape to be my porn star alter ego. . . . On any given evening I can be found checking homework and watching the news with my partner before heading to bed. I prepare a healthy, gourmet meal every night for my family and speak to my mother every day on the phone."[38] In this blog post, Sinnamon articulates the significance of what Luise White describes as "reproductive labor" for women involved in sex work.[39] Like the Kenyan sex workers in White's study of twentieth-century colonial Nairobi, black female sex workers in the twentieth- and twenty-first century United States employ illicit eroticism to do reproductive labor that often goes unacknowledged. They strategically use sex work's flexible hours and wages to ensure their and their family's livelihoods. This strategy reveals how black women strive to navigate the political economy in ways that are most beneficial for their families, even as their work is incorporated by forces of capital that require women's reproductive, intimate, and caring labor in industry and family life (to reproduce and sustain the workforce for capital). The strategic thinking of porn workers in my study is significant given the popular image of the porn performer as young, single, childless, feckless, and naïve about her involvement in a nefarious business. The ways in which porn-worker labor affects others beyond the worker herself remain largely invisible in popular and academic discourse. Sinnamon and Lola Lane show how sexual labor allowed them to pursue the dual labor, or "second shift,"[40] of mothering, never escaping the system of gendered labor exploitation of mothering under capital. Like reproductive labor in the home, sex work in pornography provides a terrain for women to struggle against and within the terms of their labor, and these struggles are compounded by race, age, and class difference. Pornography is therefore a site where black women, facing the precaritization of their work in the broader society, mobilize a kind of refusal to capitalist work discipline by choosing a form of labor seen to provide more money for less work. These women do this to support their families and communities, and in the process are saddled with the enhanced labor of mothering, which for women who are both black and sex workers poses an additional set of vulnerabilities, and a unique set of labor negotiations.

Carmen Hayes was not a mother when she decided to enter the pornography business, but she did wrestle with these considerations of family and labor. Knowing her family could not help her financially, Carmen took up exotic dancing in order to get through nursing school. Feeling stifled and unsatisfied in her job as a nurse, she soon turned to adult film. She explained:

> I was a nurse. I went to nursing school. I did in-home care, urgent care, front office, and back office work, [and worked] in the field. I started dancing to help pay for school. Because my aunties [and family] couldn't help me along the way. . . . I was also trying to be independent on my own. But I also had an itching for it, because I was always the good girl doing everything I was supposed to. I was always on honor roll and student council. I graduated with honors in school; I graduated with a yellow tassel and a yellow robe, the whole nine. I went to nursing school and I did really well and I finally graduated. [But] there was a little racism going on in the area that I chose to practice and I couldn't deal with it. And [there] was so much that came with the territory, as far as being responsible for someone's life and you have to make sure that when you are administering all these kinds of medicine that someone is not allergic to penicillin or whatever. Because of the territory, working in the emergency room, that is heavy stuff.[41]

Carmen explained that not only did she feel stressed by working with a racist doctor in a clinic or when working in the high-pressure environment of the ER, but she also struggled with working as an in-home care provider for elderly people like her grandmother. When her grandmother passed away, Carmen began to feel increasingly uncomfortable with her job.

> It's hard enough trying to deal with myself as a human being. So I just wanted to stop. I did in-home care. I lost my grandmother; she was one of my patients. . . . I loved her dearly. But also some of the other elderly people that I was taking care of, I grew attached to. And obviously with time, with whatever disorder or sickness they were going through, they passed and it was really mentally hard for me. It was one of those things where it was a no-brainer for me to start doing porn or being an exotic dancer.[42]

Carmen's testimony goes against the standard assumption that all women entering porn are uneducated, with no professional background. In fact, with the growing trend in subgenres focused on older women, such as Cougar and MILF porn, many women in their thirties and forties, coming from professional careers, are putting their sexualities to work in the porn industry. Moreover, Carmen's comment contrasts with the widely held belief that relatively high-status professions like nursing are necessarily healthier or preferred jobs for women. Although most jobs are seen as more respectable and value-added for women than pornographic entertainment work, they are not necessarily easier from a physical or emotional perspective. Further, black women have a long history of working in nursing, elder care, special needs, and child-care professions, and of facing the brunt of the backbreaking and emotionally taxing work.[43] For Carmen, negotiating racist supervisors, life or death situations in the ER, and end-of-life care was much more emotionally demanding than the emotional labor involved in sex work.

When I asked Carmen about the benefits of working in pornography, she said, "The benefits are the fast money. . . . People will make in two weeks [what] you can make in a day and maybe hours." "But the downfall is," Carmen goes on to warn, "if you are not responsible, if your head isn't on straight, it will go fast. And some girls are starstruck and get caught up in [the] game." Carmen asserted that, "Contrary of what people think, it doesn't have to be about drugs and a girl who was physically and mentally messed up in the head and she got into [pornography]. There are cases like that, but it's not all cases."[44] There are indeed cases where women enter pornography to support a drug habit or as a result of some form of abuse, but none of the women I interviewed described their own experiences in this way. This may be partly due to the fact that my informants chose to present themselves in a positive light or to keep some information private. My lack of research findings about abused or coerced women may also be due to the fact that many of the most desperate women do not stay in the industry for long—perhaps doing one or two films before they move on—and I did not have occasion to interview them since they are a marginal and transient group. However, even though it is a misleading stereotype of porn workers, the specter of the suffering, "trafficked" woman with a history of abuse and a drug habit flourishes in the popular consciousness as well as within the industry. Anecdotal stories about women brought in by agents who seem more like pimps, or lecherous boyfriends at best, circulate. According to Diana DeVoe, a black porn-star-turned-director of over one hundred films including popular film series like *Desperate Black-wives* (2005–10) and *Dymes* (2003–6), some adult film producers work with agents who make deals to pay women below-market wages and taking cuts exceeding 30 to 40 percent on the back end.[45]

Diana placed the blame on producers, explaining that they not only benefit from getting young women on the cheap, but, in a perverse way, seem to enjoy exploiting young women's labor.

> [As a director] I usually make my own schedule, but every now and then [the producer] would call me and say, "There is a girl who needs $300 right now. Could you get a location and your makeup artist together and shoot this scene? And we need to shoot today because she needs $300 today." And he loves that: he loves feeling like he got over on somebody. He feels like he won because he got a girl, who would generally not work for that [little] and he got her to a point of desperation so she has to do it. It is his bread and butter. It's the air that he breathes.[46]

Diana's description of this contemptible producer shows that there is actually a systemic benefit for producers to capitalize on desperate women and on women attached to unscrupulous "agents." Not only do some producers seem to "get off" on getting over, but they also make a lot of money off workers, especially for the lower-market gonzo videos, by paying nearly half the going rate, in the process undercutting the wages of all workers. According to BBW performer Betty Blac, producers for some of the less respected companies "regularly find women who are down on their luck," including pregnant women for the black pregnancy porn subgenre, and pay them as little as $250 per scene. Sometimes the women are promised $1,000 for a film, only to find out on set that they must perform in four sex scenes for that pay rate.[47]

As a director for hire, Diana DeVoe both witnesses and unwittingly participates in this system. I asked her how she deals with this seedy aspect of the industry, and what she thinks about the rare cases of women who are seemingly coming into porn not by making an informed decision that it is the best way to pay for school or the optimal job based on their work experience and future goals, but, as it appears from her story, because someone pressured them. Diana insisted that before every shoot she always asks the actresses if they understand the conditions under which they are agreeing to work. "When I get there the first thing I ask them is 'Do you know how much you are getting paid?'" Diana said, "Because when this particular pimp brings them, sometimes they don't know."[48] She explained that the women she encounters show their knowing authorization of their own participation in porn work, though payment is a grayer issue. Even if so-called pimps and pimp-like producers pressure, manipulate, and mislead them, at times these marginal women porn workers do refuse to do the work. "Sometimes they are like 'Fuck this, I'm out,' and other times they are like 'Yeah sure, I'm okay with

$200,'" Diana explained. Admitting that the situation exploits women, Diana also asserted that she has not seen evidence that these women were made to work in pornography without their knowledge or consent, at least not on set: "I never get a girl who gets there and is crying as she is taking her clothes off. You know the stereotype."[49]

When I pressed her on the ethics of working with women who appear to be coerced, Diana insightfully suggested that the larger structures of coercion—especially economic inequality—function as the real culprits that compel black women to perform sex work. Rather than becoming enraged at the injustice of women working under the control of a greedy agent or boyfriend, she stressed that because women's primary motivation was economic, critics might shift their focus from blame and ungrounded polemics about "trafficking" to understanding of the complexities shaping women's labor choices. Instead of assuming the women are powerless victims in their exploitation, Diana said she learned that they are conscious agents working in pornography for reasons porn observers might not expect. Diana illustrated her point with a moving story about one woman contracted through a "pimp":

> So we do the scene—and most of them are, like, dead, but this girl did a good scene, usually you get what you pay for, but this girl did pretty well. She wasn't a great looker, but she had good energy. We write her the check and she says, "Thank you so much so much for this. It's my son's birthday, he's turning five years old, I promised I would take him to Disneyland and now I can do it." Hugs, tears, "Thank you so much." She did it to take her son to Disneyland! So should I have turned her away? You never know [what someone's story is], and who am I to say, "Fuck Disneyland, go back to school?" Her son wanted to ride the damn teacups. She needed $200 to take him. And she was so happy, so happy.[50]

Whether women are motivated to enter pornography to pay for school or because they aspire only to give their children more opportunities, what is clear is that sex work offers the kind of income few other jobs can, especially for young, working-class and poor black women who are at the bottom of the labor force.[51] Black women's larger social marginalization and vulnerability within the political economy produce a context in which sex work in exotic dance or adult film provides an attractive option for gaining a higher standard of living. However, this social location also keeps them marginalized and vulnerable within the sex industry. Racism, sexism, and classism structure the terrain black women must negotiate both inside and outside of pornography.

They make choices given these overwhelming constraints. Ultimately, they are trying to make lives for themselves the best way they know how.

Once in the porn industry the question of money becomes ever more complex. If money is tied to one's erotic capital, then maintaining and enhancing that value is extremely important. For black women performers, the diminished erotic capital attached to their bodies means that they must labor harder to "catch up" to women whose desirability is attached to racial privilege, a privilege premised upon the devaluation of women of color. Yet because white women are only able to achieve their feminine desirability through the contrast to and supremacy over racial minority women, black women's erotic capital is necessarily reduced by comparison. This issue is borne out in wage competition and hierarchies that organize the industry and divide women along lines of race, where black actresses receive pay rates one-half to three-quarters of those that white actresses receive (see chapter 6).

It is also means that erotic capital is shaped by markers of racialized beauty and desirability within porn aesthetics. Lighter-but-tanned skin and long hair are most valued for women in the mainstream, heterosexual porn market, as are larger breasts, thin frames, and small waistlines (except for the fetish markets for larger-bodied women), and a pretty, feminine embodiment. For African Americans and other people of color fashioning their bodies in order to garner higher erotic capital may also mean conforming to beauty ideals within their own racial or ethnic communities as they operate in the porn marketplace. Many black women performers, for instance, cultivate a professional persona and appearance that reflect the desirability of curviness—smaller waists and ample hips and buttocks—and long, flowing (not short and kinky) hair. Many actresses work out with trainers or in dance classes to tone and shape their bodies to these ideals and to the demands of their craft, and they spend significant time on hairdressing and grooming. Consequently, porn workers expend a great deal of their earned income and time on fashioning their bodies to conform to the aesthetic standards of their trade.

In speaking to numerous performers, I found that they perform considerable unpaid labor and expend substantial wages in order to do their work. A porn actress seeking to earn $50,000 a year would need to work in five to six scenes a month if she were to earn $800 per scene, a typical rate and annual pay for black actresses in the adult industry that take into account both high-end professionals and lower-end causal workers. Of her nearly $4,200 a month of pretax earnings she may spend 30 to 35 percent, or more, on necessities for her job: $100 a month on hair (black hairstyles like authentic hair weaves, braids, and chemical relaxers can cost $200–$300 and last two to three months); $200 on manicures, pedicures, hair waxing, and other personal grooming; $200 on mandatory HIV/AIDS and STD testing (this was required every twenty-eight days for working in the professional adult film industry; recently the requirement has changed to testing every fourteen days); $300 on costumes and clothing for media appearances; $100 on cosmetics, $100 on gym memberships, exercise classes, and trainers (a fit and flexible body is often essential); $400–$625 on agents' fees; and $400 on promotional materials, consultants, other beauty and health treatments, and supplies (including birth control). These expenditures are necessary for most actresses, their gendered labor requiring actresses to spend slightly more than actors on their appearances and bodily preparations for sexual performance. In addition to expenses common for all workers such as transportation to and from work sites, taxes, and health insurance (which is purchased individually by independent contract workers), job-related expenditures of $10,000 and more for plastic surgeries such as breast enhancements are unique to sex-and-entertainment-industry workers. Other industry-related costs may be hundreds and thousands of dollars per year for hiring web designers to create and manage a performer's website, photographers, makeup artists, publicists, accountants, legal counsel, and even personal security guards for some events. For those that do not live in close proximity to the node of porn production in Southern California or who must travel for shoots or industry events elsewhere, flights and hotel expenses are significant.

Furthermore, an enormous amount of unpaid labor is spent on prepping the body for shoots (including dieting and enemas for anal sex), networking or working with agents to attain bookings, sexually transmitted infection testing, appearances for self or corporate promotion, research, education, and skill development, waiting around on set for long hours, and even mentoring other performers. For these reasons, and because of the mechanistic disposability of actresses in the adult film industry that limits their appeal to management seeking new and fresh talent for their products, many porn workers find themselves pressed to accept lower pay rates or to garner income from other sources. In the latter case, it is not uncommon for porn actresses to pursue other kinds of sex work such as exotic dancing, private escorting, webcamming, phone sex, fetish modeling, and for-pay Domination/Submission. Each of these other pursuits requires its own costs and expenditures for equipment and self-fashioning as well as unpaid labor to pursue and develop skills for the craft. They are part of a mobile and overlapping economy of activity that porn workers engage at various points in their careers. Yet they are economic activities for which being a porn star tends to garner a certain measure of prestige and added material benefit, even if outside of the sex industry these very qualities are perceived as probable hazards to one's job security. In this way, gaining a name as a porn star prior to, or in step with, these other ventures becomes an important tool in leveraging erotic capital in the sexual field, though these skills may not be assets to building opportunities for human capital in future careers outside of the sex business.

However, the field is uneven as a result of systemic racial inequality. If a typical black porn star in her late teens to middle twenties may make $50,000 or more a year from her film work—an income that, depending on whether or not she pays taxes (I calculated a 28 percent effective tax rate using only the standard deduction) or pulls in cash under the table, may be significant for a working-class or middle-class young person without a college degree at that age—white porn stars can and do make considerably more. One producer noted that it was typical for white actresses to earn $100,000 a year as contract stars, and that many actresses without exclusive contracts tying them to production companies tend to earn even more. If the pay rates for black actresses are virtually half as much as for white actresses, black actresses have to work practically twice as much to earn the same as white actresses. Instead of five to six scenes a month they would need to work ten to twelve. Filming a scene can range anywhere from two hours up to fourteen hours if actors are called to remain on set or if extensive preparation or postproduction work is required. Because of all the preparation involved and the intensity of the work, actresses typically shoot only one scene per day, unless their second scene is for the same film shoot. Taking a day's work as an average of eight hours, a black porn actress working six scenes a month would work forty-eight hours, but if she wanted to make an income close to a white porn star's she would need to work ninety-six hours, or six days longer a month in terms of a normal forty-hour work week. Since opportunities for work for black actresses are fewer because there are less roles available in porn that features black performers, one way these performers may try to bridge the gap is to take on roles that call for more intense or technical sex acts, such as anal or multi-partner sex, which garner higher pay rates. Another is to lower one's pay rate in order to appeal to the low end of the market where unscrupulous producers often hire casual and cheaper labor for their videos. And finally, as mentioned above, these actresses may feel it necessary to supplement their income with labor in other areas of the sex industry such as escorting, which is criminalized and unregulated and thus a riskier kind of work.

Considering these racialized wage inequalities, the costs of creating the body and persona of a porn star, and the incalculable unpaid and emotional or affective labor involved in porn work, many find it to be less lucrative in the long run than they had imagined when they started. Still, for many black women coming from working-class families the potential for relatively high earnings and disposable income as compared to other jobs open to them or even what their parents make is a significant factor in choosing the porn industry. There is also flexibility and sense of autonomy and creativity embedded in the work, which feature as major attractions to enter and to remain in the business as long as possible. With growing markets for older women in porn there are more opportunities for established performers to maintain careers in the business, or for women in their late twenties, thirties, forties, and more senior, to contemplate porn work as a labor option. Thanks to the interventions of veteran performers such as Nina Hartley to produce an economy of desire around sexuality of women more mature than those in the "barely legal" market, and to broader cultural shifts in the sexualization of older women in popular culture, such as the figures of Madonna in her fifties and the character Samantha (Kim Cattrall) of *Sex and the City* (1998–2004), building a career beyond the typical six to eighteen months of most young actresses is now possible. Greater visibility for pornography in popular culture also means that younger workers enter the adult entertainment industry with a certain set of knowledge and expectations about how long they intend to stay and what they want to get out of it. Nevertheless, the transience of the porn performer population not only made it difficult for me to keep track of my informants as they left (and sometimes returned and left again) the adult film industry but also reflects the precarity of porn work for most. The variability of porn labor makes it extremely difficult for workers to organize and collectively push for institutional changes that benefit labor, and it hides or obscures a class of workers and labor regimes that are instrumental to the globalized business of sexual media, U.S. cultural capitalism, and California's economy.

## Sex

"When I was younger," said India, "I was so intrigued by sex." Several performers I interviewed discussed being fascinated by pornography or curious about sexuality as youths, and having a longtime interest in sex as pleasure, rebellion, and the subversion of sexual norms. India talked about being "interested" and "intrigued" by sex as a girl, saying that she took pleasure in surreptitiously watching softcore movies on cable television and was especially fascinated by looking at men's magazines like *Players* and *Playboy*. "I remember seeing the Pam Grier issue. That's a classic one of *Players*. I just looked at it and was like wow! She's so pretty. She was a big actress at the time, and still now, and I thought she can do that and still look so beautiful doing it. And *Playboy*. I thought, wow, I'd love to do something like that one time."[52] India explained that pornographic materials featuring beautiful and glamorous women, especially black women like Pam Grier, sparked her interest in sex and inspired her imagination. Although she understood that these representations were not openly condoned, India dreamed of becoming like the dazzling and sensual women in the glossy nude pictures.

"I was so sexual when I was younger. Not molested, but just sexual." India made sure to assert that her sexuality emerged from her own desire and was not the result of abuse. "The group I was in, we were sexual and just attracted to each other."[53] Quick to point out that her early sexual explorations were with girls, not boys, India wanted to make clear that her sense of sexuality during girlhood was not a result of exploitation, but of exploration. This distinction shows India's awareness that her "risky" sexual behavior as an adult is often explained by pointing to instances of improper childhood sexualization, and often, maltreatment.[54] While sexuality between girls is cast as a further dimension of deviance for sexualized girls, India underscored how such relationships were essential to her growing sexual subjectivity.

Like India, Carmen Hayes pointed to her long-held pleasures in non-normative sexuality as a way to establish a claim for hyperconsent in her sex work: "I was very comfortable with nudity (I'm a little bit of a nudist) so it was easy for me to adapt to nudity. I was always open-minded, a little bit of a wild child. And I had been such a goody-two-shoes all my life."[55] Although as a young woman she was expected to present herself as respectable and chaste, Carmen chose to claim promiscuity as a form of rebellion. After getting top grades in high school and pursuing a nursing degree, Carmen found that she was interested in exhibitionism and sexual performance, first in exotic dance, and later in the porn industry. Similarly, Sierra described herself as a "pervert" in order to push back against the double standard that frames women interested in sex, but not love, as essentially immoral and dangerous:[56] "I'm into my sexuality. I like being a pervert. It wasn't anything that was forced on me. I didn't have a bad childhood or was raped, I just happen to enjoy sex. I always approached it with a kind of male reasoning. It was just sex. A lot of women want to talk about sex and love and all that, for me it had nothing at all to do with that. For me it was a recreational thing. Something I'd do for fun."[57]

While India aspired to be an icon of sexiness and beauty in pornographic magazines, and Carmen appropriated wildness to subvert the "goody-two-shoes" mold, Sierra saw herself as a pervert and "tomboy" with a "male reasoning" toward sex.[58] Sierra actively disidentified with the confining characteristics of traditional, feminine, romantic sexuality, and instead self-consciously modeled an active, brazen, public, and carefree sexuality, associating these qualities with her own masculinity. India, Carmen, and Sierra all responded to my questions about their sexual history by asserting, though I never asked specifically about it, that they were not molested, coerced, or raped. All three women offered a reevaluation of female sexuality in terms that disturb the sexual double standard and conventional expectations for young women's sexual expression.

Their claims reveal how many sex workers are highly alert to the fact that their mobilization of sex for money challenges hegemonic notions of sexuality as a private and reproductive matter, and that women's sexuality must necessarily cohere to concepts of purity, respectability, passivity, and fidelity. Indeed, they display a keen awareness of what Viviana Zelizer calls the "hostile worlds view." For Zelizer, the case of sex workers' use of sex for income exposes the "rigid moral boundaries between market and intimate domains."[59] The hostile worlds view is a dominant discourse that sees intimacy as private, ruled by sentiment, and solidarity, whereas the market is public and a site of calculation and efficiency. According to the hostile worlds view, when love and money come together they are imagined as producing "moral contamination."[60] As Gayle Rubin argues, because sex workers deploy exchangist modes of sex for profit, they, along with the rest of the "sexual rabble" of people having nonmonogamous, nonheterosexual, unmarried, noncommercial, nonprocreative, or non-"vanilla" sex, fall outside the "charmed circle" of dominant sexual morality and sexual hierarchy. This ideology, developed from Western religious, medical, psychiatric, and educational traditions, maintains "extreme and punitive stigma" against those on the devalued "outer limits" of the charmed circle. According to Rubin, whereas "individuals whose behavior stands high in this hierarchy are rewarded with certified mental health, respectability, legality, social and physical mobility, institutional support, and material benefits," those who fall lower on the scale are "subjected to the presumption of mental illness, disreputability, criminality, restricted social and physical mobility, loss of institutional support, and economic sanctions."[61]

As India, Carmen, and Sierra show, they understand how being placed lower on the scale of sexual hierarchy establishes them as disreputable, marginal, and vulnerable subjects. By describing their sexuality during girlhood as the basis for their continued position outside normative female sexuality, they are arguing against the common misconception that when girls display aggressive sexuality, it comes from outside of themselves, an external force of abuse, rather than inside themselves, one of self-discovery. Objectifying and policing discourses and institutions of gendered power profoundly impact girls; they are not supposed to be sexual agents who want to experiment with other children or read *Players Magazine*. Challenging these discourses, the majority of my informants emphasized individual and communal forms of erotic exploration and transgression as important to their identity formation during adolescence and to later life choices. Asserting their sexual agency in choosing to work in pornography, my informants described the industry as offering professional and personal advantages, including the opportunity to express an "erotic capacity" that is denied many women.[62] Further, my informants presented themselves as making decisions based on logic rather than powerlessness. Their comments reflect an awareness of dominant antipornography feminism that assumes women's victimization and lack of sexual agency is integral to women's experiences in the porn industry. For instance, Sierra underscores her careful analytical thinking when describing her reasoning for choosing porn labor: "I was twenty-five [when I started]. I had already been [an exotic] dancer for some time when I decided I wanted to get into the industry. I had thought about it when I was younger, but I knew this was something that would really affect my life, so I wanted to make absolutely sure that this is what I wanted to do. So I waited until I felt like it was something that I really wanted to do."[63]

Like many of the women who began working in pornography in the 1980s and '90s, Sierra started in her twenties. Rather than start porn work as soon as she hit the legal age of eighteen, as was common for performers in the 2000s, she waited. She really wanted to take time to consider what the job would offer and how it would affect her life. Many of Sierra's generation of adult actresses already had some experience in the sex industry and learned about sexual performance as exotic dancers.

Established and veteran actresses like Sierra worry that the younger women coming into pornography at eighteen, nineteen, or twenty years of age may not have skills to successfully handle the pressures and exploitations of the sex industry. They believe younger actresses are still just beginning to learn about their sexuality when they begin to commodify it as performers in porn, due to overwhelming constraints on their gaining knowledge, including poor sex education. Young women are increasingly becoming the main workforce in porn, as the adult industry focuses on building markets for youth sexuality. Some established actresses feel the age limit for actors entering the business should be raised to twenty-one. Diana DeVoe argued that the price of initial screening tests for STDs and HIV, which are required to work in any film, should be raised from $150 to $800 in order to create a disincentive for young women who might enter the industry without fully understanding what the work involves. In essence, these more established actresses worry that young women seeking opportunities for expressing sexual pleasure in pornography may, when not prepared to navigate the tricky terrain of porn work, end up confronting a tougher reality than they might expect.

Despite the potential pitfalls, self-motivated sexual exploration is a significant factor in black young women's complex considerations when deciding to work in the commercial sex industry. The desire to explore queer sexual practices motivates women like Aryana Starr to look to pornography. Aryana, who worked as a medical assistant in a cardiology office before deciding to enter the pornography business, explained: "One of the motivations for me was sexuality. Because [in] many of my previous relationships there were things that I wanted to do sexually that they couldn't understand. If I wanted two guys or two girls or even five guys, that's just me. I couldn't go to my guy at the time, and say, 'Hey this is what I want.' So at least I can live out my fantasies through doing porn and enjoy myself. Because I do enjoy myself on camera, which most people don't. You can tell on their faces."[64]

Several performers said that their choice to participate in porn was born out of the desire to explore sex and their bodies in ways that were essentially impossible in their previous lives and relationships. "A lot of my sexual firsts were on camera," said Sinnamon Love. "I love the things that I've done because I've always done things that I've wanted to experience or I can imagine having a fantasy about."[65] Like Sinnamon, Aryana found pornography work offered a chance to live out her fantasies, and to do so on camera in a way that portrayed sensuality and joy. "I'm still actively sexual and I wanted to put it on film," she explained.[66]

Sexual experimentation through porn's exhibitionist, public performance of sex provided these actresses a sense of power, heightened their fantasy imagination, and expanded their feelings of pleasure. Some of my informants felt they could experiment with queer or nonnormative sexual practices and identities in a relatively safe and professional environment through pornography. Yet while Aryana proudly claimed that her work in pornography has opened up possibilities to pursue desires previously unfulfilled, she also noted that "most people don't" enjoy their performances, and "you can tell on their faces."[67] This comment reflects the ways in which many informants described their own agency and pleasure in their work as exceptional within the industry. This rhetorical move may indicate the difficulty of acknowledging the constraints on agency and pleasure in the pornography industry for those currently working inside of it, and who have livelihoods attached to the constant assertion (especially in interviews) that they are enjoying themselves. This situation raises the questions: even when sexual pleasure is a key factor in performers' choice to work in the industry, to what extent do black women porn workers find pornography a productive space to pursue eroticism and pleasure?

Jeannie Pepper asserted that a passion for sex encouraged her to join the sex industry in the 1980s. "Hurray for sex!" she declared. "It made me feel free." She consciously rejected conceptions of sexualized black women as either deviant or victims of exploitation. Instead, she argued that black women should flip the script and take charge of their sexual agency. "How come there are not more black women doing this?" she wondered.[68] This self-determined stance, wrought by complexities of black women's sexual politics, asks a question that has been difficult to answer. Because of the brutal history of racialized sexual violence and objectification, many black women have inherited what Darlene Clark Hine calls black women's "culture of dissemblance," the tendency to mask or eschew nonnormative sex as a mechanism to protect one's sense of womanhood and identity from attack.[69] Jeannie's provocation powerfully exposes the prohibitions most black women face in confronting their sexual desires in the context of historical and stereotypical discourses about the always already deviant nature of black female sexuality, and the kinds of policing they face from within their own communities. Black feminist critics have grappled with how to account for the crucial ways in which sexual exploitation, abuse, and stereotype have affected black women's sexual identities and experiences. Yet the focus on sexuality as a site of trauma, erasure, and misrepresentation has left us without productive ways to talk about sexual agency and erotic sovereignty. In fact, this focus has made us suspicious of women's claims to agency, and almost too willing to dismiss young black women's complex deployment of sexuality in society. The focus on trauma has in some ways obscured more than revealed black women's attempts to make sense of their sexual lives. We black feminist critics have not taken seriously black women's testimony on the nature of sex as work, because we have not accounted for how these self-understandings force us to grapple with our own shame. For fear of being labeled hypersexual, deviant, or an outlaw to the black community, black feminist critics have allowed the culture of dissemblance and respectability politics to discipline and police the sexual identities, expressions, and desires of black sexual marginals, including sex workers like Jeannie Pepper. These self-imposed masks have made the desires of Jeannie, India, or Sierra invisible and illegible.

"You're not supposed to talk about liking sex because you are already assumed to be a whore," Jeannie asserted of this complex set of discourses shaping black women's sexual expression.[70] Her comment particularly addresses the discourse of black female hypersexuality in both the African American community and the broader U.S. society. Jeannie spotlights the ways in which conservative values about sexuality delimit acceptable sexual behavior to a narrowly defined heteronormativity, to which women must conform because they are already deemed whores. Within the discourse of black female hypersexuality, doing anything that seems whorish invites further ridicule of not just the woman, but of the black community as a whole. Because of this, black women in pornography must shield themselves both from the larger social stigmas of sex work and from accusations that they necessarily promote ideas about black female sexual deviance. This policing of black sexual deviance motivates a range of repressive discourses and actions by sexual marginals, and reinforces, through shaming and other mechanisms, the power of patriarchy, heterosexism, and sexual racism in the lives of black women, men, and queers. As Cathy Cohen argues, it effectively erases the political interventions of those who do not uphold ideal or respectable standards of sexual conduct, and rendering all of these nonconformists as queer outsiders to black communities, falls in line with a system of sexual value that creates black people as deviant outcasts from the charmed circle of gender-sexual normativity and political citizenship.[71]

Such ideas about hypersexuality have had immense power to define not just black womanhood, but, as in the case of the image of the sexually irresponsible welfare queen, they have had important socioeconomic effects, like the rollback of resources and services since the gains of the 1960s, to working-class and poor black women and their families. These structural and systemic ramifications of this sexual discourse have had many important effects on labor and life for black women sex workers. They shape the very options available for sex work and the highly contested nature of sexual representations within mass media and popular culture. Whorishness and hypersexuality saturate the very meaning of black women's sexuality and the ways in which black women think about their erotic choices and desires. The politics of sexuality is thus one of the most critical issues that black illicit erotic working women confront as they harness their sexualities for economic profit, personal advantage, and pleasure, against long-standing cultural and social prohibitions and intrusions. Glamour girl, pervert, wild child—these morphologies mobilize a politics of deviance to resist hypersexualization-as-harm.[72] Moving against the black community's injunctions to normalize their sexuality, and counter to dominant demands to put it at the service of state and corporate interests, black women illicit erotic workers instead perform a kind of political and cultural labor: sexual dissent.[73]

Sexual dissent, or what I term "erotic sovereignty," disrupts deep-seated discourses of sexual responsibility, gendered propriety, and racial loyalty. This dissent prioritizes, or at least aims toward, an autonomous, independent, and self-defining sexuality, while also acknowledging the forms of affiliation, relation, and responsibility that sexual subjects have to one another. Though making money is the primary motive for sex workers entering the pornography business, queer transgressions, erotic sovereignty, and sexual dissent are, if not motivations, erotic sovereignty factors in the cultural labor of black women's sex work. "I love sex. I love the sex business," contends Vanessa Blue. "I have no intention of leaving. Especially now that I'm an owner. I run my own business. I run several websites. I shoot. I do everything, top to bottom. And I want to do it because I want other girls to see that they can do it too."[74] A successful actress, director, producer, and webmistress, Vanessa asserts sexual agency and envisions an erotic imaginary in which her own black feminist pornographic gaze prioritizes black women's porn work and self-authorship. Embracing a kind of public promiscuity and sexual outlaw status, Vanessa aspires to a self-governing sexuality instead of one at the service of another producer's whims or broader social proscriptions to, as a black woman, avoid the taint of pornographic hypersexuality. Beyond identifying her own interests and needs, Vanessa also understands that her work necessarily influences others, including other sex workers.

Vanessa encourages women entering the industry to cultivate practices of self-presentation and autonomy in their work, to creatively capitalize on their own desires, and to focus on the ownership of their own sexual images and products. In these important ways, Vanessa answers Jeannie Pepper's call for more black women to take up pornography and use sex for their own needs and desires. Black women in porn are attentive actors in the regime of racial fetishism that shapes pornographic representation, and the social and legal apparatus that sustains it. As Jeannie asserts, black women are always "already assumed to be" whores. Jeannie employs her own illicit desirability in a kind of sexual repertoire: by precisely staging her sexuality so as to acknowledge the taboo desire for it, she shows that racial fetishism can actually be taken up by its objects and used differently. Intervening in pornography by creating images of black women's self-possessed sexuality, Jeannie and Vanessa enact the politics of erotic sovereignty.

While pornography, a business historically and presently run by and for men, may not allow women total sexual empowerment, the testimonies of the women I interviewed demonstrate that it holds extraordinary potential for cultivating erotic sovereignty, though most performers see it primarily as a space for earning a livelihood. "I love sex, and I love watching porn," Vanessa Blue argued, "so how do you take what you love and make money off of it? You figure it out."[75] Vanessa's commentary shows how often women in the business are attracted to the medium of pornography itself and ultimately see it as a mixed economy for sexual performance, politicized exhibitionism, and creative entrepreneurship. The adult entertainment business offers a unique setting where black women can pursue the enactment of authentic and scripted sexual desires in a relatively safe, legal, and professional environment, and can get paid for doing it. A majority of porn actresses claimed that their longtime fascination with sex factored into a primarily monetary decision to enter pornography for a period, or even make it a career. Some believed that they could use porn work to explore new practices and pleasures, but that they might also face pressures to enact sexual performances they were not particularly interested in, or willing to take on. "I set a rule for myself from the very beginning that I wouldn't do anything that I didn't find pleasurable," asserted Sinnamon. "I wouldn't do anything that I wouldn't do in my normal life."[76]

Although politicized sexual expression is a major facet of their work, many performers allude to the constraints that powerfully influence their abilities to assert this desire for expression. Many do not discuss how their own agency has been compromised in ways that may leave them feeling sexually disempowered, but they sometimes hint at the ways that others do not enjoy their work. Some performers were quite candid about the fact that they did not feel "free" enough to truly experience pleasure in their work. "I've never really had the best sexual experience on set," explained Lola Lane, "because I have that out-of-body experience. I never let go mentally, like I'm never fully relaxed."[77] Lola shows how the business of pornography can actively work against performers' desire for sovereignty in their erotic labor. The work setting influences how performers feel about their expressions of eroticism and the extent to which they might mobilize their performances to make political claims about the integrity and desirability of black female sexuality. When asked if they actually achieve orgasm while working on set, the overwhelming majority of the women I interviewed said they rarely do. "I've never really had a real orgasm on camera," Lola admits.[78] Even Vanessa Blue, who by her own account loves watching porn and making her own hardcore media, confided that she only had one authentic orgasm on camera when she was an actress.[79]

It is widely recognized that mainstream, heterosexual pornography, although highly diverse, represents a narrow set of sex practices, bodies, and desires. Pornographic media and their production practices define, or confine, the sexual performances of actors. For example, not only must actresses remain conscious of their appearance and the angles of their bodies during a scene, filming takes place in a room full of male crew members. In practice, sex work in porn is fairly procedural: a certain number of minutes performing oral sex; a number in each of several positions for penetration shots; pauses for still photographs or repositioning the camera, lights, or microphone. The reality of sex in porn often contrasts with the desires and aspirations of actresses entering the industry. Porn film sets also differed from how I, as an outsider, imagined them. Rather than spaces of erotic play and leisure, as depicted in scenes from popular movies like *Boogie Nights*, porn film shoots, as Sharon Abbott also described in her study of pornographic filmmaking, are exceedingly routine and mundane.[80] The sex is, depending on the director and production company, highly choreographed. The settings, at least for black- and interracial-cast films, are often desexualized, with scenes taking place in sterile, shabby, awkward, or uncomfortable film sets, rental homes, or hotel rooms.

"The lights are so heavy and bright that if you put an egg on your body it will sizzle and fry," Spantaneeus Xtasty, an adult film star from the 1990s, described.[81] On one set I felt dizzy and nauseous because the air was so warm due to all the lights used to illuminate the set and, because the sound of air conditioners running can be picked up on the highly sensitive microphones used, no air-conditioning was allowed during the shoot. I still remember the smell of the crew's burgers-and-fries dinner wafting through the air as I watched Marie Luv and Mark Davis perform an intense anal sex scene. In general, on sets the actors' bodies are directed in awkward and unnatural positions, with actresses being constantly reminded to "open up" for the camera by moving their hips to optimize the view of penetration. This positioning adds to the athletic nature of the sex that performers must undertake, and the hot lights and still air mean that the actors can get sweaty and tire easily. There are many pauses to reposition the cameras, lights, or microphones, so finding a comfortable rhythm for pleasurable penetration is also a challenge for performers. Although some directors and production studios allow actresses to request specific actors to work with in their scenes, most actresses do not have that luxury, and are only asked, if at all, which actors they will *not* work with. Actresses must produce enough sexual chemistry to deliver a successful scene, even if they just met the actor on set and the chemistry between them does not quite gel. If they are performing a Girl-Girl scene—as same sex scenes with women are known in the straight side of the porn industry—despite not identifying as lesbian or bisexual, or particularly enjoying sex with women, actresses must portray a believable scene. In the heterosexual market for pornography the focus is on actresses, especially their facial reactions to the sex, so the burden of developing chemistry and conveying a convincing scene for the viewer tends to rest on them to a much greater degree than on actors.

Male performers on heterosexual- and gay-market films face extreme pressure because they are required to maintain an erection and ejaculate upon the director's command. If he fails to perform, an actor usually will not get paid, and his production company loses money. Investment banker turned AVN award-winning adult performer Tyler Knight told me about his first porn shoot, and how he learned the hard way about the challenging nature of porn work for actors:

> It was a restaurant scene and there were fifteen or sixteen civilian non-porn extras there, milling about, sitting in the restaurant, whatever, and there was this contract girl, sitting at the table. I am supposed to be the waiter. I pull down my pants, trying to get my dick hard, trying, trying and trying. Nothing is working, I am up and down, up and down, up and down, crew is looking at me. . . . I mean at that point [in my life] I had only been naked in front of my girlfriends, God, my doctor, and my mom, so I'm thinking, "Fuck, this is hard." There is a camera underneath my balls, a boom mic bopped me in the head and stuff, and I just couldn't get in the zone. I couldn't focus! There is actually nothing sexual about this whatsoever, it's very clinical. So, the director Veronica Hart, a legendary performer who was then in [charge of] production at VCA, gave me a [pornographic] magazine, says, "Here, take this, go in the bathroom, jerk off. When you are hard, come back here." So, I took the magazine. I think, "This is easy. I jerk off all the time." Three strokes in, I pop in my hands. Game over. At that moment I am done. Thank you sponsors! So, at that point, my pants were [still] on set. I am actually wearing [only] a T-shirt. I am two stories up I am looking out the window, and I am actually doing physics, you know, calculating, if I

run, jump, and tuck with a certain trajectory will I injure myself or can I actually run and get to my car and get out of there in time? My car was like five blocks away. The only way it's cute if someone's running down the street with a shirt and no pants is if your name is Winnie the Pooh. So, you know, I had to go back and face the music. [Veronica] was very gracious, she said, "It's okay. It's your first scene. Change your stage name and come back." So I did.[82]

Tyler is also a creative writer and poet, and his story humanizes the story of what it means for men to perform in the adult industry, though his understanding director was much more patient and understanding of his dilemma than most other directors I have heard about in a situation like this. In order to avoid this kind of embarrassment, many adult actors have increasingly employed erection aids like Viagra, in pill or injection form, which allow them to gain and maintain erections for long periods of time. Because their careers depend on their reputation for being reliable performers, and because there is a great deal of shame in failing to achieve erection in a room full of costars and crew members, actors often risk the long-term health implications of repeated use of these medications.[83]

If an actor has difficulty getting an erection and is seen to be holding up the shoot, actresses are sometimes expected to help the actor get aroused by performing oral sex, work they do not necessarily feel they have been paid to perform. In addition, actresses report that the intense, fast-paced, athletic sex actors are expected to perform, which is rooted in a particular fetishization of male hypersexuality, takes its physical toll on them. Sasha Brabuster told me:

> What I don't like about their performance is they're doing it for the camera, which I'm not saying is wrong, but he's trying to nail you another asshole. He's trying to nail you another, you know, tomorrow. He has to do it to perform in front of the director. He's getting paid. Now you're hollerin' and beggin' for Jesus [*laughing*] but, you know it's like "Damn, I'm glad this is over. He was fine but damn that shit hurt." Where in your personal life, you are in complete control. "Get the fuck off me, get out." You know what I'm saying? So that's the only bad part about it."[84]

As Sasha describes, the nature of heterosexual porn shoots creates tension among actors, makes actresses feel they are being used and made to do extra work, and underscores the difficulties all actors face with this particular type of embodied work. The business of sex on pornography sets is never lost on the pornographic workers. Because their erotic labor is essentially routinized, managed, and disciplined for a profit, it is not surprising that my informants report difficulty in achieving sexual gratification and orgasm on set.

Spantaneeus Xtasty described how, although she very much enjoyed sex and erotic performance, when working in adult film she found it easier to divorce authentic eroticism from her work. "I always looked at it as I'm going to the office: I get up, jump in the shower, play my music, get my coffee . . . Once I get there, I'm in it. No one is ever going to see, oh, I don't feel like being here. I'm going to always make a good scene. I have to remember, I'm a product."[85] Conscious of the fact that her performance must be reliable, compelling, and convincing in order to sell, and create more demand for her work, Spantaneeus understood that her erotic performance was essential to her success in the industry. However, she also articulated how focusing on the sex as *work*, rather than as personal or authentic self-expression, in turn helped her create a distinction between her sex labor and her sex life. "There were a few times when I enjoyed myself," she shared, "but not to the point where [I thought], wow, I want to date this guy and have his babies!"[86]

While many find it necessary to maintain a distinction between sex for work and sex for personal pleasure, several actresses acknowledge that sex in pornography has its fascinations and pleasures. They maintain that what is important is seeing themselves as empowered to make choices about sex in their work or personal lives. Ultimately, they want to mobilize sex in ways they see fit, and that includes playing up hypersexuality for personal pleasure in addition to economic gain. Yet, these illicit erotic workers also understand the restrictions on sexual pleasure in an industry designed around profiting from it, and a society aimed at stigmatizing it. For instance, Vanessa Del Rio, who still maintains a large following on her popular website, refers to herself as a "slut goddess." She said, "If slut means a 'wanton, horny, nasty woman' then how can I deny that? Every piece of mail I get tells me that they love me for it. That's why I call myself a 'slut goddess.'"[87] Like Sierra, who embraces the identity of "pervert," Vanessa Del Rio shows how some women try to emphasize their desires and expertise as sex workers, as well as reworking discourses framing them as deviant, abnormal, and perverse. Vanessa Del Rio said that her Catholic upbringing played an important role in producing sexuality and eroticism as a no-go zone. "I have to deal with what I've done because I was raised Catholic," Vanessa explained. "I have the stigma on myself because society has instilled in me what I did was slutty or I was a whore. . . . There's a part of me that says, 'Oh my God' and a part of me that says, 'You go girl, I like it.' Because I did it. And I can't deny it and I will not deny it. I will not try to repent for something I found pleasurable and still do."[88]

Conscious of the prohibitions, Vanessa Del Rio defies them by building a persona that retrieves sexual agency from "sin" and "perversion." Her bold claim to inhabit the role of slut goddess and forefront her pleasure, autonomy, and desirability shows that, despite the stigma and consequences of her role in pornography, she refuses to deny or repudiate her own choices. The power of choice in sexuality is something sex workers believe most feminists eschew in their denouncements of the adult industry. Sinnamon, who has also described herself as a "slut" and uses the idea of sin in her professional persona, critiqued this view, saying, "I feel that the woman that says that that woman doesn't have a right to do [sexual labor in pornography], or that that woman isn't a feminist because she chooses to do something that's not the norm, that's not feminism because you're saying that this woman doesn't have a right to do something that she wants to do."[89] Dismissing antiporn feminist critiques, Sinnamon adopts a kind of sex-positive feminist discourse of choice and autonomy to argue for women's agency in participating in sexual expression and sexual labor. Instead of focusing on how to expand women's choices and improve their conditions, Sinnamon believes many feminists are backwardly fighting over the issue of whether pornography should be acknowledged as a form of work, when, of course, it is. Moreover, Sinnamon described the right to do sex work as equivalent with other rights to choice, privacy, and access that feminists have fought for: "Women should have the right to be able to make a choice, whether it's in employment, or social status . . . the right to abortion, or the right to choose what to do with their mind, body, and soul."[90] While some feminists might be critical of this brand of feminism, or even see Sinnamon's articulation as a form of postfeminism that reduces feminist politics to personal rights, her view is an important part of the feminist conversation and should not be dismissed.

Professional adult actresses like Sinnamon and Vanessa Del Rio argue that their use of the slut trope is a conscious attempt to negotiate the expectations and prohibitions of female sexuality. Giving voice to sexual autonomy and erotic sovereignty, these women ultimately show that sex workers have important claims to make about feminism, the uses of sexuality, and the possibilities for sex work as a site of sexual dissent as well as labor. They use sluttiness to construct professional personae that acknowledge their own exploitation of sexuality, as well as their own pleasure. The slut identity also acknowledges other people's fascination with this transgression of proper gendered bound-

FIGURE 5.1. Sinnamon Love wants to be a "voice for sex positive black feminism." Courtesy of Sinnamon Love.

aries. The use of "slut" is both about how they see themselves and how they believe others see them. Although not all performers view themselves as sluts—in fact some disidentify with this identity—many do claim that their use of sexuality for pleasure and profit defies normative expectations for women, and especially black women. Nevertheless, aside from Sinnamon, few of the women I spoke to identified with being a feminist and many tended to see feminism as a "label for members of a white women's social movement that has no concrete link to Black women or the Black community."[91]

That many black porn actresses have an ambivalent relationship to the categories of slut and feminist is not surprising given the ways in which black women have experienced both. In light of the controversy over the Slut Walks in Canada and the United States in 2011, black feminists have been especially critical of the mainstream, primarily young, white feminist movement's re-appropriations of the term "slut" as a mobilizing counterdiscourse against public sexual harassment, or what they term "slut-shaming." The Crunk Feminist Collective, a group of hip hop generation feminists of color, writes:

> For Black women, our struggles with sexuality are to find the space of recognition that exists between the hypervisibility of our social construction as hoes, jezebels, hoochies, and skanks, and the invisibility

proffered by a respectability politics that tells us it's always safer to dissemble. To reclaim slut as an empowered experience of sexuality does not move Black women out of these binaries. We are always already sexually free, insatiable, ready to go, freaky, dirty, and by consequence, unrapeable. When it comes to reclamations of sexuality, in some senses, Black women are always already fucked.[92]

Not only do the Crunk Feminists see reclaiming slut as a limited sex-positive feminist strategy more appropriate for contesting the disciplining of white female sexuality into the normativity and purity associated with privileged white womanhood, they argue that similar strategies for black women would not capture the specific ways in which black female sexuality is policed and exploited, both symbolically and materially. They find it unlikely that "sisters will be lining up to go on a symbolic 'Ho Stroll' anytime soon."[93] But perhaps we should line up on the Ho Stroll—that is if we feminists take seriously the perspectives and lessons black sex workers have to teach us about sexual rights.

Black women struggling to define and articulate their sexual selves must operate within this discursive binary, in which their representations are invariably read as invisible and hypervisible. It is within this context that black women in porn venture to make their sexuality legible and their labor livable. While black feminist analyses are helpful to understand the ho/lady binary, we must examine the tactics black women sex workers such as Sinnamon deploy as they locate themselves within this and then explode it. Black sex workers labor both within and against confining scripts of black female sexuality. Their critiques of the limiting practices of production and feminist analyses of their agency provide meaningful insights to the entrenched and thorny issue of how one claims sexual subjectivity under the neoliberal commodification of all aspects of our intimate lives. Embracing the political nature of their sexual expression within sex work—their erotic sovereignty— or holding their erotic integrity intact against the disciplinary regimes of the sex industry, these performers show that representational binaries between the respectable woman and the debased ho fail to capture the dynamic lived experience and high stakes of black female sexuality. Black women's desires exceed these binaries, and they have the capacity to destroy them.

Fame

Montana Fishburne's story illustrates how many black women entering the adult film industry desire fame, though their lower erotic capital means that they struggle to attain it against the normative hierarchy that values white femininity. Nevertheless, fame is seen as an attractive path to wealth and material resources that lie outside of their grasp. Fame is key to gaining vital social power through the expansion of a consumer and leisure-oriented lifestyle. Indeed, the popular aspiration to become a star is perhaps one of the most significant aspects of the American culture of celebrity. According to P. David Marshall, the ideological power of celebrities emerges from their "familiarity and extraordinariness": their representation of the democratic ideal that stardom is fundamentally accessible alongside the late-capitalist ideal that "decadence and excess were celebrations of the spoils of an ultimate consumer lifestyle."[94] The figure of the celebrity, seen as a product of luck or circumstance rather than necessarily merit or talent, embodies popular aspirations for both leisure and wealth. Stars perform the modern consumptive ideal, in which identity and lifestyle are sought after in the realm of "nonwork," or leisure, rather than within traditional schemas of production.

Yet stars perform a great deal of work to make themselves into commodities. Richard Dyer argues of stars: "They are both labor and the thing that labor produces."[95] "Made for profit,"[96] stars are crucial to media industries and other entities invested in the products that stars sell. Black women in pornography, situated on the margins of stardom, attempt to achieve the fundamentally accessible star ideal. They embrace the role of porn star, and in the process, hope to achieve the decadence and excess of leisure and wealth associated with the work of stars. Porn stars must create themselves as brands, marketed for consumption by an expanding fan base. Black women desiring fame must manage their personas, images, and bodies to foster the consumer following required of successful porn stars. The desire for fame does not challenge the overriding capitalist system of consumption and exploitation, but invests in it. Using illicit eroticism to work for economic success drives self-commodification, or the fabrication of one's professional persona as a consumer product and brand.

In porn, which is only one of many spaces where people are commodified, workers seek to mobilize their stardom as a commodity that exceeds any particular film or production company and garners a loyal fan following. Porn actresses' success in manufacturing their stardom has wide-ranging effects on their ability to negotiate pay rates, working conditions, advertising deals, and other opportunities. Hence, although stardom is associated with leisure, it actually requires a great deal of labor on the part of women who aspire to it. For black women with lower cultural and erotic capital than their white or brown counterparts, this labor could be greater than for other women. With little investment in their stardom by the adult film industry, black actresses must take on more work to embody the figure of the star, as well as the aspirations for leisure and wealth the star engenders. These women must market themselves within a context where they are systematically devalued. Black performers are keenly aware of how their images are merchandised in videos that are distributed and sold all over the United States and elsewhere in the world, particularly in Europe. Some in my sample voiced outrage at the fact that it is relatively common practice for companies to capitalize on their notoriety or looks by using their images on covers for movies in which they do not even appear. Yet they also spoke of the compelling pleasure they derived from being coveted by thousands of unknown fans.

"I love my fans, I really do," India told me while signing autographs on glossy photo flyers at the annual Adult Video News trade convention in Las Vegas.[97] When she signed one for me, I thought of India's longtime aspiration to be seen as a sexy and beautiful star like Pam Grier in the 1970s. For India, gaining a contract with Video Team and becoming an A-List porn actress were the closest things possible to Grier's iconic stature as a black female sex symbol. As a result, India made sure to cultivate her fans, something she continues to do in her independent music career and online talk show. At adult trade conventions many actresses are hired to sign autographs at company booths while executives make deals with distributors, retailers, and technology producers behind the scenes. During one day of convention signing, an actress may greet more than one hundred fans. Although it is exhausting to stand in six-inch stiletto heels for several hours, signing, chatting, flirting, and taking pictures with fans, performers like India realize that conventions are a major opportunity to gain visibility amid both the consumers of pornography and its corporate executives. Because of the ease with which companies use performers to sell thousands of videos, dropping them like old news when they think an actress is no longer going to make the production company money, maintaining and increasing one's fan base is a necessary professional strategy of survival for porn workers. For India, becoming a porn star was not only a means to survive in the business, but a path toward recognition and support for her dreams. She hopes to become a mainstream rapper or journalist, and eventually, a financially secure mother.

Making a name in the world of adult entertainment is the key to becoming

FIGURE 5.2. India enjoyed signing autographs at adult industry conventions. She signed this press image for the author.

a porn star. For performers, making a name includes creating a captivating persona and becoming a savvy financial manager and entrepreneur. Selling themselves as brands or commodities means that stars must spend a great deal of time on promotion, including at photo shoots, trade conventions, and entertainment-industry events, and on their websites, on social networks, and in chat rooms, to foster a fan base. The women I spoke with were hungry for the fame, visibility, and mobility that such recognition brings. Beyond the desire for starring roles, video box covers, magazine layouts, long-term contracts, and lucrative pay rates, many women spoke about using their celebrity to cultivate opportunities beyond the formal roles of porn stars. They spoke of working toward greater control over their image and work and the ability to move behind the camera or into the mainstream entertainment industry. Those interested in making a career out of the job talked about wanting to produce their own websites, direct their own films, manage their own talent agencies, and license models of their body parts for the sex-toy market. For these women, having fame means being treated as a successful star, a desirable object of beauty, and a savvy businesswoman garnering admiration, if not respect.

For many entering the business like Montana Fishburne, fame operates as a form of visibility and a form of recognition. In light of the historical invisibility of black women's lives in society and their erasure as figures of importance in dominant culture industries, these women's desire for fame may be read as a movement to capture cultural legitimacy and authority.[98] Black women's discourses of fame can be read as the articulation of a profound longing to seize the force of desire—to be both desired and desiring subjects. Essentially individualist, this longing to be a desired subject of the gaze does not guarantee the transformation of the power relations that control the process of looking and being seen. Nonetheless, illicit erotic labor in the sphere of sexual culture offers material as well as nonmaterial benefits connected to the questions of visibility, recognition, and desire. For instance, fame affords performers access to social and geographic mobility. The professional, full-time, career-oriented performers I interviewed were proud that they had attained a higher socioeconomic status as a result of their hard work in adult film, and in their own strategic labor in self-promotion. They discussed the pleasure they acquire from leasing luxury cars, buying condos and homes in trendy areas of the San Fernando Valley and Los Angeles, and traveling in style for appearances around the country, at gentlemen's clubs, adult stores, film festivals, and dance clubs. These advances are implicitly read against the shrinking opportunities for labor and social mobility that accompany their working-class roots.

Fame in pornography is both a means to and a goal of achievement. This is in part because of porn's geographic and symbolic proximity to mainstream celebrity. The adult entertainment business is located just miles from Hollywood, California, the heart of celebrity-obsessed, consumer-oriented popular culture. While some people flock to the pornography business from regions far away, most black women entering porn seem to live in nearby Los Angeles. This is a place where African American unemployment and underemployment is a significant problem, and where inner-city black, working-class women wrestle with the socioeconomic forces that compel them to struggle for survival, financial autonomy, and social access. The birthplace of gangsta rap, Los Angeles is a key zone for African American cultural production and illicit economies that produce strategies for black working-class residents to grapple with the realities of their socioeconomic exclusion and the contradictions of declining production-oriented economies and rising consumer-oriented ones.[99]

It is no wonder that, given these circumstances, young, working-class black women from Los Angeles, living in the shadows of Hollywood and Porn Valley, are drawn to an industry associated with leisure-oriented and socially relevant entertainment and celebrity culture. Like Hollywood, Porn Valley seems to offer a lucrative and carefree lifestyle, where work pivots on one's embodied resources and the performance of attractiveness, sex appeal, skill, stamina, and individuality. In an urban region with little opportunity for black women in mainstream film acting, erotic performance offers certain charms. However, the widespread commerce in professional and amateur hardcore media online, and the embedding of pornography in popular culture and everyday life, allows women all over the nation to adopt porn stardom as an increasingly visible archetype and viable career path.

Sasha Brabuster comes from Detroit, Michigan, a city that was suffering, even before the financial crisis began in 2007. Sasha frequently travels to California to shoot and described to me her excitement of imagining herself as an actress in Hollywood. Hollywood represents a compelling scene of opportunity for those who want to take advantage of resources unavailable in their hometowns, but who, like Sasha, also envisage themselves as deserving of, belonging to, or thriving in some form of stardom. When I asked Sasha to introduce herself in her interview, I was struck by how her self-presentation offers an image of a dynamic, politically engaged professional and entrepreneur who has a vision about where she wants to take her career:

Hi, I am Sasha Brabuster. The one and only original when ordinary just won't do! I'm an adult entertainer, porn star, big breasts, all natural model and website entrepreneur. I own my own website: SashaBrabuster dot com, dot net, [and] dot org. And I do acting on different websites for fetish and specialty, for big breasts and BBW. I also do charity work for Protecting Adult Welfare, PAW, and I did a fundraiser for the Free Speech Coalition for porn. I was born and raised in Detroit, Michigan, the Motor City, and I later moved to Roseville, Michigan. Now I am in California pursuing my career and surely will be going overseas, [there's] a big demand for that, and pursuing more acting and more website roles and doing more things . . . doing the Sasha Brabuster movies and [my own] makeup [line] and clothes and things of that nature.[100]

When I asked Sasha to expand on her plans to use porn stardom to make money in the long term she explained that she actually makes more money from "privates" than she does movies, and that she was keen to build up her fledgling website as a major income stream that she can rely on as she "ages out" of the adult film business.[101] In addition, the website would give her more control over her labor and allow her to distribute her image internationally:

Money is in escorting and websites; you control that. You see, you have to front money or go get an investor or a sponsor, but you control that, whereas this production guy is gonna pay you five dollars for a movie (*snaps her fingers*). . . . This is an ongoing thing, as long as you feel like taking pictures and streaming videos, you will make money, because one thing that is fact and not fiction is you gonna get old, I'm gonna get old, my titties is gonna shrivel when I am seventy, but those pictures will last forever. But with your website, you have complete control, it is worldwide, you can't do any better marketing than that, and it is directly to you, you are gonna go ahead and get the money for the website. So that is why I said I would do that. Then maybe later [I'll do] a memoir of my life with senators, athletes, celebrities, vocalists, etc. that I've seen [as an escort]. I might do that when I get bored.[102]

One aspect of fame-based mobility that performers imagine, and attempt to catalyze, includes the ability to travel nationally and abroad for performances that expand their marketability to far-reaching audiences. Although many women performers go on national tours for exotic dancing and other appearances in order to raise their star status and make needed money, only a select few black actresses have conjured the charismatic presence and star persona to invite international bookings. Like Jeannie Pepper and Angel Kelly in the 1980s, Midori, Carmen Hayes, and Spantaneeus Xtasty talked about their excitement in working and being recognized as desirable actresses outside the United States. Midori described being "sought after" in Europe, including winning awards in Poland for "Best American Actress" and being invited to perform exotic dance on several occasions. "They heard about me performing and called me. 'Would you perform for us? We'd love to have you,'" Midori recalled.[103]

"I am so happy that I got to experience that because I was starting to think that in the world white people don't give black people a chance," Midori said, laughing ruefully.[104] The attention and adoration actresses received internationally differed sharply from how they were received at home. Even though she was the first black woman to win an AVN Award for Best Supporting Actress in 2001, and one of the few black women to ever grace the cover of *Adult Video News*, Midori's achievement came at a cost. When I interviewed her she felt dejected and damaged by the hardships she had faced, and she was struggling financially to support herself and her daughter. Midori explained that while at first she had refused to acknowledge the racism at play in how black actresses like herself were treated, during the course of her career, the U.S. industry made it impossible for her to ignore. "I always wanted to make a point that yes, a black woman can be sexy, classy, and all of that. I got tired of having to sell myself all the time."[105] In Europe Midori felt special; she was regarded as classy and desirable instead of devalued and unworthy.

Carmen Hayes also recounted feeling more valued and acknowledged by her fans abroad. "They treated us like queens, like Nubian goddesses!" she said of her travels to Germany.[106] Her comment highlights the pleasure she felt in the obviously contrasting treatment; in the United States, black porn stars are rarely considered Nubian queens and goddesses. While of course this exoticism has its own problematics and perils, what is key to note is how it translates to better material conditions for black performers' work, or at least parlays into greater opportunities while at the same time functioning to challenge the ontological understanding of black sex workers as anything but regal. Spantaneeus Xtasty described touring Japan, among many other countries, and the kind of star status she occupied during the height of her career in the 1990s. Not only did she appear in a book on African American entertainers that also featured Diana Ross and Tina Turner, but she relates with pleasure how she garnered so much attention in Tokyo: "Just picture, picture, picture. Everywhere you go, paparazzi!"[107] Spantaneeus laughed about re-

FIGURE 5.3. Midori and India appear with fellow actors Sean Michaels and Mr. Marcus in this glamorous *Adult Video News* cover.

ceiving marriage proposals and even causing traffic accidents with distracted onlookers as she walked down the street: "And all I was doing was going to the 7/11!" she giggled. Spantaneeus, who grew up in Philadelphia with a performing-arts background, traveled to Japan several times, performing in topless supper clubs and providing interviews to various media outlets. She spoke with pride about learning Japanese, and about getting the opportunity to explore another country. "It's a very beautiful country, I got to go sightseeing and see Mount Fuji, and all the beautiful temples and [learn about] the whole history of Japan. Anytime I visit a country, I have to learn a little bit about the history."[108]

Jeannie Pepper was the first black porn star to tour Europe, visiting France, Germany, Italy, Switzerland, Finland, and the Netherlands. In 1986, in a photo shoot with her then husband, a German expatriate photographer known as John Dragon, Jeannie posed nude or in lingerie in parks, cafés, the countryside, porno shops, on beaches, and at famous sites like Checkpoint Charlie,

FIGURE 5.4. Jeannie Pepper stands before Checkpoint Charlie in West Berlin on her European tour in 1986. Courtesy of JohnDragon.com

the border control between East and West Germany. It was the start of a seven-year period during which she traveled and lived in Europe, and a time when she was thrilled to garner attention that she lacked in the United States. Jeannie told me: "Yes, people looked. They were fascinated. 'Who is this black lady taking off her clothes?' All the tourists were taking pictures of me too. . . . I was in the park posing for pictures and I let them take pictures of me too. They said, 'Who are you?' I said, 'I'm Jeannie Pepper from America.'"[109] For Jeannie, like so many black performers in the past, reaching beyond the confines of national and racial borders, and inhabiting the unapologetic iconicity of black women performers like Josephine Baker, was meaningful to her sense of subjectivity and grounds the way we might think about what fame means to women like her. "How were you received in Europe as a black performer?" I asked. Jeannie responded:

> Like I was a superstar. Like I was Whitney Houston, Josephine Baker, or Billie Holiday, or one of these women. Like a queen. Like they treat the white movie stars over here. They embraced me. They rolled out the red carpet, gave me whatever I want[ed], champagne . . . whatever I want[ed]. At the end of the tour I felt like Dorothy [from the *Wizard of Oz*] tapping my heels to get home. But when I saw the Eiffel Tower my eyes lit up and tears came to my eyes, I couldn't believe I was there. Me and Josephine. And I felt like Dorothy when she saw the Emerald City. . . . I [had] finally made it to Paris and Paris was my Emerald City. . . . Yes, I loved it. I said, "I know these pictures will be around hundreds and hundreds of years, I just know it. And my face will be plastered somewhere, like Marilyn Monroe." It gave me a lot of power. I feel the way I do now because I accomplished that. [It] was like my dream come true. I [said], "I made it, I made it!" I just cried.[110]

Jeannie explained that this international recognition translated into greater opportunities when she returned home and also allowed her to assert to her critical family members that, for her, stardom provided a measure of affirmation and legitimacy. "That was the best part of my career. Then coming back, everyone was like we gotta put Jeannie Pepper on. There was all this Jeannie Pepper frenzy. I ate it up! I said 'Hi, mom, you said I couldn't do it. Look I just came back from a big tour. It changed my world. I have fans all over the world. I get letters from all over the world.'"[111]

For Jeannie, Midori, Spantaneeus, and others who have fought in their careers to cultivate the star power to foster opportunities abroad, fame was as essential to their sense of agency as it was to their actual power to be mobile and marketable. Jeannie's powerful story about how emotional and deeply meaningful being seen as an icon was to her contrasts with how some black women aspiring to fame are met with more bleak realities. The first adult film shoot I visited, back in 2002 in New York City, featured two eighteen-to-twenty-year-old women shooting with an older man out of the producer's home. Every time I tried to talk to the performers in between their shoots, they would stare nervously at a glowering, obese man sitting at the kitchen table and mumble an answer or brush me off. Finally, the lurking man said to me, "They don't want to be interviewed." When I asked who he was, and why he was speaking for them, he venomously retorted, "I'm their agent and if you want to interview someone you can interview me." Though I tried, with a sickening feeling, to talk to him, the only information he offered was that his "girls" were going to be big stars in porn and were on their way to "Hollywood" to make a lot of money.

I remember thinking about his words as I watched the actresses pose for the camera with an older male actor; they seemed terribly uncomfortable, with the actor and with the situation. It was a long day too; I was there nearly twelve hours and the women had been there long before I arrived. The self-financed director did not really know what he was doing, so every setup was drawn out and exhausting for the women under the hot lights. I asked if there was food for the actors, and the production assistant pointed to a bar where potato chips and Oreo cookies were laid out next to hard liquor. "The cookies keep them going and the liquor smooths them out," he said. I did not yet know that this kind of set was common for the new upstart, semiprofessional, and amateur companies producing porn, and that a large proportion of hardcore devoted to selling black-oriented pornography since the late 1990s would be similarly organized. Given these transforming material conditions, one wonders how any black performers could attain the star power and agency of the world-traveling actresses discussed above. One of the actresses from this low-rent Queens, New York, set did go on to appear in other hardcore films and websites like ExploitedBlackTeens.com. I later saw her happily signing autographs at an adult industry convention in Atlantic City. Her "agent" was by her side, still scowling at me. I did not see her after that, and I do not know if she ever made it to Hollywood.

In recent years, many observers have noted the decline of the porn star—the particular actor with a fascination and following inside the adult world, who then crosses over into the mainstream. Real porn stars have name recognition, fan followings, and drive sales for every product they produce. "The industry isn't designed that way anymore," contends performer Candice Nicole. "You know, they shoot you for two years and then no one wants you anymore," she explained, disappointment written across her face.[112] What has changed? Candice told me what others have echoed, that since the financial crisis of 2007, and even before, adult companies have largely retreated from their star-system strategy. Instead of developing actresses into stars, they more or less ride the wave of a particular star's notoriety, organizing marketing efforts around actresses that have proven to sell well. Candice Nicole asserted, "You kind of have to have a fan base before you get into the industry to cross over to the mainstream, and Lord knows, if that happens, then good luck to you, you are one of the few exceptions."[113] Hence, while increasing numbers of black women look to pornography as a potential site for celebrity and opportunity, they are entering a business that is changing; where companies invest less in their stardom and where all women have less luck than ever breaking through the porn barrier. Yet everyone is a star, or for newbies, starlets in the porn business. Drained of the chic cultural cachet of the 1970s and '80s, "porn star" is today a rather hollow word. As Jeannie Pepper tells it, "You're not rare, you are a dime a dozen."[114]

What do we make of the motivations of black women today, particularly the young and working-class, to mobilize illicit eroticism for a chance at fame? Although there is a tremendous diversity in the social location, realities, motivations, and ambitions of black actresses in pornography, my research has found that fame is one of the central forces that attract these women across difference. To these actresses fame means a sense of legitimacy, recognition, and achievement. When they describe achieving a modicum of fame, their accounts show how it produces a feeling of affirmation and social value. It makes them feel like they are prevailing over the forceful stigma about black women's sexuality and their sexual labor, and even over the tough conditions they face in everyday life. Moreover, fame, as a kind of alternative work, allows performers to attain socioeconomic status and material resources they would not normally have access to, though this motivation may not be as significant for women from wealthy backgrounds like Montana Fishburne.

Nonetheless, in an industry where everyone is a star—or at least a fleeting starlet—black women lack the true power of stardom. Often demeaned, diminished, and used, black women often find that pornographic work largely does not include a chance at real fame, local or global. Furthermore, the fascination with fame that draws many into the porn field easily becomes a mechanism for "management" to extract and exploit their labor. In the hopes of becoming famous porn actors, performers do a lot of extra work, including signing at conventions, performing more extreme sex acts than they agreed to, or taking on extra workout regimens. These labors of self-cultivation feed the machine of profit for porn producers much more than for the actors themselves. In truth, when producers feel that performers have become too visible they often tell them they are overexposed, then deny them roles and work contracts. Consumers want to see something new, they argue. Fame depends on an investment from industry management that does not exist for many actors of color, or for actors in general, as all their bodies become exchangeable forms of capital mobilized at the discretion of management through the capitalist labor system. Because of the massive and cyclical disposability of performers in the adult industry, the reality is that the promise of fame is elusive, if not altogether an illusion that serves to make workers hyperexploitable.[115] Fame masks and obfuscates the mechanisms of commodification that make all workers submit to a system of capital that is not in their interests, does not give them true autonomy, and, for the most part, does not benefit them. This discourse of fame also obscures how rooted racial and gender difference is in the calculation of who becomes exploitable and how. "Racialized and gendered difference is absolutely necessary to the hierarchization of workers and the extraction of capital in this era," writes Grace Hong in *The Ruptures of American Capital*. "In this way, race and gender are constitutive to the operations of capital."[116] As the women of color writers in Hong's analysis capture in their texts, this ambitious drive for fame signals "the return of the repressed of capital," who are "naming their erasures at the very moment of their articulation."[117] In this way, a performer's drive for fame may reflect what Lauren Berlant terms "cruel optimism."[118] The very thing that these performers hope and strive for undermines their dreams and makes their desires impossible to fully achieve.

Yet the aspiration remains to be desired and to be understood as influencing an aspect of national culture. Fame means, fundamentally, to be seen, valued, legitimated, and remembered. It is about imagining the impossible.[119] In this sense, for black sex workers, fame remains an aspiration and perhaps today more than ever, an unattainable reality that nonetheless has a valuable meaning for how these performers wish to understand themselves and carve out a new world of possibility. Mya Lovely, a Canadian-born performer whose career lasted four years (2003–7), whom I met at the Adult Entertainment Expo in 2004, told me of her hopes for winning fame after her hit rookie performance in *Black Reign 2*. Her testimony captures the desire for and the pitfalls of stardom within the politics of disposability and erasure that encompass pornography's machine of production: "I always want to be in the spotlight. You'll see me on a feature movie or you'll see something that I produce. I'm going to start producing stuff on my own. My name will be there, I won't be forgotten."[120]

# Behind the Scenes

*Confronting Disempowerment and Creating Change*
*in Black Women's Porn Work*

Lola Lane was ready to leave porn for good. In 2009, after more than a decade in the business, she revealed to me her vision for Fantine's Dream Foundation, a nonprofit organization that would provide resources to women who wanted to leave the adult industry. Unlike Shelley Lubben's Pink Cross Foundation, which uses Christian rhetoric to coax "sex industry survivors" to renounce pornography as a sin,[1] Lola did not wish Fantine's Dream to make value claims about the morality of porn work. Against the norm of organizations designed to rescue women from the sex industry, Lola's project would help workers leave porn for other forms of employment, and to do so on their own terms. Perhaps unsurprisingly, getting out of the porn industry is much harder than getting in. As we saw in the previous chapter, some black women like Lola are drawn to porn because the alternatives are everyday nine-to-five or low-wage shift jobs that do not meet their needs—financial or otherwise. They enter because porn affords them greater economic benefits, as well as key noneconomic advantages such as the flexibility of time to pursue other interests and responsibilities and the opportunity to explore erotic performance. However, careers in pornography are difficult to sustain. As performers age, and the longer they remain in the industry, they find themselves becoming less marketable, and as a result they face rising challenges to earn a living with porn work.

Fantine, the character from the renowned Victor Hugo novel and Claude-Michel Schönberg musical *Les Misérables*, is a woman compelled to become a prostitute in order to provide for her ailing daughter. She herself is ill, but she sacrifices her body and, in the process, exposes the high costs for women struggling on their own, especially for those selling sex. Lola told me: "I don't

FIGURE 6.1. Lola Lane poses with a fan at the AVN Adult Entertainment Expo in Las Vegas in 2005. Photograph by the author.

know if you've seen the play *Les Misérables*. Fantine is the heroine. She had to be, she was working a regular job but she couldn't take care of her child, someone else did. But they were draining her money so she had to turn to prostitution so she could support her child that was staying with these people. The child got sick and needed medicine and she did this [prostitution] even when she was sick. And it's somewhat similar to myself."[2] Lola identified with Fantine: like the character, she traded sex to make a life for her child. Yet unlike Fantine, the sex Lola had was as a highly paid actress in adult film, and she chose this work even though she already had a job in retail management. For Lola, who suffers from multiple sclerosis and wrestles with chronic pain and exhaustion, porn was a lesser evil than the corporate retail industry, which was so inflexible and exhausting that it literally made her sick. "It would seem like [the industry] would be harder on your body, but it's not like going to work every single day," she explained. "My day-to-day job was very stressful. And all of that and I was having more and more relapses and when I took a break from that, the money was very little." Porn allowed her to make her own schedule and to make more money in one hour than she had in one week. A single mother, Lola could be there for her son and afford a life for him.

Lola Lane, an attractive, petite, dark-brown-skinned woman, worked in black and interracial gonzo porn for more than ten years, gaining insight into an industry that continuously revises its preferences for black women according to prevailing tastes and market trends. Appearing in over two hundred films, Lola understood the desire to pursue money, sex, and fame—the golden triad of attractions that shape the drive to become a porn star, as discussed in chapter 5. Lola witnessed and experienced for herself what happens behind the scenes of one of the most lucrative and influential industries in the nation. Normally hidden from view to spectators, the adult entertainment industry's complex sexual economy forces black women to grapple with a hierarchal system shaped by racial and gender difference and discrimination. For Lola, in spite of porn's significant appeal, issues of pay inequality, the lack of opportunities to gain stardom and success, bias, exploitation, and abuse were constituent aspects of the job. Lola was also aware of how other black women navigated this perilous terrain to make the most of their roles, challenge conditions, or reimagine their own actions. Lola understood how black women attempted to protect themselves from misuse and how they ventured to assert value, integrity, and complex personhood in their work and everyday lives. She knew well that, fundamentally, they strove to see themselves as meaningful social actors.

Rather than submit to exploitation or collude with historical representations of depraved black sexuality, some black porn actresses actively resist harm by critiquing unjust conditions and negotiating better conditions for themselves and others. As a diverse community, they respond to discrimination, bias, and harm in creative, but often complex and contradictory ways. Yet black porn actresses do more than simply react to subordination. In fact, as I have argued throughout this book, many black porn actresses engage in a dynamic politics of illicit eroticism. Employing techniques of self-fashioning, and tactics of labor and performance, they produce alternative terms for fantasizing about and desiring the black female body. In this chapter, I address the landscape of labor issues in pornographic sex work by drawing on my informants' own understandings and voices as they describe how they wrestle with and respond to structures of inequality and exploitation, often through fierce critique and shrewd practices of negotiation. I explore black women's ethics of labor rights, and their recuperative assertions of self-care and erotic sovereignty in the face of multiple entrapments offer a moral economy in which all workers may gain a sense of respect and value.

By talking to these women at the very margins of the African American and feminist movements for economic and social equality, we learn a lot about the need to exercise a radical and inclusive sexual politics that encompasses the labor struggles of sexual minorities including black sex workers in porn. Women like Lola Lane offer a view into what it means to sustain a career in the industry, and at what cost. Further, they show that the neoliberal logics in which pornography is produced and distributed today often shifts the blame for inequality and exploitation from the structures that create these conditions onto workers. Sex workers in porn become vulnerable to and held responsible for the precarity of their work, when in fact it is much larger processes, even beyond the adult industry itself, that ensure the continued life of racial and gender hierarchies and supply-and-demand logics, which have turned in on themselves to actually weaken the business of adult film production since the 1990s.

### Value in the Marketplace of Sex

"These black chicks are fucking skanks!" I overheard a man say at the AVN Adult Entertainment Expo. I had made my way through the convention floor, past the high-tech displays of the major production companies, past throngs of crowds lined up to get autographs from the biggest porn stars and *Hustler* founder Larry Flynt, to the back and side of the vast hall. Here, I found a crowd of men watching two black women in string bikinis as they did acrobatic splits and bends in a fast-paced, booty-clapping dance. Unlike the established black porn actresses standing nearby signing autographs, these women, clearly experienced exotic dancers, were hired to draw a crowd to an amateur production company. As I pushed through the shouting throng to get a better view, one young woman leaned over the display table, spread her legs wide, and rhythmically worked her shapely thighs and butt to the music. As she began to stroke her nearly exposed genitals, a dozen men with cameras pushed forward to get a close-up. This is the kind of tease some performers do to draw extra attention to themselves and their employers. I remember seeing the beads of sweat across her brow and her hair weave sticking damply to her shoulders as she danced.

It was at that moment when I heard the cruel comment of the man next to me, a well-known white director of all-white extreme hardcore. The kind of guy who profits by and takes pleasure in shoving women's heads in toilets and watching them gag and vomit during fellatio. To me, the comment was both shocking and not surprising at all. After years of research in adult industry work sites—including film sets, production offices, business conventions, awards ceremonies, and industry events—I observed other scenes like this. I have been struck by how black women are constantly disparaged, disciplined, and made vulnerable to the kinds of verbal and symbolic violence that I witnessed that day. This multidimensional, regulatory violence is integral to black women's representation and labor in pornography since its modern development, and that affects all black female performers to one degree or another. Symbolic violence pervades the ways in which black female bodies are read as oversexed, expendable, unfeminine, and unworthy. In an industry that values and trades in the sexuality of women, one would think that black women's presumed hypersexuality would give them an advantage. Ironically, however, black women porn actresses are often discredited as super-disposable "skanks."

White women are the true stars of American pornography. The young, lithe, tan, busty blonde—the iconic image of the "porn star"—is constructed as the most valuable sexual commodity. In contrast, black women are systemically positioned in spaces and roles of lesser importance to white women in the sexual marketplace of hardcore pornography, and as a result, they are more economically at risk. Although there has been tremendous, growing diversity in the kinds of bodies fetishized for particular niche markets since the 1990s—thirty-to-fifty-year-old MILFs, over-fifty GILFs (Grandmothers . . .), pregnant bodies, voluptuous bodies, transgender bodies, and disabled bodies—young white women are the primary currency of the adult entertainment business; every other body is just another fetish. White womanhood is the central fascination of the top-tier film-production companies like Hustler, Vivid, Digital Underground, and Wicked, and of adult web companies like Pornhub, xTube, and RedTube. Therefore, normative white female bodies are the key profit generators for major U.S. corporations like AT&T, TimeWarner, and DirectTV that sell hardcore and softcore video over the Internet, on pay-per-view cable channels, through video on demand, and in millions of hotel rooms each year.[3] Black women appear in interracial and white pornography to the extent that they are seen as marketable to white and nonwhite audiences. If they have "crossover" appeal and are seen as properly feminized and attractive to potential white audiences, they have a greater chance of being cast in mainstream white-cast films or in interracial genre videos. Pornographic performance and labor are, thus, raced and gendered according to long-standing sexual power relations, ideologies, and desires. Black female bodies are generally devalued in a sexual economy that reifies normative white femininity and establishes it as the measure for all women. All performers are compelled to perform in ways demanded by the political economy, but black performers perform additional labor.

Selling representations of black female sexuality as a commodity has a lot

FIGURE 6.2. White actresses are displayed prominently at the AVN Adult Entertainment Expo in 2006. Photograph by the author.

to do with how film and multimedia producers understand black women's appeal, and hence their economic value, in the market. Overwhelmingly, producers argue that there is a low demand for black women matched with white men (sometimes awkwardly termed in industry jargon "reverse interracial"), but a high demand for black men matched with white women, and to some extent, with Asian women and Latinas. These analyses are purportedly based on the evaluation of market trends; producers look at what sells and repeat the same formula again and again to maximum potential profit. Beliefs about economic value justify the sustained racialized sexism of the pornography industry's representation of black women as undesirable.

While standard supply-and-demand economics are certainly shaping the landscape of pornography's treatment and marketing of black female sexuality, I argue that there may be other structural forces at play. Thinking historically, we can say that the sexual economy for black women's bodies under slavery defined the very nature of desire for, use of, and pleasure in black women's sexuality in the United States.[4] Although in no way parallel in terms of brutality and coercion, present-day pornography recalls the past sexual economy of U.S. slavery in two important ways. First, with the economic imperative to manage and market black sexuality for profit, there is a social and political imperative to devalue the bodies that form the very basis of that profit. The illicit desire for black female sexuality, and crucial use of that sexuality for capitalistic gain, are invariably concealed and camouflaged by a kind of psychic denial and social disgust, or what I have called the myth of prohibition. When adult films like *South Central Hookers* and *Ghetto Hoes* exploit fantasies of black women, they capitalize on historical ideas about dependent black women trading on their sexualities—sexualities that black women do not deserve or have the right to mobilize for their own pleasure and liberation. The symbolic and material impoverishment of black women's value in the sexual marketplace informs these fantasies.

In turn, this impoverished valuation of black sexuality creates the rationale for sexual economic exploitation, thus sustaining a hierarchal system of embodied worth. Even though black women are actually profitable investments for adult production companies, distributors, and retailers, they are valued economically and socially as if they are worthless. Moreover, as in other industries, largely male-run porn companies use these women's sexuality to enrich themselves, yet they claim black women's lack of appeal is the reason for their marginality in the marketplace of adult entertainment. Despite its benefit for adult business interests, black female sexuality remains a site of extraction and continues to conjure ideas of illicitness and illegitimacy that then become built into the logics of black and interracial porn as domains for fantasy and labor. These powerful and long-standing mechanisms of devaluation expose black women porn workers to harassment, discrimination, and danger, as they become bodies in a system that is lucrative but never lucrative enough.

The second important way that slavery provides a lens to view the specific political economy of the pornography industry for black women workers is that labor subordination is so clearly tied to sex. Enslaved women experienced sex as the primary mechanism of their subordination as workers, breeders, and concubines. Sex saturated the economy and shaped the quotidian experience of white supremacy and racialized capital in the lives of slaves. African American women today experience sex as the chief mechanism of their subordination in the porn-industry workplace. Sex, including the practices and discourses around it, acts as a tool of sexual, racial, and labor control and renders black women a captive workforce.[5] Black women are called upon to perform sex and sexuality, but they are vilified and punished for it. Even the above-mentioned director's odious comment about the black female dancers at AVN, "These black chicks are fucking skanks," acts as a kind of disciplining speech and gesture, serving to assert racialized patriarchy both in the paternalistic control over infantilized "chicks" (and alternately and more popularly "girls"), and in white male supremacy over oversexed black "skanks." Therefore, sexual labor inequality and abuse function to discipline women workers as women and as workers.[6]

The ideological and commercial denigration of black women's bodies is integral to their denigration as workers, and their compromised desirability, exclusion, and economic vulnerability are all sexual and mutually reinforcing. Sexualized harassment and discrimination thus structure and politicize the nature of black women's work in porn, allowing it to be understood within a greater context of sexual, gender, racial, and workforce repression within advanced capitalism that has its genesis in New World slave economies. Although today this repression marginalizes black women workers from privileged positions of value in porn's sexual economy, the object of their repression is not to push women out of the workforce. On the contrary, the porn business remains enriched by black women's sustained presence as an exploitable workforce. While the sexual economy of slavery offers a compelling paradigm for the mechanisms of sexual and racial control operating in the porn industry, and in other industries as well, it also presents a model for analyzing the ways in which black women mount critical responses to sexual repression and expropriation. Reflecting the legacy of enslaved women who fought in ways large and small against slavery's tyranny, black sex workers in porn enact forms of antiracist and antisexist insurgency within a system that exploits their sexualized labor.[7]

## Managing Black Women's Labor in Porn

Segregation has long been a strategy for managing black bodies. The creation of majority black urban ghettos and the systemic exclusion of black families from white neighborhoods were two of the primary forms of racial management under Jim Crow in the United States. In the post–civil rights era, even though significant portions have traversed those boundaries to cross over into other socioeconomically defined terrains like the suburbs, black Americans remain segregated in ghettos. Not only do ghettos delimit the spatial bounds of black urban lives, but they also designate the symbolic parameters of belonging to the larger social community of the nation-state. With so much of low-end market black-oriented porn since the 1990s understood as "ghetto porn," it is clear that the devaluation of black life factors into the representational regimes and labor conditions of pornography as a cultural site and corporate business. Ghetto porn literally *ghettoizes* African American women. The reiteration of ghetto tropes in the scripted fantasies of adult video routinely sidelines black female bodies and performances in the larger porn industry. According to Lola Lane, ghetto porn calls upon black women to inhabit characters that ostensibly occupy the ghetto: prostitutes, drug fiends, easy women, and menacing men. "You're a ho," she explained of ghetto porn's constructions of black women's sexual performance. Discussing videos that market her as a "black street hooker," Lola, in a 2003 interview, asserted: "I don't really want to be seen as a hooker. I love what I do. Obviously we are having sex for money, but it can still be seen, not really as respectable, but as not so degrading."[8] Compelled to occupy this diminished and restricted position, black performers face disillusionment. For them, sexual labor should invite opportunity, not control. Like the real ghetto, ghetto porn undermines their claims for social inclusion, value, and esteem. In the process of asserting their value, however, performers sometimes privilege themselves over other sex workers, like streetwalkers.

Declaring her desire to perform in the sex film business, and to enjoy it, Lola shows that she resents the ways in which the ghetto porn genre produces an inherently devalued black female sexuality. For Lola, this construction conflicted with her personal identity and how she imagined her performance to be defined. She told me about an exchange with a director for a film where he wanted her to play what she described as a "typical ghetto girl": "And the director, he said, 'You are not coming [across] ghetto enough,' and I said well, 'I'm *not* ghetto!' And [he said], 'You're an actress, so *act*,' and I said 'Okay.'"[9] Lola took on the "ghetto ho" character even though it was very different from her own self-concept as a professional porn actress. Clearly the director felt that the performance of "ghetto-ness" was required of the role, and that Lola's embodiment alone did not communicate the particular fantasy of black women's ghetto sexuality. It was something that Lola ran up against time and time again in her career and that black performers encounter across entertainment industries. Lola relates another experience with the particular limits of the ghetto ho:

> This was funny: I did one of my first movies and I used to get my outfits made, [so] it was all glittery and fancy. Sometimes you don't know the title of the movie, they just place you somewhere. And when I saw this box cover it said *Ghetto Hoes*, I could have passed out! But here I

am and everybody else is in whatever, and I got on this fancy glittery showgirl type of dress and I'm thinking this is something that it's not. I'm thinking I'm a porn star, but [being a star is] not for black girls.[10]

Echoing the experience of Angel Kelly in the 1980s, Lola's narrative of her encounters with entrenched stereotypical roles in the 2000s illuminates how black women continue to struggle against the politics of their portrayal. Through performances of glamour, exoticism, and eroticism, they seek to enact a subversion of the familiar, well-worn stereotypes of black dysfunction and debasement, instead using their bodies and imaginations to intervene in the field of representation. Employing the aesthetics of glamour they seek to exchange disgust for desire, and denial for legitimacy. Lola went to the extreme of having her costume made by hand in the hope that she could create a performance around the enchanting and glitzy image of a Las Vegas showgirl. But her efforts were undermined by the interests of the production company to profit from the standard tropes of impoverished black femininity. Lola was, in the end, confined to the parameters of the genre within which she was allowed to operate. Yet her attempt to create her own extravagant and value-laden costume and persona shows that she not only envisioned a different image for herself, she sought to create it.

The industry's belief that it only provides supply to consumers' demand—that it simply responds pragmatically to already established fantasies, tastes, and trends—erases the actual power of the industry to influence consumer preferences and consumption practices. One reason that black women garner less interest from consumers may be the pornography industry's inability or unwillingness to centralize black women's roles, and to sustain them in the star system. Instead of being in the spotlight, black women are most often sidelined to the shadows, and undermined as expendable talent. As Lola Lane describes, even though she tried to assert a star persona in her performance, she was quickly informed that she was not there for that. The message: take off the glittery dress and be a ghetto ho. The subgenre of black pornography demands that black women appear unprepossessing, not chic and elegant. The myth that black women are unmarketable to mainstream pornography consumers explains away the systemic privileges and exclusions that define who gains and who loses. "Disguising racism as economic pragmatism" is an old strategy used by the entertainment industry, including Hollywood.[11] As Karen Alexander argues, esteemed actresses including Lena Horne, Dorothy Dandridge, and Pam Grier could only find success by "accommodating and adapting to the incapacities" of the system.[12] That is, in order to pursue their work, black film actresses had to adjust to Hollywood's covert (and often overt) racial logic in savvy ways. While they often critiqued prejudice, including their diminished star status in relationship to white actresses, and even took strong stands against the treatment of all black performers, they did, at times, accept the terms of work Hollywood offered them. Even with their accommodation to established, yet camouflaged, racial hierarchies, these actresses constantly worked to assert their economic value to the cultural marketplace and their overall social worth.

The perceived low return on investment of black women's sexuality represents the difficult situation in which black female performers find themselves. It organizes how the porn industry markets black female bodies as well as how it treats black women workers at work sites. Specifically, black women's ghettoized sexualities are deployed and circulated within a racialized and gendered political economy of explicit media in ways that mainstream performers do not experience. If pornography is the trashy, contemptible underbelly of the social corpus in dominant discourse, then black women, already known to be valueless, vulgar whores, are the degenerate hub—the bellybutton—of nonnormative sexuality threatening the very core of social standards.

Pornography's troubled position in society means that the question of labor relations in the making of mainstream sexual media products is generally overlooked. Panics about pornography's impact on mainstream culture obfuscate pressing questions about its practices as an industry. In this neoliberal moment, when the rights of workers are being eroded in a wide range of industries, the adult entertainment industry is not exceptional. But it does provide an interesting case study for how sexuality, the very quality that is commodified, also serves to undermine the industry's workers. Scholars and critics have largely elided issues of race and gender hierarchies in the work of porn actors. They focus instead on how porn oppresses women through images, not, for example, through racial inequalities in how actresses are paid. These analyses omit black professional performers' vocal critiques of the industry on wage parity, employment marginalization, and interpersonal bias, and how, given these problematic constraints, they make meaning of their participation in the pornography industry. When we interrogate the ways in which black porn actors contest the conditions driving porn's political economy, we must attend to how they also stress an alternative valuation of their embodied labor. These women show us how redressing the injurious forces of pornography's representation and labor regime mirrors a larger struggle against the historical injury of being denied social worth.

## A Woman's Worth

"I think I am still not getting equal to what the other girls are getting," Lola Lane said to me in 2003.[13] Years into her career in the porn industry, Lola succeeded in demanding a higher pay rate from producers, but she still felt that it was not the same as what white actresses were paid. Lola's comment exposes how black adult performers believe pay inequality is a key mechanism in the larger undervaluation of their labor, one bound to a racial hierarchy that defines embodied labor for all erotic performers. Although they are desired for their difference, the bodies of women of color hold much less currency compared to white female bodies, which are the most privileged and in demand by the industry. The diminished status of black female bodies is especially evident in the issue of wage inequalities, and this is one of the sorest issues for black women sex workers in the business. Concentrated in the bastardized niche genres of black and interracial porn, black actresses have largely been paid only half to three-quarters of what white female actresses earn. While pay rates have changed over time and are traditionally higher for actresses than actors, black female performers are generally paid $500–$800 for one "boy/girl" sex scene (depending on their notoriety and the company's film budget) while white actresses tend to be paid $1,000–$2,000.[14]

According to one production-company executive, the lack of parity in pay rates is the "primary issue" for black actresses: "Knowing that you could have gotten more, is really disappointing."[15] Lacey Duvalle, a former contract actress for Video Team, became a hardcore video performer at eighteen years of age and a "contract girl" three years later. At the time of her contract, Lacey was one of only a handful of black contract girls in hardcore, many of which were under contract with Video Team, including India, Alexis Amore, and Ayana Angel. With such a highly sought-after contract, India probably earned close to $50,000 a year to appear in only eight to ten films, and to make several public relations appearances.[16] Many fans and industry experts have noted the paucity of black women contract stars.[17] Black women who do gain contracts, as one performer told me, "don't get paid what white contract girls get."[18] According to Steve Hirsch, CEO of Vivid Entertainment, one of the leading studios in the adult film industry, his company awards contracts in excess of $100,000 a year—twice as much as the leading black contract workers make.[19] Vivid was the innovator of the Hollywoodesque contract-based star system in the 1980s and is a company that brought in $100 million a year in revenues at the time that Hirsch visited UCSB to speak to our students and faculty. When I questioned him about why his company only offered contracts to two black actresses ever—Heather Hunter and Tiffany Mason—and only a handful of Asian, Latina, and South Asian actresses, Hirsch insisted that his company only cared whether the actress was beautiful and possessed a tangible star quality, and that Vivid had no intentions of racially discriminating against minorities. Yet because the studio produces a standard of what it considers beautiful and marketable that is embedded in racialized ideas that privilege whiteness—notably both Heather Hunter and Tiffany Mason are light-skinned black women with long, flowing hair—it is not a bystander in the process of devaluing black women actresses in the adult industry. If obtaining a contract represents one form of job security in an industry in which independent contractors must negotiate constantly the nature of precarity in their work, while also gaining a sense of legitimacy and a wealth of opportunities that come with stardom, the exclusion of black women from contracts in top studios puts them in a position of structural deficit.[20]

Commenting on how difficult it is to attain pay rates on par with white actresses, Lollipop reveals some of the frustration that comes with constantly having one's labor depreciated. "As a black woman, I'm looking for $1,000 a pop at least. They want to say, 'Hey you look good, but here's $500.' And I'm like, well, what about my work? I'm bending over; I'm turning it up and doing *better* than my best. And still my best isn't good enough for whoever wants to shoot me."[21] Lollipop shows how the systemic underpaying of black women essentially denies their labor, ignores their performative contributions, and undermines their sense of self-worth and sense that they benefit from their work. Black actresses view the practice of underpaying black women as widespread and profoundly affecting. Sierra described how, because pay rates are usually individually negotiated, black actresses are forced to fight for decent pay every day. "The thing is, salaries aren't discussed and [producers] try to get you right then and there. You have to negotiate your own salary. . . . I've talked to [black] girls who've gotten $300–$400 to do a scene. I'm like $300 is all you got? I won't even leave my house for $300. You must be crazy! I've known a lot of white girls that come into the business and get started with regular straight scenes and get $1,000. . . . Unfortunately, most of us entering this business don't know what we're worth."[22]

Sierra's testimony reveals the acute frustration and disgust that actresses feel when they are offered performance contracts at rates far below the norm. Sierra turns down insanely low offers, she explained, because they undermine her value in the market, and thus threaten her ability to negotiate fair pay in the future. Not only does being a black woman compromise Sierra's attempt to keep her pay rate, it means that she and other black women are forced to compete for crumbs. As an established performer, Sierra faces competition from newer actresses who offer fresh faces and bodies. While starting actresses' lack of knowledge about industry standards sometimes places them at a disadvantage, veteran performers like Sierra sometimes feel threatened because they must battle to maintain their careers in a climate that favors younger women. Vulnerable to exploitation by adult filmmakers looking for the next new talent at the cheapest cost, young women entering the adult film industry are hurt not only by the coercive tactics of film companies, but also by a culture of silence about wages. The mystification about rates is something I observed in my research; it is almost considered rude to discuss one's pay rate. In fact, most of the women I interviewed talked not about what specific rates they received, but rather about what *other* actresses were paid, or how they themselves refused to work for certain, obviously low rates. The forces of exploitation, competition, and silence combine to create a system in which racial inequalities between white and nonwhite actresses are sustained, and even encouraged because the undervaluing of an entire class of workers uplifts the collective value of the industry's most prized workers and their products. Given these blatant systemic biases, I am often asked, how come the actors do not get together to create a union to ensure fairness and equity?

Unfortunately, all adult film actors are technically independent contract workers rather than salaried employees, so they lack the power to fight for transparent and equal compensation provisions, let alone other benefits like guaranteed overtime pay or travel and wardrobe allowances. In the United States, contract workers are legally excluded from the protections salaried employees receive, including bargaining rights and rules for wages and hours worked, because of their status as independent entrepreneurs. However, this has been challenged in several legal cases, particularly by workers arguing that they fill the role of employee rather than that of contract worker.[23] Adult entertainment companies benefit from the independent-contract system and may use the status of their workers to conceal their failure to act responsibly on behalf of them. Exotic dancers in California brought suit against club owners in 2009 for not awarding the minimum wages and overtime pay they felt entitled to. In *Chaves v. King Arthur's Lounge, Inc.* the court pointed to the $35 required "stage fee" for dancers to work, arguing that it failed to meet standards that independent contractors hold an "independently established trade or occupation" in a "free market."[24] The strip club argued that its principal business was that of a bar and the dancers merely provided entertainment "akin to the television and pool tables in a sports bar."[25] The court did not buy this argument, stating that it would need to be "blind to human instinct" to not see the dancers not only as more than the "wallpaper of routinely-televised matches, games, tournaments and sports talk," but as integral to the business of the strip club, and thus employees.[26] While categorically different than stripping, the status of professional adult film acting as nonunionized independent contract work allows companies to evade responsibility for normalizing working conditions, pay, and benefits.

Mainstream film, theater, and television actors created the Screen Actors Guild and Actors' Equity to address precisely this issue. Porn actors, however, lack the institutional power, organization, and social recognition to foster such a system, even though they maintain the highest status for workers in the entire sex industry. The position of porn actors as contracted workers thus contributes to the vulnerability of all sex workers. Compounded by inequalities based on gender, race, age, and class, black professional adult actresses face particular vulnerability with regards to uneven conditions of work and pay. In California, where the majority of professional pornography is produced, contract workers normally fall under the state's provision for safe and fair working conditions for all workers. Yet it is clear that fair working conditions, and to some degree safe ones as well, are not sustained equally or across the board. This is especially true for amateur, independent, or subprofessional production companies and their contractors. A suit by pornography industry actors challenging contract-worker status and claiming employee status would be a fascinating test case for the entire adult industry. If professional actors were regarded as employees, they would have rights to collective bargaining and would be able to enforce minimum standards for work in the industry, including fixed pay rates, overtime, benefits, and other protections.[27]

Although the actresses I spoke to are aware of the adult industry's abuses, many understand that the enormous diversity of companies in the field means that each film or media product has a different budget from which adult talent may be paid. Producers, manufacturers, and distributors explain the differences between productions in terms of "supply and demand," arguing that the popularity of particular pornographic genres, and the resources of the companies, are the biggest determining factors for performer pay scales. The African American actresses I interviewed tend to believe, however, that the industry follows a pattern of undercutting the wages of its female talent, especially black and other women of color. They believe that the undervaluing of their labor places them in the lowest quality, and hence lowest budgeted, pornographic productions and that their pay inequality is directly tied to the depreciation of black talent in comparison with white women's constructed desirability. Unequal pay has been a rallying point for black women in the adult industry in their struggle to be respected as workers. In the absence of a formal union, these performers have taken a stand by refusing to accept unduly low pay rates, avoiding companies with known abusive practices, and designing personae that they believe evoke value or class.

## Beauty and the Beast

"You know, I've been booked for shoots," said Lola Lane, "and they think I'm white over the phone, (because there's another Lola) and they say, 'Oh you're the black girl. We can't shoot you,' or, 'Your butt is too big.' So it can hurt your feelings."[28] For Lola, the obvious privileging of white femininity has been heartbreaking. Whiteness is the hegemonic ideal of attractiveness and desirability and, as Kemala Kempadoo argues, "white sexual labor is most valued within the global sex industry."[29] Because this unequal treatment is tied to performer wages, black female talent feel an extreme pressure to conform to standards of whiteness in order to win film roles, marketing agreements, and long-term contracts. The racial politics of beauty thus form the basis of the business of pornography. The rule tends to be: live up to the requirements of white sexual embodiment and assimilate to white beauty standards, or risk being ghettoized in the most undervalued sectors of the business. In facing beliefs about black women's supposed lack of beauty, black female performers must cultivate techniques of self-construction and self-promotion that leverage their standing in pornography, as well as in society more broadly.

The socially constituted construction of white female beauty and desirability, inherently defined against the deviant, monstrous, and repulsive black woman's body, has very real, economic implications for women of color sex workers. Being measured against an unattainable and cruel racial standard of attractiveness, desirability, and femininity is something many black women in America face every day. Black feminist scholars have discussed the multiple ways in which African American women have historically contended with these racialized beauty criteria. According to Maxine Leeds Craig, a scholar of black beauty pageants, "whether facing disparagement of their bodies in dominant cultural images or the mixture of appreciation (where alternative standards prevailed) and ridicule (where dominant standards prevailed) within African American communities, black women were diminished when their general worth was determined by their physical appearance."[30] In a business that not only trades in attractiveness and desirability but makes physical appearance the primary social capital of its workers, black actresses must negotiate their unalterable difference and measured devaluation in the interest of their own livelihoods.

As Lola's narrative shows, the preference for white actresses and the stratification of opportunities along the color line creates a tremendous sense of disappointment, frustration, and injustice among black actresses, in part because it means they are left out of potentially lucrative opportunities to work. Lola said: "You have to get that tough skin or you're not going to make it, otherwise you get low self-esteem. You are like 'Hey, what's wrong with me?' I go to these casting calls . . . and they are only looking at the white girls. It's like, 'Why am I here?' You find it humiliating."[31] Lola confided that due to her chronic MS, she experiences extreme fluctuations in her weight as well as the heavy toll of the rigors of sex work on her physical and emotional well-being. Physical and emotional labor are part of the intensive bodywork that sex workers, like workers in many other service-industry occupations, perform.[32] Lola reveals that the use of her body as the primary site of labor involved in bodywork opens her up for a unique kind of scrutiny and policing. This scrutiny has a meaningful impact on an actor's status, opportunities, and working conditions, as well as on her sense of self. Facing tremendous pressure to conform to the fairly narrow ideals of womanhood considered marketable in the mainstream adult industry, all porn actresses find ways to commodify their bodies and promote their erotic capital while also protecting their self-esteem.

One way that many actresses respond to the pressure to confront the pornstar ideal is by having some form of plastic surgery, particularly breast enhancements. The trend toward larger, surgically modified breasts in pornographic film seems to have emerged in the 1990s. This trend coincided with the popularity of the Southern California lifeguard television series *Baywatch* and its buxom leading actress, Pamela Anderson. Spantaneeus Xtasty found that modifying her breasts in the mode of her idol, country singer Dolly Parton, won her added attention during her career in the 1990s. Over a period of years, she had five surgeries to reach a size 55FF bust. Stressing that breast augmentation was her longtime dream, even before entering adult entertainment, Spantaneeus found that her larger bust allowed her to cross over into breast-fetish niche markets like *Busty Hustler*. "To have a normal or small frame and have these huge hooters," Spantaneeus asserts, "that's what I wanted. Not so big that they would just take me up in the air, but I wanted them to be abnormally big."[33] Although now she is "downsizing for the next chapter of Spantaneeus," and her own comfort, she clearly took pleasure in altering her body according to her imagination and desire. Another feature she cultivated was extremely long nails. Acquiring an "abnormally big" bust and crafting her long nails in brightly colored enamels were key tactics in Spantaneeus's efforts to stand out as unique and memorable among actresses.

Black adult actor Byron Long terms this trend in black performer embodiments mirroring norms of white femininity in pornographic media, "chocolate Barbie dolls."[34] Thinner yet busty women with narrow hips are given the most attention and access to opportunities to crossover to higher-budget pornographic film projects. According to Sinnamon Love, "The farther away [black actresses] are from the natural, voluptuous figure of a black woman, the better it is, and the more likely they are to get the jobs."[35] Black performers with more voluptuous bodies, or those with some fat or cellulite, tend to be seen as less attractive and more fitting for low-budget film work in ghetto porn and related subgenres of black and interracial porn. They are sometimes marginalized in niche markets like fat porn, where the actresses are often compared to animals like hippos and elephants. Since the early 2000s, BBW (Big Beautiful Women) pornography has gained popularity as a subgenre for women who are bigger than the norm but not quite as big as "fat porn" actresses. The black BBW niche reflects the adult industry's attempts to satisfy the desires of consumers of color to view curvier women. As a result, more full-figured actresses are gaining work opportunities in the adult film business than ever before.

Actresses like Sasha Brabuster and Betty Blac make use of the BBW market. Sasha asserted that it is not only her curves and naturally large breasts (size 44KK–JJ) that garner lucrative prospects in the business. Sasha claimed that exceptional performance skills, including a nearly double-jointed flexibility, make her more valuable in some ways than many of the women trying to break into the mainstream porn market. However, her embodiment also provided another dimension to her labor exploitation by adult industry companies. Sasha explained:

> I'm gonna tell you something about [production companies]. Let me go with you there. They gonna make you earn it. You gotta have breaks and shit! Drink your water. You know how you [have to] wipe your pussy and all that [after sex]? Them mothafuckas was talkin': "Come on Sasha!" They wanna [push me] like a damn work mule, they don't want me to rest. "I'm tired mothafucka!" These are heavy (*indicating her breasts*). . . . It's a mind game. They wanna get as much outta you as they can. You ain't gotta get fucked for nobody. You know what I'm saying?

They wanted me to do all this double-jointed, gymnastic, callisthenic, damn contortionist shit. Three hours straight. Now can I just talk about being anatomically correct, can I elaborate for a minute? I am not no fucking size 1. I never was a 1 [even] when I was a fucking baby (*laughing and shaking her head*). Ok, my titties is half my body weight. . . . Silicone has no weight. You can have a bouncing bitch for ten hours, right? If you got bowling balls on your fucking dick . . ." Picture bowling balls as your balls mothafucka and tell me that you gonna jump up and down!" It's not impossible, but it's difficult, right? So what they'll do, if you can't do it [is say], "Pshaw, we gotta go nonstop. Then something's wrong with you. Is it because you're big?" "No bitch, I'm a fucking double K mothafucka, you kidding around?"[36]

Sasha reveals the ways in which production companies demand an intense regime of labor from actors and how, though her larger size opens up job opportunities in specialty films that she may not otherwise obtain in mainstream porn, it presents a challenge. Producers that profit from her particular form of embodiment also discipline it, forcing her to perform in ways that she feels are both unnecessarily arduous and unhealthy. Sasha worries about tearing in her breast tissue from all of the bouncing required in the fast-paced athletic sex required in shoots, and she believes that producers' demands to not take breaks, to speed up her work, and to move her body in ways that ignore the costs of such mobility for someone of size are ultimately forms of exploitation that she must resist. Sasha's narration of talking back to the producers makes it unclear as to whether she actually spoke up on set about her feelings, but it is important nonetheless. It demonstrates that Sasha is critical of the conditions and expectations placed on BBW performers and that she sees herself as pushing back against these pernicious forms of labor discipline.

As newcomer BBW actress Betty Blac argues, African American BBWs are "already a subcategory of a subcategory," and a lot of the productions featuring black actresses are by studios she describes as the "more ghetto companies."[37] According to Betty, these studios "regularly find women who are down on their luck." Offering these performers $1,000 for a job, the companies then extract five scenes from them, thus paying them only $250 a scene. "I want to work for more respectable companies," Betty tells me. "BBWs are not seen as valuable at all. I feel double disposable."[38]

In addition to body size and shape, a systemic color hierarchy shapes conditions for porn work; it challenges black women workers' legitimacy and narrows their opportunities.[39] The association of lighter-skinned black women

FIGURE 6.3. "Where ordinary just won't do!" Sasha Brabuster's business card. Author's collection.

with greater sexual desirability has a long history. During the antebellum era, the so-called Fancy Trade, the trade in black women as sexual slaves popular in southern port cities, was known for prizing very light-skinned black women. These often mixed-raced or Creole women were found attractive for their approximation to the white feminine ideal, but were also desirable for their assumed racial characteristics, including potent sexual aggressiveness and exoticism. During the twentieth century, social practices that favored light skin over dark skin included black beauty pageants like Miss Bronze America, created as an alternative to all-white pageants like Miss America. Lighter-skinned actresses like Lena Horne, Eartha Kitt, and Dorothy Dandridge also gained prominence in Hollywood over darker-skinned but equally talented actresses like Ethel Waters. Fair-skinned models graced the cover of the magazines *Jet* and *Hue* in the 1950s and '60s, representing the epitome of beauty for African Americans during the civil rights movement. Even after the rise of "Black is Beautiful" as a politics of racial affirmation that celebrated brown skin and black aesthetics during the 1970s, the politics of colorism have continued. Colorism still affects the representation of black female desirability, as seen in the fairer skin tones of the top African American Hollywood actresses: Halle Berry, Zoe Saldana, Sanaa Lathan, and Queen Latifah.[40] Producing and perpetuating a hierarchal system of aesthetics and embodiment for black women in entertainment and daily life, colorism is reflected in all forms of sex work too.

Pornography's politics of colorism incite frustration among, and antipathy between, black women. With notable exceptions, darker-skinned women tend to be placed in all-black pornographic films, whereas lighter-skinned women are better able to move back and forth between all-black and interracial pornography. Many of the black women who have reached contract-star status, such as Heather Hunter, Lacey Duvalle, and Tiffany Mason, are light skinned. Those who do not fit within a desired category are subordinated or otherwise excluded from employment opportunities with evasive excuses: "We can't shoot you right now, but as soon as we're shooting something, we'll call you."[41] This was what a casting agent told brown-skinned Stacy Cash when she called to inquire about bookings. "But if you send in a picture of a girl that is lighter than you," she added, "then they'll shoot her. It depends on what their preferences are. . . . You have to work within the category that you are in."[42] Stacy is not alone in confronting painful rejection due to colorism. "There have been days that I've been cancelled for lighter girls, black girls, but lighter," Candice Nicole explained.[43]

Mya Lovely described feeling hated by other black women for her complexion. "The fact that I'm lighter skinned," she asserted, means that, "all the darker women will hate because all the white companies will hire me."[44] Mya goes on to describe how she perceives the resentment of darker-skinned actresses:

> I've been on scenes where there were all the black women and they didn't even acknowledge me, like they were too good for me, and sucking their teeth. I'm like drop it! Have fun, you are paid to be here. . . . I guess they feel like they are just oppressed or something. They have so much anger that they can't just be happy. A lot of women, black women, in this business are like that. I guess it's the business too, being turned down so many times. . . . You are too dark, you are too thick, you are too this. It can kind of turn black women angry.[45]

Mya was unhappy with the suspicion and mistrust she felt from other black female actresses; however, she saw these dynamics as playing out within an industry that makes black women constantly feel that they are not good enough. She describes the outrage black actresses feel when they are constantly rejected and told they are "too dark" or "too thick" to be cast for a role. New to the adult industry, with just twelve films under her belt when I interviewed her, Mya Lovely had already felt the effects of intra-racial antagonism spurred by these politics of desirability. When I asked if she thought that black women would be able to come together across color difference to support one another, Mya was pessimistic: "I don't think that will ever happen, unfortunately. We all wish that could happen. I think women in general wish they could get along."[46]

Competition in the adult business pits black women against each other, against other women of color, and against white women who set the bar by which they are measured. Not only does this competition contribute to a downward pressure on wages for all performers, it empowers adult manufacturers to rationalize their economic formulas in ways that never address how profoundly undervalued and diminished black sex workers are. Candice Nicole expertly broke down pornography producers' known economic rationale for privileging white women over black women: "If you put a white girl on a [video] box [cover], she will sell, like five hundred times more than what a black girl will sell and these companies need to stay in business. So they are going to put out there what they know is gonna sell, they are not gonna take a chance. So the white movies that I do do, I'm not on the box cover."[47]

Candice Nicole described how she attempted to stick up for herself and demand representation on a video box cover.[48] "I was having a conversation with a company owner. I said, 'Fuck ya'll! You done shot me about twenty to thirty times and you won't put me on a box cover.' He said, 'You are too pretty to be on a box cover. If we put a pretty girl on the box cover the shit won't sell. If we put some ugly hood bitch on the box cover it will sell.' He was like, 'You should be flattered.'"[49] Candice was shocked and furious about this producer's patronizing argument, and she was bewildered that he would argue that the video would be more marketable with an "ugly hood bitch" on the cover. "Sad to say," Candice adds, producers "don't want to see black women glamorized."[50] It seems obvious that this production company owner's statements sought to dismiss Candice's demand for greater visibility in the film's marketing materials. Given this kind of everyday manipulation and use of warped logic by production companies, it is not surprising that black actresses feel discouraged. The politics of unequal desire—on the part of viewers, manufacturers, and others—has a profound economic impact on black professional pornographic performers' work and emotional life.[51] The business of pornographic desire and desirability produces far-reaching effects that many experience as a form of injustice and injury.

## You Black Bitch

Lola Lane tells a story in which she worked for a white production company and director known for their extremely violent sex films with bizarre scenarios and antics. She thought the opportunity to work with a known director was exciting and decided to put her all into the performance. Lola describes her reaction to seeing the footage after the film came out:

> This director hadn't shot in a while and I was honored because I was going to be the only black girl in his comeback movie. And I used to love the way that they direct because they do real movies, because there's always something behind it. We were at this abandoned apartment in Hollywood and it's late and they wrote on the walls. I'm like this is a real movie. Of course, I'm the typical whore and the guy comes in and has sex with me and he kills me and I'm supposed to die. And all my girls loved the scene, but I was watching the movie (and I never watch my work but I just happened to want to watch this one because I knew I had to act) and flashing across the scene was racial comments. Like in a blink, like if you didn't really pay attention, you wouldn't have been able to see it. And I was like turn that back, and it said, "You black bitch," "black whore," something like that, it was something racial. My friends were like, "It was a really good scene," but I was hurt. Did you see what that said? But they thought I knew or that was part of the movie and they thought, "Well, how could you get mad, this is a porn movie?" and I'm like, how can I *not* be mad? I didn't know that they were going to do that, because I would have said no.[52]

Lola's astonishing story illustrates the negative ways in which black women are treated as workers, both on set and in the field of representation. The incident she describes of having racist and misogynist epithets written across her image on-screen is remarkably similar to Nyrobi Knights's experience. Nyrobi had a jewel pendant attached to her belly chain altered to appear as a mini KKK figure on a video box cover: "If you look at the backside of the video, you'll see someone has painted a KKK guy on my belly chain. It's this drawing of a guy wearing a white sheet over his head, with these little eyes and teeth peeking out, and holding a torch. I was very upset by it. The thing just disgusted me. And the folks at Rosebud [the production company] claim they don't know who put it there. But like, I mean, *fuck*, why would somebody put it there?"[53]

Lola's and Nyrobi's fury and frustration at having their images digitally manipulated and misused speaks to tensions between how black women see themselves and how others see and use them. Furthermore, these incidents exhibit the ways in which paradoxical forces of desire and disdain, as well as pleasure and control, function in the adult industry. This racist and sexist treatment, expressed even in passive and clandestine ways, is one of the major dimensions of labor exploitation that form the unequal terrain of pornography for these women. Lacking investment in their professional development, promotion for their projects and appearances, and lucrative contracts with related adult industry companies like sex-toy manufacturers, black female performers are especially vulnerable to these forms of labor subordination and abuse.

The injurious personal treatment and interactions black female performers have with casts, crews, directors, and producers inform the overall conditions of their work as well as their career paths. However, pre- and postproduction workers, such as editors, designers, casting directors, agents, public relations managers, distributors, and photographers, can all have significant impacts on work conditions and the final product as well. Unfortunately, a large number of my informants revealed having experienced rude, unprofessional, and even hostile treatment both on and off the set, behavior they identified as being racially and sexually motivated. For some actresses, these negative experiences could be very subtle or covert, while for others, abusive and biased treatment took very blatant forms.

It is common for performers to be rushed, criticized, or ignored on movie and photo sets. As Lacey Duvalle describes, "Directors will be rude to you, they'll rush you, make little comments . . . or they try to make you feel like you're not doing something right."[54] Feeling comfortable on a film set, photo shoot, or performance stage is of principal importance to adult entertainment performers precisely because their performative labor is so taxing. During hardcore sex scenes, these performers expose their naked bodies for hours under hot lights in awkward and uncomfortable positions in front of a crew of strangers, while at the same time presenting themselves as fresh, beautiful, and alluring. It is intimidating and difficult work, which is why actresses hope directors will be supportive and sensitive instead of callous and demanding. Actresses in low-end productions, as so many black actresses are, also contend with having a lack of wardrobe and makeup support when on set; they must bring their own costumes and do their own makeup, which adds to their stress on set.

Actresses are accused of having bitchy attitudes when they protest their treatment, and black women have a reputation for being divas that are especially difficult to work with. Directors complain that black women do not work hard enough, are unprofessional, lazy, do not create enough "heat," and refuse to do the real hardcore and intense sex acts that other actresses are willing to perform like double penetration, double anal, bukkake, and gang bangs. This perception that black actresses are unruly and unwilling workers is unwarranted according to some actresses, and is related to the belief that black women do not have anything to complain about and should be grateful to even be included in the business. Hyperaware of their treatment, the actresses I spoke to are critical of these excuses by management and resist being blamed for their own experiences of bias. Nyrobi Knights, for instance, described how one director treated her like "a piece of shit," even though she felt she was performing her best. "Funny thing is, I gave him a *great* scene," she said. "But he just wouldn't treat me like a human being."[55]

One racist belief that fosters the devaluation of black actresses in the adult film industry is that white actresses can lower their value by having sex with black actors, particularly with black men. Champagne, a voluptuous exotic dancer and porn actress active in the late 1990s, describes instances of being hired as the only black woman on an all-white film and the ways in which her fellow cast members and the director participated in pushing her out. On one set, she explained, "The guy who's supposed to have sex with me also has a sex scene [planned] with a white girl. And she goes crazy because she doesn't want him to fuck me and then her. The director will pat you on the back and give you twenty or thirty dollars for carfare and tell you to go home."[56] In this example, a white actress felt that even indirect sex by association with a black female actress was undesirable. Whether she was motivated by professional aspirations to keep her record "clean" or her own racial anxieties about sexual intimacy with black bodies is unclear. What is obvious, however, is that rather than challenge the racism of the white performer to provide safe, equal working conditions, the director chose to subordinate the black performer.

Although they certainly experience gender bias and oppression throughout the pornography industry, white actresses largely benefit from this racial hierarchy. For example, Marie Luv described a little-publicized trend in which some white actresses charge more for doing interracial sex scenes with black men. Marie was so frustrated by what she saw as the unfairness of white women insisting on an "interracial rate" that she decided to see if she could get away with charging more for having sex with white men. "It kinda makes me not want to be in this business because you can't tell me that that's not racist. You are going to pay a white girl more with a black man? And I did a scene with two white men and I said to them, dead serious, 'My interracial

FIGURE 6.4. Marie Luv strikes a pose at Erotica LA (2009). Photograph by the author.

rate is going to be . . .' and they *laughed* at me. It was a fucking joke! But if I was Jenna Haze and I sat there and said that they [would say], 'Let me get my checkbook.'"[57]

The fantasy of sex between white women and black men is highly complex. Rooted in historical policing of the racial-sexual border and the disciplining violence against black men's bodies this fantasy troubles white men's sense of patriarchal control over white women and produces a profound sense of anxiety for white men about their sexual displacement by the very men they subordinate. These anxieties about interracial sex are equally wrapped up in fear and pleasure, and hence, they are powerful taboos that pornography is well positioned to bring into public consciousness, to expose, rework, and commodify.

Marie Luv's claim to be similarly compensated for interracial sex with white men spotlights how black women's lower erotic capital—and their ability to make similar demands for equal treatment and pay—is essentially linked to the historical fetishism of black female sexuality as super-available to all men, especially white men. White male consumers see black women as always already hypersexual, so the interracial fantasy for them is comparatively less taboo than that of white women and black men. If black women speak up about their treatment they are often dismissed, but they nonetheless risk resisting unfair labor conditions in overt and subtle ways. Like Marie, Vanessa Blue was disgusted by the interracial rate trend and saw it as part of the overall system by which black actresses are mistreated in the porn business. She observed that "half of the white girls don't care, the other half who come in with an agent instantly, it is their agent who tells them not to do that."[58] Booking agents encourage white actresses to maximize their profit by charging more for a sex act commonly seen to degrade white women's image of racial purity and their capital in pornography. However, white actresses' personal desires are often quite different, to the point where they fetishize black men's sexuality. "But off camera, at the parties," Vanessa contends, "white girls are jocking the brothers *like dick was born*."[59] Vanessa believes white actresses enjoy the benefits of a system in which they are financially rewarded for objectifying and devaluing black people, even if they secretly desire them. As a director, Vanessa is in a position where she can refuse to pay white women more for interracial sex: "When I work with certain girls, I will try to hire from certain agencies where I know that overall the agency doesn't have an issue with it."[60] In this way, Vanessa can intervene in the political economy in order to disrupt white women's privilege.

Through interracial rates white women enjoy specific advantages in the porn business. Although they, too, face mistreatment and abuse, their erotic capital is always higher due to their racial position in regards to beauty and desirability norms. In addition, the taboo of white women's racial transgression for having sex with black men is a favored fantasy for the primarily white male viewers who buy pornography, as well as black male spectators. This fantasy exploits and uses both black men and black women, but in divergent ways. My male informants contend that the white masculine gaze uses black men to punish white women. The interracial fetish is actually a cover for white male desire to see black men's bodies.[61] I suspect that the drives, psychic and social, toward this fascination are highly varied and complicated. What seems clear is that white men and black men producing pornographic images—from professional companies that manufacture films to amateurs who create video clips for distribution online—are highly invested in the symbolic power of racial trespassing embodied in sex acts between black men and white women because it is so profitable. This fact essentially marginalizes the sexual representation and labor of black women, including in the less popular interracial films featuring black women with white men. It also adds to the competition between black women and white women for power in the adult film business.

When I met Cherry,[62] a popular adult film actress in black and interracial porn in the 2000s, she discussed her frustration with feeling ignored and undervalued. She recalled one instance when she was invited to appear in a video being shot in Northern California. Taking it in stride as part of a career that leads her all over the country for jobs and appearances, Cherry flew to the city of the shoot and was picked up at the airport by a representative from the film studio. Instead of offering to pick up her large suitcase filled with costumes for the shoot, this white male employee greeted her coolly and walked quickly in front of her as he led her to another part of the airport to pick up one of the white actresses who had also traveled to work on the film. Cherry was annoyed to see that her guide greeted the white actress warmly and professionally, and that he briskly picked up her suitcase and walked with his arms around her to the parking lot, leaving Cherry to walk behind them, struggling with her own bag.

When all three arrived at the car, the white actress, not having been introduced to Cherry as her costar, asked, "Why is this girl following us?" In addition to the embarrassment and anger over the lack of consideration offered her by the production-company employee who walked ahead of her and barely acknowledged her existence, Cherry was annoyed to learn upon arriving to the set that the company had assigned her to a double-penetration scene without her permission, knowing full well that she never performed them. "They just treated me like shit," she said, "like I didn't even matter."[63] In the end, Cherry performed the scene and did not protest the lack of professionalism and unfair treatment by the production company. "I needed the work," she said. "I had traveled all the way there. I couldn't just leave."[64] Cherry vowed to never work for that company again.

Cherry's experience is similar to Serria Tawan's story. Serria is one of the few black women to grace the pages of *Playboy* during the 2000s, a coveted job that pays $25,000. One of the benefits of becoming a *Playboy* model is gaining access to a certain level of cachet in the sex and entertainment business that ideally leads to valuable opportunities for work in softcore modeling and acting. Serria, however, found that her prized appearance in *Playboy* led nowhere. No opportunities came knocking. When she was invited to a dinner at the Playboy Mansion, Hugh Hefner's sprawling estate, Serria was surprised by what she felt was biased treatment. As all of the models were seated around an immense table with Hefner at the head, Serria, the only black woman in the room, was told to sit at a second table off in the corner of the room. Cherry's and Serria's testimonies illustrate how subtle forms of mistreatment and marginalization often undermine the ethic of care by which black porn actresses wish to be treated.

Because many black porn actresses work in other areas of the sex industry as well, it is important to note that the forms of inequality and bias apparent in the adult film business are also evident in these other domains. Prostitution is rife with abuse by law-enforcement officers and a criminal-justice system that unfairly incarcerates African American women at higher rates than women of any other race. Sex-worker activists like Gloria Lockett, Sharmus Outlaw, Carol Leigh, Rachel West, Audacia Ray, and others argue that black women and transwomen are particularly vulnerable to criminalization and, as a result, are put at risk of violence, homelessness, hunger, addiction, disease, and displacement.[65] Few studies explore the experiences of women of color in higher-end forms of prostitution that many porn actresses pursue, but because it is illegal work many of these risks born out of racialized antisex work policies and practices are also relevant for this class of laborers.

Bias in the exotic-dance industry is likewise an issue for black female sex workers. Many porn actresses begin their careers as dancers in gentlemen's clubs, which as Becki Ross has shown in the Canadian context and Siobhan Brooks and Kim Price-Glynn in the U.S. context, have a long history of racial segregation.[66] Sierra described the difficulty she had accessing opportunities to dance in white clubs both before and after she made a name for herself as a porn star. On one particular occasion she tried to get a job dancing at the Pink Pony, a well-known white club in Atlanta, Georgia, and was harshly rebuffed. She told me:

> In the South you'll never see more than two black girls on a shift in a white club. You ever notice that? I went into . . . the Pink Pony. It's a big club. They told me I could work there if I won the contest, when I went up there to apply for a job. I had to win the contest! So naïve little me goes there the next night and wins the contest! So they were like, "Well you can work here, but you can't work the night shift." I'm going like, "What? I can work here, but I can't work the night shift?" They said you can work the midshift. They show me the book and there are four girls working the midshift. It's from 4pm–12am. It's a decent

shift. . . . So being from the educated background that I am, I called the next day to make sure everything was cool. Should I go get my permit? Permits at the time were $45, which at the time for me was a little bit much, [although] less than the $300 they are now. So I call and I'm on the phone saying, "Hi, my name is Sierra. I am supposed to start today. Should I go get my permit?" And the lady goes, "Sure, no problem." Mind you we talked on the phone, and I did not tell her I was black. I don't know why. It just didn't dawn on me to also tell her that I was black! I go get my permit, put my bags in the car, go all the way up there and walk in the dressing room and I go, "Hi, I'm Sierra!" This woman's mouth dropped to the floor! She didn't even hide it! She said, "You're Sierra?" I said, "Yeah I'm Sierra." She said, "You sit there for a while." Fifteen minutes goes by, twenty-five minutes goes by, thirty-five minutes goes by. I'm like, "What's the deal? What's going on?" "Well, we have too many people working this shift. We cannot hire you for the shift." I said, "That's not true. They showed me the book last night, there are only four girls!" "Well," she says, "we really don't cater to the types of customers you would bring in." I'm like, "What? Old white men?!" (*laughing*) I pretty much only dance to rock! I don't dance to rap. I had a good following and all my customers were white men. . . . I just went home and cried and cried and cried. I had never been so insulted in my life. Now I hear it so much I forget how insulting that is. . . . I'm a pretty black girl, you know? I'm not a ghetto girl. I can understand if I was some loud ghetto girl walking in here, but even if I am loud and ghetto, if I'm pretty you should still hire me. . . . I have a fire show! I do magic tricks! I do all kinds of stuff. I actually have a SHOW! I wear big, huge Las Vegas showgirl pieces. . . . I don't understand when someone says we don't cater to your people. You are saying [audiences] are not going to like my stuff? Come on! I'm not going to do an African dance or something. There is a lot of prejudice among the strip clubs. And unfortunately, it leaks into the porn industry.[67]

Despite identifying all of the ways in which she tried to avoid stereotypes of low-class black womanhood and even cultivated a persona and performance practice that resisted the confining tropes applied to black sex workers, Sierra found that sexualized racism nonetheless defined her experiences as a stripper. When an employer attempted to bar her from working in an upscale club by requiring her to win their big dance contest, Sierra drew on her craft as a performance artist to put on a real show, with fire, magic, and elaborate feather and sequin costumes included. Although Sierra went on to win the contest—something she really wanted to do to turn the tables and empower herself in this situation—she ultimately failed to gain employment. The club management believed that her black female body would undermine the cultivated whiteness of the space. Sierra's smart and incisive critiques of the fears of black infiltration into spaces of white fantasy and sexual economy, and of the privileging of white women's erotic labor, and the seepage of these issues into the porn industry, are valuable. She argues that no matter how black women performers enact their race, gender, and class in their erotic labor, they deserve to be hired. For Sierra, employment should be fair, and racial bias is not only a painful issue, it is unjust.

### An Ethics of Power

"We are all the same," asserted Lola Lane. "I'm black and you're white, but we are still women."[68] Lola critiques the ways in which racial discrimination structures the adult industry and functions to undermine women's potential alliances across race toward a labor agenda for all sex workers. According to Lola and many of her peers, pornography, as an industry and perhaps as a cultural force too, has the capacity to respect the diversity of every worker's economic, social, and even erotic value. It is incumbent upon the industry to respond to the needs and demands of its workers. Black porn actresses theorize and negotiate inequality in at least three divergent ways. First, some performers protest and refuse to work under certain conditions, hoping their stance will force employers to realize their wrongdoing. Others, however, believe they must accept existing conditions, at least temporarily, in hopes that they will prevail over exploitation through the attainment of individual stardom. Still others opt out. Leaving the industry, perhaps after trying the first two methods of negotiation, they decide for themselves that their best interests and talents lie elsewhere. Alternately, they show that the conditions are untenable and insecure, leaving the performer without the ability to thrive financially or emotionally. In this sense, removing oneself from this labor market, even if temporarily, is a notable form of critique as well a mode of survival.

In the first set of tactics black performers mobilize illicit eroticism to navigate their work in more confrontational terms. Diana DeVoe and Lexi were good friends when I interviewed them back in 2003. Diana had years more experience than Lexi as an actress, and by that time Lexi was moving out of performance work to a role behind the scenes at a production company, and

Diana was beginning to think seriously about pursuing her aspirations to direct hardcore films. They explained that Lexi was initially bewildered and overwhelmed by the exploitative nature of the industry, and the constant attempt by studio executives to undercut her pay. Diana mentored her, providing valuable advice about how to demand her worth. She explained:

> I just told her like this: Everybody in this industry wants something from you. If they took the time to talk to you, they want something. I told her I want her to keep her rate high. I told her to not do anything she doesn't want to do because if she did that then it would make it easier for me to do the same thing. I told her just like this: "That is what I want from you. I don't want you to do $500 scenes. And if you don't do it, and I don't do it, and this girl doesn't do it, and this other girl doesn't do it, then there won't be any more $500 scenes!"[69]

Demonstrating a remarkable shrewdness, Diana explained the ways in which pay inequality serves to undermine all workers and empower management at the expense of labor. More significantly, Diana elucidates how black women's theories of empowerment and tactics of self-fashioning may be circulated and shared among their community of erotic workers. These theories and tactics are simultaneously important to black women's survival as individuals and their potential for collective dissent.

Lollipop is a good example of the second strategy. She told me: "In this industry, if you want to get yourself out there you are basically gonna accept what they have for you. If you are gonna consider yourself a star, you have to act like a star. Once you are known and you get yourself out there a little bit, people will start to recognize you."[70] For Lollipop, the lack of opportunity and other barriers black adult film actresses face can only be surpassed by accommodating to the current conditions and ultimately triumphing over them. This is an understanding born out of a prevailing neoliberal view of individualism and social responsibility: it is the responsibility of the victim to transform themselves rather than the system's responsibility to protect the victim. In fact, alongside discursive figures blaming black women for their victimization like the matriarch and the welfare queen, neoliberalism has produced an extensive discourse about black women's need to exhibit personal responsibility and undo their own conditions of inequality. When they fail, they alone are blamed.[71]

The contemporary hegemony of the concept of personal responsibility in part explains the tension between the tactics and philosophies of black sexual laborers in porn. Diana's belief in changing structures of disempowerment through confrontation and the building of strategic alliances among women rubs up against Lollipop's faith in individual agency as a path to overcoming social exclusion. These women's divergent understandings and negotiations of the unequal terrain of pornography's sexual political economy represent the essential struggle that black people face in light of the newly formulated and super-embedded structures of late capitalism. Whereas overcoming struggle is important for combating injustice and exploitation, the discourse sometimes slips into a neoliberal understanding of the victim as ultimately responsible for transforming what are actually vast structural inequities that shape her life. "It's a struggle," Lollipop declares, "but it's not something that a black woman must give up on; she just has to continue to strive and go for it if that's what she wants, and that's what I want so I'm gonna continue to strive."[72]

Lola Lane, however, decided to leave the pornography business. Ultimately, fighting issues of subordination and bias, as well as pay inequality and the constant need to fight for fair wages in the face of producers pressuring her to provide ever-cheaper work, took its toll. She was also fed up with abusive directors who wanted her to have sex with them in exchange for acting roles, and with fans who became frightening, even life-threatening, stalkers. Unlike other professional porn actresses, Lola was not interested in fame. Rather than enjoying being recognized at church or the airport, she wanted the peace of anonymity. She wanted a normal life. Lola also wanted to be there for her son, now in high school, and to finally tell him about the job she had never addressed but imagined he secretly suspected. It was important to her that when telling her son about her choices to pursue such a stigmatized profession that she could point to how it benefited them both in the long run.

> I wanted to wait until he got [to] sixteen and just talk to him because I know he'll be able to understand. I know that he probably would have understood, four years ago, three years ago, but the reason why I haven't is because I wanted to make sure that I had accomplished certain things in my life. I wanted to say, "Mommy did this to get *over here* in life. Now we're over here, I'm not saying what mommy did was bad, but she did this so that we could get here in life. So now mommy's not doing that anymore but without that there wouldn't be no *this*." I just had to make sure that I had that stabilized, because in my heart I just wanted to have that because my son has been the only real concern, not family, not friends, not the world. Protecting my son had been like the only real concern with what I've done. I'm not really ashamed of what I've

done. I just didn't want my son to be ashamed. So in my heart that was the only issue.[73]

Lola wanted to have something to show for all the years she devoted to working in porn—she wanted a sense of legitimacy, understanding, and accomplishment. In light of the overwhelming stigma associated with sex work, it is not hard to image why Lola was concerned about how her son would react to finding out his mother was a porn star. She worried that unless she proved her success and financial independence, her claims that her choice was worth it would ring hollow. But how could she explain to her son the costs of her labor, what it meant for her to fight her way through an industry that has so little perceived value? This overriding stigma, I believe, infuses the tone of Lola's testimony with regret, rather than pride in her accomplishments. As her anxious discourse reveals, these modes of negotiating inequality—accepting, fighting against, or refusing working conditions—are by no means distinct. They are overlapping and changing modes of interaction that my informants employ in dynamic ways.

When we spoke last, Lola was working on getting licensed as a real estate agent and finding ways to invest her earnings from more than a decade of work in porn. She was also working on a cookbook with her family and devising a business with her sister called *Girls on the Run*, a kind of personal concierge service. She wanted to write a book about relationships, and of course, she also discussed Fantine's Dream Foundation. Cognizant of how ex-porn organizations often frame the industry as evil and women as victims who need to wake up to their abuse, she added, "I'm not trying to stop the industry. I'm not judging anybody."[74] For Lola, the desire to help was coming from a position of sisterhood and solidarity with women who shared a common experience. Moreover, through the organization and meeting with others like her, she hoped to make sense of her own experience.

Although Lola discussed her multiple business plans and her goals for the nonprofit, she also spoke about how difficult it was to leave the business. She relied on the income to support a lifestyle to which she had become accustomed. Despite cutting back on expenses, trading in her luxury car lease for an economy option, and trying her hand at investing, Lola found her increasingly infrequent earnings from porn acting were not enough to take care of her family. "And people say, [go on] welfare. I'm not a welfare mother and that [money] is nothing compared to what I'm used to getting. And I'm supposed to survive off of that? You know it's no way when you are used to getting all this money every couple of days. You know, it's hard."[75]

Just as she did not want to be confined by the whore stigma because of her sexual labor, Lola did not want to be deemed a stereotypical black welfare mother. Moreover, leaving this stigma aside, someone whose core desires are for financial security and independence may not even consider welfare to be an option. Government entitlements do little to address the essential needs of women of color in poverty, let alone offer a middle-class standard of living.[76] Lola was forced to remain attached to the adult industry, at least until her new plans showed more promise. The difficulty exiting the industry can be viewed as an essential problematic of the profession: porn workers face narrowed opportunities to gain employment in fields outside the sex industry and are barred from some occupations—like teaching children—altogether. The question of whether to stay or leave is a difficult one. Black women porn performers contend with many issues, including how to "come out" to their families and friends, how to cope with the emotional and embodied dimensions of the work, and how to ensure their livelihoods both inside and outside of porn work.

Diana DeVoe and Lexi identify three stages black women porn workers go through. The first is naïveté, in which performers are only beginning to learn to negotiate the conditions of their labor, but lack useful knowledge about who to trust and how to advocate for themselves effectively. The second stage is rage. "At first I was like *Okay*," Lexi says in a high, sweet voice. "Afterwards I was just like, I hate everybody. I hate all of you!" Diana concurred: "The anger actually pushes you to work harder, or change something about yourself, or change something about the conditions, or it pushes you out of the business. And afterwards it pushes you towards acceptance." "Acceptance? Is that the third stage?" I asked. Diana affirmed, "That is when you either get out of the business and you decide to do something else, or when you stay in the business and fit it to suit your needs rather than trying to suit its needs."[77]

This chapter, and this book, demonstrate black women erotic performers' claims for respect. This politics of respect contrasts with the dominant politics of respectability that polices and limits black women's sexual expressions. Pornography's tiered system of erotic capital structures opportunities, conditions, relationships, and markets. Given their place at the bottom of this hierarchy, African American adult film actresses are in a unique position to offer an ethical evaluation of their industry. Black women exhibit a sexual moral economy, a system of ethics among sex workers about how relations of sexual exchange should operate.[78] This ethical framework represents black porn performers' aspirations for recognition in and control over their work, and their desire for a fair playing field for all porn workers. Shaped by the politics of illicit eroticism, this economy critiques white privilege and the systemic forces of racism and sexism in the sex industry. Moreover, this sexual moral economy values rather than stigmatizes sex work. Black women's pornographic ethics imagines sexual labor as a potential domain for their erotic sovereignty.

A black woman's moral economy that emphasizes workers' rights stands against the values of neoliberal capitalism that pornography as a business embraces. The prevailing erasure of porn performers' status as workers undermines their efforts to negotiate the precariousness of their jobs. This erasure also means that feminist and labor activists, who should be their greatest allies, typically do not see porn workers as a political constituency. Policies directed toward the porn industry, which have gone unremarked by these activists, are often couched in the language of public health, morality, and safety that invites the general public to see the pornography industry and porn workers as a threat. For instance, Measure B, the mandatory condom ordinance passed in Los Angeles in 2012, is an example of a policy that purported to protect porn workers but was designed and passed without their collaboration and input. Indeed, the L.A. County Condom Ordinance Bill was created to address a perceived threat to public health by the porn industry's barrier protection and sti testing methods, not as a work-safety issue under the province of osha.[79]

What can be done in a regulatory climate more devoted to targeting cases of obscenity than exposing violations of fair pay in sex labor markets? And in a context in which ever-greater numbers of workers are categorized as independent contractors, who lack the authority to collectively bargain for improved labor standards and benefits? Past efforts toward porn worker organizing led to informal blacklisting and backlash from industry management. Worse, this is all taking place in an era when unions are declining in all industries, giving way to a global race to the bottom for American workers. Feminists concerned with these labor issues should be the first to understand the alliances that could be forged with sex workers who share the same struggles and are doing their own theorizing about gender, race, and power.

By all accounts, we are still some time away from the emergence of a porn-actors union. This does not mean that workers are idly standing by, accepting the status quo. I have observed an extraordinary level of energy and activity among porn workers rebelling against the hierarchal and alienating aspects of their industry. They forcibly assert their value and integrity, and reimagine pornography as a sexual culture and industry that is also a site for progressive, antiracist, and antisexist politics. The rise of feminist and queer pornographies may facilitate these actors' political claims for more multidimensional representations and fair work conditions. The broader problems of sex nega-tivity and sexualized racism provide a context in which a sex-worker-friendly porn industry holds up, rather than diminishes, the rights of its most margin-alized workforce. If the adult entertainment industry can become an instru-ment of sexual freedom—a freedom belonging not solely to sexual workers but to everyone—then black women performers will have been key catalysts of this revolution.

## Epilogue  Behind the Camera

*Black Women's Illicit Erotic Interventions*

In my research on the representations and labors of black women in pornography I have interviewed dozens of performers active in the adult industry since the 1980s. These ethnographic interviews and encounters have formed the basis for this book's critical insights, as these women's voices are vital sources of knowledge about what pornography means to and for black women. When I began my fieldwork as a graduate student at New York University in 2002, there was no work being done on the topic of black women in pornography, and there were no black women working as directors in straight or queer pornography. In the mid-2000s, as a result of new technologies facilitating the production and distribution of independent pornography, increasing numbers of black women performers such as Vanessa Blue, Diana DeVoe, and Damali XXXPlosive Dares entered porn production, building on the legacy of earlier black women, like Angel Kelly in the late 1980s, who attempted to create a black women's sex cinema from inside the business. Despite utopic predictions about the future of independent digital media production, the work of black female pornographers is just one example of how independent authorship brings with it new dimensions of labor. Not only have these black women pornographers become filmmakers in the traditional sense, they must fulfill a variety of roles: director, producer, editor, screenwriter, cinematographer, public relations agent, casting agent, acting coach, mentor, and distributor, to name a few. They must make themselves experts in new media technologies, e-commerce, and social networking in order to create, promote, and sell their films. To call them simply filmmakers, or even producers, does not capture the range of labor, expertise, or creativity required in their work. Thus, while new media technologies have facilitated their move behind the camera and into new modes of independent ownership of their own images, these technologies have also demanded that black women porn producers navigate complex issues of production, distribution, and representation. As a group that is generally devalued in the marketplace, black women porn directors must develop and pursue tactics to revalue black women in their media and assert their own value as media makers in the adult industry.

Pornography created by black women attempts to expand black women's sexual representations, performances, and labor beyond the current limits of the mainstream porn industry and the confines of pervading stereotypes. Vanessa's *Dark Confessions* (2007), Diana's *Desperate Blackwives* series (2005–10), and Damali's *Maneater: The Prelude* (2010) all display an interest in creating more dynamic roles for black actresses in porn. This work helps us imagine a pornography that could include voluptuous sites for black women's intervention, imagination, and activism. Vanessa Blue's film work explores power reversals and role play, while Diana DeVoe's large body of work tends to engage the issue of class by presenting black women as bored, conniving upper-income housewives, just like the reality TV stars they parody, or as cute and stylish hip hop generationers who counter the image of the abject, low-class "ghetto ho."

Black women filmmakers who are not adult actors, such as Shine Louise Houston (*The Crash Pad*, *Superfreak*, *Champion*), Nenna Feelmore Joiner (*Tight Places: A Drop of Color*, *Hella Brown*), Abiola Abrams aka Venus Hottentot (*AfroDite Superstar*), and Tune (*Day Dreamin'*), also constitute part of this new black women's sex cinema. Shine's and Nenna's work, which has garnered significant attention from queer and transgender communities of color, draws on performers and representations traditionally excluded from both mainstream heterosexual and alternative lesbian porn. Their work emphasizes the sheer range of embodiments, attractions, acts, and desires possible between black women, other women of color, white people, and gender-queer and transgender persons—figurations absent in most porn. This new school of black women porn filmmakers creates visual texts that forcefully intervene in the existing landscape of pornographic media and that prioritize complex views of desire and relation over static notions of race and gender performance. It also upsets ideas about consumption and the notion that black pornography can only ever be offered up for someone else's fantasy—the purported white male gaze. Although this work addresses and appeals to a wide audience, these filmmakers create images that make sure to address other black women. As black women making pornography from their own perspectives, these filmmakers also show the diversity of viewpoints, positions, and gazes employed by black women as spectators.

Yet black women porn filmmakers—both performers-turned-directors and nonperformers—face a number of constraints. There are still far fewer black women active in directing and producing their own videos or video series than black men, who have benefited from the patronage of white male owners of major and minor production houses. Moreover, black women's porn production work is not as well financed as that of black men. Unlike the predominantly white male directors, producers, and distributors who run the porn industry, and the many white female directors who have innovated a veritable feminist pornography movement since the 1980s, black women do not have the capital, privilege, or influence to truly compete in the multibillion-dollar trade of pornography. They must either rely on traditional "boy's club" networks for production or distribution, or invent new modes to produce, or distribute their work directly to consumers, all of which tend to limit their sales. A reason they have to become so good at many facets of making and marketing porn is that they often lack the resources to do otherwise. As Vanessa Blue explains, for black women sex workers, gaining access to the means of production often involves negotiating a set of barriers and exploitations that do not exist for others: "I see that there are no women of my skin tone [making porn]. I see that there are very few white women doing it. But what's stopping us from doing it? The more I talked to people about it, the more I found out the truth. I had to fuck a few people to get some more information, and I did."[1] As a woman of color in the sex industry no one takes you seriously, Vanessa told me, and they are certainly not willing to invest in you without some personal gain.

Black women pornographers confront material constraints as they enact expansive, and even radical, views of black sexuality against deeply fraught imaginings of black being. They work to challenge the representation of black women's bodies as simultaneously desirable and undesirable objects. In the adult industry, where excessive sexuality would seem to be an asset, black women's presumed hypersexuality may actually undermine their value. Whether located in the mainstream heterosexual market of pornography or on its marginalized outer limits, this disabling discursive construction of black female sexuality provides an inescapable text that black women behind the camera must confront and grapple with as they strive to author a pornographic imaginarium of and for themselves.

I use the term "illicit eroticism" throughout this book to conceptualize how black women sex workers employ their mythic racialized hypersexuality in the sexual economy. Because they make use of a sexuality intertwined with notions of deviance and pathology, I argue that black illicit erotic workers are positioned as sexual outlaws. From this position, they convert forbidden and proscribed sexual desires, fantasies, and practices (including prostitution) into a form of defiant "play-labor."[2] The tactics of illicit eroticism, as described in this book, are threefold. First, black women in pornography use illicit eroticism to intervene in the realm of *representation*, working around, against, and through often-stereotypical roles to produce illicit erotic images of black female sexuality. Second, black female porn performers use illicit eroticism in the realm of *personal development and exploration*, using erotic performance as an opportunity to have new sexual experiences, and presenting themselves and their biographical experiences as courageous, groundbreaking, and transcendent, not exploited or victimized. Finally, illicit eroticism is useful to black women navigating the field of pornography as an *industry*. The industrial tactics of illicit eroticism include black women's use of their sexual capital for material survival, the ways in which their participation in the industry may provide space for future actresses to enter, and their ability to take control of the means of production. It is to this goal of controlling the means of production to which I turn in this epilogue. This third mode of industrial illicit eroticism may also be called "activist production." That is, illicit eroticism also captures how black sex workers advocate for just conditions in the sexual economy and greater personal autonomy in the choice of sexual labor. Illicit erotic activism includes making porn that undermines, or reimagines, the status quo of black representational politics and organizes labor to improve conditions for sex workers. Illicit erotic activism thus theorizes the involvement, incorporation, and interventions of black women in feminist pornography and as feminist pornographers. These multiple and dynamic mobilizations are only just beginning to be examined by scholars and critics.

## Control

Vanessa Blue decided to become a porn director because of her grandparents. "My grandparents had a whole room dedicated to smut," she explained. "Smut and two Lazy Boys."[3] I had gone to visit Vanessa in her Woodland Hills condo to talk to the performer-turned-director and webmistress about her life and latest work. She told me about how she grew up with porn in her home, so it was in no way foreign to her. When Vanessa began to perform in the late 1990s, it was her grandparents in Nebraska who found out first. "I'm looking at this movie *Dirty Debutantes #61*, and that sure does look like you," she recalled her grandmother saying, hilariously exaggerating her aged voice on the phone. "After that first scene and everybody found out, I was like fuck

FIGURE E.1. Multitalented former adult film actress Vanessa Blue is now a producer, director, and dominatrix. Courtesy of Vanessa Blue, DominaX.com.

it. I might as well finish what I started," Vanessa explained, shrugging her shoulders.[5]

"But what exactly drove you to start making your own porn, not just acting in it?" I asked. "I always loved porn and I always wanted to make it and to be a part of it," Vanessa asserted. "I liked watching people be free and enjoy themselves, and I liked shooting it. I always wanted to be behind the camera. . . . [I thought] Let me see if I can become the director." Being confronted by her grandmother about working as a porn actress forced Vanessa to think about what she really wanted. Her family did not celebrate her work in the sex industry, but they understood it. What her family really wanted was for her to control her labor, rather than be controlled by someone else. If the sex industry offered that opportunity, then she should take it. Her grandparents sternly told her: "We are not saying it is wrong that you do porn, it's not. Just don't let these people fuck you. Don't stay there getting fucked. Figure out a way to make money off of it if that's what you like."[6]

After many stops and starts, Vanessa Blue took her grandparents' advice and taught herself filmmaking and web design. She built her own editing studio from her earnings as a porn actress, exotic dancer, phone sex worker, fetish model, dominatrix, and private escort. She has directed over twenty hardcore videos and dozens of digital shorts, which are distributed by major companies like Adam and Eve, Hustler, and Evil Angel's Justin Slayer International. She also distributes her work through her suite of members-only websites and privately owned video hosting sites like Clips4Sale.com. Though Vanessa is working to make a living outside of the corporate adult entertainment industry's influence, she remains very much tied to it. Vanessa is a compelling example of the possibilities and limits of pornography as a space where black women vie to gain greater control over their labor but are nonetheless cleaved to the industry's inexorable capitalistic apparatus.

For Vanessa, control doesn't just mean achieving independence from porn producers who make a great deal of money off of her work as a performer while also treating her as a disposable working body; it means being able to decide when, where, and how she wants to employ her labor. It means avoiding working under unethical directors and producers who create exploitative and unsafe work environments, and treat her with little care, interest, or respect. There is a less tangible aspect to gaining control over the means of production in porn work as well: authorship. To create the terms of one's own performance and to catalyze one's own fantasies into the sex scene—these dimensions of a more autonomous sexual labor allow Vanessa to see herself as much more empowered behind the camera.

Moving behind the camera is a kind of mobility that allows sex workers greater agency to traverse the barriers placed around them in the porn business. This maneuver reveals the material factors that restrict the movement of sex workers, as well as the factors that could facilitate performers' ability to claim the means of production.[7] As my research has shown, maneuvers by black female workers like Vanessa Blue to reappropriate their images for their own profit and politics are shaped by the oppressive power of race in the structural and social relations of the porn industry. All of porn's workers are subject to the disciplining force of racialized sexuality, even the idealized white female porn star. However, as I demonstrate in the previous chapter, women of color are specifically devalued within porn's tiered system of racialized erotic capital.[8] Within this hierarchy the low value attributed to black bodies mobilizes the fetishism driving their representations. Not only does black-cast pornography tend to be organized around a view of black sexual deviance and pathology—often a low-budget affair presenting pimps and players trolling the 'hood for hoes and hookers—but black porn actors tend to be paid rates half to three quarters of what white actors earn. In this way, black labor in porn mirrors the exploitation of black labor in "legitimate" arenas like service sector blue- and pink-collar jobs, where black workers confront systemic inequality, prejudice, and occupational health risks. In order to understand the ways in which black pornographers like Vanessa Blue come to self-authorship and to make critical interventions in the porn industry—and what is at stake in this important move—we must take seriously the overwhelming discursive and institutional restrictions placed on black women in porn. We must also take seriously these producers' tactics of illicit eroticism, through which they simultaneously claim and challenge restrictive discourses about black women's sexuality and worth.

Damali Dares explained how a sense of feminism motivated her to direct, produce, and star in *Maneater: The Prelude*, a film depicting a sexy detective who uses her sexuality to catch men who cheat. "Some guys would say I'm a man hater and I'm not," Damali said. "I just hate ignorant people, guys or other females who try to take advantage of people. I've always been an activist and I'm always standing up for the underdog. So [the idea for the film] kind of came from both me as a person and also wanting to do that superhero type, save the world, one female at a time. It was really about empowering females."[9] Though Damali was sometimes construed as a "man hater" for being outspoken about sexism, racism, and homophobia, she turned this established antifeminist attack into "man eater," for a film that went on to be nominated for a Feminist Porn Award in 2010. Casting herself both as the detective heroine who catches "guys who victimize women," and as the cuckolded wife who becomes empowered by learning the truth of her husband's infidelity, Damali uses her dual role to portray women in charge of their lives, employing the good girl / bad girl binary in order to dismantle it.

The phenomenon of black female porn makers must be evaluated in light of black sex workers' continued attempts to survive and succeed against tremendous barriers. Black women performers-turned-directors face barriers that other black women pornographers do not. When they continue to perform in their own films, they are implicated as sex workers in ways that black women directors coming from film schools and other paths not related to the sex industry avoid. Directors like Vanessa Blue and Damali Dares also maintain other kinds of ties to the sex business through their performer websites, exotic dancing, or BDSM work. Thus producing porn for them is, in addition to controlling their images and asserting creative self-authorship, part of an overall strategy to extend their professional persona into a lucrative brand, one with many formats, audiences, and streams of income.

Vanessa Blue welcomed me with a warm and mischievous smile. I followed her, barefoot and dressed in a colorful, flowing sundress, into her home office. Explaining that she was in the middle of some important edits for a new project, Vanessa sat down at her desk with a confident grace, like the conductor of an orchestra, eminently sure the various parts of the symphony will coalesce, forming a masterpiece. The room was cluttered with equipment, yet organized. On her desk a Mac laptop was open to the movie editing software Final Cut Pro. Notes, technical books, hard drives, and DVDs occupied the rest of the desk surface. A high-definition digital video camera stood on a tripod at the center of the room, aimed at a canopy bed swathed in red satin and covered in velvet pillows. This was where Vanessa shot many of her videos. As she told me, she likes "watching people be free and enjoy themselves." Vanessa was drawn to the idea of creating an environment where performers could take pleasure in their performances. "I knew I wanted to get behind the camera," she told me, "and I wanted to control the scene so that either I could get to fuck the way I wanted to fuck or produce the scenes that I knew this industry was missing."

"What is the porn industry missing?" I asked. "As a performer," Vanessa explained, "sitting on the set and watching the director leave the room and leave the cameraman to finish the scene, to direct and make those people fuck a certain way." She shook her head in disgust. "I grew up with an appreciation for smut, and it broke my heart that smut was being made by people who really didn't care."[10] This statement powerfully indicts the management of porn production, which has standardized the filming of sex scenes to the extent that actors often feel they are handled more as automatons than real people, and directed to have sex that is mechanical, perfunctory, and even unerotic. This industrial mass-production schema is thought necessary to provide the market with a constant stream of pornographic media options that satisfy every taste at the cheapest cost. It replicates exactly what seems to sell and innovates only when other styles outsell the dominant.

"Fucking" the way Vanessa wanted would mean having more freedom to decide how sex should proceed. She described her ideal interaction as more organic and dynamic, thus more erotic. For Vanessa, this style meant *not* following a predictable formula, but following a new calculus of her imagination. Vanessa Blue rejects the politics of disposability that turns porn's workers, like women of color working under the conditions of neoliberal capital around the world, into "a form of industrial waste" to be "discarded and replaced."[11]

"My fans will not want to hear this," she explained, "but when I was working [as a performer in the mainstream adult industry], it was a means to an end, and the end was to direct."[12] For Vanessa, acting was a means to transition from being a contracted worker in the formulaic milieu of gonzo porn, to being the creator of the image and taking control of the terms of sexual labor. Now Vanessa shoots films that she makes and she performs in roles that she designs. In the process of converting her labor from contracted worker to creative author, Vanessa presents black women's sexuality in ways that highlight this drive for authorship and self-determination. She aspires to eschew the framework of the stereotyped black sexuality dominant in most porn, yet much of her work remarks on blackness in ways that show its inextricable connection to systems of power. Vanessa exposes how black feminist porn must contend with race, as black female sexuality is sutured to racial histories that inform our contemporary fantasies and sexual economies.

In her adult feature (full-length narrative) films, like *Dark Confessions*, *Taking Memphis*, and *Black Reign*, Vanessa emphasizes the sexual autonomy of her female characters. Employing tactics that serve to humanize the performers and the characters, her camera closes in on and lingers on performer faces, offering representations of embodiment beyond the often fractured "tits and ass" styling of so much pornographic media. Vanessa creates a space for black eroticism and black subjectivity, centering themes of intimacy, mischief, inverted power dynamics, and role play. Vanessa's presentation of cross and interracial intimacy pushes against the notion that relationships between black men and women, and black women and white men, are inherently alienating and objectifying.

In *Dark Confessions* Vanessa employs the trope of the confession to elicit testimonials from couples about their fantasies, and as the box cover advertises, "revealing their darkest desires." Vanessa takes on the role of the confessor, sitting invisibly behind the camera as she draws out the sexual fantasies of five black male-female couples in this film, which is distributed by Adam and Eve, and marketed for a heterosexual "couples" audience. Although this narrative leaves certain porn conventions intact, such as the use of conventional gender roles, and the address of "couples porn" to straight couples, it opens up interesting possibilities for black heterosexual desire and erotic intimacy. Each interview, filmed in a series of medium shots in black-and-white, presents a heterosexual couple sitting side by side, holding or leaning on one another. These professional porn actors portray a familiarity and closeness that is not usually present in much black-cast porn, where normally a series of sex acts are strung together with little plot, characterization, or opportunity for the actors to speak. Here the actors improvise from the outline of a script, yet their articulations are fluid as they play off one another to construct an image of a relationship that may appear familiar to heterosexual audiences. Vanessa probes them with questions: How did you meet? How's the sex? What's your fantasy? As in most documentary-influenced genres, the spectators of this performance become invested in the notion of its authenticity and realness. But this is a longed-for illusionary authenticity. It is through the process of confession that we invest in its actuation. While reproducing regulatory regimes of power on the subject, the discourses of sex produced by the confessional in this film present performances of black intimate disclosure, subjectivity, and relation rare in pornographic film.[13] Both members of each couple speak about their sexual desires, and their conversation becomes the launching pad for the performance of the described fantasies, a kind of continued conversation among sexual partners as well as an alternative space for portraying the possibilities for subjectivity attached to these "dark confessions."

One fantasy scenario in *Dark Confessions* takes place between Marie Luv and Tyler Knight, two actors whose powerful chemistry translates to the sex scene. In their confessional Marie aggressively asserts her desire to be the submissive. She says of her fantasy in the confessional pre-scene interview: "I want you to just take me, just take me!" Tyler, her partner in the scene, endearingly nods and smiles, "Whatever you want, I'm happy to do it." Shot in an industrial-looking set with concrete walls and chain-link fencing, the sex scene recalls the urban settings that much of black pornography uses to locate black characters in spaces that connote their racialized sexuality as inhabiting and consuming the city. However, Marie's retro 1980s glam eye shadow, and Vanessa's creative use of pixilation, cross fades, and kaleidoscopic editing effects, mean that the scene feels more like a sci-fi, futurist fantasy than an anachronistic imaginary of black sex happening in the midst of urban blight. Moreover, Vanessa Blue gave her actors the space to be cocreators in the fantasies they portray. Having visited Marie on the set of *Rough Sex*—a feature by feminist director Tristan Taormino in which Marie performed in a sex scene that she designed based on her own fantasy about coercive sex[14]—I argue that Marie's articulation of her desire to be "taken" by Tyler appears to further reflect the performer's own wishes to explore BDSM sex. One of Marie's actual fantasies is extreme submission (what some might call rape fantasy), and in *Dark Confessions*, Marie and Tyler both enthusiastically play with power, consent, trust, and questions of who is in control of the sex act. Tyler moves and holds Marie's body with force, and their athletic, fast-paced sex conveys the urgency and excitement that her character says she wants. At one point, during animated cunnilingus play, Tyler asks Marie to smother him—that is sit on his face so that he cannot breathe—which is a particular submissive fetish that many black men, usually called upon to play the dominant role, are rarely shown performing, especially with other black women.[15]

FIGURE E.2. Marie Luv and Tyler Knight in Vanessa Blue's *Dark Confessions* (2007).

Vanessa Blue confronts the issue of power head-on, especially in short films made for her websites DominaX.com and FemmeDomX.com. Using BDSM fetishism—particularly the fantasy of black women dominating white men—Vanessa queers racial and gender hegemonies by exposing their very constructedness. By creating fantasies that explode assumptions about what constitutes proper gendering of, and appropriate pleasure and pain for, the black body, she suggests that social power is changeable and that racialized sexuality can be toyed with for her own ends. "Kink" is an underexplored arena of black sexual culture, and a technology of the self that is, if acknowledged in the public domain at all, seen as the epitome of deviant sexuality.[16] The performances in Vanessa's BDSM video shorts are very different from the sensuality of the feature film *Dark Confessions*. They involve ropes, chains, whips, torches, clamps, gags, harnesses, and other tools that are associated with the historical, nonconsensual mutilation and punishment of the black body, but that are used in this context to expose power as a terrain of (consensual) play in fantasy. Here, black dominatrixes, Vanessa included, torture white and black men by making them crawl, beg, and subject themselves to all manner of abuse, including by painting their faces with lipstick and otherwise emasculating them with taunting acts. While this type of humiliation relies on fixed and immutable gender-sex binaries and thus evinces some of the limitations of this kind of representation, it subverts other aspects of porn convention, including the representation of black women as they are shown being "worshipped" and adored by white and black men together. In these shorts, black women take charge of the scene by prioritizing their own desires to act on the bodies of men. Ever playful, Vanessa's "tickle torture" films for her planned website EbonyTickle.com show how kink can be mediated in ways that create a permissible environment where black women can be seen to play with the ever-dangerous position of subordination and powerlessness — here, in the excruciating and taunting tickling of submissive female performers tied to Vanessa's bed. Through the performance of subjection as submissives in Ebony Tickle, or of merciless domination as dominatrixes, black actresses in Vanessa's work show the significance of racialized kink fetishism as a market in the pornography industry for black women looking to capitalize on, and sometimes revise, the sexual scripts available for them.

Vanessa Blue's illicit erotic activism displays the use of what may be generally understood as super-deviant sexualities to empower black women's sexual performances in pornography. For Vanessa, black women's performances of submissiveness or domination can be enjoyable acts, and ones that might encourage black women spectators to explore their own "darkest desires," even if they borrow from tropes of black women as emasculating Sapphires and uncoercible, always already hypersexual Jezebels. Though her interest is not in presenting a narrative of racial progress, in overthrowing patriarchy, or in making sexually emancipatory or pleasurable texts outside the marketplace or external to legacies of sexual myth, Vanessa's intervention is, I argue, progressive. Her work asks viewers to think about what we might learn from pornography's most marginalized: how our pleasure is indeed tied to historical realities of our pain.

Despite its reputation as super-deviant, BDSM work can be some of the most desirable for porn performers, since fetish work often does not require penetrative sex, but instead the performance of a dominant or submissive role in non-penetrative sex acts that are seen as less taxing on the sex worker's body. What does it mean that this relatively low-intensity labor is tied up with brutal inheritances of sexual expropriation and sexual myth? Could taking pleasure in the most deviant articulations of black sexual deviance offer a radical tool to negotiate and transform how power acts on our bodies and communities? Black women's objectification in pornography has a long history, emerging from New World slavery as a pornographic, voyeuristic, sexual economy. Yet since the earliest photographic and film productions of sexually explicit material made for sale in a pornographic market of images, black models and actresses returned the objectifying gaze, and gestured to their own subjective understandings as sex workers and as sexual subjects. If black women's sex cinema offers a new frontier to present the inextricable bind between sexual labor and sexual fantasy, the task is to explore it as a new kind of voice in pornography, one that is never divorced from the marketplace, but shines a light on the ways in which black women's sexualities are intimately linked with the illicit erotic project of authorship and control.

### Superfreaks: Black Art-Porn Entrepreneurs

Abiola Abrams, aka Venus Hottentot, brought her background in film studies, art, and creative writing to her collaboration with feminist-pornography pioneer Candida Royalle in *AfroDite Superstar* (Femme Productions, 2007). Royalle's Femme Productions produced the film and guaranteed its audience would be women and couples interested in her quasi-softcore aesthetic while Abrams's location as a media figure in black popular culture assured *AfroDite Superstar* an audience among African Americans. Moreover, as a black entertainment industry journalist, novelist, and outsider to the porn industry, Abrams had more opportunity to insert a political message into her film. She used goddess imagery and black feminist poetry by the likes of Audre Lorde to critique hip hop's misogynist depictions of violence toward black women, and the problematic lack of images of black women's sexuality that capture their agency and investigate their desires. Abrams entered the project without conceptualizing it as pornography (for the purposes of titillation and masturbation), but as a "sex film" that would offer a political statement about the richness and complexity of black women's fantasy lives.[17] However, Abrams's reliance on Candida Royalle's production company and on porn actors to carry the film, including India, Mr. Marcus, and Justin Long, as well as the less experienced leading actress Simone Valentino, meant that Abrams's film would be marketed as a porn film even while it circulated as a black feminist art statement of sorts. "I had to have five sex scenes in the film no matter what. So for me that was a difficulty creatively because there is one scene in the film that is there only because the distributor wanted it to be. They were like, 'You can go off on whatever weird, artsy path you want to go on as long as we've got five sex scenes. That's what our objective is.'"[18] Abrams's experience underscores Angela Carter's insistence that pornography "can never be art for art's sake. Honourably enough, it always has work to do."[19]

Yet the work done by porn—political, economic, social, or otherwise—builds on the backs of its sex workers. Abiola Abrams wanted to shoot a narrative film, with a longer-than-normal script (for porn) that required actors to learn their parts, but she quickly learned that most performers are sex workers who do not have the luxury to explore artistic practice at the expense of their survival.[20] They, for instance, cannot afford to donate extra time for a film in which they are only paid an acting rate normally calculated for a specific kind of sex act and scene, but are expected to work longer hours or extra days than is common on most one-day porn shoots. Abrams told me how she called agents in L.A. from her New York City production studio, telling them about the script and what the film was about in the hope they would recommend appropriate actors to fill the parts:

> One agent said, "We don't care about that. We care about the money. You are offering to pay them what they make in an hour or a day. And you want to pay them that for a week?" He said, if the women came to do the film, he wanted them to escort on the side to make up the money while they work on the film. That was shocking to me. I was thinking of them as just performers and so it was really interesting. I found that there were people working at different levels in the industry, so the people who worked in my film were the people that are at the top in the industry. The people who I was trying to hire from the agent were on the fringes. I realized everyone is not India or Mr. Marcus.[21]

Although Abrams made the assumption—inaccurate in my experience—that top-tier actors do not engage in other kinds of income-generating activities such as illegal prostitution and escorting to supplement their income and pay for travel, her comments reveal how sometimes filmmakers with a progressive artistic and political vision can contribute to the erasure of porn performance as sex work. Abrams's shock that actors would want to prioritize earnings over art underscores the problematic invisibility of the struggles of sex workers to gain access to varied representations and roles as they simultaneously seek opportunities for lucrative pay inside and outside of porn work. Because women and men of color are already economically marginalized, this need to seek better pay or flexible work conditions in order to supplement earnings is even more significant. It is also significant that Abrams did find actors willing to sacrifice some of their normal earnings to make the film. Though it is not clear if they, too, pursued escorting off set, they apparently believed in her vision and thus made the choice to catalyze their illicit erotic labor in the interest of work and politics.

Abiola Abrams wanted to send a message to audiences of her "sex film" about the varied range of black women's beauty. "I knew that when I was casting this film, I felt I wanted to show different kinds of black women that were just absent from media, period, across the board," said Abiola. "I wanted to show women with different shades of brown and natural textured hair in a beautiful and powerful light. I also wanted to only cast women with real body parts. I wanted to show women with a lack of artifice. My cinematographer was annoyed that I didn't use body paint on the lead, Simone Valentino's, stretch marks, but I wanted the stretch marks there. Most of the women watching have stretch marks! And Simone is beautiful regardless." Women performers like Sinnamon Love or Vanessa Blue would certainly question the logic that "real body parts" and "lack of artifice" are requisite elements of authentic beauty—they both fiercely defend breast enhancements as tools of their trade and aspects of their attempts to express self-esteem and self-authorship. However, Abrams's point that to provide a wider range of images of beauty for black women would constitute an intervention into porn, hip hop, and popular culture is well taken. This is another example in which the desire to produce varied and diverse images of black women's sexuality for consumption relies upon the sexual labor of workers, yet fails to consider the reality of the sexual economy in shaping what constitutes marketable racialized and sexed bodies for these same workers. Even though many viewers may find it laudable that Abrams wanted to keep Simone Valentino's stretch marks in the film, her choice as director may undermine Valentino's marketability for other kinds of porn work. Her aesthetics of naturalism also marginalizes actresses that have changed their bodies in ways they deem important for their careers in sex work.

Black feminist and queer filmmakers coming from outside the industry produce for a different market and face a different set of expectations from their audiences than black performers-turned-producers of porn. For the former, consumers are largely women of color, trans folk, and other queer people looking to find authentic images of themselves and their sexual communities. These authentic representations are, while problematic to define, often lacking in porn. The sense of authenticity in this queer porn is underscored by the fact that sometimes the sex workers employed for these films are a part of queer communities. Actors in these films may even be renowned performance artists and actors from the San Francisco Bay area, the queerporn San Fernando Valley.[22] Both Shine Louise Houston and Nenna Feelmore Joiner use queer people of color from their own circles of friends and collaborators in their films and market, in part, to those same circles, though their work reaches many more markets in the United States and abroad). Even as the consumption of their work extends much farther afield, this local community-based approach also presents a kind of political intervention.

That said, independently produced queer porn has a complex relationship to the ethics of sex work. On the one hand, these indy-queer and sex-positive feminist producers work hard to treat their performers with an ethics of care, including by allowing performers to have a say about the conditions of their work, or by providing safer sex barriers, food, and wardrobe support on set. Yet because these filmmakers, as independent producers on a tight budget, tend to work with performers drawn from their communities who are working less for a paycheck and more for the experience of making alternative art or exploring sex on camera, they pay much lower rates (usually by several hundred dollars) than typical pro-amateur, low-budget, wall-to-wall production companies in Porn Valley. Since indy-porn work is more of a labor of love than a lucrative industry, whether an ethics of care and sense of political artistic activism outweigh equal pay remains a question. For instance, Nenna Joiner tells performers who show up to casting calls asking about the pay rates, "You don't really want to do this" because it involves "more than just the money."[23] While Nenna wants to remind performers that they should be mindful of how their images will be permanently circulated—and hence they should seriously consider what irreversible and potentially negative impacts their performance may have on their lives—this care for performer well-being also marginalizes sex workers who do want to put money issues first and see their fair pay as the most important approach to their well-being. In addition, the lower pay on many of these independent sets means that workers must lower their rates if they wish to perform in spaces where they may experience greater care and respect, and enhanced autonomy in their performances. As black BBW performer Betty Blac points out, Girl-Girl sex scenes, whether for a mainstream company or a queer feminist indy company, are, compared to Boy-Girl sex, always more work for less pay. However, she enjoys working for queer feminist producers like Shine Louise Houston and Courtney Trouble, despite the lower pay, because it feeds her desire for both a political and a creative outlet for her sex work. Betty Blac hopes to become a director herself one day soon: she says, "I don't want to be seen through other people's lenses anymore."[24]

Though black performers-turned-directors employ filmmaking as a politically charged facet of their strategic sexual labor, black women filmmakers who are not performers do not engage illicit erotics in the same way. Rather than use their own sexualities for commoditized gains, they propel the sexualities of others to enact fantasies of their design. While this relationship necessarily contains elements of exploitation, as in the relationship of factory owners or shop managers to their assembly line workers, it is also a relationship that allows for the cocreation of commercial representations that intervene in, and sometimes expand, the narrowed landscape of possibilities for black female sexuality in today's culture. That is not to say that these black women auteurs do not deploy their own embodiments, and specifically the deviance attached to their black female bodies, in the pornoscape. Shine Louise Houston, for instance, launches her body into her texts in unexpected and subversive ways. In *Superfreak* she appears as the ghost of notoriously naughty funk singer Rick James, whose hit "Super Freak" (1981) describes "a very kinky girl, the kind you don't take home to mother." Inhabiting James's spirit, Shine brings to life a trickster figure bent on turning one character after another into a "superfreak." Using her own body to set in motion the pleasure-inducing, orgiastic scene, Shine moves from the role of cultural producer (to represent or depict sex) to that of sexual laborer (to trade on sex) to sexual intellectual (whose role is to critique sex labor and sex representations, as I do) to the role of superfreak (who performs elements of all of the above). This schema, offered by L. H. Stallings in a radical theory of black erotic rebellion she terms "the politics of hoin,'" opens up ways of thinking about the black women pornographers not so much divided by their interests in and differing relationships to the porn industry as united by a shared politics—porn as a site of possibility for black women's own intervention and critique.[25] At the very least, the potential is there to theorize forms of collaboration and possibilities for revolution by black women porn management and workers.

What does it mean to be a superfreak and is that a good thing for black women? As black women, the respectability-dissemblance framework has overwhelmed our ability to think of sex apart from the threat of harm to our womanhood and to our communities.[26] Through the prioritization of normative gender and sexual codes, behaviors, and relations we have sought to recuperate ourselves from myths associated with black sexual deviance, and the systemic violence attached to those myths. Pornography offers a site to study how the myths of black sexual deviance and black female hypersexuality attach to fantasies and to labor arrangements, as well as a site to make visible the pleasures taken in the queerness of superfreakiness.[27] These directors show the significant overlaps between sex work, cultural production, and cultural critique, and the ways in which progressive representational politics must always be invested in a progressive labor politics. Black women porn directors' body of work exposes the defiant sensibilities, subversive politics, and voluptuous potential of illicit eroticism as a framework for thinking about how minoritized subjects may use sexuality to imagine otherwise.[28]

As I have argued throughout this book, black women's representation and pleasure are inextricably bound up with capitalist markets, traumatic racial history, respectability-dissemblance politics, and social stigma and hierarchy. The new wave of erotic texts produced by black women are not simply positive representations that upset a large and enduring archive of negative representations, because they are not solely in the service of a racial-progress narrative, or the overthrow of patriarchy or pornography. These are muddy, ambivalent explorations into unknown territory, where power is a toy and sex may be a practice of freedom for a moment, even if it is for sale. This book asks us to think about what black feminists might learn from pornography's outlaws. Black women are claiming a pornographic gaze for themselves. We must explore the radical possibilities and constraints that their work offers and exposes. There exists a generalized resistance, by academics and others, to taking seriously how black women exist within and shape the life of pornography, in part due to a politics that has circumscribed our ability to understand and appreciate black women's varied experiences of eroticism and pleasure in the context of always present exploitation and pain. But what if pleasure is one of the most radical tools black women can mobilize to intervene in their oppression?

Often I have been asked if black women pornographers really flip the script on objectification and exploitation, or if they are simply complicit in reproducing bad stereotypes. I believe this question is, in essence, a trap. As I have shown throughout this book, black women's objectification in pornography has a long history and at its foundation is linked to the voyeuristic use of their bodies as slaves and colonized subjects, and the rationales attached to that nonconsensual use. Showing the critical importance of sexual autonomy and erotic sovereignty for African Americans since that time, some black women performers have employed the terms of their objectification to resist their conditions, and to imagine themselves against the grain, through the tactics of illicit eroticism. I have traced particular moments when these interventions seem especially striking, particularly given the context of performers' lives and of the image-making process. Illicit erotic efforts to return the gaze and to recapture erotic sovereignty from sexual devaluement take place under the imposition of varied and profound exploitation, abuse, and constraint. Because performers labor within the demands of pornographic capitalism, their attempts to seize agency in their images and performances are sutured to hegemonic forces that necessarily re-exploit them and others.

Nevertheless, aware of these dangers, black women pornographic producers at times show an alternative way of seeing. This way of seeing, and moving within, the sexual economy is not primarily concerned with delineating what is an inherently positive or negative representation, what is a good or bad use of black female sexuality. Ambivalent about the expectation to "flip the script" of black women's sexual stereotyping, my informants show that their interest lies in disidentifying with the expectation that they represent a monolithic figure—positive or negative—of black women's eroticism. For them, porn is or can be a space where black women try on roles, perform imaginaries against expectations, and revel in the practice of making black women's bodies into desirable texts for a diversity of viewers, including other black women. The black woman porn spectator is a subject that deserves further study. Caught in a struggle over how black women are represented or represent themselves sexually, we have not undressed how black women *see* sexually. That question is still on the table. And in light of the enormous shifts in media technologies and mediated sociality, black women are now positioned in new ways as both producers and consumers, as image makers and as spectators. Principally, though, my informants believe that increasing their access to and control over the means of production is the best way to improve the images and experiences of black women workers in porn.

This book has also traced a genealogy of black women's performances in porn in order to initiate a discussion of what black women's sexual subjectivities might look like in a pornetrated society. With today's neoliberal shaping of the political economy and social life around contingent and vulnerable labor, I have presented ways in which sex work is seen to offer both a site for sexual subjectivity and an opportunity for material benefit and survival. Sexual labor forms an important thread in the history of black women's pornography. From the earliest stag films to theatrical film, video, and digital media, the spectacularization of black women's sexual images has required black women's labor. Deploying illicit eroticism, black women sex workers in pornography, I argue, made use of the ideas about their taboo sexuality by employing them for erotic work.

Given the necessity to make the sexualized world of black womanhood livable, I have highlighted how black women venture to negotiate the sexual economy in ways that retain their complex personhood and move toward erotic sovereignty. I have additionally pointed to moments when these women express subjectivity or agency within or outside of the pornographic text. Ethnographic interviews with black porn actresses provided the critical insights in this study, and the voices of these women are vital sources of knowledge about what pornography means to black women. Black women in porn are articulate about what it means to make their sexuality visible and their labor sexual. Critical of the exploitations of an industry that profits from leveraging racial hierarchies of erotic capital among their workers and from commoditizing base racial stereotypes in its rush to produce ever more porn products for a hungry market, these women explain that porn needs to be transformed. They aspire to pornography as a venue for something more humanizing, more equitable, more interesting, and more hospitable to new ways of thinking. But they also show that porn is not so different than other industries in the late-capitalist United States, and that the struggles black women face in porn are part of the broader struggles faced by all black women in America.

# Notes

Preface. Confessions

1. Gilman, "Confessions of an Academic Pornographer," 28.

2. For black feminist work on the iconicity of the Hottentot Venus and about Sara Baartman herself, see for example: Alexander, *The Venus Hottentot*; Parks, *Venus*; Sharpley-Whiting, *Black Venus*; Willis, *Black Venus 2010*; Hobson, *Venus in the Dark*; Chase–Riboud, *Hottentot Venus*; Maseko, *The Life and Times of Sara Baartman*; Magubane, "Which Bodies Matter?"; Fleetwood, *Troubling Vision*; Qureshi, "Displaying Sarah Baartman, the 'Hottentot Venus'"; and Nash, "Strange Bedfellows." For other work on the Hottentot Venus, see Crais and Scully, *Sara Baartman and the Hottentot Venus*; Holmes, *The Hottentot Venus*; Bancel et al., *Human Zoos*; Skelly, *No Strangers to Beauty*; Gould, *The Flamingo's Smile* and *The Mismeasure of Man*; Hall, "The Spectacle of the 'Other'"; and Gilman, "Black Bodies, White Bodies."

3. See Saar's statements in the anonymous article (credited to Juliette Bowles Harris), "Extreme Times Call for Extreme Heroes"; also Gilman, "Confessions of an Academic Pornographer," 29.

4. See for example, Walker and Vergne, *My Complement, My Enemy, My Oppressor, My Love.*

5. Higginbotham, *Righteous Discontent.*

6. Hine, "Rape and the Inner Lives of Black Women in the Middle West."

7. Gardner, "Racism in Pornography and the Women's Movement," 105; Forna, "Pornography and Racism," 105–6.

8. Collins, *Black Feminist Thought*, 144–45.

9. Walker, "Coming Apart," 42.

10. Collins, *Black Feminist Thought*, 137.

11. Lorde, "The Uses of the Erotic: The Erotic as Power."

12. These feminists all signed on to the Feminist Anti-Censorship Taskforce (FACT) Amici Curiae Brief to the U.S. Court of Appeals protesting the passage of the Dworkin-MacKinnon Ordinance, which would have criminalized pornography, in Indianapolis in 1985. The FACT Brief was originally filed in April of 1985 and published

as "Brief Amici Curiae of Feminist Anti-Censorship Taskforce," *University of Michigan Journal of Law Reform* 21, no. 1 and 2 (fall 1987–winter 1988). Here I am citing the FACT Brief that appears as appendix A in Duggan and Hunter, *Sex Wars*, 207–47, 235–36.

13. Cohen, "Deviance as Resistance."

14. Cohen, "Deviance as Resistance," 30.

15. Cruz, "Pornography," 223–24.

16. Stallings, "'Mutha' Is Half a Word!," 6.

17. King, "Multiple Jeopardy, Multiple Consciousness," 312.

18. Hammonds, "Black (W)holes and the Geometry of Black Female Sexuality," 309.


### Introduction. Brown Sugar

Jeannie Pepper, personal interview with author, December 8, 2002.

1. Pepper, "A Special Achievement Presentation Award to the Legendary Jeannie Pepper, from 1982 to 2002, Twenty Years of Hot Sizzling Sex."

2. I use first names when discussing porn actresses throughout this book because not all actors take on last names for their personas, and those who do often do not use them. Using performers' entire professional pseudonym or just their first name allows me to maintain equality in how they are discussed.

3. Jeannie Pepper, personal interview with author, December 8, 2002.

4. Sex work is defined by Ronald Weitzer as "the exchange of sexual services, performances, or products for material compensation. It includes activities of direct physical contact between buyers and sellers (prostitution, lap dancing) as well as indirect sexual stimulation (pornography, stripping, telephone sex, live sex shows, erotic webcam performances)." Weitzer, "Sex Work: Paradigms and Policies," 1.

5. Mintz, *Sweetness and Power*.

6. Davis, "Don't Let Nobody Bother Yo' Principle!," 117.

7. Brown, "Eating the Dead," 117.

8. Mintz, *Sweetness and Power*, 43.

9. It is precisely for this lyrical ambiguity as both bawdy and loving, both dangerous and attractive, that the words "brown sugar" have been taken up by artists, entertainers, and poets. See, for example, the song "Brown Sugar" from *Sticky Fingers* (1971) by the Rolling Stones.

10. See, for example, hooks, "Selling Hot Pussy."

11. Stallings, "Gender Realism, Poor Black Women, and the Politics of Hoin' and Hustlin.'"

12. Kendrick, *The Secret Museum*, 31.

13. Kipnis, *Bound and Gagged*, 164.

14. On the history and social implications of pornography, see also Mowry, *The Bawdy Politic in Stuart England, 1660–1714*; Hunt, "Introduction: Obscenity and the Origins of Modernity, 1500–1800" and "Pornography and the French Revolution"; and Ferguson, "Pornography: The Theory."

15. Escoffier, *Bigger than Life*, 1.

16. I use the terms "pornography industry," "porn industry," "porn business," "adult industry," and "adult entertainment industry" interchangeably. These terms refer to the system of production, distribution, and consumption of adult media, products, and performance labor as discussed in this book. They include the people, technologies, modes of exchange and marketing, trade organizations, communication entities, and work sites and labor norms that allow the industry to function. Whereas these terms have different valences outside of the industry, with porn/pornography industry sometimes taking on negative connotations, especially in the writings of antiporn critics, I use all of these terms because adult-industry professionals use them as well. Adult industry or adult entertainment industry is often used in professional settings, and porn more informally, but there is great diversity and fluidity in their use by my informants. My use of porn/pornography industry instead of adult industry in places is not meant to undermine the legitimacy of the entity that I am naming, though I acknowledge that "pornography" is a highly problematic term, tied to its connotations with obscenity, and defining it is an extremely subjective enterprise.

There is no clear information about the revenues of the adult entertainment industry because companies are private and do not share their financial data. It has been extremely difficult for researchers to develop accurate numbers, and most estimates are controversial. According to *Top Ten Reviews*, in 2006, revenue from video rentals and sales was $3.62 billion, and Internet porn sales earned $2.8 billion. Cable TV, Pay Per View, mobile phone, and in-room hotel rentals were problematically lumped together with phone sex revenues at $2.19 billion. These numbers have surely shifted in the last few years as new mobile technologies increase the consumption of Internet-based porn, and the financial crisis diminishes revenues for the adult entertainment industry across the board. See Ropelato, "Internet Pornography Statistics." See also statistics from 1997–2003 in Schlosser, *Reefer Madness*; Rich, "Naked Capitalists; and Slade, *Pornography and Sexual Representation*.

17. Williams, *Porn Studies*, 1; Weitzer, "Sex Work."

18. Paasonen, *Pornification*, 2.

19. On pornification see Paasonen, *Pornification*, 8. On "pornetration" see Hebdige, "Flat Boy vs Skinny."

20. On "bad sex," see Berlant and Warner, "Sex in Public"; and Rubin, "Thinking Sex."

21. Attwood, "Reading Porn," 99; Lumby, *Bad Girls*, 117.

22. Laura Kipnis argues that pornography, "in essence, is an oppositional political form." Kipnis, *Bound and Gagged*, 123. See also Mowry, *The Bawdy Politic*. Both authors discuss pornography as a dimension of free speech and speech critical of state and social authority.

23. McClintock, "Gonad the Barbarian and the Venus Flytrap," 115; Williams, "Porn Studies," 3. See also Juffer, *At Home with Pornography*; and Attwood, "Reading Porn."

24. Fung, "Looking for My Penis," 161.

25. Arthurs, *Television and Sexuality*, 41–42.

26. Paasonen, Nikunen, and Saarenmaa, "Pornification and the Education of Desire," 8.

27. Kipnis, *Bound and Gagged*.

28. On racialization, see Omi and Winant, *Racial Formation*. For scholarly studies of pornography that examine race, see Shimizu, *The Hypersexuality of Race*; Fung, "Looking for My Penis"; Williams, "Skin Flicks on the Racial Border"; Bernardi, "Interracial Joysticks"; Hoang, "The Resurrection of Brandon Lee"; Penley, "Crackers and Whackers"; Nash, "The Black Body in Ecstasy"; and Cruz, "Berries Bittersweet."

29. Hall, *Representation*.

30. Hall, *Representation*.

31. Davis, "Don't Let Nobody Bother Yo' Principle."

32. Hall, *Representation*, 268.

33. Adrienne Davis uses the term "sexual economy" to theorize the important interaction between enslaved black women's sexual expropriation and the political economy of the antebellum era. I find it a useful concept to describe the historical and continuing relationship between sexual knowledge, sexual power, and the political economy in advanced capitalism. See Davis, "Don't Let Nobody Bother Yo' Principle."

34. Green, "The Social Organization of Desire," 32. See also Brooks, *Unequal Desires*.

35. Brooks, *Unequal Desires*, 29.

36. While this work focuses on black women, I reference research I conducted with Latinas, Asian women, and black men. Adequate research has not been done on any of these groups, and unfortunately this study cannot address the specific experience of these sex workers or the complexity of their relationship to black women. Asian men and Latinos are rare in the heterosexual sector of the pornography business and little work has been done on them either.

37. On the growing significance of the global sexual marketplace for black women see, for example, Kempadoo and Doezema, *Global Sex Workers*; Kempadoo, *Sun, Sex, and Gold*; Wekker, *The Politics of Passion*; Collins, "New Commodities."

38. Harley, Wilson, and Logan, "Introduction." See also Blair, *I've Got to Make My Own Livin'*; Hicks, *Talk with You like a Woman*; and Dill and Johnson, "Between a Rock and a Hard Place."

39. Kelley, *Yo' Mama's Disfunktional!*, 45–46.

40. Marx, *Capital*.

41. Harley, "'Working for Nothing but a Living,'" 51.

42. Shimizu, *The Hypersexuality of Race*, 30.

43. Shimizu, *The Hypersexuality of Race*, 22.

44. Wanzo, "Beyond a 'Just Syntax,'" 137.

45. Wanzo, "Beyond a 'Just Syntax,'" 138.

46. In a conversation between myself and Xavier Livermon, assistant professor of African and African Diaspora studies at the University of Texas at Austin, we discussed how the ingénue-meets-sexpot performance of Britney Spears would never stand in for all white women's performances. Viewers understand she is just one person in a range of varied representations offered by other entertainers and actresses like Lady Gaga or Julia Roberts. Xavier Livermon, conversation with author, December 8, 2011.

47. Wanzo, "Beyond a 'Just Syntax,'" 137.

48. Muñoz, *Disidentifications*.

49. Hall, *Representation*.

50. "Complex personhood," writes Gordon, "means that the stories people tell about themselves . . . are entangled and weave between what is immediately available as a story and what their imaginations are reaching towards." Gordon, *Ghostly Matters*, 4.

51. Muñoz, *Disidentifications*, 4.

52. In developing this concept I draw upon Bataille's discussion of sovereign subjects and eroticism. I also relate erotic sovereignty to Alexander's concept of "erotic autonomy." However, for me, erotic sovereignty conveys the processural desire to reclaim the body and eroticism for a range of purposes and in the always existing context of sexual economy, racialization, and racism. See Bataille, *Erotism*; Alexander, *Pedagogies of Crossing*.

53. Mahmood, "Feminist Theory, Embodiment, and the Docile Agent," 203.

54. Mahmood, "Feminist Theory, Embodiment, and the Docile Agent," 217.

55. Dworkin, "Against the Male Flood," 523.

56. Russell, "Pornography and Rape," 50. See also Dworkin and MacKinnon, *Pornography and Civil Rights*, 36. More recent work by antipornography feminist critics like Gail Dines and Robert Jensen argues that a culture of abuse created by porn has saturated U.S. national culture, hijacked our values, warped our identities and sexual practices, and now threatens to "ruin" sex itself. See Dines, *Pornland*; Jensen, *Getting Off*; Boyle, *Everyday Pornography*; Paul, *Pornified*; Sarracino and Scott, *The Porning of America*.

57. Duggan, "Introduction," in *Sex Wars*, 7.

58. Walker, "Coming Apart"; Collins, *Black Feminist Thought*; Forna, "Pornography and Racism"; Gardner, "Racism in Pornography and the Women's Movement."

59. Although it is not within the scope of this book to fully account for black female pornography consumers or spectators, their critical readings of pornography are important because they impact the subjective experiences of black women porn producers.

60. Tirrant, "Is Porn Racist?"; Dines, "Yes, Pornography Is Racist"; Hernandez, "Rethinking Porn. Really"; Shabazz, "Ghetto Gaggers"; Rivas, "Porn Stars of Color Face Racial Inequality and Wage Gap Too"; Snow, "Interracial Sex Still Taboo for Many Porn Stars"; Goff, "Is the Porn Industry Racist?"; Stewart, "Porn Performers Agree."


## Chapter 1. Sepia Sex Scenes

1. It was common for stag-film producers and salesmen to release more than one version of a film, and as a result there is another version of *The Golden Shower* titled *Miss Park Avenue Takes a Bath*. Dave Thompson describes the latter film as having some of the same footage in his book, *Black and White and Blue*, 112, 114, 117–18.

2. I use this term to describe a range of facial manipulations used by black performers like Bert Williams and George Walker, as discussed by Daphne Brooks in *Bodies in Dissent*, 235–38.

3. Bruno, *Streetwalking on a Ruined Map*, 3.

4. Bruno, *Streetwalking on a Ruined Map*, 4–5.

5. For scholarship in early visual pornography, see Williams, *Hard Core*; Kendrick, *The Secret Museum*; Waugh, *Hard to Imagine*; Sigel, "Filth in the Wrong People's Hands."

6. Kaplan, *Looking for the Other*; Wallace, *The Imperial Gaze*.

7. In response to Guy Debord's concept of spectacle in "Society of the Spectacle," see for instance, Markovitz, *Racial Spectacles*, 3–6.

8. Rony, *The Third Eye*; Jenkins, *What Made Pistachio Nuts?*, 264.

9. See, for instance, Cohen, *Punks, Bulldaggers, and Welfare Queens*.

10. Hall, "What Is the 'Black' in Black Popular Culture?"

11. Davis, *Blues Legacies and Black Feminism*, 4.

12. On the grain of the voice see Moten, *In the Break*.

13. Spillers, "Mama's Baby, Papa's Maybe."

14. Russo, "Female Grotesques," 1–13.

15. Hartman, *Scenes of Subjection*.

16. Hartman, *Scenes of Subjection*, 7.

17. Hartman, *Scenes of Subjection*, 7, 57.

18. Hartman, *Scenes of Subjection*, 57.

19. Johnson, *Soul by Soul*, 148–49.

20. Johnson, *Soul by Soul*, 149.

21. Johnson, *Soul by Soul*, 149.

22. Johnson, *Soul by Soul*, 149.

23. Davis, "Don't Let Nobody Bother Yo' Principle," 108. Davis coined the term "sexual economy," which I use throughout this book. Katz also notes that "the courts of the slave system served the interests of the holding class. . . . Since the law did not permit testimony by a Negro, whether enslaved or free, against a white person in court, the Negro woman could not seek redress from the inhumanities inflicted upon her." Katz, "The Negro Woman and the Law," 278–86. See also Hartman, *Scenes of Subjection*, 84.

24. Davis, "Don't Let Nobody Bother Yo' Principle," 109.

25. Spillers, "Mama's Baby, Papa's Maybe," 67.

26. Davis, "Don't Let Nobody Bother Yo' Principle," 117.

27. Roach, *Cities of the Dead*, 215. As Roach explains, the fancy-girl auctions were especially prevalent in New Orleans: "The sale of quadroons (one quarter of African-descended females) and octoroons proved an exceptionally popular New Orleans specialty, performed in an atmosphere charged not only with white privilege but with male privilege" (215). Further, the practice of *plaçage* was a popular "Creole custom of arranging extra-marital liaisons with educated mulattas" (217). See also Davis, "Don't Let Nobody Bother Yo' Principle," 116; Stevenson, *Life in Black and White*, 180.

28. Davis, "Don't Let Nobody Bother Yo' Principle," 115.

29. Johnson, *Soul by Soul*, 148.

30. Collins, "Economies of the Flesh."

31. Gilman, "Black Bodies, White Bodies," 216.

32. Hall, "The Spectacle of the 'Other,'" 265.

33. Flower and Murie, "Account of the Dissection of a Bushwoman," 189–208.

34. Hall, "The Spectacle of the 'Other,'" 266.

35. Morton, *Crania Americana*, 90.

36. Morgan, "Some Could Suckle over Their Shoulder," 108.

37. Morgan, "Some Could Suckle over Their Shoulder," 56. See also Ms. 12405, p364/f295, British Library, London, 2.

38. Sharpley-Whiting, *Black Venus*, 17.

39. Sharpley-Whiting, *Black Venus*, 24.

40. Sharpley-Whiting, *Black Venus*, 24. Sharpley-Whiting translates and quotes from Cuvier, "Extraits d'observations faites," 214.

41. Sharpley-Whiting, *Black Venus*, 7.

42. Gilman, "Black Bodies, White Bodies," 226, 229.

43. Somerville, *Queering the Color Line*.

44. Italians Guilio Romano, Marcantonio Raimondi, and Pietro Aretino coordinated erotic and explicit illustrations, engravings, and sonnets in the first mass-distributed early pornographic work known as *I modi: The Sixteen Pleasures* in 1524, which ignited a firestorm of controversy and was subsequently outlawed and destroyed (save a surviving woodcut) by Pope Clement VII. See Hughes, "Between the Sistine and Disney," 6; and Haslam, "Views form the Gallery."

45. Hunt, *The Invention of Pornography*, 10–11.

46. In France after 1852, académies had to be registered with the authorities prior to sale. In the next year, close to 40 percent of the photographs registered were nude studies, but by 1860 there were none. As a result of campaigns for censorship of pornographic materials, they were driven underground. There were also very many sold underground in England and the United States. See the documentary film Bailey and Barbato, dir., *Pornography*.

47. See my forthcoming chapter, "Exotic/Erotic/Ethnopornographic."

48. See, for example, Eugéne Delacroix's *Odalisque* (1847). Malek Alloula points out that the French word Odalisque, which first appeared in the language in the early seventeenth century, is derived from the Turkish *odaliq*, meaning chambermaid. He observes, "Initially a chambermaid or a slave in the service of the women of the harem, the odalisque was metamorphosized by Orientalist painting . . . into the subliminated image of the one enclosed by the harem. This jewel of the prohibited space is endowed by the Western imagination with a strong erotic connotation." Alloula, *The Colonial Harem*, 130–31.

49. Gilman, "Black Bodies, White Bodies," 209.

50. Willis and Williams, *The Black Female Body*, 39.

51. Of the lace-covered sofa, Willis and Williams note: "The same type of crudely manufactured lace appears in numerous French postcards of nudes from the same period, but rarely with such lack of arrangement. Though this is a machine-made fabric, lace making was lower-class women's work, and it thus has a symbolic significance as the backdrop on which she rests. In spite of its traditional iconographic meaning, this lace does not connote innocence, gentility, beauty or finery. Like the woman dis-

played it is to be understood as cheap, decorative, and readily available." Willis and Williams, *The Black Female Body*, 51.

52. Despite the evidence of the lace, it is unclear to me if this model was a brothel worker or a concubine and whether she was enslaved or a freedwoman. There is little known of the negotiations of black women in brothels and as concubines during the 1850s and '60s, the period in which this daguerreotype was taken. Herbert Gutman notes cases of "colored concubines" in Yazoo, Mississippi, suing for property rights and demanding marriage rights from their "sweethearts." He also cites cases of black women refugees working as prostitutes around Union Army soldiers following the war. Gutman, *The Black Family in Slavery and Freedom*, 392–93, 613.

53. Sigel, "Filth in the Wrong People's Hands," 867–73.

54. Waugh, "Homosociality in the Classical American Stag Film," 285–26.

55. Black migration, which consisted of several waves, began with moves to urban centers in the South and to the West in the late 1870s, such that many blacks were already urbanized prior to their arrival in northern cities. See Marks, *Farewell—We're Good and Gone*.

56. D'Emilio and Freedman, *Intimate Matters*, 295.

57. Carby, "Policing the Black Woman's Body in an Urban Context," 739.

58. Regester, "The Construction of an Image and the Deconstruction of a Star," 31–84.

59. On the overlap between black women's performance cultures, commodification, and desire, and black women's negotiations of these, see Brown, *Babylon Girls*.

60. Mumford, *Interzones*.

61. D'Emilio and Freedman, *Intimate Matters*, 295.

62. Blacks were forced to live in or near these areas because of racially restrictive residential covenants that enforced segregation. Carby, "Policing the Black Woman's Body in an Urban Context," 754.

63. D'Emilio and Freedman, *Intimate Matters*, 296.

64. Aside from Cynthia Blair's work, most of the historical studies of prostitution in the United States during the early twentieth century provide only passing mention of the issue of black women as prostitutes. Hazel Carby's research on middle-class efforts to police the boundaries of black women's sexuality discusses vaudeville as a labor option of "clean work" as opposed to domestic labor for black women, and the entertainment industry's close relationship to illicit commercial sex. In her autobiography, Billie Holiday discusses her miserable experience as a domestic servant and her falling into prostitution as a young woman living in poverty and a new migrant to New York City in the 1920s. Holiday also describes being arrested and imprisoned in a women's workhouse when she refused to have sex with one of her clients who was particularly violent toward her. See Blair, *I've Got to Make My Own Livin'*; Gross, *Colored Amazons*; Hicks, *Talk with You like a Woman*; Gilfoyle, *City of Eros*; Rosen, *The Lost Sisterhood*; Carby, "Policing the Black Woman's Body in the Urban Context"; Holiday, *Lady Sings the Blues*.

65. The authors argue that the "lower class" distinguishes between professional prostitutes and "freebys" who are not so much involved in commercial transactions as

they are positioned as "casual pick-ups" available for a "good time" to lower-class men. Drake and Cayton, *Black Metropolis*, 595.

66. Drake and Cayton, *Black Metropolis*, 596.

67. Drake and Cayton, *Black Metropolis*, 596.

68. Drake and Cayton, *Black Metropolis*, 597.

69. Drake and Cayton, *Black Metropolis*, 596.

70. "The Report on the Sub-Committee on Crime and Delinquency of the City-Wide Citizen's Committee on Harlem (1942)," 5. Cited in Myrdal and Bok, *An American Dilemma*, 974. See also D'Emilio and Freedman, *Intimate Matters*, 295.

71. Myrdal and Bok, *An American Dilemma*, 597.

72. Myrdal and Bok, *An American Dilemma*, 597–98.

73. Myrdal and Bok, *An American Dilemma*, 598.

74. Myrdal and Bok, *An American Dilemma*, 598.

75. Gross, *Colored Amazons*, 82.

76. D'Emilio and Freedman, *Intimate Matters*, 297, originally quoted in Staples, *The Black Family*, 372.

77. de Leeuw, *Sinful Cities of the Western World*, 266; cited in Myrdal and Bok, *An American Dilemma*, 1268.

78. Malcolm X, Haley, and Handler, *The Autobiography of Malcom X*, 136–38.

79. Blair, *I've Got to Make My Own Livin'*; Hunter, *To 'Joy My Freedom*; Wolcott, *Remaking Respectability*; Gross, *Colored Amazons*; Hicks, *Talk with You like a Woman*.

80. In thinking about the survival strategies of people living at the fringes and how the dreams, desires, and imaginations of the dispossessed are never entirely contained by the forces of capital, I am indebted to Tamara Spira and others who attended my workshop at the Center for the Study of Women in Society at the University of Oregon. Tamara Spira, conversation with author, Eugene, OR, April 17, 2013. See also Davis, "Reflections of the Black Woman's Role in the Community of Slaves"; Davis and Tadiar, *Beyond the Frame*; and Agathangelou and Ling, *Transforming World Politics*.

81. Waugh, "Homoerotic Representation in the Stag Film, 1920–1940," 4–19, 6.

82. Waugh, "Homoerotic Representation in the Stag Film, 1920–1940," 7.

83. Waugh, "Homoerotic Representation in the Stag Film, 1920–1940," 7.

84. Di Lauro and Rabkin, *Dirty Movies*, 54.

85. Waugh posits that of the stag films made before World War II, only 180 remain, mainly in archives and private collections. Of these, 100 are American, 50 French, and the rest Latin American, Austrian, and Spanish. Waugh, "Homoerotic Representation in the Stag Film, 1920–1940," 6.

86. Joseph Slade says that one thousand of the seventeen hundred stags were made in the United States. Meade, dir., *American Stag*. See also Slade, *Pornography in America*.

87. Everett, *Returning the Gaze*.

88. Di Lauro and Rabkin, *Dirty Movies*, 101.

89. On racial intimacy and black women as renowned stag performers, see Vogel, *The Scene of Harlem Cabaret*; see also Brown, *Babylon Girls*.

90. Mumford, *Interzones*.

91. Schaefer, "*Bold! Daring! Shocking! True!*," 278–80.

92. Schaefer, "*Bold! Daring! Shocking! True!*," 281.

93. By my use of the term "race porn" I do not mean to suggest that it was similarly manufactured or had similar goals as the "race films" of the era, made primarily by black directors (like Oscar Micheaux) for black audiences with themes of racial uplift and black middle-class values. I use "race porn" to delineate the centrality of racialization as a process created in the making or viewing of such material, particularly racial desire. On "race films" see Gaines, *Fire and Desire*.

94. Penley, "Crackers and Whackers," 313.

95. Penley disagrees with Peter Lehman's reading of "fleeting moments of humor in porn," instead seeing humor as much more critical to the overall structure of the stag (Penley, 314). Here I am interested in both possibilities in race porn: that humor structures the "dirty joke" and that humor offers more "fragmentary pleasures" for the viewer, and in my examination, the performer/sex worker herself. See Lehman, "Revelations about Pornography," 3–15.

96. Bogle, *Toms, Coons, Mulattoes, Mammies, and Bucks*, 7.

97. Penley, "Crackers and Whackers," 316.

98. Freud, *The Joke and Its Relationship to the Unconscious*, 92–97.

99. Freud, *The Joke and Its Relationship to the Unconscious*, 92–97.

100. On black women as trickster figures see Stallings, "'Mutha' Is Half a Word!"

101. Jules-Rosette, *Josephine Baker in Art and Life*.

102. Russo, "Female Grotesques."

103. Gunning, "The Cinema of Attraction," 65–70.

104. Brown, *Babylon Girls*, 92–127; Mizejewski, *Ziegfeld Girl*, 120–35.

105. Mizejewski, *Ziegfeld Girl*, 130–31.

106. Williams, "'White Slavery' versus the Ethnography of 'Sexworkers,'" 126–27.

107. Here by asserting this actress's role as a sex worker I disagree with Linda Williams that "the word 'sexworker' is . . . anachronistic for the period" and "has a euphemistic tinge of political correctness that does not fit the historical attitudes towards women who performed sex for hire from the teens through the late sixties and toward the women who can be seen to repeat those acts in the stag film archives" (124). I use sex worker precisely because it describes their work. I make clear that these sex workers are also actresses and performers, but that as participants in pornography they were likely prostitutes or involved in other kinds of sexual labor and performance. Williams seems concerned that the term "sexworker" does not capture the degree to which these women were constrained by their position. The women working in stag film may have been coerced, but using this term highlights their labor in ways that are obscured by a sole focus on their victimization. The term "sex worker" has been expanded over the years by feminist theorists and activists to include a variety of persons involved in the sex industry in various historical periods. I argue that the term allows for complexity and difference among sex workers rather than proscribing one identity, experience, or narrative.

108. Hartman, *Scenes of Subjection*.

109. This tactic is seen in the performances of other actresses at the time. For instance, consider Candy Barr's refusal to perform a blow job on another actor in the stag film *Smart Aleck* (1951).

## Chapter 2. Sexy Soul Sisters

1. Hotmovies.com, "Sex with Soul." See also video compilation *Sex With Soul*, Historic Erotica, 2005.

2. Of course, the civil rights movement was also a time when the black middle class actively sought to disassociate with what they saw as the problematic sexual deviance of the working class and in the process sought to police the gender performance and sexual behaviors of homosexuals, sex workers, and other "deviants." However, I aim to open up these gender and sexual performances and behaviors of the black working class as examples of how, despite the will of political elites such as Adam Clayton Powell and Dr. Martin Luther King Jr., African Americans were expressing and exploring sexual issues, identities, and practices in new ways. On gender and sexual policing during the civil rights era see Russell, "The Color of Discipline."

3. Rare Celebrities, "Legendary Ebony Porn Actress Desiree West-Biography."

4. The video was removed from YouTube, most likely for violating YouTube's policy of censoring nudity. Many fans had commented on the YouTube page as well as on other blogs on which the video was posted, but those comments have also been erased due to the removal.

5. Excalibur Films, "Desiree West Biography."

6. Bennett, *The Negro Mood*, 89.

7. Green and Guillory, "By Way of an Introduction," 1.

8. Green and Guillory, "Question of a 'Soulful Style,'" 259.

9. Green and Guillory, "Question of a 'Soulful Style,'" 259; see also Tate et al., "Ain't We Still Got Soul?"

10. Hall, "The Long Civil Rights Movement and the Political Uses of the Past," 1235.

11. Davis, "Afro Images," 23–31.

12. Bennett, "The Soul of Soul," 114.

13. Green and Guillory, "Question of a 'Soulful Style,'" 251–52.

14. Van Deburg, *New Day in Babylon*.

15. Gertzman, *Bookleggers and Smuthounds*.

16. D'Emilio and Freedman, *Intimate Matters*, 287.

17. D'Emilio and Freedman, *Intimate Matters*, 287.

18. Duggan and Hunter, *Sex Wars*, 19–21.

19. Duggan and Hunter, *Sex Wars*, 19–21.

20. Nye, *Sexuality*, 381.

21. Slade, "Erotic Motion Pictures and Videotapes," 107.

22. Some argue that violence was a substitute for the constraints on showing sexuality in film. See *American Grindhouse*; Sconce, *Sleaze Artists*.

23. Delany, *Times Square Red, Times Square Blue*.

24. D'Emilio and Freedman, *Intimate Matters*, 277.

25. Slade, "Violence in the Hardcore Pornographic Film."

26. Slade, "Violence in the Hardcore Pornographic Film," 160.

27. Ford, *A History of X*, 49.

28. Camille Paglia interviewed in Bailey and Barbato, dir., *Inside Deep Throat*.

29. Bailey and Barbato, dir., *Inside Deep Throat*.

30. Blumenthal, "Hardcore Grows Fashionable—and Very Profitable."

31. Although the $600 million figure is cited in the documentary film *Inside Deep Throat*, others believe the lower figure, estimated by the FBI, is more accurate. The confusion relates to the fact that the film was distributed by Mafia networks attached to the Peraino family, who were believed to inflate revenue reports in order to launder money from illegal activities.

32. Slade, *Pornography and Sexual Representation*.

33. Williams, "Skin Flicks on the Racial Border."

34. McClintock, *Imperial Leather*.

35. Shimizu, *The Hypersexuality of Race*.

36. Slade, *Pornography in America*.

37. Thanks to Albert Steg for making me aware of these performers and for screening these rare 16 mm and 8 mm films for me.

38. See Heller, "Inter-Racial Porno Movies," 91; Boone, "Black Girl in a White World," 52–56.

39. A "white coater" is a term for sexploitation films of the 1960s and early '70s that were prefaced or narrated by an actor portraying a doctor or psychiatrist. Often dressed in a white coat, the doctor provided the educational pretext necessary to circumvent U.S. obscenity laws. See Cook, *Lost Illusions*.

40. Schaefer, *Bold! Daring! Shocking! True!*, 265–85.

41. Schaefer, *Bold! Daring! Shocking! True!*, 281, 280. See also Fredrickson, *The Black Image in the White Mind*, 275–82.

42. Asante, *Afrocentricity*, 66. Cress Welsing quoted in Hemphill, *Ceremonies*. Both are discussed in Stallings, "'Mutha' Is Half a Word!,'" 153.

43. Stallings, "'Mutha' Is Half a Word!,'" 153.

44. Guerrero, *Framing Blackness*, 85–86.

45. Guerrero, *Framing Blackness*, 86. Not all films deemed part of Blaxploitation were exploitation films. Classic exploitation films sought to exploit a particular racy topic or to shamelessly pander to a particular audience, and were usually cheaply made films produced and marketed outside of Hollywood and its distribution networks. Yet films like *Cotton Comes to Harlem* and *Cleopatra Jones* were made on big budgets by big Hollywood studios, while *The Spook Who Sat by the Door* took on important political questions that hardly pandered to its audience. Hence, because many black-cast, black-oriented and black-produced films were considered part of the genre, the designation Blaxploitation film does not represent the tremendous diversity of so many films created during this period. However, scholars continue to debate the

conventions of the genre. See Lawrence, *Blaxploitation Films of the 1970s*; and Simon, "The Stigmatization of 'Blaxploitation.'"

46. Schaefer, *Bold! Daring! Shocking! True!*

47. Hall, *Representation*, 270.

48. Hall, *Representation*, 270.

49. Hall, *Representation*, 271.

50. Hall, *Representation*, 271.

51. Dyer, *White*.

52. Jaggi, "Twentieth-century fox."

53. Jaggi, "Twentieth-century fox."

54. Jaggi, "Twentieth-century fox."

55. Jaggi, "Twentieth-century fox."

56. Robinson, "Blaxploitation and the Misrepresentation of Liberation," 6.

57. Robinson, "Blaxploitation and the Misrepresentation of Liberation," 5.

58. Robinson, "Blaxploitation and the Misrepresentation of Liberation," 6.

59. Robinson, "Blaxploitation and the Misrepresentation of Liberation," 11.

60. Hall, *Representation*, 263.

61. America Distribution Corporation was owned by the same person (Bentley Morris) as Holloway House publishing, which was known for many of the "black experience novels" of the time, such as the work of Donald Goines as well as *Pimp* and *Trick Baby* by Robert Beck (under the pen name Iceberg Slim).

62. Neal, *Soul Babies*.

63. Lewis, "Letter to the Editor."

64. On the casting-couch trope and the classic stag film *The Casting Couch*, known for its portrayal of ambitious aspiring actresses pressed for sex by unseemly directors, see Williams, *Hard Core*; and Di Lauro and Rabkin, *Dirty Movies*.

65. Martial arts themes were very popular among African American audiences of Blaxploitation and represent an important commingling of black and Asian American culture at the time. See Prashad, *Everybody Was Kung Fu Fighting*.

66. Arthur Bell, cited in Bogle, *Blacks in American Films and Television*, 133.

67. Bogle, *Blacks in American Films and Television*, 133.

68. Penley, "Crackers and Whackers."

69. Linda Williams argues that the racial difference between the actors in pornographic film creates a specific and powerful erotic charge. She writes specifically about the contrast between black men and white women but I think this racialized tension creates interest and heightened eroticism in scenes between black women and white men as well, though of course because of the different history between these couplings, the erotic charge works differently. See Williams, "Skin Flicks on the Racial Border."

70. "Colonial fantasy" is a term used by Homi Bhabha in "The Other Question."

71. Marcus, *The Other Victorians*, 269.

72. Fanon, *Black Skin, White Masks*.

73. Slade, *Pornography in America*.

74. JanMohamed, "Sexuality on/of the Racial Border."

75. I am drawing again on Linda Williams's argument that racial differences charge interracial pornography with a special form of intensity due to the powerful investments and desires rooted in race. Williams draws upon Abdul JanMohamed for her argument about these erotics on the racial border. See Williams, "Skin Flicks on the Racial Border"; JanMohamed, "Sexuality on/of the Racial Border."

76. Brown cited in Rickford and Rickford, *Spoken Soul*, 3–4.

77. Rickford and Rickford, *Spoken Soul*, 4–5.

78. Williams, "Skin Flicks on the Racial Border," 286; JanMohamed, "Sexuality on/ of the Racial Border."

79. Moynihan, *The Negro Family*.

80. Although E. Franklin Frazier discussed "black matriarchy" as problematic, his thesis did not see it as being the *primary* cause of African American political and social powerlessness and economic marginalization, as the Moynihan Report later argued. See Frazier, *The Negro Family in the United States*.

81. The image of the "black matriarch" had a profound influence on social discourse around gender roles in the black community and inspired a lasting debate among scholars. In response to Moynihan, Herbert Gutman asserted that the black family and gender roles were essentially adaptive to histories of slavery and marginalization, with black women as assets rather than detriments to the black family's stability. Black feminist scholar Linda La Rue critiqued Moynihan's view as well: "He does not recognize the liberation struggle and the demands that it has placed on the black family" (168). See Gutman, *The Black Family in Slavery and Freedom*; La Rue, "The Black Women's Movement and Liberation." See also Ladner, *Tomorrow's Tomorrow*; Staples, "The Myth of the Black Matriarchy," 8–16; and Hernton, *Sex and Racism in America*.

82. Roberts, *Killing the Black Body*, 207. See also Mink, "Welfare Reform in Historical Perspective," 879, 891; Mink, *The Wages of Motherhood*; Gordon, *Pitied but Not Entitled*.

83. Jill Quadagno argues that the abolishment of War on Poverty programs, through the design of a strategic, conservative white backlash, was linked to the black civil rights movement's increasing and threatening demands for political and economic justice. Quadagno, *The Color of Welfare*.

84. Sugrue, *The Origins of the Urban Crisis*.

85. *Plessy v. Ferguson*, 163 U.S. 537 (1896); D'Emilio and Freedman, *Intimate Matters*, 106.

86. *Loving v. Virginia*, 388 U.S. 1 (1967); Pascoe, "Miscegenation Law," 50.

87. Cleaver, *Target Zero*, 47.

88. Pseudonyms were common: virtually every performer used them because it was still illegal to perform in sex films in California and New York during the 1970s and early 1980s.

89. Harris, "Revolutionary Black Nationalism," 169.

90. Brown, *A Taste of Power*.

91. La Rue, "The Black Women's Movement and Liberation."

92. hooks, "Eating the Other."

Chapter 3. Black Chicks

1. O'Toole, *Pornocopia*, 104. In fact, many argue that the adult industry's use of the Sony VHS format secured the dominance of VHS, while JVC's resistance to the porn industry using their Beta video format forced Beta to become obsolete. See Slade, "Erotic Motion Pictures and Videotapes," 107; Van Scoy, "Sex Sells, so Learn a Thing or Two from It," 64.

2. Videocassette recorders were invented in the 1950s, but VHS entered the market in 1971, remaining a specialty technology until the early 1980s.

3. Holliday, "The Changing Face of Adult Video," 15.

4. "Who Rents Adult Tape?," 27. According to this graph, which includes rentals from general video stores as well as all-adult video stores, women account for 47 percent of renters. Of these renters 29 percent are listed as "Women and Men Renters," 15 percent are "Women Alone," and 3 percent are "Women with Women Renters."

5. Bailey, dir., *Pornography*.

6. Higgins, cited in Bailey, dir., *Pornography*.

7. Holliday, "The Changing Face of Adult Video," 88.

8. *Adult Video News 1986–87 Buyer's Guide*. See also "Charting the Adult Industry," 26.

9. Bailey, dir., *Pornography*.

10. Thomas, "The Marketing of Three Major Titles," 1.

11. Paone, "Combating the Adult Video Glut," 8.

12. Paone, "Combating the Adult Video Glut," 8.

13. "Consumer Feedback: Problems with Shot-On-Video Features," 4.

14. Fishbein, "Where Are We Spiralling to Now?," 63.

15. Fishbein, "Where Are We Spiralling to Now?," 63.

16. Fishbein, "Where Are We Spiralling to Now?," 63.

17. "Retail Feedback," 6; "Consumer Feedback: Favorite Sub-Genres," 6.

18. "Retail Feedback," 6; "Consumer Feedback: Favorite Sub-Genres," 6.

19. In this way, black and interracial video—which function differently in terms of representation, but because they are lumped together in the adult-business discourse during this period in time I will refer to generally as "black pornography"—was both a valued and devalued product.

20. Goldsby, "Queen for 307 Days," 117–18.

21. Goldsby, "Queen for 307 Days," 121.

22. Margold's comment is cited in the post "Racism" on LukeFord.com, which is no longer accessible. Margold reiterated it in an interview with me at his residence in 2002. Bill Margold, personal interview with author, November 26, 2002; "Racism," LukeFord.com.

23. Black pornography in the video era also included Latino and Asian actors. However, despite the occasional inclusion of people of other races and ethnicities, black-cast films were still categorized as black. The category interracial films indicated black-white sex acts. The separate Latino market was not developed until the late 1990s, but during the 1980s films featuring Vanessa Del Rio were advertised to both black and Latino men in urban markets. Some advertisements for Vanessa Del Rio's films used

both Spanish and English. The Asian market also took off in the late 1990s, sparked largely by films made in east and Southeast Asia and sold in the United States. American pornography featuring Asian women, however, was mainly marketed to white men rather than Asian men. Asian male actors are extremely rare in the heterosexual market to this day, though actor Brandon Lee gained notoriety in the gay pornography market during the early 2000s. The heterosexual Asian films made in the United States often feature interracial pairings of Asian women and black men. During the 1970s and '80s, Mai Lin was the best-known Asian American porn actress. She made a brief comeback in the 1990s. Annabel Chong followed Mai Lin as the best-known actress in the late 1990s and early 2000s. She became famous for her film *World's Biggest Gang Bang* (1995) in which she had sex with 251 men over ten hours, a record at the time. There are no published academic studies on Latina actresses in pornography that I know of. On Asian porn actresses see Shimizu, *The Hypersexuality of Race*. See also Hoang, "The Resurrection of Brandon Lee"; and Fung, "Looking for My Penis."

24. Lott, *Love and Theft*.

25. Lott, *Love and Theft*, 6–9.

26. Lott, *Love and Theft*, 6–9.

27. Omi and Winant, *Racial Formation*.

28. Here I agree with Daniel Bernardi that pornography "engages in overt and implicit, complex if not always explicit forms of racism" but I disagree that pornography, as a genre, constitutes an "ideology of hate" or a form of hate speech. By offering an analysis of racist and racialist pornography I am attempting to complicate the discussion of race in porn by arguing that some representations that exploit racial difference are not designed or performed as racist expressions, even though their historical references, codes, and labor conditions can be seen as racist. While the implied spectator for these representations is clearly a white male, the fact that black actors assert their own interpretations of the roles, and that black spectators may be doing the same, similarly complicates how racism is employed in these cultural products. By employing the terms racialism and racialization, I hope to expand the field of this discourse on the work of racial desire in porn as a necessarily contested process, not to elide the ways in which a lot of porn is actually severely racist. See Bernardi, "Interracial Joysticks," 240.

29. "Black Bun Busters," 13.

30. Fishbein, "How to Sell Adult Tapes," 18.

31. Guerrero, *Framing Blackness*, 165.

32. Fishbein, "How to Sell Adult Tapes," 18.

33. Fishbein, "Where Are We Spiralling to Now?," 84.

34. McMahon, "Displaying Adult Tapes," 14.

35. Bright, "The Image of the Black in Adult Video," 64.

36. Bright, "The Image of the Black in Adult Video," 56.

37. United States Department of Justice, *Attorney General's Commission on Pornography, Final Report*.

38. Until 1987 it was illegal to shoot pornography in Los Angeles County. With *Hal Freeman v. State of California*, the shooting of pornographic movies, which had been

hampered by vice police raids under charges of prostitution and pandering, was legalized.

39. Fishbein, "The Decade in Review." See also, O'Toole, *Pornocopia*, 106–11.

40. In response to this state repression, the industry organized collectives to take on anti-obscenity prosecutions, which they viewed as violations of their First Amendment rights. The Adult Video Association sued the U.S. government to challenge the constitutionality of numerous federal obscenity prosecutions in 1987 under the Racketeer Influenced and Corrupt Organizations Act (RICO), eventually winning its case. In addition, the Free Speech Coalition, the industry's trade organization, organized to combat obscenity and censorship laws beginning in 1991. Fishbein, "The Decade in Review, Part 2," 66.

41. Bright, "The Image of the Black in Adult Video," 56.

42. Bright, "The Image of the Black in Adult Video," 64.

43. Suggs, "Hard Corps," 39.

44. Zbryski, "Review of *Black Dynasty*," 24.

45. Fishbein, "Review of *More Chocolate Candy*" and "Review of *Chocolate Bon Bons*," both on page 20.

46. In videos, much of the sex was shot by one or two cameras, so that all that the editor could do was make the frame alternate between a wide view and a close-up of penetration—usually with brief inserts of the performers' faces. In order to prolong scenes, editors often spliced in duplicate footage within the sex act in postproduction. This process added to the repetitive quality of the sex, as did many videos' utter lack of story line. Kernes, Guest Lecture in Film Studies 150.

47. Bill Margold, phone conversation with author, June 27, 2004.

48. Bill Margold has been a big supporter of this project and kindly provided contacts, shared his vast knowledge of the history of the porn industry, raised funds to support my research, and offered to help me honor Angel Kelly by inducting her into the Legends of Erotica Hall of Fame. His organization Protecting Adult Welfare (PAW) works to support the needs of actors (especially young women new to the industry) with counseling and resource recommendations. We met for an interview in 2002 when I first began my fieldwork, and he reiterated several of the comments I cite here. Bill Margold, personal interview with author, November 26, 2002.

49. Bright, "The Image of the Black in Adult Video," 56.

50. Fishbein, "Where Are We Spiralling to Now?," 84.

51. Fishbein, "Where Are We Spiralling to Now?," 63. Emphasis in original.

52. Fishbein, "Where Are We Spiralling to Now?," 63.

53. Bill Margold, personal interview with author, November 26, 2002.

54. Bright, "The Image of the Black in Adult Video," 56.

55. Bright, "The Image of the Black in Adult Video," 56.

56. Irving, "Director's Corner: Gregory Dark," 53.

57. Kipnis, *Bound and Gagged*, 161.

58. Collins discusses the ways in which "freak" has taken on specifically racialized and sexualized connotations in black popular culture over the past thirty years. Collins, *Black Sexual Politics*.

59. Irving, "Director's Corner: Gregory Dark," 53.

60. Petkovich, "Dark World," 43.

61. Petkovich, "Dark World," 43.

62. Here I draw on the work of Anne McClintock. Although she is not referring to interracial pornography specifically, her point here about the role of sexual risk is insightful. McClintock, "Gonad the Barbarian and the Venus Flytrap," 125.

63. Bill Margold, phone conversation with author, June 27, 2004. Jack Baker is the pseudonym for the actor John Anthony Bailey, who was a 1970s television actor. He appeared in several popular television shows, including *Good Times* (CBS, 1974–79), *The Jeffersons* (CBS, 1975–85), *M*A*S*H* (CBS, 1972–83), and *Wonderbug* (ABC, 1976–78), in which he had a major role. Baker, who was one of the most prolific black porn actors during the 1980s and appeared in many non-sex roles, also worked as a dialogue coach on numerous adult films. According to the Internet Adult Film Database, he died of cancer in 1994. "Jack Baker," Internet Adult Film Database.

64. Since the 1960s, the discourse on welfare policy has framed poor black women as the embodiment of the stigmatized "welfare mother." Although black women were never the majority of recipients of Aid for Families with Dependent Children (AFDC), they came to signify a dominant ideological contempt for "the culture of poverty" during the black militancy of the 1960s and the retrenchment of social welfare spending under Reagan, Bush, and Clinton in the 1980s and '90s. According to this powerful and politically useful stereotype, poor black women are portrayed as unforgivingly manipulative and lazy. See Lubiano, "Black Ladies, Welfare Queens and State Minstrels."

65. Cherry Layme is billed (incorrectly) as "Charry Lei-Me" in the credits to *Let Me Tell Ya 'Bout Black Chicks*. IAFD, "Let Me Tell Ya 'Bout Black Chicks." Accessed March 27, 2014. http://www.iafd.com/title.rme/title=let+me+tell+ya+bout+black+chicks /year=1985/let-me-tell-ya-bout-black-chicks.htm.

66. This choice represents a real labor option for many black women sex workers. I would add that it might have been a choice for Sahara herself, but without her biographical information, it would be impossible to assume that she chose to work in hard core over a "working-class job" or poverty. She may have come from a middle-class family and had many more options than most black sex workers. I discuss these issues of motivation and choice for sexual labor in pornography in chapter 5.

67. Gilman, *Difference and Pathology*, 27.

68. She also makes a contemporary pop-culture reference to *Ghostbusters* and the Billboard number one hit of the same name by black musician Ray Parker Jr.

69. Aside from Jeannie Pepper, I was not able to locate the actresses involved in *Let Me Tell Ya 'Bout White Chicks*.

70. Jeannie Pepper, personal interview with the author, December 8, 2002.

71. Jeannie Pepper, personal interview with the author, December 8, 2002.

72. Jeannie Pepper, personal interview with the author, December 8, 2002.

73. Jeannie Pepper quoted in Bright, "The Image of the Black in Adult Video," 62.

74. Bright, "The Image of the Black in Adult Video," 62.

75. Bright, "The Image of the Black in Adult Video," 61.

76. Bright, "The Image of the Black in Adult Video," 61.

77. Suggs, "Hard Corps," 39.

78. Angel Kelly, personal interview with author, April 21, 2003.

79. I thank "GregWn" for posting this interview on YouTube, and then when You-Tube removed it, probably for copyright reasons, brazenly reposting it. Without collectors like GregWn it would be much harder to find archival sources that include the voices and images of black women adult performers. There is clearly interest in this archive. As of May 2013 the second posting of the video had over thirty-one thousand hits. GregWn, "Angel Kelly and Heather Hunter Discuss 'Adult Entertainment'—1990 Part 1 of 5."

80. Angel Kelly, personal interview with author, April 21, 2003.

81. Bright, "The Image of the Black in Adult Video," 63.

82. Angel Kelly, phone interview with author, September 16, 2013.

83. Angel Kelly, personal interview with author, April 21, 2003.

84. *Adam Film World Guide* (1991), 30.

85. Angel Kelly, personal interview with author, April 21, 2003.

86. Drea was, for a time, Bill Margold's wife and collaborator.

87. Angel Kelly, personal interview with author, April 21, 2003.

88. Angel Kelly, personal interview with author, April 21, 2003.

89. Angel Kelly, personal interview with author, April 21, 2003.

90. According to Nina Hartley, the Pink Ladies Social Club was short-lived because they were seen as a threat to the industry for calling out unfair labor practices and as a result members were quickly blacklisted. Nina Hartley, conversation with author, May 29, 2013.

91. Angel is not credited as a director for *Little Miss Dangerous* (1989) on the Internet Adult Film Database. Instead Chi Chi LaRue is credited as the director. However, according to Angel she did work in a codirectorial role on this film.

92. Angel Kelly, personal interview with author, April 21, 2003.

93. Angel Kelly, personal interview with author, April 21, 2003.

94. Sadly this interview, which Angel says she did not realize would sound as negative about her career and the porn industry as it did when published, is something that Angel says she regrets. It caused her to lose both friends and opportunities in the industry and she felt that the author was more interested in telling a sensational story than showing a nuanced view of her life and career. Because of this negative experience Angel was reluctant to allow me to interview her when we first met in 2003. Thankfully she changed her mind. Interestingly, this *Essence Magazine* article was later reprinted in the antiporn feminist volume *Making Violence Sexy*, edited by Diana E. H. Russell, which proves that antiporn feminism is also less interested in telling a nuanced story of the lives of porn's workers than they are in telling a sensational narrative about pornography's harms to women. See Campbell, "A Portrait of Angel."

95. Campbell, "A Portrait of Angel."

# Chapter 4. Ho Theory

1. Salomon, "Snoop Dogg Ventures into the World of Porn"; Edlund, "Hip-Hop's Crossover into the Adult Aisle."

2. Erotic Networks Press Release, "The Erotic Networks Releases Snoop Dogg's Doggy Style."

3. Edlund, "Hip-Hop's Crossover into the Adult Aisle," n.p.

4. Salomon, "Snoop Dogg Ventures into the World of Porn."

5. Majors, "The Porn-to-Rap Connection," n.p.

6. Weasels, "Porn 101," n.p.

7. Railton and Watson, "Naughty Girls and Red Blooded Women," 52.

8. Weasels, "Porn 101," n.p.

9. A full discussion of the video vixen as a trope in contemporary discussions of hip hop and gender is beyond the scope of this project. However, there are some interesting similarities to porn performance in the fact that the video vixen's sexual labor is used to create wealth for the producers of black cultural products. Black women might see both the video vixen and the porn star as potentially offering economic opportunity, social mobility, and a measure of glamour. Both figures tend to ignite intense controversy, but the video vixen has in many ways been the more visible figure, through her representation in hip hop videos and some popular tell-all memoirs, how-to guides, and documentaries. See Steffans, *Confessions of a Video Vixen*, *The Vixen Diaries*, and *The Vixen Manual*; Bryan, *It's No Secret*; Gibson, dir., *Kiss and Tail*. For scholarship on the hip hop model or video vixen and for insight into the black feminist critique of black women's representation in rap music video, see Pough et al., *Home Girls Make Some Noise*; Carpenter, "An Interview with Joan Morgan"; Morgan, *When Chickenheads Come Home to Roost*; Fitts, "Drop It like It's Hot"; Emerson, "Where My Girls At?"; Cheney, *Brothers Gonna Work It Out*; Hunter, "Shake It, Baby, Shake It"; Perry, "Who(se) Am I?"; Rose, *Hip Hop Wars*; Sharpley-Whiting, *Pimps Up, Ho's Down*. See also Cercone, "Hoopty Hoop Hip Hop Feminism: the Manifesta."

10. Collins, *Black Sexual Politics*; Pough, *Check It While I Wreck It*; Rose, *Longing to Tell*.

11. See for instance, Dines, *Pornland*.

12. Lyrics are sourced from RapGenius.com. All subsequent citations are sourced from this website. "Sir-Mix-a-Lot–Baby Got Back Lyrics," RapGenius.com.

13. Hobson, "The 'Batty' Politic," 95–96.

14. On hip hop as commentary on social issues see Kelley, *Race Rebels*; Rose, *Black Noise*; Perry, *Prophets of the Hood*; Pough, *Check It While I Wreck It*; Kitwana, *The Hip-Hop Generation*; Ogbar, *Hip-Hop Revolution*; Chang, *Can't Stop, Won't Stop*; Watkins, *Hip Hop Matters*; Cobb, *To the Break of Dawn*; and Forman and Neal, *That's the Joint!*

15. Christian Mann, personal interview with the author, November 27, 2002.

16. Christian Mann, personal interview with the author, November 27, 2002.

17. Christian Mann, personal interview with the author, November 27, 2002.

18. Miami bass is a form of music that emerged from the black Miami ghettos such as Liberty City and Overtown, known for "booming, low bass frequencies guaranteed to make the most expensive car stereo systems shudder and rattle the windows of

homes throughout the neighborhood." In addition, it was "sometimes dubbed 'booty' music after the part of the body most likely to shake to the bass, and most likely to be discussed in the lyrics." Unterberger, *Music USA*, 144.

19. Sharpley-Whiting, *Pimps Up Ho's Down*, 61–63.

20. Kelley, *Race Rebels*.

21. Wall-to-wall is a genre of porn that features sex scenes with little narrative, plot, or script. These videos focus on sex rather than constructing a story about the characters in the scenes. They are marketed to consumers who prefer to view sex acts without an elaborate fantasy structure.

22. Physical violence is rarely actuated on the female performers, however. This violence is usually depicted as occurring between men. In "Donkey Punching," which is a tiny subniche of extreme porn in which women are (consensually) punched at the moment of the man's orgasm, supposedly forcing them to tighten their PC muscles to intensify the orgasm, I have not found many black women in that genre. Censorship restrictions have pushed the porn industry to police itself and bar images that explicitly depict violence against women in order to avoid prosecution. Although some scholars read roughness in sex as violence, specifically studying a range of acts like slapping or pinching, I do not believe that it is reasonable to equate these acts with violence. Intense sexual performance might involve these acts, but the question of whether it constitutes violence rather than playfulness absolutely depends on the context.

23. Kelley, *Yo' Mama's Disfunktional!*, 181.

24. Rose, *Black Noise*.

25. See Wilson, "Tip Drills, Strip Clubs, and Representation in the Media"; Sharpley-Whiting, *Pimps Up Ho's Down*.

26. Rose, *The Hip Hop Wars*.

27. Shock G, personal interview with the author, January 11, 2004.

28. Gray, *Watching Race*; Perry, *Prophets of the Hood*.

29. Kelley, *Race Rebels*; Perry, *Prophets of the Hood*.

30. Perry, *Prophets of the Hood*, 120.

31. Lyrics are sourced from RapGenius.com. "Goldie Loc–Lets Roll Lyrics," RapGenius.com.

32. Quinn, "Who's the Mack," 121–22.

33. On rappers as black capitalists, see Hunter, "Shake it, Baby, Shake it."

34. Lil Jon, personal interview with the author, January 11, 2005.

35. When this occurred during my interview with Lil Jon at the AVN Convention in Las Vegas in 2005, I was shocked, but in order to keep the interview going I did not reprimand him. I was offended that he touched my breasts without consent, but it was one of the many "colorful" interactions I have had in the course of my over ten years of research in the adult industry. I was eager to see how he behaved with the performers and with me, as an academic, so I merely observed his actions, which were extremely physical and flirtatious with most of the women at the Video Team booth. Yet I believe his touching my breast during the interview to have been a tactic to avoid answering my pressing questions about sexism and misogyny in rap culture by dis-

tracting and charming me. My interview with Lil Jon—who was at the convention to promote his hip hop porn projects—did not last long, however, as some of my porn-actress informants came over and a conversation ensued about the previous night's activities.

36. On the stud or Mandingo figure, see Wells-Barnett, *Southern Horrors*; Hodes, *White Women, Black Men*; McBride, *Why I Hate Abercrombie and Fitch*; Richeson, "Sex, Drugs, and the Race-to-Castrate"; Scott, *Extravagant Abjection*; and Miller-Young and Livermon, "Black Stud. White Desire."

37. See also my discussion of black men as studs in the chapter "The Doctor" in Ross, *The Money Shot*.

38. Guerrero, *Framing Blackness*.

39. McBride, "Can the Queen Speak?," 364.

40. Sharpley-Whiting, *Pimps Up Ho's Down*, 58.

41. Candice Nicole, personal interview with author, June 13, 2009.

42. Hammonds, "Toward a Genealogy of Black Women's Sexuality."

43. Sasha Brabuster, personal interview with the author, January 25, 2005.

44. Sierra, personal interview with the author, April 28, 2003.

45. India, personal interview with author, November 23, 2002.

46. India, personal interview with author, November 23, 2002.

47. Sinnamon Love, personal interview with the author, December 5, 2002.

48. Sinnamon Love, personal interview with the author, December 5, 2002.

49. Love, public lecture in Film Studies 150.

50. Sinnamon Love, public lecture in Film Studies 150.

51. Mercer and Julien, "Race, Sexual Politics and Black Masculinity."

52. Black feminist students at Spelman College staged a protest against Nelly's visit to their campus as a way to call attention to the way in which they felt rappers should be confronted and made responsible for their misogynistic lyrics and videos. One of their protest slogans asked the question, "We Love hip hop, but does hip hop love us?" See Watkins, *Hip Hop Matters*, 216–19.

53. In thinking about these performing bodies as sites of defiance in a political economy of pleasure, I am informed by the work of University of Surrey professor Melissa Blanco Borelli who writes about mulata performance in Afro-Cuban dance that she calls hypnosis. On erotic capital I am drawing on Adam Green. Borelli, "Mulata Performances by a River"; Green, "The Social Organization of Desire."

54. Gross, *Colored Amazons*, 73–100. Gross explains that black women were not the only badger thieves, but those that were black women tended to victimize white men. In addition, though they posed as prostitutes, not all badger thieves were or had been prostitutes. Badger thieves used negative stereotypes about black female hypersexuality to "trick the tricks"—to "expose white men's immorality in trying to purchase sex and in attempting to engage in interracial intercourse," and in the process, "capitalize on their former exploitation" (78). Many white male victims of badger thieving did not report the crimes because of the shame that would incur if it was found they patronized black prostitutes, and were robbed by a woman.

55. Gross, *Colored Amazons*, 79.

56. Gross, *Colored Amazons*, 72, 74.

57. Bailey, *Butch Queens Up in Pumps*.

58. Here I am thinking about this self-making and self-mastery in terms of what Michel Foucault discusses as a technology of the self in his lectures on ethics and subjectivity. See Foucault, *Technologies of the Self*.

59. Thomas, "Modern Blackness," 43.

60. Cohen, "Deviance as Resistance."

61. Carpenter, "An Interview with Joan Morgan," 766.

## Chapter 5. (Black) Porn Star

1. Warren, "Montana Fishburne Speaks."

2. "A-List Hollywood Daughter Montana Fishburne Makes XXX Debut with Vivid Entertainment." See also Montana Fishburne's interview in XBIZTV, "Montana Fishburne Talks Sex Tape with XBIZ."

3. See *Kim Kardashian Superstar, Featuring Hip Hop Star Ray Jay* and *1 Night in Paris*, both distributed by Vivid. Pamela Anderson and Tommy Lee were some of the earliest adopters of the sex tape. See Kleinhans, "Pamela Anderson on the Slippery Slope."

4. Williams, "Laurence Fishburne's Daughter: A New Kind of Sex Tape"; and Williams, "'Real Housewives.'"

5. Szalai, "Vivid."

6. Carlton Jordan, "Pt. 2 Laurence Fishburne's 18-Year Old Daughter is Officially a Porn Star!"

7. Szalai, "Vivid." It was rumored that Kardashian made about $25,000 by selling her tape to Vivid. See The Stilts and Devoe Show.

8. Montana Fishburne discussed her desire to explore her sexuality, have fun, and seek out pleasure in several interviews. See Grossberg, "Montana Fishburne Does Porn to 'Explore Sexuality'"; Warren, "Montana Fishburne Speaks"; XBIZTV, "Montana Fishburne Talks Sex Tape with XBIZ."

9. During the 1970s and '80s there were not many black women actresses in the commercial pornography business. Today there are hundreds, perhaps thousands, of mostly casual workers coming in and out of the adult movie industry, and many more in other sectors of the commercial sex industry. There is no way to know exactly how many black women have been in pornography because the industry does not retain demographic data about its workers. My broad estimate comes from examining the number of actresses in black and interracial hard-core videos since the 1970s on the Internet Adult Film Database (IAFD).

10. On the historical intimate labor of black women, especially as domestic workers in the United States, see Glenn, "From Servitude to Service Work," 43; and Jones, *Labor of Love, Labor of Sorrow*. On the growing significance of the global sexual marketplace for black women, see Kempadoo and Doezema, *Global Sex Workers*;

Kempadoo, *Sun, Sex, and Gold*; Wekker, *The Politics of Passion*. On care work as global intimate labor, see Ehrenreich and Hochschild, *Global Woman*.

11. Agustín, *Sex at the Margins*, 21.

12. Harley, "Working for Nothing but a Living," 48–66.

13. Kelley, *Yo' Mama's Disfunktional!*, 45–46.

14. Collins, "New Commodities, New Consumers," 297–317.

15. Foucault, *The History of Sexuality*, Vol. 3, 46.

16. On black women's unemployment and underemployment, and the issue of economic pressures on black women's single-headed households, see Brown, "Explaining the Black-White Gap in Labor Force Participation among Women Heading Households," 236–52; James, Grant, and Cranford, "Moving Up, but How Far?"; Harley, Wilson, and Logan, "Introduction: Historical Overview of Black Women and Work"; and Thornton Dill and Johnson, "Between a Rock and a Hard Place."

17. Lowe, *The Body in Late-Capitalist USA*, 17–46, 103–11; On flexible accumulation, see Harvey, *The Condition of Postmodernity*.

18. Black women are cited as having a 61.6 percent participation rate in the labor force. They had the highest rate of participation among all women: white women had 58.9 percent, Hispanic women had 55.3 percent, and Asian women had 58.2 percent. United States Department of Labor, "Employment Status of Women and Men in 2005."

19. Lowe, *The Body in Late-Capitalist USA*, 127.

20. This assertion may be borne out by examining the increasing numbers of black women incarcerated for prostitution. Sex workers are usually charged with drug offenses or public order offenses, rather than for "soliciting." Lyderson, "'Our Bodies Are Not a Sacrifice'"; see also Brooks, "Sex Work and Feminism."

21. Lowe, *The Body in Late-Capitalist USA*, 17–28; Cunningham and Zalokar, "The Economic Progress of Black Women."

22. Glenn, "From Servitude to Service Work"; Hunter, *To 'Joy My Freedom*; Terborg-Penn and Milkman, "Survival Strategies among Afro-American Women Workers"; Woody, *Black Women in the Workplace*; Wallace, Datcher, and Malveaux, *Black Women in the Labor Force*.

23. Glenn, "From Servitude to Service Work," 20–22; Jones, *Labor of Love*; Brewer, "Theorizing Race, Class, and Gender," 29–38; and Enobang, "The Creation of Restricted Opportunity due to the Intersection of Race and Sex," 247–65.

24. Glenn, "From Servitude to Service Work," 14; Boris, *Home to Work* and Boris and Klein, *Caring for America*.

25. According to the Bureau of Labor Statistics, black women with college degrees had a 6.9 percent unemployment rate in 2009 versus white women who had a 4 percent rate of unemployment. For women with only high school degrees, the rates of unemployment are higher, with black women at 11.4 percent and white women at 7.4 percent. See Multimedia Graphic "Racial Differences in Joblessness" in Luo, "In Job Hunt, College Degree Can't Close Racial Gap."

26. "Black America: Nearer to Overcoming."

27. Agustín, *Sex at the Margins*; Bernstein, *Temporarily Yours*; Chapkis, *Live Sex Acts*; Chapkis, "Power and Control in the Commercial Sex Trade," 81–201.

28. I thank Heather Berg for talking this point out with me, and letting me riff on her important theoretical work on sex work from a labor perspective. See Berg, "Working for Love, Loving for Work."

29. On the "Desire Industry," see Brooks, *Unequal Desires*.

30. This assertion may seem obvious to my readers but is actually a radical assertion given the tendency in radical cultural feminism to deny sex work as work. Jeffries, *The Industrial Vagina*, 19.

31. Dee, personal interview with author, January 11, 2004.

32. Lexi, personal interview with author, January 11, 2003.

33. Crystal, personal interview with author, January 9, 2003.

34. Sandi Beach, personal interview with author, January 9, 2003.

35. Angel Eyes, personal interview with author, January 10, 2003.

36. Lola Lane, personal interview with author, January 10, 2003.

37. Love, "Life, Love and Sinn."

38. Love, "Life, Love and Sinn."

39. White, *The Comforts of Home*, 12. See also Prescod-Roberts, "Bringing It All Back Home." On reproductive labor I am informed by Dalla Costa and James, *The Power of Women and the Subversion of the Community*; Fortunati, *The Arcane of Reproduction*; Federici, *Revolution at Point Zero*.

40. Hochschild, *The Second Shift*.

41. Carmen Hayes, phone interview with author, February 8, 2010.

42. Carmen Hayes, phone interview with author, February 8, 2010.

43. Here I am thinking of Eileen Boris and Jennifer Klein's important work on black women domestic, special needs, and elder-care workers. See Boris and Klein, *Caring for America*.

44. Carmen Hayes, phone interview with author, February 8, 2010.

45. A normal agent's cut is 10 to 15 percent.

46. Diana DeVoe, personal interview with author, June 20, 2010.

47. Betty Blac, phone interview with author, September 20, 2013.

48. Diana DeVoe, personal interview with author, June 20, 2010.

49. Diana DeVoe, personal interview with author, June 20, 2010.

50. Diana DeVoe, personal interview with author, June 20, 2010.

51. Lowe, *The Body in Late-Capitalist USA*, 25.

52. India, personal interview with author, November 23, 2002.

53. India, personal interview with author, November 23, 2002.

54. Child sexual abuse (CSA) as a factor leading women into "adult sexual risk behavior," including prostitution and other sex work, is overcited in the psychological literature. See, for example, Senn and Carey, "Child Maltreatment and Women's Adult Sexual Risk Behavior," 324–35; and McClanahan et al., "Pathways into Prostitution among Female Jail Detainees and Their Implications for Mental Health Services," 1606–13.

55. Carmen Hayes, phone interview with author, February 8, 2010.

56. Nussbaum, *Sex and Social Justice*, 287.

57. Sierra, personal interview with author, April 28, 2003.

58. Sierra, personal interview with author, April 28, 2003.

59. Zelizer, "The Purchase of Intimacy," 22.

60. Zelizer, "The Purchase of Intimacy," 22.

61. Rubin, "Thinking Sex," 150–53.

62. Rubin, "Thinking Sex," 150.

63. Sierra, personal interview with author, April 28, 2003.

64. Aryana Starr, personal interview with author, June 13, 2009.

65. Love, "Black Actors in Adult Film."

66. Aryana Starr, personal interview with author, June 13, 2009.

67. Aryana Starr, personal interview with author, June 13, 2009.

68. Jeannie Pepper, personal interview with author, December 8, 2002.

69. Hine, "Rape and the Inner Lives of Black Women in the Middle West."

70. Jeannie Pepper, personal interview with author, December 8, 2002.

71. Cohen, "Punks, Bulldaggers, and Welfare Queens."

72. Cohen, "Deviance as Resistance," 43. I am also informed here by Celine Parreñas Shimizu's concept of productive perversity here. Her concept describes the ways in which minorities may employ perversity, nonnormativity, and hypersexuality "to create new morphologies in representation and in history." Shimizu, *The Hypersexuality of Race*, 26.

73. Here I am drawing on Lisa Duggan and Nan Hunter's discussion of sexual dissent in *Sex Wars* to tease out the political dimensions of erotic sovereignty.

74. Vanessa Blue, personal interview with author, January 10, 2004.

75. Vanessa Blue, personal interview with author, January 10, 2004.

76. Sinnamon Love, personal interview with author, December 8, 2002.

77. Lola Lane, personal interview with author, June 14, 2009.

78. Lola Lane, personal interview with author, June 14, 2009.

79. Here I am not attempting to privilege female orgasm as the test for authentic sexual pleasure. It is a significant question because by definition the porn scene ends with the cathartic release of energies and the resolution to the conflict between characters in the scene with the "money shot." The money shot, Linda Williams argues, may be a compensatory act that focuses on visualizing the male orgasm precisely because the female orgasm cannot be so easily visualized. Porn actresses must compensate for their invisible orgasm with a lot of enthusiastic gestural and audible performance. See Williams, *Hard Core*.

80. Abbott, "Creating a Scene," 380–89.

81. Spantaneeus Xtasty, phone interview with author, February 4, 2010.

82. Tyler Knight, personal interview with author, August 15, 2008.

83. Tyler Knight, personal interview with author, August 15, 2008.

84. Sasha Brabuster, personal interview with author, January 25, 2005.

85. Spantaneeus Xtasty, phone interview with author, February 4, 2010.

86. Spantaneeus Xtasty, phone interview with author, February 4, 2010.

87. Winbush, "The Diva of Sex."

88. Winbush, "The Diva of Sex."

89. Love, "Black Actors in Adult Film."

90. Love, "Black Actors in Adult Film."

91. Hence they are like the black women rappers that Tricia Rose discusses. Rose, *Black Noise*, 177.

92. The Crunk Feminist Collective, "I Saw the Sign but Did We Really Need a Sign?"

93. The Crunk Feminist Collective, "Slut Walks v. Ho Strolls."

94. Marshall, "The Cinematic Apparatus," 236.

95. Dyer, *Heavenly Bodies*, 5.

96. Dyer, *Heavenly Bodies*, 5.

97. India, personal interview with author, November 23, 2002.

98. On the invisibility of black performers, see Alexander, "Fatal Beauties"; Mask, *Divas on Screen*. On the trauma of invisibility, see also Rose, "Race, Class, and the Pleasure/Danger Dialectic."

99. Kelley, *Race Rebels*.

100. Sasha Brabuster, personal interview with author, January 25, 2005.

101. Although there has been a growing market for MILF porn, which stands for Mothers I'd Like to Fuck, women over thirty years of age still have fewer opportunities in the business. There is scant research on the topic of "aging out," but I am inspired by the research being done by adult performer and scholar Dylan Ryan.

102. Sasha Brabuster, personal interview with author, January 25, 2005.

103. Midori, personal interview with author, December 9, 2002.

104. Midori, personal interview with author, December 9, 2002.

105. Midori, personal interview with author, December 9, 2002.

106. Carmen Hayes, phone interview with the author, February 8, 2010.

107. Spantaneeus Xtasty, phone interview with the author, February 4, 2010.

108. Spantaneeus Xtasty, phone interview with the author, February 4, 2010.

109. Jeannie Pepper, personal interview with author, December 8, 2002.

110. Jeannie Pepper, personal interview with author, December 8, 2002.

111. Jeannie Pepper, personal interview with author, December 8, 2002.

112. Candice Nicole, personal interview with the author, June 13, 2009.

113. Candice Nicole, personal interview with the author, June 13, 2009.

114. Jeannie Pepper, personal interview with author, December 8, 2002.

115. For an excellent analysis of disposability of workers in late capital, see Bales, *Disposable People*; Ehrenreich and Hochschild, *Global Woman*; and Wright, *Disposable Women and Other Myths of Global Capitalism*.

116. Hong, *The Ruptures of American Capital*, xxiii–xxiv.

117. Hong, *The Ruptures of American Capital*, xxiii–xxiv.

118. Berlant, *Cruel Optimism*.

119. Here I am implicitly linking my informants to the tradition of women of color feminism outlined by Hong in *The Ruptures of American Capital*, xxv.

120. Mya Lovely, personal interview with author, January 11, 2004.

## Chapter 6. Behind the Scenes

1. See the Pink Cross Foundation, http://thepinkcross.org/.

2. Lola Lane, personal interview with author, 2009.

3. PBS Frontline: American Porn, "Interview with Bill Ascher," "Interview with Dennis McAlpine," Johnston, "Indications of a Slowdown in Sex Entertainment Trade."

4. As always I attribute my use of the term "sexual economy" to Adrienne Davis. See Davis, "Don't Let Nobody Bother Yo' Principle."

5. Davis, "Don't Let Nobody Bother Yo' Principle." Also Davis, "The Sexual Economy of Slavery."

6. Davis, "Slavery and the Roots of Sexual Harassment."

7. Davis, "Reflections on the Black Woman's Role in the Community of Slaves."

8. Lola Lane, personal interview with author, January 10, 2003.

9. Lola Lane, personal interview with author, June 14, 2009.

10. Lola Lane, personal interview with author, June 14, 2009.

11. Alexander, "Fatal Beauties," 50.

12. Alexander, "Fatal Beauties," 53.

13. Lola Lane, personal interview with author, January 10, 2003.

14. Vanessa Blue, personal interview with author, August 13, 2008.

15. Anonymous, personal interview with the author, December 5, 2002.

16. Most informants did not share their yearlong contract rates, or too many economic details. This rate was the average contract rate for actresses awarded by Video Team for 2000–2004.

17. See, for instance, this thread by fans and industry insiders on a popular adult-industry discussion forum: "Why Won't Vivid, Wicked and DP Get Black Woman?"

18. Angel Eyes, personal interview with author, January 10, 2003.

19. Hirsch, Lecture in Film Studies 150.

20. Not all contract workers, however, possess the same labor rights as pornography-company employees, such as job security or health benefits.

21. Lollipop, personal interview with author, June 13, 2009.

22. Sierra, personal interview with author, April 28, 2003.

23. In *Estrada v. FedEx* (2007) the court's ruling hinged on the question of how workers become categorized as employee or contractor, and whether corporations use "contract worker" status to evade responsibilities and to cut their own labor costs. By using the "guise of an independent contractor model," FedEx concealed how contract workers were in fact integral to and integrated in the company's operation; that the drivers were in fact employees. Crain, Kim, and Selmi, *Work Law*, 86.

24. Crain, Kim, and Selmi, *Work Law*, 89.

25. Crain, Kim, and Selmi, *Work Law*, 88.

26. Crain, Kim, and Selmi, *Work Law*, 88.

27. The California Labor Code "does not expressly define 'employee'" so there is no clear answer to whether the performers in adult film would meet the common law test of employment. The test for whether a person counts as an employee includes numerous factors: how much control the employer (or principal) has over the supervision,

direction, nature, time, and payment of the worker's work, and the skill required for that work. Even if the skill required for erotic labor is unrecognized and contractors work for numerous companies at any given time, adult media production companies do exercise a tremendous degree of supervision over the work of their contractors.

28. Lola Lane, personal interview with author, January 10, 2003.

29. Kempadoo and Doezema, *Global Sex Workers*, 11.

30. Craig, *Ain't I a Beauty Queen*, 6.

31. Lola Lane, personal interview with author, January 10, 2003.

32. Wolkowitz, "The Social Relations of Body Work." Dewey, *Neon Wasteland*, 160–90.

33. Spantaneeus Xtasty, phone interview with author, February 4, 2010.

34. Byron Long, personal interview with author, January 10, 2003.

35. Sinnamon Love, personal interview with author, December 5, 2002.

36. Sasha Brabuster, personal interview with author, January 25, 2005.

37. Betty Blac, personal interview with author, September 20, 2013.

38. Betty Blac, personal interview with author, September 20, 2013.

39. Research shows that colorism exists throughout the labor market. See Harrison, Reynolds-Dobbs, and Thomas, "Skin Color Bias in the Workplace."

40. Mask, *Divas on Screen*.

41. Stacy Cash, personal interview with author, January 10, 2004.

42. Stacy Cash, personal interview with author, January 10, 2004.

43. Candice Nicole, personal interview with author, June 13, 2009.

44. Mya Lovely, personal interview with author, January 11, 2004.

45. Mya Lovely, personal interview with author, January 11, 2004.

46. Mya Lovely, personal interview with author, January 11, 2004.

47. Candice Nicole, personal interview with author, June 13, 2009.

48. This is important because movie covers are a primary form of advertising in an industry where, in the absence of movie trailers, DVD designs (even on websites) are one of the key ways consumers evaluate if the movie is appealing enough to rent or purchase. It is also a primary way that actresses can cultivate audience recognition and a fan following.

49. Candice Nicole, personal interview with author, June 13, 2009.

50. Candice Nicole, personal interview with author, June 13, 2009.

51. Brooks, *Unequal Desires*.

52. Lola Lane, personal interview with author, June 14, 2009.

53. Petkovich, *The X Factory*, 107.

54. Lacey, personal interview with author, December 5, 2002.

55. Petkovich, *The X Factory*, 107.

56. Chavez interview with Champagne, "Actor's Spotlight: Champagne, A Cool Sip of Champagne."

57. Marie Luv, personal interview with author, June 13, 2009.

58. Vanessa Blue, personal interview with author, August 17, 2008.

59. Vanessa Blue, personal interview with author, August 17, 2008.

60. Vanessa Blue, personal interview with author, August 17, 2008.

61. I am drawing on conversations with several porn actors to make this point, but especially actor Tyler Knight and male escort Damien Decker. Tyler Knight, personal interview with author, August 15, 2008; Damien Decker, personal interview with author, March 22, 2010.

62. I am using a pseudonym to protect the identity of the performer.

63. Cherry (pseudonym), personal conversation with author, January 11, 2004.

64. Cherry (pseudonym), personal conversation with author, January 11, 2004.

65. See Brooks, "Working the Streets"; and Lockett, "What Happens When You Are Arrested," "Leaving the Streets," and "Destroying Condoms." See also, Berger, *Workable Sisterhood*, Carter and Giobbe, "Duet"; and West, "US PROstitutes Collective."

66. Ross, "Spectacular Striptease"; Brooks, *Unequal Desires*; Brooks, "Dancing toward Freedom"; Brooks, "Exotic Dancing and Unionizing"; and Price-Glynn, *Strip Club*. For scholarship highlighting the roles of gender and class, see Dewey, *Neon Wasteland*; Frank, *G-Strings and Sympathy*; Frank and Carnes, "Gender and Space in Strip Clubs"; Kay, "Naked but Unseen"; Trautner, "Doing Gender, Doing Class"; Egan, *Flesh for Fantasy*; and Barton, *Stripped*.

67. Sierra, personal interview with author, April 28, 2003.

68. Lola Lane, personal interview with author, January 10, 2003.

69. Diana DeVoe and Lexi, joint personal interview with author, January 11, 2003.

70. Lollipop, personal interview with author, June 13, 2009.

71. Collins, *Black Sexual Politics*; Roberts, *Killing the Black Body*.

72. Lollipop, personal interview with author, June 13, 2009.

73. Lola Lane, personal interview with author, June 14, 2009.

74. Lola Lane, personal interview with author, June 14, 2009.

75. Lola Lane, personal interview with author, June 14, 2009.

76. See for example, Boris, "When Work Is Slavery"; Smith, *Welfare Reform and Sexual Regulation*; Gordon, *Women, the State, and Welfare*; and Burnham, "Racism in U.S. Welfare Policy."

77. Diana DeVoe and Lexi, joint personal interview with author, January 11, 2003.

78. While there is a great deal of anthropological literature on moral economy, here I am drawing on the work of Ara Wilson on the moral economy of sex workers in Thailand. See Wilson, *The Intimate Economies of Bangkok*.

79. The state regulation of sex work and pornography is a central concern for sex work scholars. See for example, Dewey and Kelly, *Policing Pleasure*; Weitzer, *Sex for Sale*.

### Epilogue. Behind the Camera

1. Vanessa Blue, personal interview with author, August 13, 2008.

2. Kelley, *Yo' Mama's Disfunktional!*, 45–46.

3. Vanessa Blue, personal interview with author, August 13, 2008.

4. I refer to my research interlocutors by their first name rather than their last name only to create consistency between those who employ last names in their professional personas and those who do not.

5. Vanessa Blue, personal interview with author, August 13, 2008.

6. Vanessa Blue, personal interview with author, August 13, 2008.

7. This aspect of my argument is informed by Jane Juffer's work on the domestication of pornography and erotica and women's access to these forms. However, Juffer advocates for prioritizing "material transgression" and "material factors that restrict movement" across boundaries for they allow "the ability of women to literally enter into the means of production, to step across the threshold of an adult video store, to access an online sex toy shop, to buy a volume of literary erotica" over the feminist sex positive "valorization of individuals' subversive abilities to appropriate texts," whereas I see a dual focus on material and textual appropriation and constraint as productive for my purposes here. Juffer, "There Is No Place Like Home," 56.

8. On erotic capital see Green, "The Social Organization of Desire"; and Brooks, *Unequal Desires.*

9. Damali XXXPlosive Dares, personal interview with author, March 24, 2010.

10. Vanessa Blue, personal interview with author, August 13, 2008.

11. Wright, *Disposable Women and Other Myths of Global Capitalism,* 2.

12. Vanessa Blue, personal interview with author, August 13, 2008.

13. On the confessional as site for the production of sexual truth see Foucault, *History of Sexuality,* vol. 1. My thinking on Reality TV is shaped by Weber, *Makeover TV,* and Murray and Ouelette, *Reality TV.*

14. This scene with Mark Davis was later edited out of the movie due to concerns that the kinky sex acts and level of violence would not pass the approval process at Vivid Entertainment, the production company and distributor, and that an interracial, black-white sex scene in which coercive sex is the fantasy might be too controversial for audiences.

15. Sinnamon Love laments the lack of black-cast kink fetish scenes and rough sex scenes in her essay in *The Feminist Porn Book.* See Love, "A Question of Feminism."

16. McClintock, "Maid to Order." There is a paucity of research on black women or men and kink or BDSM, but a few popular articles and blog essays or interviews exist. See Hernandez, "Playing with Race"; North, "When Prejudice Is Sexy"; Plaid, "Interview with the Perverted Negress."

17. Abiola Abrams, personal interview with author, April 10, 2009.

18. Abiola Abrams, personal interview with author, April 10, 2009.

19. Carter, *The Sadeian Woman,* 12.

20. Berg, "Working for Love, Loving for Work."

21. Abiola Abrams, personal interview with author, April 10, 2009.

22. For useful work on authenticity in porn, see Bakehorn, "Making Authenticity Explicit" and "Women Made Pornography"; Ryan, "Fucking Feminism."

23. Nenna Feelmore Joiner, phone interview with author, June 28, 2013.

24. Betty Blac, phone interview with author, September 20, 2013.

25. Stallings, "Superfreak."

26. On the "politics of respectability," see Higginbotham, *Righteous Discontent.* Related to respectability politics is black women's "culture of dissemblance"—their

strategies of masking, avoiding, and resisting racialized sexual stereotyping. See Hine, "Rape and the Inner Lives of Black Women in the Middle West."

27. On deviance as a site of potential for black (sexual) politics, see Cohen, "Deviance as Resistance."

28. See Stallings, "*'Mutha' Is Half a Word!*"

# Bibliography

Abbott, Sharon. "Creating a Scene: The Work of Performing Sex." In *Sexualities: Identities, Behaviors, and Society*, edited by Michael S. Kimmel and Rebecca F. Plante, 380–90. New York: Oxford University Press, 2004.

Abbott, Sharon. "Motivations for Pursuing an Acting Career in Pornography." In *Sex for Sale: Prostitution, Pornography, and the Sex Industry*, edited by Ronald Weitzer, 17–34. New York: Routledge, 2000.

*Adam Film World Guide: Directory of Adult Films*, vol. 5, no. 9, 1991.

*Adult Video News 1986–87 Buyer's Guide*. 1986.

Agathangelou, Anna M., and Lily H. M. Ling. *Transforming World Politics: From Empire to Multiple Worlds*. New York: Routledge, 2009.

Agustín, Laura. *Sex at the Margins: Migration, Labour Markets and the Rescue Industry*. New York: Zed Books, 2007.

Alexander, Elizabeth. *The Venus Hottentot*. Charlottesville: University Press of Virginia, 1990.

Alexander, Karen. "Fatal Beauties: Black Women in Hollywood." In *Stardom: Industry of Desire*, edited by Christine Gledhill, 46–57. London: Routledge, 1991.

Alexander, M. Jacqui. *Pedagogies of Crossing: Meditations on Feminism, Sexual Politics, Memory, and the Sacred*. Durham, NC: Duke University Press, 2005.

Alexander, Michelle. *The New Jim Crow: Mass Incarceration in the Age of Colorblindness*. Rev. ed. New York: New Press, 2012.

"A-List Hollywood Daughter Montana Fishburne Makes XXX Debut with Vivid Entertainment." *Vivid News*, July 30, 2010. Accessed August 4, 2010. http://vivid.com/news/2010–07–30/alist-hollywood-daughter-montana-fishburne-makes-xxx-debut-with-vivid-entertainment.

Allen, Jafari S. "Blackness, Sexuality, and Transnational Desire: Initial Notes toward a New Research Agenda." In *Black Sexualities: Probing Powers, Passions, Practices and Politics*, edited by Juan Battle and Sandra A. Barnes, 311–26. New Brunswick, NJ: Rutgers University Press, 2010.

Allen, Scott. "Review of *Black Girls Do It Better*." *Adult Video News*, July 1986, 52.

Allen, Scott. "Interview: Linda Wong." *Adult Video News*, March 1985, 19, 24.

Alloula, Malek. *The Colonial Harem*. Minneapolis: University of Minnesota Press, 1986.

"American Porn." *Frontline*. PBS. February 21, 2002.

Anzaldúa, Gloria. *Making Face, Making Soul/Haciendo Caras: Creative and Critical Perspectives by Feminists of Color*. San Francisco, CA: Aunt Lute Foundation Books, 1990.

Apter, Emily. *Fetishism as Cultural Discourse*. Ithaca, NY: Cornell University Press, 1993.

Arthurs, Jane. *Television and Sexuality: Regulation and the Politics of Taste*. New York: McGraw-Hill International, 2004.

Asante, Molefi K. *Afrocentricity: The Theory of Social Change*. Chicago: African American Images, 2003.

Attwood, Feona. "Reading Porn: The Paradigm Shift in Pornography Research." *Sexualities* 5, no. 1 (2002): 91–105.

Attwood, Feona, ed. *Mainstreaming Sex: The Sexualisation of Western Culture*. New York: Palgrave Macmillan, 2009.

Attwood, Feona, ed. *Porn.com: Making Sense of Online Pornography*. New York: Peter Lang, 2010.

"AVN's Ultimate Guide to Stocking Ethnic Fare: Hot Chocolate, Spicy Señioritas, and Aromatic Asians." *Adult Video News Ethnic Video Supplement* 178 (April 1998).

Bailey, Fenton, and Randy Barbato, dir. *Pornography: The Secret History of Civilization*. KOCH Entertainment LP, 2006.

Bailey, Fenton, and Randy Barbato, dir. *Inside Deep Throat*. Universal Studios Home Entertainment, 2005.

Bailey, Marlon M. *Butch Queens Up in Pumps: Gender, Performance, and Ballroom Culture in Detroit*. Ann Arbor: University of Michigan Press, 2013.

Bailey, Moya. "'The Illest': Disability as Metaphor in Hip Hop Music." In *Blackness and Disability: Critical Examinations and Cultural Interventions*, edited by Christopher Bell, 141–48. Berlin: LIT Verlag, 2011.

Bakehorn, Jill A. "Making Authenticity Explicit: How Women-Made Pornography Constructs Sex." PhD diss., University of California, Davis, 2010.

Bakehorn, Jill A. "Women-Made Pornography." In *Sex for Sale: Prostitution, Pornography, and the Sex Industry*, edited by Ronald Weitzer, second edition, 91–114. New York: Routledge, 2010.

Bakhtin, Mikhail Mikhaïlovich. *Rabelais and His World*. Cambridge, MA: MIT Press, 1968.

Bakhtin, Mikhail Mikhaïlovich, and Michael Holquist. *The Dialogic Imagination: Four Essays*. Austin: University of Texas Press, 1982.

Bales, Kevin. *Disposable People: New Slavery in the Global Economy*. Los Angeles: University of California Press, 2012.

Bambara, Toni. *The Black Woman: An Anthology*. New York: New American Library, 1970.

Bancel, Nicolas, Pascal Blanchard, Gilles Boëtsche, Eric Deroo, and Sandrine Lemaire, eds. *Human Zoos: From the Hottentot Venus to Reality Shows*. Liverpool, UK: Liverpool University Press, 2009.

Barthes, Roland. *Camera Lucida: Reflections on Photography*. New York: Hill and Wang, 1981.

Barton, Bernadette. *Stripped: Inside the Lives of Exotic Dancers*. New York: New York University Press, 2006.

Bataille, Georges. *Erotism: Death and Sensuality*, trans. Mary Dalwood. San Francisco: City Lights, 1986.

Bateman, Anne. "Black Video: Forward or Back?" *Adult Video News*, June 1999.

Battle, Juan, and Sandra A. Barnes, eds. *Black Sexualities: Probing Powers, Passions, Practices and Politics*. New Brunswick, NJ: Rutgers University Press, 2010.

Beale, Frances. "Double Jeopardy: To Be Black and Female." In *Words of Fire: An Anthology of African-American Feminist Thought*, edited by Beverly Guy-Sheftall, 146–56. New York: New Press, 1995.

Bell, Christopher, ed. *Blackness and Disability: Crucial Examinations and Cultural Interventions*. Berlin: LIT Verlag, 2011.

Bennett, Lerone. *The Negro Mood, and Other Essays*. Chicago: Johnson Publishing, 1964.

Bennett, Lerone. "The Soul of Soul." *Ebony*, December 1961, 111–14.

Berg, Heather. "An Honest Day's Wage for a Dishonest Day's Work: (Re)Productivism and Refusal." *WSQ*. Forthcoming.

Berg, Heather. "Working for Love, Loving for Work: Labor Discourse in Feminist Discourses of Sex Work." *Feminist Studies*. Forthcoming.

Berger, Michele Tracy. *Workable Sisterhood: The Political Journey of Stigmatized Women with HIV/AIDS*. Princeton, NJ: Princeton University Press, 2004.

Berlant, Lauren. *Cruel Optimism*. Durham, NC: Duke University Press, 2011.

Berlant, Lauren, and Michael Warner. "Sex in Public." *Critical Inquiry* 24, no. 2 (1998): 547–66.

Bernardi, Daniel. "Interracial Joysticks: Pornography's Web of Racist Attractions." *Pornography: Film and Culture*, edited by Peter Lehman, 220–43. New Brunswick, NJ: Rutgers University Press, 2006.

Bernstein, Elizabeth. *Temporarily Yours: Intimacy, Authenticity, and the Commerce of Sex*. Chicago: University of Chicago Press, 2007.

Bernstein, Elizabeth, and Laurie Schaffner, eds. *Regulating Sex: The Politics of Intimacy and Identity*. New York: Routledge, 2005.

Bhabha, Homi. "The Other Question: The Stereotype and Colonial Discourse." *Screen* 24 (1983): 18–36.

Bielby, William. "Minimizing Workplace Gender and Racial Bias." *Contemporary Sociology* 29, no. 1 (2000): 120–29.

"Black America: Nearer to Overcoming: Barack Obama's Success Shows That the Ceiling Has Risen for African-Americans but Many are Still Close to the Floor." *Economist*, August 5, 2008. Accessed June 8, 2011, http://www.economist.com/node/11326407.

"Black and Interracial Videography." *Adult Video News*, April 1987, 64–65.

"Black Bun Busters Is First All-Black Anal Tape." *Adult Video News Confidential*, June 1985, 13.

Blair, Cynthia M. *I've Got to Make My Own Livin': Black Women's Sex Work in Turn-of-the-Century Chicago*. Chicago: University of Chicago Press, 2010.

Blue, Vanessa. "Black Actors in Adult Film." Presentation at the University of California, Santa Barbara, Santa Barbara, CA, May 25, 2010.

Blumenthal, Ralph. "Hard-Core Grows Fashionable—and Very Profitable." *New York Times*, January 21, 1973.

Bogle, Donald. *Blacks in American Films and Television: An Encyclopedia*. New York: Simon and Schuster, 1989.

Bogle, Donald. *Toms, Coons, Mulattoes, Mammies, and Bucks: An Interpretive History of Blacks in American Films*. New York: Viking Press, 1973.

Boone, Barney "Black Girl in a White World." *Adam Film World*, February 1973, 52–56.

Borelli, Melissa. "Mulata Performances by a River: Ninón Sevilla, Olga Guillot and Representations of Afro-Cuban Dance." Paper presented at the annual meeting of the American Studies Association, Renaissance Hotel, Washington, DC, December 29, 2013.

Boris, Eileen. *Home to Work: Motherhood and the Politics of Industrial Homework in the United States*. New York: Cambridge University Press, 1994.

Boris, Eileen. "When Work Is Slavery." In *Whose Welfare?*, edited by Gwendolyn Mink, 36–55. Ithaca, NY: Cornell University Press, 1999.

Boris, Eileen, and Jennifer Klein. *Caring for America: Home Health Workers in the Shadow of the Welfare State*. New York: Oxford University Press, 2012.

Bowles, Juliette. "Extreme Times Call for Extreme Heroes." *International Review of African American Art* 14, no. 3 (1997): 2–15.

Boyle, Karen, ed. *Everyday Pornography*. New York: Routledge, 2010.

Branch, Enobong Hannah. "The Creation of Restricted Opportunity due to the Intersection of Race and Sex: Black Women in the Bottom Class." *Race Gender and Class* 14, no. 3/4 (2007): 247–64.

Brandt, Eric. *Dangerous Liaisons: Blacks, Gays and the Struggle for Equality*. New York: New Press, 1999.

Brewer, Rose M. "Black Women in Poverty: Some Comments on Female-Headed Families." *Signs* 13, no. 2 (1988): 331–39.

Brewer, Rose M. "Theorizing Race, Class and Gender: The New Scholarship of Black Feminist Intellectuals and Black Women's Labor." *Race, Gender and Class* 6, no. 2 (1999): 29–47.

Bright, Susie. "The Image of the Black in Adult Video." *Adult Video News*, April 1987, 54–64.

Bright, Susie. *Susie Bright's Erotic Screen: The Golden Hardcore and the Shimmering Dyke-Core*. E-book. Bright Stuff, 2011.

Brooks, Daphne. *Bodies in Dissent: Spectacular Performances of Race and Freedom, 1850–1910*. Durham, NC: Duke University Press, 2006.

Brooks, Siobhan. "Dancing toward Freedom." In *Whores and Other Feminists*, edited by Jill Nagle, 252–55. New York: Routledge, 1997.

Brooks, Siobhan. "Exotic Dancing and Unionizing: The Challenges of Feminist and Antiracist Organizing at the Lusty Lady Theater." In *Feminism and Antiracism: International Struggles for Justice*, edited by France Winddance Twine and Kathleen M. Blee, 59–70. New York: NYU Press, 2001.

Brooks, Siobhan. "Sex Work and Feminism: Building Alliances through a Dialogue between Siobhan Brooks and Professor Angela Davis." *Hastings Women's Law Journal* 10, no. 1 (1999): 181–87.

Brooks, Siobhan. *Unequal Desires: Race and Erotic Capital in Stripping*. Albany, NY: SUNY Press, 2010.

Brooks, Siobhan. "Working the Streets: Gloria Lockett's Story." *SCAPA LV: Sin City Alternative Professionals' Association*, n.d. Accessed December 12, 2013, http://www.scapa-lv.org/Resources/aboutsexwork/people/glorialockett.htm.

Brown, Elaine. *A Taste of Power: A Black Woman's Story*. New York: Anchor Books, 1992.

Brown, Jayna. *Babylon Girls: Black Women Performers and the Shaping of the Modern*. Durham: Duke University Press, 2008.

Brown, Vincent. "Eating the Dead: Consumption and Regeneration in the History of Sugar." *Food and Foodways* 16, no. 2 (2008): 117–26.

Browne, Irene. "Explaining the Black-White Gap in Labor Force Participation among Women Heading Households." *American Sociological Review* 62, no. 2 (1997): 236–52.

Bruno, Giuliana. *Streetwalking on a Ruined Map: Cultural Theory and the City Films of Elvira Notari*. Princeton, NJ: Princeton University Press, 1993.

Bryan, Carmen. *It's No Secret: From Nas to Jay-Z, from Seduction to Scandal—a Hip-Hop Helen of Troy Tells All*. New York: Pocket Books, 2006.

Bugner, Ladislas. *The Image of the Black in Western Art*. Cambridge, MA: Harvard University Press, 1976.

Burnham, Linda. "Has Poverty Been Feminized in Black America?" *Black Scholar* 16, no. 2 (March 1985): 14–24.

Burnham, Linda. "Racism in US Welfare Policy." In *Sing, Whisper, Shout, Pray!: Feminist Visions for a Just World*, edited by Dorothy Abbott, M. Jacqui Alexander, Lisa Albrecht, Sharon Day, and Mab Segrest, 58–77. Fort Bragg, CA: EdgeWork Books: 2003.

Califia, Patrick. *Public Sex: The Culture of Radical Sex*. 2nd ed. San Francisco, CA: Cleis Press, 2000.

Campbell, Bebe Moore. "A Portrait of Angel: The Life of a Porn Star." *Essence Magazine*, vol. 21, no. 7, November 1990, 63–64, 120.

Carby, Hazel. "'On the Threshold of Woman's Era': Lynching, Empire, and Sexuality in Black Feminist Theory." *Critical Inquiry* 12, no. 1 (1985): 262–77.

Carby, Hazel. "Policing the Black Woman's Body in an Urban Context." *Critical Inquiry* 18, no. 4 (1992): 738–55.

Carby, Hazel. *Reconstructing Womanhood: The Emergence of the Afro-American Woman Novelist*. New York: Oxford University Press, 1987.

Carlson, Shirley. "Black Ideals of Womanhood in the Late Victorian Era." *Journal of Negro History* 77, no. 2 (1992): 61–73.

Carpenter, Faedra Chatard. "An Interview with Joan Morgan." *Callaloo* 29, no. 3 (2006): 764–72.

Carter, Angela. *The Sadeian Woman: And the Ideology of Pornography*. New York: Penguin, 1979.

Carter, Vednita and Evelina Giobbe. "Duet: Prostitution, Racism, and Feminist Discourse." In *Prostitution and Pornography: Philosophical Debate About the Sex Industry*, edited by Jessica Spector, 17–39. Stanford, CA: Stanford University Press, 2006.

Cercone, Katie. "Hoopety Hoop Hip Hop Feminism: the Manifesta." *Revolt Magazine* 1, no. 2 (May/June 2012). Revoltmagazine.org. Accessed March 27, 2014. http://revoltmagazine.org/Issue_02/Articles/HIP_HOP_FEMINIST_article.htm.

Chang, Jeff. *Can't Stop, Won't Stop: A History of the Hip-Hop Generation*. New York: Picador, 2005.

Chapkis, Wendy. *Live Sex Acts: Women Performing Erotic Labor*. London: Cassell, 1997.

Chapkis, Wendy. "Power and Control in the Commercial Sex Trade." In *Sex for Sale: Prostitution, Pornography, and the Sex Industry*, edited by Ronald Weitzer, 179–200. New York: Routledge, 2000.

"Charting the Adult Industry." *Adult Video News*, January 1992, 26–28.

Chase-Riboud, Barbara. *Hottentot Venus: A Novel*. New York: Random House Digital, 2007.

Chateauvert, Melinda. *Sex Workers Unite: A History of the Movement from Stonewall to Slutwalk*. Boston, MA: Beacon Press, 2014.

Cheney, Charise. *Brothers Gonna Work It Out: Sexual Politics in the Golden Age of Rap Nationalism*. New York: NYU Press, 2005.

Chisholm, Shirley. "Facing the Abortion Question." In *Words of Fire: An Anthology of African-American Feminist Thought*, edited by Beverly Guy-Sheftall. 390–95. New York: New Press, 1995.

Clarke, Cheryl. *Humid Pitch: Narrative Poetry*. Ann Arbor, MI: Firebrand Books, 1989.

Clarke, Cheryl. "Lesbianism: An Act of Resistance." In *Words of Fire: An Anthology of African-American Feminist Thought*, edited by Beverly Guy-Sheftall, 242–52. New York: New Press, 1995.

Clarke, Cheryl. *Living as a Lesbian: Poetry*. Ann Arbor, MI: Firebrand Books, 1986.

Cleaver, Eldridge. *Soul on Ice*. New York: Delta Publishing, 2003.

Cleaver, Eldridge. *Target Zero: A Life in Writing*. London: Macmillan, 2007.

Cobb, William Jelani. *To the Break of Dawn: A Freestyle on the Hip Hop Aesthetic*. New York: NYU Press, 2007.

Cohen, Cathy J. "Deviance as Resistance: A New Research Agenda for the Study of Black Politics." *Du Bois Review: Social Science Research on Race* 1, no. 1 (2004): 27–45.

Cohen, Cathy J. "Punks, Bulldaggers, and Welfare Queens: The Radical Potential of Queer Politics?" *GLQ* 3 (1997): 437–65.

Collins, Lisa. "Economies of the Flesh: Representing the Black Female Body in Art."

In *Skin Deep, Spirit Strong: The Black Female Body in American Culture*, edited by Kimberly Wallace-Sanders, 99–127. Ann Arbor: University of Michigan Press, 2002.

Collins, Patricia Hill. *Black Feminist Thought: Knowledge, Consciousness, and the Politics of Empowerment*. Rev. 2nd ed. New York: Routledge, 2000.

Collins, Patricia Hill. *Black Sexual Politics: African Americans, Gender, and the New Racism*. New York: Routledge, 2004.

Collins, Patricia Hill. "New Commodities, New Consumers." *Ethnicities* 6, no. 3 (2006): 297–317.

Collins, Patricia Hill. "The Social Construction of Black Feminist Thought." In *Words of Fire: An Anthology of African-American Feminist Thought*, edited by Beverly Guy-Sheftall, 338–57. New York: New Press, 1995.

Combahee River Collective. "A Black Feminist Statement." In *This Bridge Called My Back: Writings by Radical Women of Color*, edited by Cherrie Moraga and Gloria Anzaldua, 234–45. New York: Kitchen Table Press, 1984.

Comella, Lynn. "From Text to Context: Feminist Porn and the Making of a Market." In *The Feminist Porn Book: The Politics of Producing Pleasure*, edited by Tristan Taormino, Celine Parreñas Shimizu, Constance Penley, and Mireille Miller-Young, 79–93. New York: Feminist Press at CUNY, 2013.

Comella, Lynn. "Remaking the Sex Industry: The Adult Expo as a Microcosm." In *Sex for Sale: Prostitution, Pornography, and the Sex Industry*, edited by Ronald Weitzer, 285–306. New York: Taylor and Francis, 2010.

Conlin, John O. "Review of *Black Mariah*," *Adult Video News*, October 1991, 32.

"Consumer Feedback: The Ten Biggest Problems With Adult Video Today." *Adult Video News Confidential*, January 1986, 6.

"Consumer Feedback: Favorite Sub-Genres." *Adult Video News Confidential*, February 1986, 6.

"Consumer Feedback: Problems with Shot-On-Video Features." *Adult Video News Confidential*, August 1985, 4.

Cook, David A. *Lost Illusions: American Cinema in the Shadow of Watergate and Vietnam, 1970–1979*. New York: Simon and Schuster, 2000.

Cornell, Drucilla. *Feminism and Pornography*. Oxford: Oxford University Press, 2000.

Craig, Maxine Leeds. *Ain't I a Beauty Queen?: Black Women, Beauty, and the Politics of Race*. New York: Oxford University Press, 2002.

Crain, Marion G., Pauline T. Kim, and Michael L. Selmi. *Work Law: Cases and Materials*. Second Edition. LexisNexis, 2010.

Crais, Clifton C., and Pamela Scully. *Sara Baartman and the Hottentot Venus: A Ghost Story and a Biography*. Princeton, NJ: Princeton University Press, 2009.

Creekmur, Corey. *Out in Culture: Gay, Lesbian, and Queer Essays on Popular Culture*. Durham, NC: Duke University Press, 1995.

Crenshaw, Kimberle. "Mapping the Margins: Intersectionality, Identity Politics, and Violence against Women of Color." *Stanford Law Review* 43, no. 6 (1991): 1241–99.

Cripps, Thomas. *Black Film as Genre*. Bloomington: Indiana University Press, 1978.

Cripps, Thomas. *Making Movies Black: The Hollywood Message Movie from World War II to the Civil Rights Era*. New York: Oxford University Press, 1993.

Cripps, Thomas. *Slow Fade to Black: The Negro in American Film, 1900–1942.* New York: Oxford University Press, 1993.

Crunk Feminist Collective. "How do you solve a problem like Montana?" August 17, 2010. Accessed August 20, 2010, https://crunkfeministcollective.wordpress.com/tag/montana-fishburne/.

Crunk Feminist Collective. "I Saw the Sign But Did We Really Need a Sign?: SlutWalk and Racism." October 6, 2011. Accessed October 23, 2011, http://www.crunkfeminist collective.com/2011/10/06/i-saw-the-sign-but-did-we-really-need-a-sign-slutwalk -and-racism/.

Crunk Feminist Collective. "Slut Walks v. Ho Strolls." May 23, 2011. Accessed October 23, 2011, http://www.crunkfeministcollective.com/2011/05/23/slutwalks-v-ho -strolls/.

Cruz, Ariane. "Berries Bittersweet: Visual Representations of Black Female Sexuality in Contemporary American Pornography." PhD diss. University of California, Berkeley: African American Studies, 2010.

Cruz, Ariane. "Pornography: A Black Feminist Woman Scholar's Reconciliation." In *The Feminist Porn Book: The Politics of Producing Pleasure*, edited by Tristan Taormino, Celine Parreñas Shimizu, Constance Penley, and Mireille Miller-Young, 215–27. New York: Feminist Press at CUNY, 2013.

Cunningham, James S., and Nadja Zalokar. "The Economic Progress of Black Women, 1940–1980: Occupational Distribution and Relative Wages." *Industrial and Labor Relations Review* 45 (1992): 540–55.

Cuvier, Georges. "Extraits d'observations faites sur le cadavre d'une femme connue à Paris et à Londres sous le nom de Vénus Hottentot," *Discours sur les révolutions du globe.* Paris: Passard, 1864.

Dalla Costa, Mariarosa, and Selma James, *The Power of Women and the Subversion of the Community.* Bristol, UK: Falling Wall Press, 1972.

Dalton, Karen. "Josephine Baker and Paul Colin: African American Dance Seen through Parisian Eyes." *Critical Inquiry* 24, no. 4 (1998): 903–34.

Daniels, Karu F. "Montana Fishburne: Up, Close & Extremely Personal." *AOL Black Voices Entertainment Newswire*, August 6, 2010. Accessed August 12, 2010, http://www.bvnewswire.com/2010/08/06/montana-fishburne-interview/.

Davis, Adrienne D. "Don't Let Nobody Bother Yo' Principle: The Sexual Economy of American Slavery." In *Sister Circle: Black Women and Work*, edited by Sharon Harley and the Black Women and Work Collective, 103–27. New Brunswick, NJ: Rutgers University Press, 2002.

Davis, Adrienne D. "Slavery and the Roots of Sexual Harassment." In *Directions in Sexual Harassment Law*, edited by Catharine A. MacKinnon and Reva B. Siegel, 457–78. New Haven, CT: Yale University Press, 2004.

Davis, Adrienne D. "The Sexual Economy of Slavery: Reflections on Yinka Shonibare's Mother and Father Worked So Hard So I Could Play." Presentation, Black Sexual Economies: Transforming Black Sexualities Research. Washington University School of Law, September 28, 2013.

Davis, Angela. "Afro Images: Politics, Fashion, and Nostalgia." In *Soul: Black Power,*

*Politics, and Pleasure*, edited by Richard C. Green, 23–31. New York: NYU Press, 1998.

Davis, Angela. *Blues Legacies and Black Feminism: Gertrude "Ma" Rainey, Bessie Smith, and Billie Holiday*. New York: Pantheon Books, 1998.

Davis, Angela. "Race and Criminalization: Black Americans and the Punishment Industry." In *The House That Race Built: Black Americans, US Terrain*, edited by Wahneema Lubiano, 264–69. New York: Pantheon Books, 1997.

Davis, Angela. "Reflections on the Black Woman's Role in the Community of Slaves." *Black Scholar* 12, no. 6 (November 1981): 2–15.

Davis, Angela. *Women, Race, and Class*. London: Women's Press, 1981.

Davis, Angela, and Neferti X. M. Tadiar, eds. *Beyond the Frame: Visual Representations of Women of Color*. New York: Palgrave Macmillan, 2005.

Dean, Tim. *Unlimited Intimacy: Reflections on the Subculture of Barebacking*. Chicago: University of Chicago Press, 2009.

Delacoste, Frédérique. *Sex Work: Writings by Women in the Sex Industry*. Pittsburgh, PA: Cleis Press, 1987.

Delany, Samuel R. *Times Square Red, Times Square Blue*. New York: NYU Press, 2001.

D'Emilio, John, and Estelle B. Freedman. *Intimate Matters: A History of Sexuality in America*. 2nd ed. Chicago: University of Chicago Press, 1997.

Dewey, Susan. *Neon Wasteland: On Love, Motherhood, and Sex Work in a Rust Belt Town*. Berkeley: University of California Press, 2011.

Dewey, Susan and Patty Kelly, eds. *Policing Pleasure: Sex Work, Policy, and the State in Global Perspective*. New York: New York University Press, 2011.

DeWitt, Clyde. "Ten Years of Persecution: The Adult Entertainment Industry vs. The Government." *Adult Video News 10th Anniversary Supplement*, 1992.

Di Lauro, Al, and Gerald Rabkin. *Dirty Movies: An Illustrated History of the Stag Film, 1915–1970*. New York: Chelsea House, 1976.

Dines, Gail. "King Kong and the White Woman: Hustler Magazine and the Demonization of Black Masculinity." *Violence Against Women* 4, no. 3 (June 1998): 291–307.

Dines, Gail. *Pornland: How Porn Has Hijacked Our Sexuality*. Boston: Beacon Press, 2010.

Dines, Gail. "The White Man's Burden: Gonzo Pornography and the Construction of Black Masculinity." *Yale Journal of Law and Feminism* 18, no. 1 (2006): 283–97.

Dines, Gail. "Yes, Pornography Is Racist," *Ms. Magazine* blog, August 27, 2010. Accessed December 12, 2013, http://msmagazine.com/blog/2010/08/27/yes-pornography-is-racist/.

Ditmore, Melissa Hope, Antonia Levy, and Alys William. *Sex Work Matters: Exploring Money, Power, and Intimacy in the Sex Industry*. New York: Zed Books, 2010.

Drake, St. Clair, and Horace R. Cayton. *Black Metropolis: A Study of Negro Life in a Northern City*. Chicago: University of Chicago Press, 1970.

Drenner, Elijah, dir. *American Grindhouse*. Lux Digital Pictures, 2010.

Driskill, Qwo-Li. "Stolen from Our Bodies: First Nations Two-Spirits/Queers and the Journey to a Sovereign Erotic." *Studies in American Indian Literatures* 16, no. 2 (2004): 50–64.

Duggan, Lisa *Sapphic Slashers: Sex, Violence, and American Modernity*. Durham, NC: Duke University Press, 2000.

Duggan, Lisa, and Nan Hunter. *Sex Wars: Sexual Dissent and Political Culture*. New York: Routledge, 1995.

Dunn, Stephanie. *Baad Bitches and Sassy Supermamas: Black Power Action Films*. Urbana: University of Illinois Press.

Durham, Meenakshi Gigi, and Douglas Kellner. *Media and Cultural Studies: Keyworks*. Malden, MA: Blackwell Publishing, 2006.

Dworkin, Andrea. "Against the Male Flood." In *Pornography: Women, Violence, and Civil Liberties*, edited by Catherine Itzin, 515–35. Oxford: Oxford University Press, 1992.

Dworkin, Andrea, and Catharine A. MacKinnon. *Pornography and Civil Rights: A New Day for Women's Equality*. Minneapolis, MN: Organizing Against Pornography, 1988.

Dyer, Richard. *Heavenly Bodies: Film Stars and Society*. Second edition. New York: Routledge, 2004.

Dyer, Richard. *White*. New York: Routledge, 1997.

Edlund, Martin. "Hip-Hop's Crossover to the Adult Aisle." *New York Times*, March 7, 2004. Accessed December 12, 2013, http://www.nytimes.com/2004/03/07/arts/music-hip-hop-s-crossover-to-the-adult-aisle.html.

Egan, Danielle and Katherine Frank, eds. *Flesh for Fantasy: Producing and Consuming Exotic Dance*. New York: Thunder's Mouth Press, 2006.

Ehrenreich, Barbara, and Arlie Russell Hochschild, eds. *Global Woman: Nannies, Maids, and Sex Workers in the New Economy*. New York: Metropolitan Books, 2003.

Emerson, Rana A. "'Where My Girls At?': Negotiating Black Womanhood in Music Videos." *Gender & Society* 16, no. 1 (February 2002): 115–35.

Enobang, Hanna Branch. "The Creation of Restricted Opportunity due to the Intersection of Race and Sex." *Race, Gender, and Class* 14, no. 3/4 (2007): 247–65.

Erotic Networks Press Release. "The Erotic Networks Releases Snoop Dogg's Doggy Style." *Adult Industry News*, July 9, 2001. Accessed December 1, 2006, http://www.ainews.com/Archives/Story2076.phtml#axzz1gIYnxMAq.

Escoffier, Jeffrey. *Bigger than Life: The History of Gay Porn Cinema from Beefcake to Hardcore*. Philadelphia: Running Press, 2009.

Evans, Jessica, and Stuart Hall. *Visual Culture: The Reader*. Thousand Oaks, CA: SAGE, 1999.

Everett, Anna. *Returning the Gaze: A Genealogy of Black Film Criticism, 1909–1949*. Durham, NC: Duke University Press, 2001.

Excalibur Films. "Desiree West Biography." Accessed June 1, 2011, http://www.excaliburfilms.com/pornlist/starpgs/Desiree_West.html.

Fanon, Frantz. *Black Skin, White Masks*. Berkeley, CA: Grove Press, 2008.

Federici, Silvia. *Revolution at Point Zero: Housework, Reproduction, and the Feminist Struggle*. Oakland, CA: PM Press, 2012.

Ferguson, Frances. "Pornography: The Theory." *Critical Inquiry* 21, no. 3 (1995): 670–95.

Fishbein, Paul. "The Decade in Review," in 3 parts, *Adult Video News* 4, no. 7 (December 1989), *Adult Video News* 5, no. 1 (January 1990), and *Adult Video News* 5, no. 2 (February 1990).

Fishbein, Paul. "How to Sell Adult Tapes: Marketing All-Black or Interracial Cassettes." *Adult Video News Confidential*, July 1985.

Fishbein, Paul. "How to Sell Adult Tapes: Selling an Individual Star." *Adult Video News Confidential*, August 1985.

Fishbein, Paul. "The Next 10 Years: How to Improve the Adult Video Business." *Adult Video News 10th Anniversary Supplement*, 1992.

Fishbein, Paul. "Review of *Chocolate Bon Bons*." *Adult Video News*, May 1986, 20.

Fishbein, Paul. "Review of *More Chocolate Candy*." *Adult Video News*, May 1986, 20.

Fishbein, Paul. "Where Are We Spiralling to Now? A Challenge to the Industry." *Adult Video News*, September 1989.

Fitts, Mako. "'Drop It Like It's Hot': Culture Industry Laborers and Their Perspectives on Rap Music Video Production." *Meridians* 8, no. 1 (2007): 211–35.

Fleetwood, Nicole R. *Troubling Vision: Performance, Visuality, and Blackness*. Chicago: University of Chicago Press, 2011.

Flower, William Henry and James Murie. "Account of the Dissection of a Bushwoman." *Journal of Anatomy and Physiology* 1, no. 2 (1867): 189–208.

Foner, Philip. *Women and the American Labor Movement: From Colonial Times to the Eve of World War I*. New York: Free Press, 1979.

Ford, Luke. *A History of X: 100 Years of Sex in Film*. Amherst, MA: Prometheus Books, 1999.

Ford, Luke. "Racism," Lukeford.com. Accessed November 16, 2002, http://lukeford .com/racism [discontinued link].

Forman, Murray, and Mark Anthony Neal, eds. *That's the Joint! The Hip-Hop Studies Reader*. 2nd ed. New York: Routledge, 2012.

Forna, Aminatta. "Pornography and Racism: Sexualizing Oppression and Inciting Hatred." In *Pornography: Women, Violence and Civil Liberties*, edited by Catherine Itzin, 102–12. New York: Oxford University Press, 1991.

Fortunati, Leopoldina. *The Arcane of Reproduction: Housework, Prostitution, Labor and Capital*. Brooklyn, NY: Autonomedia, 1996.

Foucault, Michel. *Discipline and Punish: The Birth of the Prison*. New York: Pantheon Books, 1977.

Foucault, Michel. *The History of Sexuality*, Vol. 1: *An Introduction*. New York: Pantheon Books, 1978.

Foucault, Michel. *The History of Sexuality*, Vol. 3: *The Care of the Self*, trans. Robert Hurley. New York: Vintage Books, 1986.

Foucault, Michel. *Power/Knowledge: Selected Interviews and Other Writings, 1972–1977*. New York: Pantheon Books, 1980.

Foucault, Michel. *Technologies of the Self: A Seminar with Michel Foucault*, edited by Luther H. Martin, Huck Gutman, and Patrick H. Hutton. Amherst: University of Massachusetts Press, 1988.

Frank, Katherine. *G-Strings and Sympathy: Strip Club Regulars and Male Desire*. Durham, NC: Duke University Press, 2002.

Frank, Katherine and Michelle Carnes. "Gender and Space in Strip Clubs." In *Sex For Sale: Prostitution, Pornography, and the Sex Industry*, second edition, edited by Ronald Weitzer, 115–38. New York: Routledge, 2010.

Frazier, Edward. *The Negro Family in the United States*. Rev. and abridged ed. Chicago: University of Chicago Press, 1966.

Fredrickson, George. *The Black Image in the White Mind: The Debate on Afro-American Character and Destiny, 1817–1914*. New York: Harper and Row, 1971.

Freud, Sigmund. *The Joke and Its Relation to the Unconscious*. New York: Penguin, 2003.

Fung, Richard. "Looking For My Penis: The Eroticized Asian in Gay Porn Video." In *How Do I Look?* edited by Bad Object Choices, 145–68. Seattle, WA: Bay Press, 1991.

Fusco, Coco. "Hustling for Dollars: Jineterismo in Cuba." In *Global Sex Workers: Rights, Resistance, and Redefinition*, edited by Kamala Kempadoo, 151–66. New York: Routledge, 1998.

Gaines, Jane. *Fire and Desire: Mixed-Race Movies in the Silent Era*. Chicago: University of Chicago Press, 2001.

Gaines, Kevin. *Uplifting the Race: Black Leadership, Politics, and Culture in the Twentieth Century*. Chapel Hill: University of North Carolina Press, 1996.

Gardner, Tracey A. "Racism in Pornography and the Women's Movement." In *Take Back the Night: Women on Pornography*, edited by Laura Lederer, 105–14. New York: Morrow, 1980.

Gates, Henry. *Figures in Black: Words, Signs, and the "Racial" Self*. New York: Oxford University Press, 1987.

Gertzman, Jay A. *Bookleggers and Smuthounds: The Trade in Erotica, 1920–1940*. Philadelphia: University of Pennsylvania Press, 2011.

Gibson, Pamela Church and Roma Gibson, eds. *Dirty Looks: Women, Pornography, Power*. London: BFI, 1993.

Gibson, Pamela Church, ed. *More Dirty Looks: Gender, Pornography and Power*. London: BFI, 2004.

Gibson, Thomas, dir. *Kiss and Tail: The Hollywood Jumpoff*. Image Entertainment, 2009.

Giddings, Paula. "The Last Taboo." In *Words of Fire: An Anthology of African-American Feminist Thought*, edited by Beverly Guy-Sheftall, 414–28. New York: New Press, 1995.

Giddings, Paula. *When and Where I Enter: The Impact of Black Women on Race and Sex in America*. New York: William Morrow, 1984.

Gilfoyle, Timothy. *City of Eros: New York City, Prostitution, and the Commercialization of Sex, 1790–1920*. New York: W. W. Norton, 1992.

Gillespie, Michael. "Reckless Eyeballing: Coonskin, Film Blackness, and the Racial Grotesque." In *Contemporary Black American Cinema: Race, Gender and Sexuality at the Movies*, edited by Mia Mask, 56–86. New York: Routledge, 2012.

Gilman, Sander L. "Black Bodies, White Bodies: Toward an Iconography of Female

Sexuality in Late Nineteenth-Century Art, Medicine, and Literature." *Critical Inquiry* 12, no. 1 (1985): 204–42.

Gilman, Sander L. "Confessions of an Academic Pornographer." In *Kara Walker: My Complement, My Enemy, My Oppressor, My Love*, essays by Philippe Vergne, Sander L. Gilman, Kevin Young, Thomas McEvilley, Robert Storr, and Yasmil Raymond, 27–36. Minneapolis, MN: Walker Art Center, 2007.

Gilman, Sander L. *Difference and Pathology: Stereotypes of Sexuality, Race, and Madness*. Ithaca, NY: Cornell University Press, 1985.

Gilman, Sander L. *Sexuality: An Illustrated History*. New York: Wiley, 1989.

Glenn, Evelyn Nakano. "From Servitude to Service Work: Historical Continuities in the Racial Division of Paid Reproductive Labor." *Signs* 18, no. 1 (October 1, 1992): 1–43.

Goff, Keli. "Is the Porn Industry Racist?" *The Root*, April 3, 2013. Accessed December 12, 2013, http://www.theroot.com/articles/culture/2013/04/pornindustry_racism _whats_behind_it.html.

Goldman, L. R. "Interview: Candida Royalle." *Adult Video News*, July 1985, 38.

Goldsby, Jacqueline. "Queen for 307 Days: Looking B(l)ack at Vanessa Williams and the Sex Wars." In *Sisters, Sexperts, Queers: Beyond the Lesbian Nation*, edited by Arlene Stein, 165–188. New York: Plume, 1993.

Gomez, Jewelle. *The Gilda Stories: A Novel*. Ithaca, NY: Firebrand Books, 1991.

Gomez, Jewelle and Tristan Taormino. *The Best Lesbian Erotica of 1997*. Berkeley, CA: Cleis Press, 1996.

Gordon, Avery F. *Ghostly Matters: Haunting and the Sociological Imagination*. Minneapolis: University of Minnesota Press, 2008.

Gordon, Linda. "Black and White Visions of Welfare Activism, 1890–1945." *Journal of American History* 78 (1991): 551–90.

Gordon, Linda. *Pitied but Not Entitled: Single Mothers and the History of Welfare*. Cambridge, MA: Harvard University Press, 1995.

Gordon, Linda. *Women, the State, and Welfare*. Madison: University of Wisconsin Press, 1990.

Gould, Stephen. *The Flamingo's Smile: Reflections in Natural History*. New York: W. W. Norton, 1985.

Gould, Stephen. *The Mismeasure of Man*. New York: W. W. Norton, 1996.

Gramsci, Antonio. *Selections from the Prison Notebooks of Antonio Gramsci*. New York: International Publishers, 1971.

Gray, Herman. *Watching Race: Television and the Struggle for Blackness*. Minneapolis: University of Minnesota Press, 1995.

Green, Adam Isaiah. "The Social Organization of Desire: The Sexual Fields Approach." *Sociological Theory* 26, no. 1 (March 1, 2008): 25–50.

Green, Richard C., and Monique Guillory. "By Way of an Introduction." In *Soul: Black Power, Politics, and Pleasure*, edited by Richard Green, 1–4. New York: NYU Press, 1998.

Green, Richard C., and Monique Guillory. "Question of a 'Soulful Style': Interview with Paul Gilroy." In *Soul: Black Power, Politics, and Pleasure*, edited by Richard Green, 250–68. New York: NYU Press, 1998.

GregWn, "Angel Kelly and Heather Hunter Discuss 'Adult Entertainment'—1990 Part 1 of 5." YouTube. September 3, 2010. Accessed December 1, 2010 [discontinued link], http://www.youtube.com/watch?v=jGBjhZz1Xfo.

Grisby Bates, Karen. "Let's Not Indulge in Society's 'Chocolate' Fantasies: Black Women Posing Nude Feed an Image of the Wanton Hussy That So Many Others Have Worked to Disavow." *Los Angeles Times*, September 3, 1997. Late edition, sec. B7.

Gross, Kali N. *Colored Amazons: Crime, Violence, and Black Women in the City of Brotherly Love, 1880–1910.* Durham, NC: Duke University Press, 2006.

Grossberg, Josh. "Montana Fishburne Does Porn to 'Explore Sexuality.'" *E! Online*, August 10, 2010. Accessed August 12, 2010, http://www.eonline.com/news/194561 /montana-fishburne-does-porn-to-explore-sexuality.

Grosz, E. *Volatile Bodies: Toward a Corporeal Feminism.* Bloomington: Indiana University Press, 1994.

Guerrero, Ed. *Framing Blackness: The African American Image in Film.* Philadelphia: Temple University Press, 1993.

Guha, Ranajit. "The Prose of Counter-Insurgency." In *Selected Subaltern Studies*, edited by Ranajit Guha and Gayatri Chakravorty Spivak, 45–84. New York: Oxford University Press, 1988.

Guillory, Monique, and Richard C. Green. "By Way of an Introduction." In *Soul: Black Power, Politics, and Pleasure*, edited by Richard C. Green, 1–4. New York: NYU Press, 1998.

Gunning, Tom. "The Cinema of Attractions: Early Film, Its Spectator and the Avant-Garde." *Wide Angle* 8, no. 3/4 (1986): 63–70.

Gutman, Herbert. *The Black Family in Slavery and Freedom, 1750–1925.* New York: Pantheon Books, 1976.

Guy-Sheftall, Beverly. "The Body Politic: Black Female Sexuality and the Nineteenth-Century Euro-American Imagination." In *Skin Deep, Spirit Strong: The Black Female Body in American Culture*, edited by Kimberly Wallace-Sanders, 13–35. Ann Arbor: University of Michigan Press, 2002.

Guy-Sheftall, Beverly. *Daughters of Sorrow: Attitudes Toward Black Women, 1880–1920.* Brooklyn, NY: Carlson Publishing, 1990.

Guy-Sheftall, Beverly, ed. *Words of Fire: An Anthology of African-American Feminist Thought.* New York: New Press, 1995.

Halberstam, J. Jack. *Gaga Feminism: Sex, Gender, and the End of Normal.* Boston: Beacon Press, 2013.

Halberstam, Judith. *Female Masculinity.* Durham, NC: Duke University Press, 1998.

Halberstam, Judith. "Mackdaddy, Superfly, Rapper: Gender, Race, and Masculinity in the Drag King Scene." *Social Text* 52/53 (1997): 104–31.

Halberstam, Judith. *The Queer Art of Failure.* Durham, NC: Duke University Press, 2011.

Hall, Jacqueline Dowd. "The Long Civil Rights Movement and the Political Uses of the Past." *Journal of American History* 91, no. 4 (2005): 1233–63.

Hall, Jacqueline Dowd. "The Mind That Burns in Each Body: Women, Rape, and Racial Violence." In *Powers of Desire: The Politics of Sexuality*, edited by Ann Snitow, 329–33. New York: Monthly Review Press, 1983.

Hall, Ronald E. *Racism in the 21st Century: An Empirical Analysis of Skin Color*. East Lansing, MI: Springer, 2008.

Hall, Stuart. *Representation: Cultural Representations and Signifying Practices*. Thousand Oaks, CA: SAGE, 2007.

Hall, Stuart. "The Spectacle of the 'Other.'" In *Representation: Cultural Representations and Signifying Practices*, edited by Stuart Hall, 223–90. Thousand Oaks, CA: SAGE, 2007.

Hall, Stuart. "What Is the 'Black' in Black Popular Culture?" In *Black Popular Culture*, edited by Gina Dent, 21–33. New York: New Press, 1998.

Hall, Stuart. "The White of Their Eyes: Racist Ideologies of the Media." In *Gender, Race, and Class in Media: A Text-Reader*, edited by Gail Dines and Jean M. Humez, 89–94. Thousand Oaks, CA: SAGE, 1995.

Hammonds, Evelynn. "Black (W)holes and the Geometry of Black Female Sexuality." In *Skin Deep, Spirit Strong: The Black Female Body in American Culture*, edited by Kimberly Wallace-Sanders, 301–20. Ann Arbor: University of Michigan Press, 2002.

Hammonds, Evelynn. "Missing Persons: African American Women, AIDS, and the History of Disease." In *Words of Fire: An Anthology of African-American Feminist Thought*, edited by Beverly Guy-Sheftall, 434–50. New York: New Press, 1995.

Hammonds, Evelynn. "Toward a Genealogy of Black Female Sexuality: The Problematic of Silence." In *Feminist Genealogies, Colonial Legacies, Democratic Futures*, edited by Jacqui Alexander and Chandra Talpade Mohanty, 170–82. New York: Routledge, 1997.

Hanson, Dian. *Vanessa Del Rio: Fifty Years of Slightly Slutty Behavior*. Los Angeles: Taschen Books, 2010.

Haraway, Donna. *Simians, Cyborgs, and Women: The Reinvention of Nature*. New York: Routledge, 1991.

Hare, Nathan, and Julia Hare. *Crisis in Black Sexual Politics*. San Francisco, CA: Black Think Tank, 1989.

Harley, Sharon. "'Working for Nothing but a Living': Black Women in the Underground Economy." In *Sister Circle: Black Women and Work*, edited by Sharon Harley and the Black Women and Work Collective, 48–66. New Brunswick, NJ: Rutgers University Press, 2002.

Harley, Sharon, Francille Rusan Wilson, and Shirley Wilson Logan. "Introduction: Historical Overview of Black Women and Work." In *Sister Circle: Black Women and Work*, edited by Sharon Harley and the Black Women and Work Collective, 1–10. New Brunswick, NJ: Rutgers University Press, 2002.

Harrington, Imani. "Aid of America." In *The Black Women's Health Book: Speaking for Ourselves*, edited by Evelyn White, 187–88. Seattle, WA: Seal Press, 1990.

Harris, Jessica Christina. "Revolutionary Black Nationalism: The Black Panther Party." *Journal of Negro History* 85, no. 3 (July 1, 2000): 162–74.

Harrison, Matthew S., Wendy Reynolds-Dobbs, and Kecia M. Thomas. "Skin Color Bias in the Workplace: The Media's Role and Implications Toward Preference." In *Racism in the 21st Century*, edited by Ronald E. Hall, 47–62. New York: Springer New York, 2008.

Harris-Perry, Melissa V. *Sister Citizen: Shame, Stereotype, and Black Women in America*. New Haven, CT: Yale University Press, 2011.

Hartman, Saidiya. *Scenes of Subjection: Terror, Slavery, and Self-Making in Nineteenth-Century America*. New York: Oxford University Press, 1997.

Harvey, David. *The Condition of Postmodernity: An Enquiry into the Origins of Cultural Change*. Malden, MA: Blackwell, 1990.

Haslam, Fiona. "Views from the Gallery." *BMJ: British Medical Journal* 311, no. 7021 (1995): 1712.

Hebdige, Dick. "Flat Boy vs. Skinny: Takashi Murakami and the Battle for 'Japan,'" in *©Murakami*, organized by Paul Schimmel, 14–51. Los Angeles: Museum of Contemporary Art/Rizzoli International Publications, Inc., 2007.

Heller, Cord. "Inter-Racial Porno Movies." *Adam Film World*, October 1973.

Hemphill, Essex. *Ceremonies: Prose and Poetry*. Berkeley, CA: Cleis Press, 2000.

Hernandez, Daisy. "Playing With Race." *Colorlines*, December 1, 2004. Accessed April 2 2014, http://colorlines.com/archives/2004/12/playing_with_race.html.

Hernandez, Daisy. "Rethinking Porn. Really." *Colorlines*, April 22, 2009. Accessed March 25, 2014, http://colorlines.com/archives/2009/04/rethinking_porn_really.html.

Hernton, Calvin. *Sex and Racism in America*. New York: Grove Press, 1977.

Hicks, Cheryl D. *Talk with You like a Woman: African American Women, Justice, and Reform in New York, 1890–1935*. Chapel Hill: University of North Carolina Press, 2010.

Higginbotham, Evelyn. "African-American Women's History and the Metalanguage of Race." *Signs: Journal of Women in Culture and Society* 17, no. 2 (1992): 251–74.

Higginbotham, Evelyn. "Beyond The Sound of Silence: Afro-American Women in History." *Gender and History* 1, no. 1 (1989): 50–67.

Higginbotham, Evelyn. *Righteous Discontent: The Women's Movement in the Black Baptist Church, 1880–1920*. Cambridge, MA: Harvard University Press, 1993.

Hine, Darlene Clark. *Black Women in United States History*. Brooklyn, NY: Carlson Publishing, 1990.

Hine, Darlene Clark. "Rape and the Inner Lives of Black Women in the Middle West: Preliminary Thoughts on the Culture of Dissemblance." In *Words of Fire: An Anthology of African-American Feminist Thought*, edited by Beverly Guy-Sheftall, 380–87. New York: New Press, 1995.

Hine, Darlene Clark, Wilma King, and Linda Reed, eds. *"We Specialize in the Wholly Impossible": A Reader in Black Women's History*. Brooklyn, NY: Carlson Publishing, 1995.

Hines, Claire, and Darren Kerr, eds. *Hard to Swallow: Hard-Core Pornography on Screen*. New York: Columbia University Press, 2012.

Hirsch, Steven. Lecture in Film Studies 150, University of California, Santa Barbara, Santa Barbara, CA, May 20, 2004.

Hoang, Nguyen Tan. "The Resurrection of Brandon Lee: The Making of a Gay Asian American Porn Star." In *Porn Studies*, edited by Linda Williams, 223–70. Durham, NC: Duke University Press, 2004.

Hobson, Janell. "The 'Batty' Politic: Toward an Aesthetics of the Black Female Body." *Hypatia* 18, no. 4 (2003): 87–105.

Hobson, Janell. *Venus in the Dark: Blackness and Beauty in Popular Culture*. New York: Routledge, 2005.

Hochschild, Arlie. *The Second Shift*. New York: Penguin Books, 2003.

Hodes, Martha. *Sex, Love, Race: Crossing Boundaries in North American History*. New York: NYU Press, 1999.

Hodes, Martha. *White Women, Black Men: Illicit Sex in the Nineteenth-Century South*. New Haven, CT: Yale University Press, 1997.

Holiday, Billie. *Lady Sings the Blues*. Garden City, NY: Doubleday, 1956.

Holland, Sharon Patricia. *The Erotic Life of Racism*. Durham, NC: Duke University Press, 2012.

Holliday, Jim. "The Changing Face of Adult Video." *Adult Video News*, March 1987, 15, 88.

Holliday, Jim. "Only the Best: A Decade of Distinction and Discord Plus the Holliday 'Best of the Decade Honors.'" *Adult Video News 10th Anniversary Supplement*, 1992.

Holmes, Rachel. *The Hottentot Venus: The Life and Death of Saartjie Baartman: Born 1789–Buried 2002*. New York: Bloomsbury, 2007.

Honey, Michael. *Black Workers Remember: An Oral History of Segregation, Unionism, and the Freedom Struggle*. Berkeley: University of California Press, 1999.

Hong, Grace. *The Ruptures of American Capital: Women of Color Feminism and the Culture of Immigrant Labor*. Minneapolis: University of Minnesota Press. 2006.

Honour, Hugh. *The Image of the Black in Western Art*. Cambridge, MA: Harvard University Press, 1989.

hooks, bell. "Eating the Other: Desire and Resistance." In *Black Looks: Race and Representation*, 21–40. Boston: South End Press, 1992.

hooks, bell. *Reel to Real: Race, Sex, and Class at the Movies*. New York: Routledge, 1996.

hooks, bell. "Selling Hot Pussy: Representation of Black Female Sexuality in the Cultural Marketplace." In *Black Looks: Race and Representation*, 61–78. Brooklyn, NY: South End Press, 1992.

hooks, bell. *Talking Back: Thinking Feminist, Thinking Black*. Toronto: Between the Lines, 1988.

Hughes, Albert, and Allen Hughes. *American Pimp*. MGM Home Entertainment, 2000.

Hughes, Robert. "Between the Sistine and Disney: The Licentious Genius of Mantua's Giulio Romano." *Time*, June 11, 1989.

Hull, Gloria, Patricia Bell Scott, and Barbara Smith, eds. *All the Women Are White, All the Blacks Are Men, but Some of Us Are Brave: Black Women's Studies.* Old Westbury, NY: Feminist Press, 1982.

Hunt, Lynn Avery, ed. *The Invention of Pornography: Obscenity and the Origins of Modernity, 1500-1800.* New York: Zone Books, 1993.

Hunt, Lynn Avery. "Pornography and the French Revolution." In *The Invention of Pornography: Obscenity and the Origins of Modernity, 1500-1800,* edited by Lynn Hunt, 301–40. New York: Zone Books, 1993.

Hunter, Heather, and Michelle Valentine. *Insatiable: The Rise of a Porn Star.* New York: St. Martin's Griffin, 2008.

Hunter, Margaret. "Shake It, Baby, Shake It: Consumption and the New Gender Relation in Hip-Hop." *Sociological Perspectives* 54, no. 1 (Spring 2011): 15–36.

Hunter, Tera. *To 'Joy My Freedom: Southern Black Women's Lives and Labors after the Civil War.* Cambridge, MA: Harvard University Press, 1997.

Hyde, H. Montgomery. *A History of Pornography.* New York: Farrar, Straus and Giroux, 1965.

IAFD: Internet Adult Film Database. Accessed March 27, 2014, http://www.iafd.com/.

Ignique, Ferro. "They Call Me Mr. Marcus." *Adult Video News Ethnic Video Supplement* 178 (April 1998).

Ignique, Ferro. "Toy(s of Color) Story." *Adult Video News Ethnic Video Supplement* 178 (April 1998).

Irving, Lee. "Director's Corner: Gregory Dark." *Adult Video News,* December 1985, 48–53.

Irving, Lee. "Exclusive Interview: Vanessa Del Rio." *Adult Video News,* August 1986, 16, 18.

Itzin, Catherine. *Pornography: Women, Violence and Civil Liberties.* New York: Oxford University Press, 1991.

"Jack Baker." IAFD. Accessed March 27, 2014. http://www.iafd.com/person.rme/per fid=jbaker/gender=m/jack-baker.htm.

Jacobs, Katrien. *Netporn: DIY Web Culture and Sexual Politics.* Lanham, MD: Rowman and Littlefield Publishers, 2007.

Jacobs, Katrien, Matteo Pasquinelli, and Marije Janssen eds. *C'Lick Me: A Netporn Studies Reader.* Amsterdam: Institute of Network Cultures, 2007.

Jaggi, Maya. "Twentieth-century fox." *Guardian* (Manchester), March 7, 1998, 15.

James, Angela D., David M. Grant, and Cynthia Crawford. "Moving Up, but How Far? African American Women and Economic Restructuring in Los Angeles, 1970–1990." *Sociological Perspectives* 43, no. 3 (2000): 399–420.

James, Selma. *Sex, Race, and Class: The Perspective of Winning, A Selection of Writings, 1952-2011.* Oakland, CA: PM Press.

JanMohamed, Abdul. "Sexuality on/of the Racial Border: Foucault, Wright, and the Articulation of Racialized Sexuality." In *Discourses of Sexuality: from Aristotle to AIDS,* edited by Donna C. Stanton, 94–116. Ann Arbor: University of Michigan Press, 1992.

Jeffries, Sheila. *The Idea of Prostitution.* North Melbourne, Australia: Spinefex Press, 1997.

Jeffries, Sheila. *The Industrial Vagina: The Political Economy of the Global Sex Trade.* New York: Routledge, 2009.

Jenkins, Henry. *What Made Pistachio Nuts? Early Sound Comedy and the Vaudeville Aesthetic.* New York: Columbia University Press, 1992.

Jenkins, Reese. *Images and Enterprise: Technology and the American Photographic Industry 1839-1925.* Baltimore, MD: Johns Hopkins University Press, 1987.

Jennes, Valerie. *Making It Work: The Prostitutes' Rights Movement in Perspective.* New York: Aldine De Gruyter, 1993.

Jensen, Robert. *Getting Off: Pornography and the End of Masculinity.* Cambridge, MA: South End Press, 2007.

Jewell, K. *From Mammy to Miss America and Beyond: Cultural Images and the Shaping of US Social Policy.* London: Routledge, 1993.

Johnson, E. Patrick. *Appropriating Blackness Performance and the Politics of Authenticity.* Durham, NC: Duke University Press, 2003.

Johnson, E. Patrick, and Mae Henderson, eds. *Black Queer Studies: A Critical Anthology.* Durham, NC: Duke University Press, 2005.

Johnson, Walter. *Soul by Soul: Life Inside the Antebellum Slave Market.* Cambridge, MA: Harvard University Press, 1999.

Johnston, David Cay. "Indications of a Slowdown in Sex Entertainment Trade." Late Edition, *New York Times*, January 4, 2007, C6.

Jones, Jacqueline. *Labor of Love, Labor of Sorrow: Black Women, Work, and the Family from Slavery to the Present.* New York: Basic Books, 1985.

Jones, Jacquie. "The New Ghetto Aesthetic." *Wide Angle* 13, nos. 3/4 (1991): 32–43.

Jordan, Carlton. "Pt. 1 Laurence Fishburne's 18-Year Old Daughter is Officially a Porn Star!" YouTube. July 29, 2010. Accessed April 3, 2014, https://www.youtube.com/watch?v=c4f9QIPoQWU.

Jordan, Carlton. "Pt. 2 Laurence Fishburne's 18-Year Old Daughter is Officially a Porn Star!" YouTube. July 29, 2010. Accessed April 3, 2014, https://www.youtube.com/watch?v=obXlOJkA824#t=3m34s.

Jordan, June. "A New Politics of Sexuality." In *Words of Fire: An Anthology of African-American Feminist Thought*, edited by Beverly Guy-Sheftall, 407–12. New York: New Press, 1995.

Juffer, Jane. *At Home with Pornography: Women, Sex, and Everyday Life.* New York: NYU Press, 1998.

Juffer, Jane. "There's No Place Like Home: Further Developments on the Domestic Front." *More Dirty Looks: Gender, Pornography and Power*, edited by Pamela Church Gibson, 45–58. London: British Film Institute, 2004.

Jules-Rosette, Bennetta. *Josephine Baker in Art and Life: The Icon and the Image.* Champaign: University of Illinois Press, 2007.

Kaplan, E. Ann. "Is the Gaze Male?" In *Powers of Desire: The Politics of Sexuality*, edited by Ann Snitow, Christine Stansell, and Sharon Thompson, 309–25. New York: Monthly Review Press, 1983.

Kaplan, E. Ann. *Looking for the Other: Feminism, Film and the Imperial Gaze.* New York: Psychology Press, 1997.

Kappeler, Susanne. *The Pornography of Representation*. Minneapolis: University of Minnesota Press, 1986.

Kapsalis, Terri. "Mastering the Female Pelvis: Race and the Tools of Reproduction." In *Skin Deep, Spirit Strong: The Black Female Body in American Culture*, edited by Kimberly Wallace-Sanders, 263–300. Ann Arbor, MI: University of Michigan Press, 2002.

Katz, Maude White. "The Negro Woman and the Law." In *Black Women in United States History*, edited by Darlene Clark Hine, 309–17. Brooklyn, NY: Carlson Publishing, 1990.

Kauanui, J. Kēhaulani. "A Fraction of National Belonging: 'Hybrid Hawaiians,' Blood Quantum, and the Ongoing Search for Purity." In *Beyond the Frame: Visual Representations of Women of Color*, edited by Angela Davis and Neferti X. M. Tadiar, 153–68. New York: Palgrave Macmillan, 2005.

Kay, Kerwin. "Naked but Unseen: Sex and Labor Conflict in San Francisco's Adult Theaters." *Sexuality and Culture* 3 (1999): 39–68.

Kearnes, Mark. "Video Team Finds Nothing Eccentric About Afro-Centric." *Adult Video News Ethnic Video Supplement* 178 (April 1998).

Kelbaugh, Ross J. *Introduction to African American Photographs, 1840–1950: Identification, Research, Care & Collecting*. Gettysburg, PA: Thomas Publications, 2005.

Kelley, Robin D. G. *Freedom Dreams: The Black Radical Imagination*. Boston: Beacon Press, 2003.

Kelley, Robin D. G. *Race Rebels: Culture, Politics, and the Black Working Class*. New York: Simon and Schuster, 1996.

Kelley, Robin D. G. *Yo' Mama's Disfunktional! Fighting the Culture Wars in Urban America*. Boston: Beacon Press, 1998.

Kempadoo, Kamala. "Introduction: Globalizing Sex Workers' Rights." In *Global Sex Workers: Rights, Resistance, and Redefinition*, edited by Kamala Kempadoo and Jo Doezema. New York: Routledge, 1998.

Kempadoo, Kamala. *Sun, Sex, and Gold: Tourism and Sex Work in the Caribbean*. Lanham, MD: Rowman and Littlefield, 1999.

Kempadoo, Kamala, and Jo Doezema. *Global Sex Workers: Rights, Resistance, and Redefinition*. New York: Routledge, 1998.

Kendrick, Walter, and Walter M. Kendrick. *The Secret Museum: Pornography in Modern Culture*. Berkeley: University of California Press, 1987.

Kennedy, Florynce. "A Comparative Study: Accentuating the Similarities of the Societal Position of Women and Negroes." In *Words of Fire: An Anthology of African-American Feminist Thought*, edited by Beverly Guy-Sheftall, 102–6. New York: New Press, 1995.

Kernes, Mark. Guest lecture in Film Studies 150, UC Santa Barbara, Santa Barbara, CA, May 16, 2004.

Kernes, Mark. "Distributors as Manufacturers: The Next Wave Is Here." *Adult Video News*, September 1992, 14–16.

Kessler-Harris, Alice. "Where Are the Organized Women Workers?" *Feminist Studies* 3, no. 1/2 (October 1975): 92–110.

King, Deborah. "Multiple Jeopardy, Multiple Consciousness: The Context of a Black Feminist Ideology." In *Words of Fire: An Anthology of African-American Feminist Thought*, edited by Beverly Guy-Sheftall, 294–318. New York: New Press, 1995.

Kipnis, Laura. *Bound and Gagged: Pornography and the Politics of Fantasy in America*. Durham, NC: Duke University Press, 1998.

Kipnis, Laura. *Ecstasy Unlimited: On Sex, Capital, Gender, and Aesthetics*. Minneapolis: University of Minnesota Press, 1993.

Kitwana, Bakari. *The Hip Hop Generation: Young Blacks and the Crisis in African-American Culture*. New York: Basic Books, 2002.

Kleinhans, Chuck. "Pamela Anderson on the Slippery Slope." In *The End of Cinema as We Know It: American Films of the Nineties*, edited by Jon Lewis. New York: New York University Press, 2001.

Knight, Tyler. "Black Actors in Adult Film." Presentation at the University of California, Santa Barbara, Santa Barbara, CA, May 25, 2010.

Korstad, Robert, and Nelson Lichtenstein. "Opportunities Found and Lost: Labor, Radicals, and the Early Civil Rights Movement." *Journal of American History* 75, no. 3 (1988): 786–811.

Koskoff, Harriet, and KQED-TV (San Francisco, CA). *Patently Offensive Porn under Siege*. Filmmakers Library, 1991.

Kulick, Don. *Travesti: Sex, Gender, and Culture among Brazilian Transgendered Prostitutes*. Chicago: University of Chicago Press, 1998.

Ladner, Joyce A. "Racism and Tradition: Black Womanhood in Historical Perspective." In *The Black Woman Cross-Culturally*, edited by Filomina Steady, 269–88. Rochester, NY: Schenkman Publishing Company, 1981.

Ladner, Joyce A. *Tomorrow's Tomorrow: The Black Woman*. Garden City, NY: Doubleday, 1972.

Langley, Erika. *The Lusty Lady*. New York: Scalo, 1997.

La Rue, Linda. "The Black Women's Movement and Liberation." In *Words of Fire: An Anthology of African-American Feminist Thought*, edited by Beverly Guy-Sheftall, 164–75. New York: New Press, 1995.

Lawrence, Novotny. *Blaxploitation Films of the 1970s: Blackness and Genre*. New York: Psychology Press, 2007.

Lederer, Laura. *Take Back the Night: Women on Pornography*. New York: William Morrow, 1980.

Lehman, Peter. "Revelations about Pornography." *Film Criticism* 20 (1995): 1–2.

Lerner, Gerda. *Black Women in White America: A Documentary History*. New York: Vintage Books, 1992.

Lewis, Charles D. "Letter to the Editor." *Players*, March 1974, 26.

Lewis, Jon. *Hollywood v. Hard Core: How the Struggle over Censorship Created the Modern Film Industry*. New York: NYU Press, 2002.

Lidchi, Henrietta. "The Poetics and the Politics of Exhibiting Other Cultures." In *Representation: Cultural Representations and Signifying Practices*, edited by Stuart Hall, 151–222. Thousand Oaks, CA: SAGE, 1997.

Linz, Daniel, Edward Donnerstein, Bradley J. Shafer, Kenneth C. Land, Patricia L.

McCall, and Arthur C. Graesser. "Discrepancies between the Legal Code and Community Standards for Sex and Violence: An Empirical Challenge to Traditional Assumptions in Obscenity Law." *Law and Society Review* 29, no. 1 (January 1, 1995): 127–68.

Lockett, Gloria. "Black Prostitutes and AIDS." In *The Black Women's Health Book: Speaking for Ourselves*, edited by Evelyn C. White. Seattle, WA: Seal Press, 1994.

Lockett, Gloria. "Destroying Condoms." In *Sex Work: Writings by Women in the Sex Industry*, edited by Frederique Delacoste and Priscilla Alexander, 158. New York: Cleis Press, 1998.

Lockett, Gloria. "Leaving the Streets." In *Sex Work: Writings by Women in the Sex Industry*, edited by Frederique Delacoste and Priscilla Alexander, 96–7. New York: Cleis Press, 1998.

Lockett, Gloria. "What Happens When You Are Arrested." In *Sex Work: Writings by Women in the Sex Industry*, edited by Frederique Delacoste and Priscilla Alexander, 39–40. New York: Cleis Press, 1998.

Logan, Mark. "Editorial: Black, Asian and Beyond." *Adult Video News Ethnic Video Supplement* 178 (April 1998).

Lorde, Audre. Sister Outsider: Essays and Speeches by Audre Lorde. Ithaca, NY: Crossing Press, 1984.

Lott, Eric. *Love and Theft: Blackface Minstrelsy and the American Working Class*. New York: Oxford University Press, 1993.

Love, Sinnamon. "Black Actors in Adult Film." Presentation at the University of California, Santa Barbara, Santa Barbara, CA, May 25, 2010.

Love, Sinnamon. "Life, Love and Sinn: An Assumption of Immortality." *The Well Versed*, October 11, 2011. Accessed December 15, 2010 [discontinued link], http://thewellversed.com/2010/11/11/life-love-and-sinn-an-assumption-of-immortality/.

Love, Sinnamon. Public lecture in Film Studies 150, from UC Santa Barbara, Santa Barbara, CA, May 25, 2011.

Love, Sinnamon. "A Question of Feminism." In *The Feminist Porn Book: The Politics of Producing Pleasure*, edited by Tristan Taormino, Celine Parreñas Shimizu, Constance Penley, and Mireille Miller-Young, 97–104. New York: The Feminist Press, 2013.

Loving v. Virginia, 388 U.S. 1 (1967).

Lowe, Donald M. *The Body in Late-Capitalist USA*. Durham, NC: Duke University Press, 1995.

Lubiano, Wahneema. "Black Ladies, Welfare Queens and State Minstrels." In *Race-ing Justice, En-Gendering Power: Essays on Anita Hill, Clarence Thomas, and the Construction of Social Reality*, edited by Toni Morrison, 323–63. New York: Pantheon Books, 1992.

Lubiano, Wahneema. *The House That Race Built: Black Americans, U.S. Terrain*. New York: Pantheon Books, 1997.

Lumby, Catharine, Kath Albury, and Alan McKee. *The Porn Report*. Carlton, AU: Melbourne University Publishing, 2008.

Lumby, Catharine. *Bad Girls: The Media, Sex, and Feminism in the 90s*. Victoria: Allen & Unwin, 1997.

Luo, Michael. "In Job Hunt, College Degree Can't Close Racial Gap." *New York Times*, November 30, 2009. Accessed February 11, 2011, http://www.nytimes.com/2009/12/01/us/01race.html?ref=bureauoflaborstatistics.

Lutz, Catherine, and Jane Lou Collins. *Reading National Geographic*. Chicago: University of Chicago Press, 1993.

Lydersen, Kari. "Our Bodies Are Not a Sacrifice: Prostitution and Progressive Approaches." *Women and Prison: A Site for Resistance*. (n.d.). Accessed July 23, 2008, http://womenandprison.org/sexuality/karilydersen.htm.

Lydersen, Kari. "Sexuality, Women and Prison: A Site for Resistance." *Women and Prison: A Site for Resistance*. (n.d.) Accessed January 8, 2012, http://womenandprison.org/sexuality/kari-lyderson.html.

MacKinnon, Catharine A. *Feminism Unmodified: Discourses on Life and Law*. Cambridge, MA: Harvard University Press, 1987.

MacKinnon, Catharine A. *Only Words*. Cambridge, MA: Harvard University Press, 1993.

Magubane, Zine. "Which Bodies Matter? Feminism, Poststructuralism, Race, and the Curious Theoretical Odyssey of the 'Hottentot Venus.'" *Gender and Society* 15, no. 6 (2001): 816–34.

Mahmood, Saba. "Feminist Theory, Embodiment, and the Docile Agent: Some Reflections on the Egyptian Islamic Revival." *Cultural Anthropology* 16, no. 2 (May 1, 2001): 202–36.

Majors, Frank. "The Porn-to-Rap Connection." *Adult Video News*, January 21, 2003.

Malcolm X and Alex Haley. *The Autobiography of Malcolm X as Told to Alex Haley*. New York: Ballantine Books, 1992.

Manatu, Norma. *African American Women and Sexuality in the Cinema*. Jefferson, NC: McFarland, 2003.

Manring, Maurice M. *Slave in a Box: The Strange Career of Aunt Jemima*. Charlottesville: University of Virginia Press, 1998.

Marcus, Steven. *The Other Victorians: A Study of Sexuality and Pornography in Mid-Nineteenth-Century England*. New Brunswick, NJ: Transaction Publishers, 2009.

Mardonov, Dr. "Monique est la Mode." *Adult Video News Ethnic Video Supplement* 178 (April 1998).

Markovitz, Jonathan. *Racial Spectacles: Explorations in Media, Race, and Justice*. New York: Taylor and Francis, 2011.

Marks, Carole. *Farewell—We're Good and Gone: The Great Black Migration*. Bloomington: Indiana University Press, 1989.

Marshall, P. David. "The Cinematic Apparatus and the Construction of the Film Celebrity." In *The Film Cultures Reader*, edited by Graeme Turner. New York: Routledge, 2002.

Martin, Biddy. "Feminism, Criticism and Foucault." In *Feminism and Foucault: Reflections on Resistance*, edited by Irene Diamond and Lee Quinby, 3–20. Lebanon, NH: Northeastern University Press, 1988.

Marx, Karl. *Capital: A Critique of Political Economy. The Process of Production of Capital.* Vol. 1. Moscow, USSR: Progress Publishers, 1986.

Maseko, Zola. *The Life and Times of Sara Baartman: "The Hottentot Venus."* New York: Icarus Films, 1998.

Mask, Mia. *Divas on Screen: Black Women in American Film.* Urbana: University of Illinois Press, 2009.

McBride, Dwight A. "Can the Queen Speak? Racial Essentialism, Sexuality and the Problem of Authority." *Callaloo* 21, no. 2 (1998): 363–79.

McBride, Dwight. *Why I Hate Abercrombie & Fitch: Essays on Race and Sexuality.* New York: NYU Press, 2005.

McClanahan, Susan F., Gary M. McClelland, Karen M. Abram, and Linda A. Teplin. "Pathways into Prostitution among Female Jail Detainees and Their Implications for Mental Health Services." *Psychiatric Services* 50, no. 12 (1999): 1606–13.

McClintock, Anne. "Maid to Order: Commercial Fetishism and Gender Power." *Social Text* 37 (Winter 1993): 87–116.

McClintock, Anne. "Gonad the Barbarian and the Venus Flytrap: Portraying the Female and Male Orgasm." In *Sex Exposed: Sexuality and the Pornography Debate*, edited by Lynne Segal and Mary McIntosh, 111–31. New Brunswick, NJ: Rutgers University Press, 1993.

McClintock, Anne. *Imperial Leather: Race, Gender, and Sexuality in the Colonial Contest.* New York: Routledge, 1995.

McClintock, Anne, Aamir Mufti, and Ella Shohat, eds. *Dangerous Liaisons: Gender, Nation, and Postcolonial Perspectives.* Minneapolis: University of Minnesota Press, 1997.

McGlotten, Shaka and Dána-Ain Davis, eds. *Black Genders and Sexualities.* New York: Palgrave Macmillan, 2012.

McGruder, Kevin. "Pathologizing Black Sexuality: The U.S. Experience." In *Black Sexualities: Probing Powers, Passions, Practices and Politics*, edited by Juan Battle and Sandra A. Barnes, 311–26. New Brunswick, NJ: Rutgers University Press, 2010.

McMahon, Thomas. "Displaying Adult Tapes." *Adult Video News*, November 1986, 14–15.

McNair, Brian. *Porno? Chic! How Pornography Changed the World and Made It a Better Place.* New York: Routledge, 2013.

McNair, Brian. *Striptease Culture: Sex, Media and the Democratization of Desire.* New York: Psychology Press, 2002.

McNeil, Leggs, and Jennifer Osborne. *The Other Hollywood: The Uncensored Oral History of the Porn Industry.* New York: It Books, 2005.

Meade, Benjamin, dir. *American Stag.* Corticrawl Productions, 2006.

Mercer, Kobena. *Welcome to the Jungle: New Positions in Black Cultural Studies.* New York: Routledge, 1994.

Mercer, Kobena, and Isaac Julian. "Race, Sexual Politics and Black Masculinity: A Dossier." In *Male Order: Unwrapping Masculinity*, edited by Rowena Chapman and Jonathan Rutherford, 97–164. London: Lawrence and Wishart, 1988.

Michaels, Tobias. "Review of *Let Me Tell Ya 'Bout Black Chicks*." *Adult Video News*, November 1985, 24.

Miller-Young, Mireille. "Exotic/Erotic/Ethnopornographic: Black Women, Desire, and Labor in the Photographic Archive." Forthcoming.

Miller-Young, Mireille. "Hip Hop Honeys and Da Hustlaz: Black Sexualities in the New Hip Hop Pornography." *Meridians* 8, no. 1 (April 2008): 261–92.

Miller-Young, Mireille. "Let Me Tell Ya 'Bout Black Chicks: Black Women in 1980s Video Pornography." In *Blackness and Sexualities*, edited by Michelle Wright and Antje Schuhmann, 143–64. Berlin: LIT Verlag, 2007.

Miller-Young, Mireille. "Putting Hypersexuality to Work: Black Women and Illicit Eroticism in Pornography." *Sexualities* 13, no. 2 (April 2010): 219–235.

Miller-Young, Mireille. "Sexy and Smart: Black Women and the Politics of Self-Authorship in Netporn." In *C'Lick Me: A Netporn Studies Reader*, edited by Katrien Jacobs, Matteo Pasquinelli and Marije Janssen, 205–16. Amsterdam: Institute of Network Cultures, 2007.

Miller-Young, Mireille, and Xavier Livermon. "Black Stud, White Desire: Black Masculinity in Cuckold Photography and Sex Work." Lecture, Black Sexual Economies: Conference on Transforming Black Sexualities Research, Washington University Law, St. Louis, MO, September 28, 2013.

Mink, Gwendolyn. *The Wages of Motherhood: Inequality in the Welfare State, 1917–1942*. Ithaca, NY: Cornell University Press, 1996.

Mink, Gwendolyn. "Welfare Reform in Historical Perspective." *Connecticut Law Review* 26 (spring 1994): 879–99.

Mintz, Sidney Wilfred. *Sweetness and Power: The Place of Sugar in Modern History*. New York: Penguin Books, 1986.

Mitchell, Janet, and Patricia Loftman. "HIV Infection, AIDS, and Black Women." In *The Black Women's Health Book: Speaking for Ourselves*, edited by Evelyn C. White, 319–22. Seattle, WA: Seal Press, 1994.

Mizejewski, Linda. *Ziegfeld Girl: Image and Icon in Culture and Cinema*. Durham, NC: Duke University Press, 1999.

Mohanty, Chandra Talpade. "Under Western Eyes: Feminist Scholarship and Colonial Discourses." In *Dangerous Liaisons: Gender, Nation, and Postcolonial Perspectives*, edited by Anne McClintock, Aamir Mufti, and Ella Shohat, 255–75. Minneapolis: University of Minnesota Press, 1997.

Monto, Martin. "Why Men Seek Out Prostitutes." In *Sex for Sale: Prostitution, Pornography, and the Sex Industry*, edited by Ronald John Weitzer, 67–84. New York: Routledge, 2000.

Moore, Darrell. "The Frame of Discourse: Sexuality, Power, and the Incitement to Race." *Philosophy Today* 42, no. 1 (1998): 94–107.

Morel, India. *Infamous: Memoirs of a XXX Star*. Create Space Independent Publishing Platform, 2013.

Morgan, Jennifer L. "'Some Could Suckle over Their Shoulder': Male Travelers, Female Bodies, and the Gendering of Racial Ideology, 1500–1770." *William and Mary Quarterly* 54, no. 1 (1997): 167–92.

Morgan, Joan. *When Chickenheads Come Home to Roost: A Hip-Hop Feminist Breaks It Down*. New York: Simon and Schuster, 2000.

Morgan, Robin. "Theory and Practice: Pornography and Rape." In *Take Back the Night: Women on Pornography*, edited by Laura Lederer, 134–40. New York: William Morrow 1980.

Morrison, Toni. *Race-ing Justice, En-Gendering Power: Essays on Anita Hill, Clarence Thomas, and the Construction of Social Reality*. New York: Pantheon Books, 1992.

Morton, Samuel George. *Crania Americana: or a Comparative View of the Skulls of Various Aboriginal Nations of North and South America*. Philadelphia: J. Dobson, 1839.

Moten, Fred. *In the Break: The Aesthetics of the Black Radical Tradition*. Minneapolis: University of Minnesota Press, 2003.

Mowry, Melissa M. *The Bawdy Politic in Stuart England, 1660–1714: Political Pornography and Prostitution*. Burlington, VT: Ashgate Publishing, 2004.

Moynihan, Daniel. *The Negro Family: The Case for National Action*. Reprint. Westport, CT: Greenwood Press, 1981.

Mumford, Kevin J. *Interzones: Black/White Sex Districts in Chicago and New York in the Early Twentieth Century*. New York: Columbia University Press, 1997.

Muñoz, José Esteban. *Disidentifications: Queers of Color and the Performance of Politics*. Minneapolis: University of Minnesota Press, 1999.

Murray, Susan, and Laurie Ouellette, eds. *Reality TV: Remaking Television Culture*. New York: New York University Press, 2009.

Myrdal, Gunnar. *An American Dilemma: the Negro Problem and Modern Democracy*. Piscataway, NJ: Transaction Publishers, 1944.

Nagle, Jill. *Whores and Other Feminists*. New York: Routledge, 1997.

Nash, Jennifer C. "The Black Body in Ecstasy: Reading Race, Reading Pornography." PhD diss., Harvard University, 2009.

Nash, Jennifer C. "Strange Bedfellows: Black Feminism and Antipornography Feminism." *Social Text* 26, no. 4 97 (2008): 51–76.

Neal, Mark Anthony. *Soul Babies: Black Popular Culture and the Post-Soul Aesthetic*. New York: Psychology Press, 2001.

Needham, Gerald. "Manet, 'Olympia,' and Pornographic Photography." In *Woman as Sex Object: Studies in Erotic Art, 1730–1970*, edited by Thomas B. Hess and Linda Nochlin. New York: Newsweek, 1972.

North, Anna. "When Prejudice Is Sexy: Inside the Kinky World of Race-Play." *Jezebel*, March 14, 2012. Accessed April 2 2014, http://jezebel.com/5868600/when-prejudice-is-sexy-inside-the-kinky-world-of-race-play/all.

Nussbaum, Martha C. *Sex and Social Justice*. New York: Oxford University Press, 2000.

Nye, Robert A. *Sexuality*. New York: Oxford University Press, 1999.

Ogbar, Jeffrey O.G. *Hip-Hop Revolution: The Culture and Politics of Rap*. Lawrence: University of Kansas Press, 2007.

Ohmann, Richard Malin. *Selling Culture: Magazines, Markets, and Class at the Turn of the Century*. London: Verso, 1996.

Omi, Michael, and Howard Winant. *Racial Formation in the United States: From the 1960s to the 1990s*. New York: Psychology Press, 1994.

O'Toole, Laurence. *Pornocopia: Porn, Sex, Technology and Desire*. London: Serpent's Tail, 1999.

Owens, Brent, and Out of Pocket Productions. *Pimps Up, Ho's Down: The Director's Cut*. DVD. Los Angeles, CA: Delta Entertainment, 1999.

Paasonen, Susanna, Kaarina Nikunen, and Laura Saarenmaa, eds. *Pornification: Sex and Sexuality in Media Culture*. New York: Berg, 2007.

Paasonen, Susanna, Kaarina Nikunen, and Laura Saarenmaa, "Pornification and the Education of Desire." In *Pornification: Sex and Sexuality in Media Culture*, edited by Susanna Paasonen, Kaarina Nikunen and Laura Saarenmaa, 1–20. New York: Berg, 2007.

Page, Enoch H. and Matt U. Richardson. "On the Fear of Small Numbers: A Twenty-First Century Prolegomenon of the U.S. Black Transgender Experience." In *Black Sexualities: Probing Powers, Passions, Practices, and Politics*, edited by Juan Battle and Sandra A. Barnes, 311–26. New Brunswick, NJ: Rutgers University Press, 2010.

Paone, John. "1986 In Review." *Adult Video News Confidential*, January 1986, 12–15.

Paone, John. "Combating the Adult Video Glut: First of Three Parts." *Adult Video News Confidential*, February 1986, 8–11.

Paone, John. "Combating the Adult Video Glut: Second of Three Parts." *Adult Video News Confidential*, March 1986, 8, 14, 18.

Paone, John. "Combating the Adult Video Glut: Third of Three Parts." *Adult Video News Confidential*, April 1986, 16, 18.

Paone, John. "Interview: Perry Ross of Fantasy of Home Video." *Adult Video News Confidential*, May 1987, 18, 21.

Parks, Suzan-Lori. *Venus: A Play*. New York: Dramatists Play Service, 1998.

Pascoe, Peggy. "Miscegenation Law, Court Cases, and Ideologies of 'Race' in Twentieth-Century America." *Journal of American History* 83, no. 1 (1996): 44–69.

Paul, Pamela. *Pornified: How Pornography Is Transforming Our Lives, Our Relationships, and Our Families*. New York: Macmillan, 2007.

PBS Frontline: American Porn. "Interview with Bill Ascher," July 2001. Accessed April 2, 2014, http://www.pbs.org/wgbh/pages/frontline/shows/porn/interviews/asher.html.

PBS Frontline: American Porn. "Interview with Dennis McAlpine," August 2001. Accessed April 2, 2014, http://www.pbs.org/wgbh/pages/frontline/shows/porn/interviews/mcalpine.html.

Penley, Constance. "Crackers and Whackers: The White Trashing of Porn." In *Pornography: Film and Culture*, edited by Peter Lehman, 99–117. New Brunswick, NJ: Rutgers University Press 2006.

Pepper, Jeannie. "A Special Achievement Presentation Award to the Legendary Jeannie Pepper, from 1982 to 2002, Twenty Years of Hot Sizzling Sex." Speech, October 9, 2002. East Coast Video Show After Party, Atlantic City, NJ.

Perry, Imani. *Prophets of the Hood: Politics and Poetics in Hip Hop*. Durham, NC: Duke University Press, 2004.

Perry, Imani. "Who(se) Am I?: The Identity and Image of Women in Hip Hop." In *Gender, Race, and Class in Media: A Text-Reader*, edited by Gail Dines and Jean McMahon Humez, 136–48. Thousand Oaks, CA: SAGE, 2003.

Petkovich, Anthony. "Dark World: An Interview with the Salvador Dali of Porn, Gregory Dark." In *The X Factory: Inside the American Hardcore Film Industry*. Manchester, UK: Critical Vision, 2002.

Pink Cross Foundation. 2013. Accessed April 1, 2014, https://www.thepinkcross.org/.

Plaid, Andrea. "Interview with the Perverted Negress." *Racialicious—the Intersection of Race and Pop Culture*, July 10, 2009. Accessed April 2, 2014, http://www.raciali cious.com/2009/07/10/interview-with-the-perverted-negress/.

Plessy v. Ferguson, 163 U.S. 537 (1896).

Poole, Deborah. *Vision, Race, and Modernity: A Visual Economy of the Andean Image World*. Princeton, NJ: Princeton University Press, 1997.

Porter, Judith, and Louis Bonilla. "Drug Use, HIV, and the Ecology of Street Prostitution." In *Sex for Sale: Prostitution, Pornography, and the Sex Industry*, edited by Ronald Weitzer, 103–37. New York: Routledge, 2000.

Pough, Gwendolyn D. *Check It While I Wreck it: Black Womanhood, Hip-Hop Culture, and the Public Sphere*. Lebanon: UPNE, 2004.

Pough, Gwendolyn D., Elaine Richardson, Aisha Durham, and Rachel Raimist, eds. *Homegirls Make Some Noise!: Hip Hop Feminism Anthology*. Mira Loma, CA: Parker Publishing, 2007.

Poulson-Bryant, Scott. *Hung: A Meditation on the Measure of Black Men in America*. New York: Harlem Moon, 2005.

Power, Nina. *One Dimensional Woman*. Hants, UK: Zero Books, 2009.

Prashad, Vijay. *Everybody Was Kung Fu Fighting: Afro-Asian Connections and the Myth of Cultural Purity*. Boston: Beacon Press, 2002.

Pratt, Mary Louise. "Scratches on the Face of the Country; Or, What Mr. Barrow Saw in the Land of the Bushmen." *Critical Inquiry* 12, no. 1 (October 1, 1985): 119–43.

Prescod-Roberts, Margaret. "Bringing It All Back Home." In *Black Women: Bringing It All Back Home*, edited by Margaret Prescod, 13–40. Bristol, UK: Falling Wall Press, 1980.

Price-Glynn, Kim. *Strip Club: Gender, Power, and Sex Work*. New York: New York University Press, 2010.

Prince, Stephen. "The Pornographic Image and the Practice of Film Theory." *Cinema Journal* 27, no. 2 (January 1, 1988): 27–39.

"Prostitution in New York City." *Nation*, March 25, 1936, 369.

Quadagno, Jill S. *The Color of Welfare: How Racism Undermined the War on Poverty*. New York: Oxford University Press, 1996.

Quinn, Eithne. "Who's the Mack: The Performativity and Politics of the Pimp Figure in Gangsta Rap." *Journal of American Studies* 34, no. 1 (2000): 115–36.

Qureshi, Sadiah. "Displaying Sara Baartman, the Hottentot Venus.'" *History of Science* 42 (2004): 233–57.

Raiford, Leigh. *Imprisoned in a Luminous Glare: Photography and the African American Freedom Struggle*. Chapel Hill: University of North Carolina Press, 2011.

Railton, Diane, and Paul Watson. "Naughty Girls and Red Blooded Women: Representations of Female Heterosexuality in Music Video." *Feminist Media Studies* 5, no. 1 (2005): 51–63.

Railton, Diane, and Paul Watson. "Sexed Authorship and Pornographic Address Music Video." In *Pornification: Sex and Sexuality in Media Culture*, edited by Susanna Paasonen, Kaarina Nikunen, and Laura Saarenmaa, 115–25. Oxford, UK, Berg Publishers, 2007.

Ramos, Norma. "Pornography Is a Social Justice Issue." In *Feminism and Pornography*, edited by Drucilla Cornell, 45–47. New York: Oxford University Press, 2000.

Rap Genius. "Goldie Loc—Let's Roll Lyrics." Accessed March 27, 2014, http://rap genius.com/Goldie-loc-lets-roll-lyrics.

Rap Genius. "Sir Mix-a-Lot—Baby Got Back Lyrics." Accessed March 27, 2014, http:// rapgenius.com/Sir-mix-a-lot-baby-got-back-lyrics.

Rare Celebrities. "Legendary Ebony Porn Actress Desiree West—Biography." Accessed June 21, 2013, http://www.rarecelebrities.co.uk/desireewest/desireewestbiography .html.

Ray, Audacia. *Naked on the Internet: Hookups, Downloads, and Cashing in on Internet Sexploration.* Berkeley, CA: Seal Press, 2007.

Regester, Charlene. "The Construction of an Image and the Deconstruction of a Star—Josephine Baker Racialized, Sexualized, and Politicized in the African American Press, the Mainstream Press, and FBI Files." *Popular Music and Society* 24, no. 1 (2000): 31–84.

"Retail Feedback: Carrying Sub-Genres." *Adult Video News Confidential*, February 1986, 6.

Rhines, Jesse Algeron. *Black Film, White Money.* New Brunswick, NJ: Rutgers University Press, 1996.

Rich, Frank. "Naked Capitalists," *New York Times*, May 20, 2001.

Rich, Grant Jewell, and Kathleen Guidroz. "Smart Girls Who Like Sex: Telephone Sex Workers." In *Sex for Sale: Prostitution, Pornography, and the Sex Industry*, edited by Ronald Weitzer, 35–48. New York: Routledge, 2000.

Richardson, Mattie Udora. "No More Secrets, No More Lies: African American History and Compulsory Heterosexuality." *Journal of Women's History* 15, no. 3 (2003): 63–76.

Richeson, Marques P. "Sex, Drugs, and the Race-to-Castrate: A Black Box Warning of Chemical Castration's Potential Racial Side Effects." *Harvard BlackLetter Law Journal* 25 (2009): 95–131.

Rickford, John R., and Russell John Rickford. *Spoken Soul: The Story of Black English.* Hoboken, NJ: Wiley, 2000.

Ringlero, Aleta. "Prairie Pinups: Reconsidering Historic Portraits of American Indian Women." In *Only Skin Deep: Changing Visions of the American Self*, edited by Coco Fusco and Brian Wallis, 183–98. New York: International Center of Photography/ Harry N. Abrams, 2003.

Rivas, Jorge. "Porn Stars of Color Face Racial Inequality and Wage Gap Too." *Colorlines*, November 14, 2012. Accessed November 15, 2012, http://colorlines.com

/archives/2012/11/porn_stars_of_color_face_racial_inequality_and_wage_gap_too
.html.

Roach, Joseph R. *Cities of the Dead: Circum-Atlantic Performance*. New York: Columbia University Press, 1996.

Roberts, Dorothy E. *Killing the Black Body: Race, Reproduction, and the Meaning of Liberty*. New York: Vintage, 1999.

Robinson, Cedric J. *Black Marxism: the Making of the Black Radical Tradition*. Chapel Hill: University of North Carolina Press, 1983.

Robinson, Cedric J. "Blaxploitation and the Misrepresentation of Liberation." *Race and Class* 40, no. 1 (1998): 1–12.

Robinson, Cedric J. *Forgeries of Memory and Meaning: Blacks and the Regimes of Race in American Theater and Film before World War II*. Chapel Hill: University of North Carolina Press, 2007.

Rock, Leif. "Black Videos Keep Flyin' out of the Back Door." *Adult Video News Ethnic Video Supplement* 178 (April 1998).

Rock, Leif. "Booty on the Web." *Adult Video News Ethnic Video Supplement* 178 (April 1998).

Rogers, Molly. *Delia's Tears: Race, Science, and Photography in Nineteenth-Century America*. New Haven, CT: Yale University Press, 2010.

Rony, Fatimah Tobing. *The Third Eye: Race, Cinema, and Ethnographic Spectacle*. Durham, NC: Duke University Press, 2004.

Ropelato, Tony. "Internet Pornography Statistics," *Top Ten Reviews*, Accessed June 22, 2011, http://internet-filter-review.toptenreviews.com/interest-pornography-statistics.html.

Rose, Tricia. *Black Noise: Rap Music and Black Culture in Contemporary America*. Middletown, CT: Wesleyan University Press, 1994.

Rose, Tricia. *The Hip Hop Wars: What We Talk about When We Talk about Hip Hop—and Why It Matters*. New York: Basic Civitas, 2008.

Rose, Tricia. *Longing to Tell: Black Women Talk about Sexuality and Intimacy*. New York: Macmillan, 2004.

Rose, Tricia. "Race, Class, and the Pleasure/Danger Dialectic: Rewriting Black Female Teenage Sexuality in the Popular Imagination." *Black Renaissance/Renaissance Noire* 1, no. 31 (1998): 171–90.

Rose, Tricia. "Rewriting the Pleasure/Danger Dialectic: Black Female Teenage Sexuality in the Popular Imagination." In *From Sociology to Cultural Studies: New Perspectives*, edited by Elizabeth Long, 185–202. Malden, MA: Blackwell, 1997.

Rosello, Mireille. *Declining the Stereotype: Ethnicity and Representation in French Cultures*. Hanover, NH: University Press of New England, 1998.

Rosen, Ruth. *The Lost Sisterhood: Prostitution in America, 1900–1918*. Baltimore, MD: Johns Hopkins University Press, 1982.

Ross, Becki and Kim Greenwell. "Spectacular Striptease: Performing the Sexual and Racial Other in Vancouver, B.C., 1945–1975." *Journal of Women's History* 17, no. 1 (Spring 2005): 137–64.

Ross, Gene. "*Adult Video News*: The First Five Years," *Adult Video News*, February 1988, 46–48.

Ross, Gene. "Actress/Screenwriter: Angel Kelly." *Adult Video News*, January 1990, 14, 68.

Ross, Gene. "Introducing AVN's March Cover Girl: Heather Hunter." *Adult Video News*, March 1989, 15–16.

Ross, Lawrence. *Money Shot: The Wild Nights and Lonely Days Inside the Black Porn Industry*. New York: Running Press, 2007.

Rotenberg Collection. *Forbidden Erotica*. London: Taschen, 2001.

Rowe, Kathleen. *The Unruly Woman: Gender and the Genres of Laughter*. Austin: University of Texas Press, 1995.

Rubin, Gayle. "Thinking Sex: Notes for a Radical Theory of the Politics of Sexuality." In *Pleasure and Danger: Exploring Female Sexuality*, 267–93. London: Pandora Press, 1984.

Russell, Diana E. H. *Making Violence Sexy: Feminist Views on Pornography*. New York: Teachers College Press, 1993.

Russell, Diana E. H. "Pornography and Rape: A Causal Model." In *Feminism and Pornography*, edited by Drucilla Cornell, 48–93. New York: Oxford University Press, 2000.

Russell, Thaddeus. "The Color of Discipline: Civil Rights and Black Sexuality." *American Quarterly* 60, no. 1 (March 2008): 101–28.

Russo, Mary. *Female Grotesques: Carnival and Theory*. Center for Twentieth Century Studies. Milwaukee: University of Wisconsin Press, 1985.

Rutter, Jared. "The Big New Wave of Porn Parodies: For an Increasing Number of Studies the XXX Parody Has Been Turning Laughter into Gold." *Adult Video News*, July 2009.

Ruvolo, Julie. "How Much of the Internet is Actually for Porn." Forbes.com, September 7, 2011. Accessed September 14, 2011, http://www.forbes.com/sites/julieruvolo/2011/09/07/how-much-of-the-internet-is-actually-for-porn/.

Ryan, Dylan. "Fucking Feminism." In *The Feminist Porn Book: The Politics of Producing Pleasure*, edited by Tristan Taormino, Celine Parreñas Shimizu, Constance Penley, and Mireille Miller-Young, 121–29. New York: The Feminist Press, 2013.

Salazai, Georg. "Vivid: A New Business Model for Porn." *Hollywood Reporter*, September 2, 2010. Accessed September 3, 2010, http://www.hollywoodreporter.com/news/vivid-new-business-model-porn-27414.

Salomon, Yves. "Snoop Dogg Ventures into the World of Porn." *Adult Industry News*, February 26, 2001. Accessed August 28, 2002, http://www.ainews.com/Archives/Story1547.phtml.

Santiago, Roberto. "Sex, Lust and Videotapes: How Pornography Affects Black Couples." *Essence Magazine*, vol. 21, no. 7, November 1990, 62–64, 120.

Sarracino, Carmine, and Kevin M. Scott. *The Porning of America: The Rise of Porn Culture, What It Means, and Where We Go from Here*. Boston: Beacon Press, 2009.

Sawicki, Jana. "Identity, Politics and Sexual Freedom: Foucault and Feminism." In

*Feminism and Foucault: Reflections on Resistance*, edited by Irene Diamond and Lee Quinby. Lebanon, NH: Northeastern University Press, 1988.

Schaefer, Eric. *"Bold! Daring! Shocking! True!": A History of Exploitation Films, 1919–1959*. Durham, NC: Duke University Press, 1999.

Schlosser, Eric. *Reefer Madness: Sex, Drugs and Cheap Labor on the American Market*. Wilmington, MA: Mariner Books, 2003.

Sconce, Jeffrey, ed. *Sleaze Artists: Cinema at the Margins of Taste, Style, and Politics*. Durham, NC: Duke University Press, 2007.

Scott, Daerick. *Extravagant Abjection: Blackness, Power, and Sexuality in the African American Literary Imagination*. New York: NYU Press, 2010.

Scott, James C. *Weapons of the Weak: Everyday Forms of Peasant Resistance*. New Haven, CT: Yale University Press, 1985.

Scott, Patricia Bell. "Debunking Sapphire: Toward a Non-Racist and Non-Sexist Social Science." In *All the Women Are White, All the Blacks Are Men, but Some of Us Are Brave: Black Women's Studies*, edited by Gloria Hull, Patricia Bell Scott, and Barbara Smith, 85–92. Old Westbury, NY: Feminist Press at CUNY, 1982.

Segal, Lynne, Pamela Church Gibson, and Roma Gibson. "Does Pornography Cause Violence? The Search for Evidence." *Dirty Looks: Women, Pornography, Power*, edited by Pamela Church Gibson and Roma Gibson, 5–21. London: BFI, 1993.

Segal, Lynne, and Mary McIntosh. *Sex Exposed: Sexuality and the Pornography Debate*. New Brunswick, NJ: Rutgers University Press, 1993.

*Sex with Soul*. Historic Erotica, 2005.

"Sex with Soul," *Hotmovies.com*, n.d. Accessed April 1, 2014, http://www.hotmovies.com/video/65895/Sex-With-Soul/.

Senn, Theresa, and Michael Carey. "Child Maltreatment and Women's Adult Sexual Risk Behavior: Childhood Sexual Abuse as a Unique Risk Factor." *Child Maltreatment* 15, no. 4 (2010): 324–35.

Shabazz, Jamel. "Ghetto Gaggers: A Nation Can Rise No Higher than Its Women." *Hycide*, n.d. Accessed January 29, 2013. http://hycide.com/GHETTO-GAGGERS.

Sharpley-Whiting, T. Denean. *Black Venus: Sexualized Savages, Primal Fears, and Primitive Narratives in French*. Durham, NC: Duke University Press, 1999.

Sharpley-Whiting, T. Denean. *Pimps Up, Ho's Down: Hip Hop's Hold on Young Black Women*. New York: NYU Press, 2007.

Shimizu, Celine Parreñas. *The Hypersexuality of Race: Performing Asian/American Women on Screen and Scene*. Durham, NC: Duke University Press, 2007.

Sigel, Lisa Z. "Filth in the Wrong People's Hands: Postcards and the Expansion of Pornography in Britain and the Atlantic World, 1880–1914." *Journal of Social History* 33, no. 4 (2000): 859–85.

Simon, Richard. "The Stigmatization of 'Blaxploitation.'" In *Soul: Black Power, Politics, and Pleasure*, edited by Richard Green, 236–49. New York: NYU Press, 1998.

Simpson, Rennie. "The Afro-American Female: The Historical Context of the Construction of Sexual Identity." In *Powers of Desire: The Politics of Sexuality*, edited by Ann Barr Snitow, Christine Stansell, and Sharon Thompson, 229–35. New York: Monthly Review Press, 1983.

Skelly, Julia. *No Strangers to Beauty: Black Female Artists and the Hottentot Venus Body*. Saarbrücken, Germany: VDM Publishing, 2008.

Slade, Joseph W. "Erotic Motion Pictures and Videotapes." *Pornography in America: A Reference Handbook*. Santa Barbara, CA: ABC-CLIO, 2000.

Slade, Joseph W. *Pornography and Sexual Representation: A Reference Guide* 193, no. 6859. Westport, CT: Greenwood Publishing, 2001.

Slade, Joseph W. *Pornography in America: A Reference Handbook*. Santa Barbara, CA: ABC-CLIO, 2000.

Slade, Joseph W. "Violence in the Hard-core Pornographic Film: A Historical Survey." *Journal of Communication* 34, no. 3 (1984): 148–63.

Smith, Anna. *Welfare Reform and Sexual Regulation*. New York: Cambridge University Press, 2007.

Smith, Barbara. *Home Girls: A Black Feminist Anthology*. Piscataway, NJ: Rutgers University Press, 2000.

Smith, Barbara. "Some Home Truths: On the Contemporary Black Feminist Movement." In *Words of Fire: An Anthology of African-American Feminist Thought*, edited by Beverly Guy-Sheftall, 254–67. New York: New Press, 1995.

Smith, Shawn Michelle. *American Archives: Gender, Race, and Class in Visual Culture*. Princeton, NJ: Princeton University Press, 1999.

Smith, Shawn Michelle. *Photography on the Color Line: W.E.B. Du Bois, Race, and Visual Culture*. Durham, NC: Duke University Press, 2004.

Smith, Valerie. *Representing Blackness: Issues in Film and Video*. Piscataway, NJ: Rutgers University Press, 1997.

Snead, James A., and Colin MacCabe. *White Screens, Black Images: Hollywood from the Dark Side*. London: Psychology Press, 1994.

Snitow, Ann Barr, Christine Stansell, and Sharon Thompson. *Powers of Desire: The Politics of Sexuality*. New York: Monthly Review Press, 1983.

Snorton, C. Riley, ed. "The Queerness of Hip Hop/The Hip Hop of Queerness." *Palimpsest* 2, no. 2 (2013).

Snow, Aurora. "Interracial Sex Still Taboo for Many Porn Stars." *Daily Beast*, March 5, 2013. Accessed December 13, 2013, http://www.thedailybeast.com/articles/2013/03/05/interracial-sex-still-taboo-for-many-porn-stars.html.

Soble, Alan. *Pornography: Marxism, Feminism, and the Future of Sexuality*. New Haven, CT: Yale University Press, 1986.

Solinger, Rickie. "Race and 'Value': Black and White Illegitimate Babies, in the USA, 1945–1965." *Gender and History* 4, no. 3 (1992): 343–63.

Solomon-Godeau, A. "Reconsidering Erotic Photography: Notes for a Project of Historical Salvage." *Photography at the Dock: Essays on Photographic History, Institutions, and Practices*, 220–37. Minneapolis: University of Minnesota Press, 1991.

Somerville, Siobhan B. *Queering the Color Line: Race and the Invention of Homosexuality in American Culture*. Durham, NC: Duke University Press, 2000.

Sonn, Kurt, "Black Adult Video: What It Is, What It Was, and What It Shall Be." *Adult Video News Ethnic Video Supplement* 178 (April 1998).

Spiegelman, Art. "Those Dirty Little Comics." Introduction to *Tijuana Bibles: Art and*

*Wit in America's Forbidden Funnies, 1930s–1950s*, by Bob Adelman, 4–10. New York: Simon and Schuster / Editions Erotic Print Society, 2006.

Spillers, Hortense. J. "Mama's Baby, Papa's Maybe: An American Grammar Book." *Diacritics* 17, no. 2 (1987): 65–81.

Stack, Carol B. "Sex Roles and Survival Strategies in an Urban Black Community." In *The Black Woman Cross-Culturally*, edited by Filomina Chioma Steady, 349–368. Cambridge, MA: Schenkman Publishing, 1981.

Stallings, LaMonda Horton. "Gender Realism, Poor Black Women, and the Politics of the Hoin' and Hustlin." Paper presented at the annual meeting of the National Women's Studies Association, Atlanta, GA, November 13, 2009.

Stallings, LaMonda Horton. *"'Mutha' Is Half a Word!": Intersections of Folklore, Vernacular, Myth, and Queerness in Black Female Culture*. Columbus: Ohio State University Press, 2007.

Stallings, LaMonda Horton. "Superfreak: The Black Lesbian Gaze and Black Lesbian Porn," Paper presented at Race, Sex, Power: New Movements in Black and Latina/o Sexualities, University of Illinois, Chicago, April 12, 2008.

Stallybrass, Peter, and Allon White. *The Politics and Poetics of Transgression*. Ithaca, NY: Cornell University Press, 1986.

Staples, Robert. *The Black Family: Essays and Studies*. Belmont, CA: Wadsworth Pub. Co., 1999.

Staples, Robert. *The Black Woman in America: Sex, Marriage, and the Family*. Chicago: Nelson-Hall Publishers, 1973.

Staples, Robert. "The Myth of the Black Matriarchy." *Black Scholar* 12, no. 6 (1981): 26–34.

Steady, Filomina Chioma. *The Black Woman Cross-Culturally*. Cambridge, MA: Schenkman Publishing, 1981.

Steffans, Karrine. *Confessions of a Video Vixen*. New York: HarperCollins, 2005.

Steffans, Karrine. *The Vixen Diaries*. New York: Grand Central Publishing, 2007.

Steffans, Karrine. *The Vixen Manual: How to Find, Seduce and Keep the Man You Want*. New York: Grand Central Publishing, 2009.

Stein, Arlene, ed. *Sisters, Sexperts, Queers: Beyond the Lesbian Nation*. New York: Plume, 1993.

Steinem, Gloria. "Erotica and Pornography: A Clear and Present Difference." *Take Back the Night: Women on Pornography*, 35–39. New York: William Morrow, 1980.

Sterry, David Henry, and R. J. Martin, Jr. eds. *Hos, Hookers, Call Girls, and Rent Boys: Professionals Writing on Life, Love, Money, and Sex*. Brooklyn, NY: Soft Skull Press, 2009.

Stevenson, Brenda, E. *Life in Black and White: Family and Community in the Slave South: Family and Community in the Slave South*. New York: Oxford University Press, 1996.

Stewart, Dodai. "Porn Performers Agree: The Porn Industry is Racist." *Jezebel*, April 5, 2013. Accessed April 25, 2013, http://jezebel.com/5993788/porn-performers-agree -the-porn-industry-is-racist.

Stiffler, David, ed. *The Secret Museum of Mankind*. New York: Manhattan House, 1941.

The Stilts and DeVoe Show. August 4, 2010, http://www.latalkradio.com/Players /Devoe-080410.shtml.

Strossen, Nadine. *Defending Pornography: Free Speech, Sex, and the Fight for Women's Rights.* New York: NYU Press, 2000.

Sturken, Marita and Lisa Cartwright. *Practices of Looking: An Introduction to Visual Culture.* New York: Oxford University Press, 2009.

Suggs, Donald. "Hard Corps: A New Generation of People of Color Penetrates Porn's Mainstream." *Village Voice*, August 21, 1997.

Sugrue, Thomas J. *The Origins of the Urban Crisis: Race and Inequality in Postwar Detroit.* Princeton, NJ: Princeton University Press, 2005.

Szalai, Georg. "Vivid: A New Business Model for Porn." *Hollywood Reporter*, September 2, 2010, http://www.hollywoodreporter.com/news/vivid-new-business-model -porn-27414.

Tagg, John. *The Burden of Representation: Essays on Photographies and Histories.* Minneapolis: University of Minnesota Press, 1988.

Tarrow, Sidney G. *Power in Movement: Social Movements and Contentious Politics*, 2nd ed. Cambridge Studies in Comparative Politics. Cambridge: Cambridge University Press, 1998.

Tate, Greg. *Everything but the Burden: What White People Are Taking from Black Culture.* New York: Broadway Books, 2003.

Tate, Greg, Portia Maultsby, Thulani Davis, Clyde Taylor, and Ishmael Reed. "Ain't We Still Got Soul?" In *Soul: Black Power, Politics, and Pleasure*, edited by Richard Green, 269–83. New York: NYU Press, 1998.

Tatum, Stephanie. L. "Black Female Sex Workers: Racial Identity, Black Feminist Consciousness, and Acculturated Stress." In *Black Sexualities: Probing Powers, Passions, Practices and Politics*, edited by Juan Battle and Sandra A. Barnes, 311–26. New Brunswick, NJ: Rutgers University Press, 2010.

Teish, Luisah. "A Quiet Subversion." *Take Back the Night: Women on Pornography*, edited by Laura Lederer, 105–8. New York: William Morrow, 1980.

Terborg-Penn, Rosalyn, and Ruth Milkman. "Survival Strategies among Afro-American Women Workers: A Continuing Process." *Women, Work, and Protest: A Century of Women's Labor History.* Boston: Routledge, 1985.

Terrell, Mary Church. "The Progress of Colored Women." *Words of Fire: An Anthology of African American Feminist Thought*, edited by Beverly Guy-Sheftall, 64–68. New York: New Press, 1995.

Terrlonge, Pauline. "Feminist Consciousness and Black Women." In *Words of Fire: An Anthology of African-American Feminist Thought*, edited by Beverly Guy-Sheftall, 490–502. New York: New Press, 1995.

Terry, Jennifer, and Jacqueline Urla. "The Antropometry of Barbie: Unsettling Ideals of the Feminine Body in Popular Culture." In *Deviant Bodies: Critical Perspectives on Difference in Science and Popular Culture*, edited by Jennifer Terry and Jacqueline Urla. Indianapolis: Indiana University Press, 1995.

Terry, Jennifer, and Jacqueline Urla. *Deviant Bodies: Critical Perspectives on Difference in Science and Popular Culture.* Bloomington: Indiana University Press, 1995.

Thomas, Alex. "The Marketing of Three Major Titles." *Adult Video News Confidential*, March 1985.

Thomas, Deborah A. "Modern Blackness: 'What We Are and What We Hope to Be.'" *Small Axe* 6, no. 2 (2002): 25–48.

Thompson, Dave. *Black and White and Blue: Adult Cinema from the Victorian Age to the VCR*. Toronto: ECW Press, 2007.

Thornton Dill, Bonnie, and Tallese Johnson. "Between a Rock and a Hard Place: Mothering, Work, and Welfare in the Rural South." In *Sister Circle: Black Women and Work*, edited by Sharon Harley and the Black Women and Work Collective, 67–83. New Brunswick, NJ: Rutgers University Press, 2002.

Tirrant, Shira. "Is Porn Racist?" *Ms. Magazine* blog, August 18, 2010. Accessed August 19, 2010, http://msmagazine.com/blog/blog/2010/08/16/is-pornography-racist/.

Trautner, Mary Nell. "Doing Gender, Doing Class: The Performance of Sexuality in Exotic Dance Clubs." *Gender and Society* 19, no. 6 (December 2005): 771–88.

Troeller, Linda, and Marion Schneider. *The Erotic Lives of Women*. New York: Scalo, 1998.

Trouillot, Michel-Rolph. *Silencing the Past: Power and the Production of History*. Boston: Beacon Press, 1995.

Turan, Kenneth, and Stephen F. Zito. *Sinema: American Pornographic Films and the People Who Make Them*. New York: New American Library, 1975.

Turner, Graeme. *The Film Cultures Reader*. New York: Psychology Press, 2002.

Ulysse, Gina A. *Downtown Ladies: Informal Commercial Importers, a Haitian Anthropologist, and Self-Making in Jamaica*. Chicago: University of Chicago Press, 2007.

United States Commission on Civil Rights. *The Economic Status of Black Women: An Exploratory Investigation*. By Nadja Zalokar. Washington, D.C.: United States Government Printing Office, 1990.

United States Department of Justice. *Attorney General's Commission on Pornography: Final Report*, vol. 1, "Introduction: The Commission and Its Mandate" (July 1986). By Henry E. Hudson, Diane D. Cusack, Park Elliot Dietz, James Dobson, Father Bruce Ritter, Frederick Schauer, Deanne Tilton-Durfee, Judith Becker, and Ellen Levine. Washington, D.C.: United States Government Printing Office, 1986.

United States Department of Labor, Women's Bureau. "Employment Status of Women and Men in 2005." Washington, D.C.: United States Government Printing Office, 2005, http://www.dol.gov/wb/factsheets/Qf-ESWM05.htm. Accessed July 23, 2008.

Unterberger, Richie. *Music USA: The Rough Guide*. London: Rough Guides, Ltd., 1999.

Vance, Carole S. *Pleasure and Danger: Exploring Female Sexuality*. New York: Pandora, 1992.

Van Deburg, William L. *New Day in Babylon: The Black Power Movement and American Culture, 1965–1975*. Chicago: University of Chicago Press, 1992.

Van Scoy, Kayte. "Sex Sells, So Learn a Thing or Two From it." *PC Computing* 13, no. 1 (2000): 64.

Vergne, Philippe. *Kara Walker: My Complement, My Enemy, My Oppressor, My Love*. Minneapolis, MN: Walker Art Center, 2007.

Vogel, Shane. *The Scene of Harlem Cabaret: Race, Sexuality, Performance*. Chicago: University of Chicago Press, 2009.

Walcott, Rinaldo. "Somewhere Out There: The New Black Queer Theory." In *Blackness and Sexualities*, edited by Michelle Wright and Antje Shuhmann, 29–40. Berlin: LIT Verlag, 2007.

Walker, Alice. "Coming Apart." In *You Can't Keep a Good Woman Down*. New York: Houghton Mifflin Harcourt, 2004.

Walker, Alice. "Porn." In *Feminism and Pornography*, edited by Drucilla Cornell, 600–605. New York: Oxford University Press. 2000.

Wallace, Michele. "The Imperial Gaze: The Venus Hottentot, Human Display and World's Fairs." In *Black Venus 2010: They Called Her "Hottentot,"* edited by Deborah Willis, 149–54. Philadelphia: Temple University Press, 2010.

Wallace, Michele, and Gina Dent. *Black Popular Culture*. New York: New Press, 1998.

Wallace, Michelle, and Beverly Guy-Sheftall. "Anger in Isolation: A Black Feminist's Search for Sisterhood." In *Words of Fire: An Anthology of African American Feminist Thought*, 220–30. New York: New Press, 1995.

Wallace, Phyllis A., Linda Datcher, and Julianne Malveaux. *Black Women in the Labor Force*. Cambridge, MA: MIT Press, 1982.

Wallace-Sanders, Kimberly. *Skin Deep, Spirit Strong: the Black Female Body in American Culture*. Ann Arbor: University of Michigan Press, 2002.

Wallis, Brian. "Black Bodies, White Science: Louis Agassiz's Slave Daguerreotypes." *American Art* 9, no. 2 (July 1, 1995): 39–61.

Wanzo, Rebecca. "Beyond a 'Just' Syntax: Black Actresses, Hollywood and Complex Personhood." *Women and Performance: a Journal of Feminist Theory* 16, no. 1 (2006): 135–52.

Wanzo, Rebecca. *The Suffering Will Not Be Televised: African American Women and Sentimental Political Storytelling*. Albany, NY: SUNY Press, 2009.

Warren, Peter. "Montana Fishburne Speaks." *Adult Video News*, August 6, 2010. Accessed August 7, 2010, http://business.avn.com/articles/video/avn-Exclusive -Montana-Fishburne-Speaks-406615.html.

Warren, Peter. "Vivid Sells Out 'Montana Fishburne' on 3rd Shipping Day." *Adult Video News*, August 5, 2010. Accessed August 5, 2010, http://business.avn.com /articles/video/Vivid-Sells-Out-Montana-Fishburne-on-3rd-Shipping-Day-406307 .html.

Watkins, S. Craig. *Hip Hop Matters: Politics, Pop Culture, and the Struggle for the Soul of a Movement*. Boston: Beacon, 2005.

Waugh, Thomas. *Hard to Imagine: Gay Male Eroticism in Photography and Film from Their Beginnings to Stonewall*. New York: Columbia University Press, 1996.

Waugh, Thomas. "Homoerotic Representation in the Stag Film, 1920–1940: Imagining an Audience." *Wide Angle* 14, no. 2 (1996): 4–21.

Waugh, Thomas. "Homosociality in the Classical American Stag Film: Off-Screen, On-Screen." *Sexualities* 4, no. 3 (2001): 275–91.

Waugh, Thomas. "Men's Pornography: Gay vs. Straight." In *Out in Culture: Gay, Les-*

*bian, and Queer Essays on Popular Culture*, edited by Corey K. Creekmur and Alexander Doty. Durham, NC: Duke University Press, 1995.

Weasels, P. "Porn 101: Hip Hop Porn Primer." *GameLink*, n.d. Accessed December 13, 2013, http://www.gamelink.com/news.jhtml?id=news_nt_primer_hip_hop_porn.

Weathers, Mary Ann. "An Argument for Black Women's Liberation as a Revolutionary Force." In *Words of Fire: An Anthology of African American Feminist Thought*, edited by Beverly Guy-Sheftall, 158–61. New York: New Press, 1995.

Weber, Brenda R. *Makeover TV: Selfhood, Citizenship, and Celebrity*. Durham, NC: Duke University Press, 2009.

Webster, Paula. "Pornography and Pleasure." In *Caught Looking: Feminism, Pornography and Censorship*, edited by Kate Ellis, Nan Hunter, Beth Jaker, Barbara O'Dair, and Abby Tallmer, 30–35. East Haven, CT: Long River, 1986.

Weitzer, Ronald. *Legalizing Prostitution: From Illicit Vice to Lawful Business*. New York: NYU Press, 2012.

Weitzer, Ronald, ed. *Sex for Sale: Prostitution, Pornography, and the Sex Industry*. 2nd ed. New York: Routledge, 2010.

Weitzer, Ronald. "Sex Work: Paradigms and Policies." In *Sex for Sale: Prostitution, Pornography, and the Sex Industry*, 2nd ed., edited by Ronald Weitzer, 1–13. New York: Routledge, 2010.

Weitzer, Ronald. *Sex for Sale: Prostitution, Pornography, and the Sex Industry*. New York: Taylor and Francis, 2000.

Weitzer, Ronald and Melissa Ditmore. "Sex Trafficking: Facts and Fictions." In *Sex for Sale: Prostitution, Pornography, and the Sex Industry*, 2nd ed., edited by Ronald Weitzer, 325–52. New York: Routledge, 2010.

Wekker, Gloria. *The Politics of Passion: Women's Sexual Culture in the Afro-Surinamese Diaspora*. New York: Columbia University Press, 2006.

Wells-Barnett, Ida B. *Southern Horrors: Lynch Law in All Its Phases* [1892, 1893, 1894]. Ebook: Project Gutenberg, 2005. Accessed March 27, 2014, http://www.gutenberg.org/files/14975/14975-h/14975-h.htm.

West, Rachel. "US PROStitutes Collective." In *Sex Work: Writings by Women in the Sex Industry*, edited by Frederique Delacoste and Priscilla Alexander, 279–89. New York: Cleis Press, 1998.

Whisnant, Rebecca, and Christine Stark. *Not for Sale: Feminists Resisting Prostitution and Pornography*. North Melbourne, AU: Spinifex Press, 2005.

White, Deborah Gray. *Aren't I a Woman?* New York: W. W. Norton, 1999.

White, Deborah Gray. *Too Heavy a Load: Black Women in Defense of Themselves, 1894–1994*. New York: W. W. Norton, 1999.

White, E. Frances. *Dark Continent of Our Bodies: Black Feminism and The Politics of Respectability*. Philadelphia: Temple University Press, 2001.

White, Luise. *The Comforts of Home: Prostitution in Colonial Nairobi*. Chicago: University of Chicago Press, 1990.

"Who Rents Adult Tape?" *Adult Video News*, January 1992, 27.

"Why Won't Vivid, Wicked and DP Get Black Woman?" *Adult DVD Talk*. Accessed

June 3, 2013. http://forum.adultdvdtalk.com/why-wont-vivid-wicked-and-dp-get
-black-woman.

Williams, Eric Eustace. *Capitalism and Slavery*. Chapel Hill: University of North Carolina Press, 1944.

Williams, Erica Lorraine. *Ambiguous Entanglements: Sex Tourism in Bahia*. Urbana:
University of Illinois Press, 2013.

Williams, Linda. *Hard Core: Power, Pleasure, and the "Frenzy of the Visible."* Berkeley:
University of California Press, 1989.

Williams, Linda. "Porn Studies: Proliferating Pornographies On/Scene: An Introduction." In *Porn Studies*, edited by Linda Williams, 1–23. Durham, NC: Duke University Press, 2004.

Williams, Linda. "Skin Flicks on the Racial Border: Pornography, Exploitation and
Interracial Lust." In *Porn Studies*, edited by Linda Williams, 271–308. Durham, NC:
Duke University Press, 2004.

Williams, Linda. "'White Slavery' versus the Ethnography of 'Sexworkers': Women in
Stag Films at the Kinsey Archive." *Moving Image* 5, no. 2 (2005): 107–34.

Williams, Mary Elizabeth. "Laurence Fishburne's Daughter: A New Kind of Sex Tape."
Salon.com, August 2, 2010. Accessed August 3, 2010, http://www.salon.com/life
/feature/2010/08/02/laurence_fishburne_daughter_porn.

Williams, Mary Elizabeth. "'Real Housewives': Spare Us Your Sex Tapes." Salon.com,
June 8, 2010. Accessed August 4, 2010, http://www.salon.com/2010/06/08/danielle
_staub_sex_tape_fatigue/.

Williams, Patricia J. *Seeing a Color-Blind Future: The Paradox of Race*. New York:
Noonday Press, 1997.

Williams, Raymond. *Problems in Materialism and Culture: Selected Essays*. New York:
Verso, 1980.

Willis, Deborah, ed. *Black Venus 2010: They Called Her "Hottentot,"* Philadelphia:
Temple University Press, 2010.

Willis, Deborah, ed. *Picturing Us: African American Identity in Photography*. New
York: New Press, 1996.

Willis, Deborah, and Carla Williams, eds. *The Black Female Body: A Photographic History*. Philadelphia: Temple University Press, 2002.

Willis, Ellen. "Feminism, Moralism, and Pornography." In *Powers of Desire: The Politics of Sexuality*, edited by Ann Barr Snitow, Christine Stansell, and Sharon Thompson. New York: Monthly Review Press, 1983.

Winbush, Jeff. "The Diva of Sex: The Vanessa Del Rio Interview." G21.com, n.d.,
http://www.generator21.net/g21archive/bare23.html.

Wilson, Ara. *The Intimate Economies of Bangkok: Tomboys, Tycoons, and Avon Ladies
in the Global City*. Berkeley: University of California Press, 2004.

Wilson, Joycelyn A. "Tip Drills, Strip Clubs, and Representation in the Media: Cul-
tural Reflections and Criticisms from the POV of an African American Female
Southern Hip-Hop Scholar." In *Home Girls Make Some Noise!: Hip Hop Femnism
Anthology*, edited by Gwendolyn D. Pough, Elaine Richardson, Aisha Durham, and
Rachel Raimist. Mira Loma, CA: Parker Publishing, 2007, 170–84.

Wolcott, Victoria W. *Remaking Respectability: African American Women in Interwar Detroit*. Chapel Hill: University of North Carolina Press, 2001.

Wolf, Naomi. *The Beauty Myth: How Images of Beauty Are Used against Women*. New York: HarperCollins, 2002.

Wolkowitz, Carol. "The Social Relations of Body Work." *Work, Employment and Society* 16, no. 3 (2002): 497–510.

Woody, Bette. *Black Women in the Workplace: Impacts of Structural Change in the Economy*. Westport, CT: Greenwood Press, 1992.

Wray, Matt, and Annalee Newitz, eds. *White Trash: Race and Class in America*. London: Psychology Press, 1997.

Wright, Melissa W. *Disposable Women and Other Myths of Global Capitalism*. New York: Routledge, 2006.

Wright, Michelle. *Becoming Black: Creating Identity in the African Diaspora*. Durham, NC: Duke University Press, 2004.

Wright, Michelle and Antje Schuhmann, eds. *Blackness and Sexualities*. Berlin: LIT Verlag, 2007.

Wyatt, Gail Elizabeth. *Stolen Women: Reclaiming our Sexuality, Taking Back Our Lives*. New York: Wiley, 1997.

X, Nelson. "Black Humor: The Marketing of Racial Stereotypes in Interracial Porn, an AVN Discussion." *Adult Video News*, February 2009.

XBIZTV. "Montana Fishburne Talks Sex Tape with XBIZ." YouTube, August 16, 2010. Accessed April 3, 2014, https://www.youtube.com/watch?v=ozV-bVBbnHU.

Zbryski, Alvin. "Review of *Black Dynasty*." *Adult Video News*, June 1985.

Zelizer, Viviana and A. Rotman. *The Purchase of Intimacy*. Princeton, NJ: Princeton University Press, 2007.

# Index

Abrams, Abiola, 275–76

abuse, 194n54, 248–51, 254–55. *See also* pay inequality; treatment of actresses, personal

academic pornographers, vii–ix

*académies*, 35–36

activists and activism: Damali, 269; illicit erotic, 264; labor, 138, 139, 261–62

actors: black, 156–62, 206–7

actors: white, *92, 94*, 95, 96, 97, 205

actresses, black: background of, 189; as film-makers, 263–65; in the marketplace of sex, 229–33; personal treatment of, 248–56. *See also* motivations of actresses

actresses, white: interracial sex with, 162–63; in the marketplace of sex, 230, *231*; pay rates of, 195; preferences for, 241–42; racial anxieties of, 250–51

*Adam Film World*, 136

Adult Video Association, 115n38

Adult Video News (AVN): Adult Entertainment Expo, 104–5, *231*; awards, 142; on black-cast videos, 112; covers, 138, *219*; Fishburne in, 180; Hall of Fame, 1, 140, 169; on video glut, 108

advertising and advertisements: at Adult Entertainment Expo, *231*; to blacks, 84; box covers, 138, *219*, 247, 248–49; Dark Brothers, *122*; ghetto porn, 152; India's, *214*; penises in, 75; racialized, 74. *See also* websites

aesthetics and aesthetism, 46, 66, 97

*Africanus Sexualis (Black Is Beautiful)*, 76–78

afrocentric views of sexuality, 76–77

*AfroDite Superstar*, 275

agentive black subjectivity: 1930s–1940, 45; agency in relation to, 16–17; of Angel, *135*–36, 137–39; in *Black Chicks*, 128–29, 131–32; in Blaxploitation, 81; of blues women, 29–30; within capitalism, 280–81; Davis on, 29–30; of Del Rio, 209; fetishism in relation to, 27; of Grier, 82; in hip hop porn, 145–46; of hip hop porn, 154; as insurgency, 28–29; in kkk *Night Riders*, 62–65; in *Lialeh*, 87–88; in photographic porn, 40–41; pleasure and, 200–201; in porno, 67; in prostitution, 49; in rape fantasies, 59, 62–63; of rappers, 159; of sex workers, 25; significance of, 6; slut identity as, 209–10; in soul porn, 67, 68, 69; in stag films, 61–62; through facial stunting, 25; through subversion, 132–34; of West, 102. *See also* black feminist pornographies; labor, control of; motivations of actresses

aging out, research on, 217n101

Alexander, Karen, 235

*Alice in Blackland*, 137

*Alice in Whiteland*, 137

Alloula, Malek, 36n48

amateur porn, 150

America Distribution Company, 82

Angel (Eyes), motivations of, 187

Angel (Kelly): agency of, 137–39; aspirations of, 16; on *Black Chicks*, 133; in *The Call Girl*, 134; career of, 14; rebirth of, 104; significance of, 140; on *Welcome to the Jungle*, 15; on working conditions, 135–36

*Angkor*, 51

antiporn feminists, 19, 139n94, 165, 199

Arnone, Joe, 114

Arrow Home Video, 114

artists, use of sexuality, viii

Aryana (Starr), 200

Asante, Molefi, 77

Asian actors and actresses, 75, 110n23

*As Nasty as They Wanna Be*, 150, 151

audiences: Blaxploitation film, 80; of soul porn, 68, 83–84, 86; voyeurism and, 56, 80–81, 88–89, 154, 157–58; white, 51–52, 66, 67–68, 110. *See also* consumers and consumption

AVN. *See Adult Video News* (AVN)


Baartman, Saartjie (Sara) (Hottentot Venus), vii, viii, 33–35

*Baby Got Back*, 147–48, 150

*Babysitter*, 58

"badger game," 176

Baker, Jack, 121, 123, 124

Baker, Josephine, 13, 20, 46, 55–56

*Baywatch*, 242–43

BDSM fetishism, 273–74

Beach, Sandi, 186

beauty: butt worship and, 150; historical aspects, 40, 41; racial politics of, 241–43, 247

Beavers, Louise, 63

*Behind the Green Door*, 73–75

Bennett, Lerone, 69

Bercovichy, Barron, 76, 85

Berg, Heather, 185n28

Berlant, Lauren, 224

Bernardi, Daniel, 112n28

Betty (Blac), 191, 243–44, 278

Big Beautiful Women (BBW) pornography, 243

*Birth of a Nation*, 60

black and interracial video, 107n4

black art-porn entrepreneurs, 275–82

*Black Bandit, The*, 58

*Black Bun Busters*, 112

black-cast and interracial pornography: *Behind the Green Door*, 74–75; *Bubble Gum Honey*, 75; complexities of, 111–12; demand for, 109–10; growth of, 106; photographic, 35–36, 37, 38–40, 42; rate differential, 252; sexploitation, 76; *Sex with Soul*, 66; *Sex World*, 71, 95; significance of, 252–53; in soul porn era, 98–99; in stag films, 50–51, 52, 58–60; of the video era, 109; Video Team, 147; Williams on, 96n75. *See also* hip hop pornography; photographic pornography; soul porn; video pornography

*Black Chicks*. See *Let Me Tell Ya 'Bout Black Chicks*

*Black Dynasty*, 116

*Black Female Body, The* (Willis), 36, 38

black feminist pornographies: Abrams, 275–76; academic, vii–xii; concept of, 28–29; Dares, Damali, 269; DeVoe, Diana, 190–92, 199–200, 256–57; gaze theory of, 63–65, 203; history of, 29–35; lens of, 17; Pinky's, 171–77; producers and directors, 263–68; significance of, 279–81. *See also* Sinnamon (Love); Vanessa (Blue)

black feminists: Abrams, 275–76; artists, viii; on beauty, 241; Carby, 47n64; Clark, ix; Collins, ix, 121n58, 182–83; Crenshaw, 151; Crunk Feminist Collective, 210–11; Dares, 269; exploitation and, 201; Harley, 12–13; producers, 277–78; Spillers, 30, 33; Stallings, x–xi, 78, 279. *See also* feminists and feminism; Sinnamon (Love); Vanessa (Blue)

"Black is Beautiful," 70, 245

*Black Is Beautiful* (*Africanus Sexualis*), 76–78

*Black Lovers*, 52

black male actors. *See* actors, black

black matriarchy discourse, 97–98

Black Panther Party, 99–100

black power era, 67

"black stud" in advertising, 75

costumes, self-styled, 137–38
*Cotton Comes to Harlem*, 78n45
Cougar porn, 189–90
couples photographs, 38–39, 40
couples porn, 271
"crafting," 176
Craig, Maxine Leeds, 241
Crenshaw, Kimberlé, 151
"Creole Queens," 57
*Critical Inquiry*, vii
Crunk Feminist Collective, 210–11
Cruz, Ariane, x
Crystal, motivations of, 186
culture of dissemblance, ix, x, 201, 279, 280
Cuvier, Georges, 34

Damiano, Gerard, 73
Damien (Decker), 252n61
dancing and dancers: booty antics, 171–72;
    burlesque, 50, 68, 89; exotic, 139, 155,
    173–74; labor relations, 239–40; treatment
    of, 254–55
*Dancing Darkies*, 54
Dark Brothers, 120–25
*Dark Confessions*, 271–73
*Darkie Rhythm*, 52, 53–55, 57
dark-skinned women, 40–41, 246
Dashiel, 75
Davis, Adrienne, 33
Davis, Angela, 29–30, 63–64, 80
Davis, Mark, 205, 272n14
Davis, Tina, 120
Decker, Damien, 252n61
*Deep Throat*, 73
Del Rio, Vanessa, 110n23, 132–33, 208–9
D'Emilio, John, 46, 72
deviance, politics of, x, 68n2, 202, 203, 274,
    279
Diana (DeVoe), 190–92, 199–200, 256–57, 264
*Difference and Pathology* (Gilman), vii
digital media, impact of, 18
directors and directing: Abrams, 275–76;
    Angel Kelly, 138; black, 52n93; Dares, 269;
    DeVoe, 190–92, 199–200, 256–57, 264;
    Dodson, 80–81; Drea, 137; Hart, 206;

Jennings, 99–100, 101; Joiner, 264, 277, 278;
    of *Little Miss Dangerous*, 138n91; Michaels,
    162; Spinelli, 70–71, 90; Taormino, 272;
    treatment of actors by, 248; Vanessa Blue,
    252, 266–68
Dirty Rap, 148–49
discrimination, racial. *See* labor conditions
    and practices; racist and racialist pornog-
    raphy; stereotypes and stereotyping; treat-
    ment of actresses, personal
disidentification, concept of, 15–16
dissemblance, culture of, ix, x, 201, 279, 280
*Doc Black*, 52
Dodson, Tamara, 80–81
*Doggystyle*, 142, 157–58
domestic work and workers. *See* maids and
    maid roles
dominatrixes, *267*, *273*
Dominique (Simone), 149
*double focus*, 9
Dragon, John, 3, 219
Drake, St. Clair, 47
Drea, 137
Duggan, Lisa, 19–20
"dusky belles," 57
Duvalle, Lacey, 153–54, 237
Dyer, Richard, 212

early pornography. *See* stag films
*Eastsidaz, The*, 158
economic inequality. *See* pay inequality
Éditions Astarté, 38
educational motivations, 186, 187, 189
Edwards, Nancy, 75
employee status, 239–41
employment, wage economy, 184
entertainers, black women: Baker, 13, 20, 46,
    55–56; blues women, 29–30; colorism and,
    245–46; Holiday, 47n64; porn actors and,
    63; porn industry in relation to, 235–36
erections, gaining and maintaining, 206–7
erotic capital, maintaining and enhancing,
    193–94
erotic sovereignty, 16, 63–64, 203–4, 228. *See
    also* illicit eroticism

Goldsby, Jackie, 110
gonzo style porn, 150, 153–54
Great Depression, 47
Great Migration, 44–46
Green, Adam, 174n53
Grier, Pam, 80–81, 82, 84, 197
Gross, Kali N., 48, 49, 176
Guccione, Bob, 110
*Guess Who Came at Dinner*, 132
Gutman, Herbert, 38n52, 97n81

Hal Freeman v. State of California, 115n38
Hall, Stuart, 78–79
Hammonds, Evelyn, xi
handmaids, 37
Harley, Sharon, 12–13
Hart, Veronica, 206
Hartman, Saidiya, 31–32
Hayes, Carmen, 189–90, 197, 218
Henri Pachard (Ron Sullivan), 107
*Her Maid Raped*, 59
Hicks, Cheryl, 49
Higgins, Bill, 107, 108
Hine, Darlene Clark, ix, 201
hip hop pornography: agency in, 145–46, 154; ghetto in, 155; ghetto porn in relation to, 152–53; hypersexual aspects of, 156–57; impact of, 18; industry of, 142; influences, 143; labor relations in, 165–67; Mann on, 149; men in, 160–62; *My Baby Got Back*, 147; origin of, 147–49; pimp figure in, 157–60; sex workers on, 165–66. *See also* ho figure; ho theory
Hippolyte, Gregory (Greg Dark). *See* Dark Brothers
Hirsch, Steve, 237–38
ho figure: actresses on, 165–67; appropriation of, 165, 171–72; in ghetto porn, 234–35; Ho Stroll, 211; origin of, 18; relations with black community, 163–64; significance of, 144–45, 179; theorizing, 18, 147, 174, 176–77
Holiday, Billie, 47n64
Holliday, Jim, 107, 108
Hollywood film and TV industry: *Baywatch*,

242–43; blacks in, 80; colorism in, 245–46; nudity in, 72; porn actors and, 63; porn industry compared to, 235–36
home video. *See* video pornography
Hong, Grace, 224, 224n119
HoodHunter.com, 153, 154
Ho Stroll, 211
*Hot Chocolate*, 118–19
ho theory, 18, 147, 174, 176–77. *See also* ho figure
*Hotter Chocolate*, 137
Hottentot Venus (Sara Baartman). *See* Baartman, Sara
Houston, Shine Louise, 264, 277, 278, 279
"How Do You Want It?," 140
*How Rastus Gets His Turkey*, 54
"How to sell Adult Tapes: Marketing All-Black or Interracial Cassettes," 112
*Hue*, 68
humor, 23, 38, 54–55
Hunter, Tera, 49
*Hustlaz: Diary of a Pimp*, 142
Hustler Productions, 142
hustling women. *See* prostitutes and prostitution
hypersexuality: appropriation of, 177–78; attitudes toward, 171; disciplinary aspects, 13; of the ho, 144–45; labor of, 9; leveraging, 6; male, 156–58, 206–7; of the pimp, 159–60; policing of, 128, 202; of the stud, 160–62; in the video era, 106
*Hypnotist, The*, 23–25, 56

IAFD (Internet Adult Film Database), 180n9
illicit eroticism: concept of, 182; disidentification compared to, 15–16; erotic sovereignty in relation to, 63–64, 203–4, 228; framework of, 10; in the marketplace of sex, 229–33; nature of, 183; politics of, 228, 260–61; role of, 18–19; tactics of, 265–66
"The Image of the Black in Adult Video," 116
*Imitation of Life*, 57–58
*I modi: The Sixteen Pleasures*, 35n44
incest, 120
India: on fame, 213; image of, *214, 219*; on

labor relations, 166–68; motivations of, 196–201

*In Living Color*, 149

*In Loving Color*, 147

*Inside Deep Throat*, 73n31

international bookings and fame, 218–20

Internet Adult Film Database (IAFD), 180n9

interracial pornography. *See* black-cast and interracial pornography

interzones, 46, 48–49, 51

Ivory Snow soap, 74

Jameson, Jenna, 7

Jazz Age sex industry, 46

Jean Idelle, 68

Jeannie (Pepper): aspirations of, 16; on *Black Chicks*, 129–30, 131; career of, 1; erotic sovereignty of, 4–5, 204; in Europe, 2–3, *11*, 219, *220*, 221; on fame, 223; as fan, 20; on fans abroad, 218; illicit eroticism of, 10; motivations of, 132, 201; self-representation and, 14; sex and, 201; voodoo girl role, 57

Jennings, David, 99–100, 101

*Jet*, 67

Johnson, Walter, 32

Joiner, Neena Feelmore, 264, 277, 278

Jones, Mick, 75

Juffer, Jane, 268n7

Julien, Isaac, 173

Julien, Max, 159

Kardashian, Kim, 180

Kelley, Robin, 12

Kelly, Angel. *See* Angel (Kelly)

Kempadoo, Kemala, 241

Kendrick, Walter, 6

Keyes, Johnnie, 74

King, Deborah, xi

kink in black sexual culture, 273–74

Kinsey Institute, 38

Kipnis, Laura, 121

kkk*Night Riders* (1939), 59–65

Klein, Jennifer, 190n43

Knight, Nyrobi, 248–49

Knight, Tyler, 61, 162, 206–7, 272, *273*

Ku Klux Klan (kkk): actresses on, 130–31; Angel on, 133; in *Black Chicks*, 126–29; imagery, 248–49; kkk *Night Riders*, 59–65

labor: activists, 138, 139, 261–62; feminists and, 201; historical aspects, 31–35; managing, 233–41; physical and emotional, 242; porn as a site of, 64; reproductive, 188; in stag films, 24; unpaid, 193–96

labor, control of: by freaks and feminists, 275–82; nature of, 268; significance of, 281; by Vanessa, 270–74; Vanessa on, 266–67

labor conditions and practices: abusive aspects, 248–51; Angel on, 133; antebellum, 38; challenging, 16; contestation of, 28–29; of independent workers, 239–41; interventions in, 62–63; managing, 233–38; negotiating, 155–56, 165–69; response to, 138n90; Sasha on, 243–44; significance of, 228, 236; structural problems of, 167–68. *See also* pay inequality; treatment of actresses, personal

Lacey (Duvalle), 153–54, 237

Lady Stephanie, 125

Lane Lola. *See* Lola (Lane)

language in *Sex World*, 96–97

La Rue, Linda, 98n81, 100

Latino market, 110n23

laws and legislation: circumventing, 76n39; Comstock Law of 1873, 71; Estrada v. FedEx, 239n23; Hal Freeman v. State of California, 115n38; Loving v. Virginia, 99; Measure B, 261; Miller v. California, 71–72; Personal Responsibility and Work Opportunity Act, 164; Plessy v. Ferguson, 98–99; re: contract worker status, 239–40; RICO, 115n38; slave era, 33n23

*Leaky Sink*, 58

Lee, Brandon, 110n23

Legends of Erotic Hall of Fame, 117n48, 140

Lehman, Peter, 54n94

Leigh, Jennifer, 85

Leslie, John: images of, *92*, *94*; in *Sex World*, 90, *95*, 96, 97; on *Sex World*, 101

Penley, Constance, 54

*Penthouse Magazine*, 110

Pepper, Jeannie. *See* Jeannie (Pepper)

Personal Responsibility and Work Opportunity Act, 164

Pertillar, Lawrence, 85

perversion politics, x, 203n72

Petkovich, Anthony, 121

photographic pornography: couples, 38–40; gaze theory applied to, *43*; impact of, 35–36; interracial, 38–39, 40; maid in, *37*; prettiness and confidence in, *44*; significance of, 40–41

pimp figure, 142, 156–60, 191

Pink Cross Foundation, 226

Pink Ladies Social Club, 138, 139

Pink Pony, 245–55

Pinky: *Big Ass Boot Camp*, 173; image of, *175*; significance of, 171–72; songs of, 174–76; "Trick Off," 177

plastic surgery, 242

*Playboy*, 66, 82, 197, 253–54

*Players*, 82–84, 196–97

*Playgirl*, 82

play-labor, 12, 266

pleasure. *See* sex as motivation

"porno chic," 73

pornography: commercialization of, 72; definition of, 6; historical aspects, 17, 41, 44; origin of, 35; pornification of culture, 7; role of, 8–9. *See also* black feminist pornographies; hip hop pornography; photographic pornography; soul porn; stag films

pornography industry: complexity of, 20; demographics, 180n9; economic aspects, 108–9; Essex Video, 114; exiting, 259–60; growth of, 106–8; Hollywood compared to, 235–36; impact of, 7–8; music industry compared to, 143; neoliberal aspects, 164; policing of, 114–15; Porn Valley, 216; sales, 142; sex industries compared to, 185; tiered economy of, 161. See also *Adult Video News* (*AVN*); production and distribution

porn stardom. *See* fame

Porn Valley, 216

power, an ethic of, 256–62, 266–75

precarity of work, 188, 196

President's Commission on Obscenity and Pornography, 71

*Price of Pleasure, The* (Sun), 7

primitivism, African, 45

production and distribution: Betty on, 244–45; black women in, 263–65; box cover politics and, 247; companies, 230; Dark Brothers, 120–25; Femme Productions, 275–77; film sets, 204–8; gaining control of, 281; manufacturers, 114; Margold, 110, 117, *118–19*, 120; marketing, 109–14; producers, 67–68, 191; props and sets, 36; quality in, 108–9; sales, 142; Sasha on, 243–44; Slade on, 50n85; Vanessa on, 266–68; of video porn, 108, 114; Vivid Entertainment, 180–81, 237; Web companies, 230. *See also* black feminist pornographies; marketing; pornography industry; Video Team

productive perversity, 203n72

prostitutes and prostitution: abuse and, 254; as badger thieves, 176n54; in boudoir photos, 36, 38; consumers of, 48–49; in early porn, 44; in ghetto porn, 152; historical aspects, 47n64; incarceration rates, 184n20; in interzones, 48–49; in *South Central Hookers*, 167–68; white, 46–47

Protecting Adult Welfare (PAW), 117n48

public sex, 7

Punany Poets, 170

Purdie, Bernard "Pretty," 84–85

"Pussy Sells," 158

Quadagno, Jill, 98n83

quality of pornography, 108–9

queer pornographies: exploration of, 200; impact of, 261–62; marketing, 110n23; sex workers compared to, 163; Shine and Neena, 264; significance of, 277–78; of soul porn era, 82

Quinn, Eithne, 159

sex work and workers (*continued*)
community, 163–64; scope of, 12; sexual
rights, 209–11. *See also* actors, black;
actresses, black; actresses, white; dancing
and dancers; prostitutes and prostitution
*Sex World*: images of, *92, 93, 94*; Leslie on,
101; nature and purpose of, 90–91; racialized sexuality in, 95–96; racism in, 100;
significance of, 70–71; West in, 96–102
Shakur, Tupac, 140
Sharpley-Whiting, T. Denean, 164
*Sheba Baby* (1975), 80
Sierra: choices of, 199; labor negotiations,
165–67; motivations of, 197, 198; on pay inequality, 238; on racism, 255–56
Simone (Valentino), 275
Simone, Dominique, 149
Sinnamon (Love): on beauty, 243; career of,
169–71; on feminism, 209; as feminist,
*210*; motivations of, 187–88; "A Question
of Feminism," 272n15; on representation,
168–69; set experiences of, 204
Sir-Mix-a-Lot, 147–48, 150
*Skinflicks* (Jennings), 99
skin tones, 40–41, 57–58, 245–46
Slade, Joseph, 49n79, 73
slavery: antebellum, 38; colorism in, 245;
porn compared to, 231–32; pornographic
aspects of, 32–33; sexual economy of, 96,
232; spectacle of, 31, 34–35; stud figure in
relation to, 162
slut identity, 208–9
Smokey, 75
*Snoop Dogg's Doggy-style*, 142, 157–58
soap, trope of, 74
social media, 104
Sonny Boy (Tony El-Ay), 120
Sony vhs, 139
*Sorority Pink*, 138
soul porn: aesthetic of, 97; concept of, 17, 66;
definition of, 67; Golden Age in relation
to, 72–73; *Lialeh*, 84–85; magazines, 81–84;
race porn, 17, 49–58; *Sex World*, 90–102;
significance of, 102; soul in relation to,
69, 70

South, Jim, 161
*South Central Hookers*, 152, 167–68
Spantaneeus (Xtasty), 153, 205, 208, 218–19,
242–43
spectacle of black bodies: linked to imperial
gaze, 27; lynching, 40; rereading, 27–29,
32; in slavery, 31; voyeurism and the, 56,
80–81, 154, 157–58. *See also* consumers and
consumption; gaze theory
speech, black vernacular, 96–97
Spelman College, 174n52
Spillers, Hortense, 30, 33
Spinelli, Anthony, 70–71, 90
Spira, Tamara, 49n79
Stacey (Cash), 246
stag films: black cast, 52; consumers and consumption of, 50–51; excavating, 26–27;
facial stunting in, 24, 55–56; humor in,
23, 54–55; with Jim Crow themes, 58–59;
nature and purpose of, 49–50; production and distribution of, 50; racial aspects
of, 51; rape in, 58, 59–62; reading, 30–31;
rereading, 27–29; sexism and, 74; "sex
workers" in, 61–62; significance of, 25–26;
soul porn compared to, 66; women's labor
in, 63–64. *See also* race porn
Stagliano, John (Buttman), 149–50
Stallings, L.H., x–xi, 78, 279
Starr, Aryana, 200
Steed, Jake, 162
Steg, Albert, 75n37
Stepin Fetchit, 63
stereotypes and stereotyping, 154; aggressive
black matriarch, 97–98, 100; appropriation of, 13–14, 15; caricatures, 120–21; Dark
Brothers' use of, 126; demand for, 116;
hypersexuality, 78, 95; impact of, 144–45;
reappropriation of, 5; representation in relation to, 81; response to, 63; in the video
era, 106; welfare mother, 126, 173, 202, 257,
260; of white men, 154
Stewart, Kelly, 75
*Streetwalking on a Ruined Map* (Bruno), 26
strippers and stripping, 139, 155, 173–74
stud figure, 160–63